Evangelical Missiological Society Series

no. **19**

REFLECTING GOD'S GLORY TOGETHER

DIVERSITY IN EVANGELICAL MISSION

Other Books in the EMS Series

No. 1   *Scripture and Strategy: The Use of the Bible in Postmodern Church and Mission*, David Hesselgrave

No. 2   *Christianity and the Religions: A Biblical Theology of World Religions*, Edward Rommen and Harold Netland

No. 3   *Spiritual Power and Missions: Raising the Issues*, Edward Rommen

No. 4   *Missiology and the Social Sciences: Contributions, Cautions, and the Conclusions*, Edward Rommen and Gary Corwin

No. 5   *The Holy Spirit and Mission Dynamics*, Douglas McConnell

No. 6   *Reaching the Resistant: Barriers and Bridges for Mission*, Dudley Woodberry

No. 7   *Teaching Them Obedience in All Things: Equipping for the 21st Century*, Edgar Elliston

No. 8   *Working Together With God to Shape the New Millennium: Opportunities and Limitations*, Kenneth Mulholland and Gary Corwin

No. 9   *Caring for the Harvest Force in the New Millennium*, Tom Steffen and Douglas Pennoyer

No. 10 *Between Past and Future: Evangelical Mission Entering the Twenty-first Century*, Jonathan Bonk

No. 11 *Christian Witness in Pluralistic Contexts in the Twenty-First Century*, Enoch Wan

No. 12 *The Centrality of Christ in Contemporary Missions*, Mike Barnett and Michael Pocock

No. 13 *Contextualization and Syncretism: Navigating Cultural Currents*, Gailyn Van Rheenen

No. 14 *Business as Mission: From Impoverished to Empowered*, Tom Steffen and Mike Barnett

No. 15 *Missions in Contexts of Violence*, Keith Eitel

No. 16 *Effective Engagement in Short-Term Missions: Doing it Right!* Robert J. Priest

No. 17 *Missions from the Majority World: Progress, Challenges, and Case Studies*, Enoch Wan and Michael Pocock

No. 18 *Serving Jesus with Integrity: Ethics and Accountability in Mission*, Dwight P. Baker and Douglas Hayward

ABOUT EMS
WWW.EMSWEB.ORG

The Evangelical Missiological Society is a professional organization with more than 350 members comprised of missiologists, mission administrators, teachers, pastors with strategic missiological interests, and students of missiology. EMS exists to advance the cause of world evangelization. We do this through study and evaluation of mission concepts and strategies from a biblical perspective with a view to commending sound mission theory and practice to churches, mission agencies, and schools of missionary training around the world. We hold an annual national conference and eight regional meetings held throughout the United States and Canada.

Evangelical Missiological Society Series
no. **19**

REFLECTING GOD'S GLORY TOGETHER

DIVERSITY IN EVANGELICAL MISSION

A. SCOTT MOREAU / BETH SNODDERLY
EDITORS

Available at missionbooks.org

Reflecting God's Glory Together: Diversity in Evangelical Mission

Copyright © 2011 by Evangelical Missiological Society

All rights reserved. No part of this book may be reproduced, stored in a retrieval system, or transmitted in any form or by any means—electronic, mechanical, photocopy, recording, or otherwise—without prior written permission from the publisher, except brief quotations used in connection with reviews in magazines or newspapers. For permission, email permissions@wclbooks.com. For corrections, email editor@wclbooks.com.

Scriptures taken from the Holy Bible, New International Version®, NIV®. Copyright © 1973, 1978, 1984 by Biblica, Inc.™ Used by permission of Zondervan. All rights reserved worldwide. www.zondervan.com

Published by William Carey Publishing (formerly William Carey Library)
10 W. Dry Creek Cir | Littleton, CO 80120 | www.missionbooks.org

William Carey Publishing is a ministry of Frontier Ventures
Pasadena, CA | www.frontierventures.org

Melissa Hicks, copyeditor
Hugh Pindur, interior designer
Mike Riester, cover designer
Rose Lee-Norman, indexer

ISBNs: 978-1-64508-495-2 (paperback), 978-0-87808-889-8 (epub)

Printed Worldwide

27 26 25 24 23   2 3 4 5 6   IN

Library of Congress Cataloging-in-Publication Data

Reflecting God's glory together : diversity in evangelical mission / A. Scott Moreau and Beth Snodderly, editors.

   p. cm.
Includes bibliographical references and index.
ISBN 978-1-64508-495-2
1. Missions. 2. Evangelistic work. 3. Cultural pluralism. I. Moreau, A. Scott, 1955- II. Snodderly, Beth. III. William Carey Library.
BV2063.R425 2011
266--dc23
                    2011026896

CONTENTS

Foreword
    Enoch Wan xi

Introduction
    A. Scott Moreau xiii

Contributors xv

Part I: Case Studies and Experiments in Diversity

1. Can Multicultural Social Theory Help Us in Leading Multicultural Faith Communities?
    Dan Sheffield 3

2. Mission by the Immigrant Churches: What Are They Doing?
    Chin (John) T. Wang 21

3. Diversity of Ghanaian Diaspora in the US: Ministering to the Ghanaian Communities through Ghanaian Congregations
    Enoch Wan and Yaw Attah Edu-Bekoe 35

4. Diaspora Church Planting in a Multicultural City: A Case Study of Greenhills Christian Fellowship
    Sadiri Joy Tira and Narry F. Santos 63

5. "Kids These Days!" Generational Issues in Missions Mobilization
    Lisa La George 91

6. From Kitchen Table to Boardroom Table: Diversity Issues in Global Mission Leadership
    Gil Odendaal 103

Part II: The Challenges of Diversity in Teams

7. The Multifaceted Journey Toward Globalization in Mission: Lessons in Flexibility, Humility, and Community
   Donna Downes 125

8. Effective Cross-cultural Ministry Teams
   George Brown 141

9. Missionary Member Care in a Culturally Diverse Ministry Team
   Ejin Cho 163

10. Global Leadership in Missions: Reflections on the Issues Facing a Global Leader in a Multicultural Mission Organization
    Sunny Eunsun Hong 177

11. A Multicultural Team-building Workshop
    Sheryl Takagi Silzer 197

12. A Biblical Understanding of the Diversity of Paul's Missionary Coworkers
    William Brooks 209

Part III: Understanding and Facing Diversity

13. Different for God's Greater Glory: Benefits of and Barriers to Embracing Ethnic and Generational Diversity in Mission Leadership
    Kenhiti Katayama and John Kilmarnock 229

14. Understanding the Importance of Diversity in Missions: An African American Perspective
    Gabriel B. Tait 241

15. The Story of Alma: Diversity in Evangelical Mission Today
    Rodney Orr 263

16. Generational Diversity and WorldViews in Missions Today: A Study of the Millennial Generation
    Dale Wolyniak 273

17. A Biblical Balance Between Christian Unity and Ethnic Diversity
    Carlos G. Martin 289

18. Diversity, Donations, and Disadvantage: The Implications of Race, Class, and Gender for Personal Fund-raising in Evangelical Missions
    Samuel L. Perry 307

19. Understanding the Effects of Diversity in Mission from a Social Science Perspective
    David R. Dunaetz 335

Index 355

Scripture Index 387

Figures

Figure 1: The Akan (Ghanaian) Cosmology and Worldview. 38

Figure 2: Cultural Integration/Variation and Readiness Scale. 42

Figure 3: The Congregation Type and Church Planter's Option Scale. 51

Figure 4: Elmer Learning Cycle 118

Figure 5: The Prototype Social Games 154

Figure 6: Situational Leadership Model 156

Tables

Table 1: Comparison between Ghanaian Traditional and Western Mind-sets 39

Table 2: Ethnic Distribution of Ghanaians 41

Table 3: Ministering to Ghanaian Diaspora Communities in the USA 44

Table 4: Ministering through Ghanaian Diaspora Congregations in the USA 45

Table 5: OBG and LBG Morality and Values Differences. 46–47

Table 6: The PEACE Plan. 106

Table 7: Information on Paul's Coworkers. 221–23

Table 8: Tendencies of workers from the four generations. 275

FOREWORD

Diversity/variety is by divine design at creation. Diversity is referenced seven times in the creation account (see Gen 2:11, 12, 21, 24, 25), is seen in Christ's salvation deliverance (i.e., both Jew and Greek, slave and free, male and female, Gal 3:26–29), is demonstrated in members of the "Body of Christ," and is by endowed gifts of the Holy Spirit (Rom 12; 1 Cor 14; Eph 4:11–16). Even in the apocalyptic vision of John, the multitude before the throne and in front of the Lamb included those from "every nation, tribe, people and language" (Rev 7:9–10).

The theme of this EMS annual monograph is "diversity." It is a collection of papers from 2010, presented in two stages. They were first presented at regional conferences and then selectively chosen to be included for presentation at the national EMS conference by participants who themselves are diverse in ethnicity, race, class, and gender.

As a professional society, EMS in recent years has gradually morphed into a more diverse organization. We can identify several indicators of this encouraging shift:

- Membership: Increasing diversity by the addition of a "student membership" category, offering a reduced student membership fee and special student discounts for the annual conference registration fees.
- Participants and presenters: In recent years we have seen more diversity in gender, age, and ministry among individuals active in EMS. There has been a significant increase in the number of seminarian and female presenters at both regional and national EMS conferences. A case in point is that in recent years, the North-Central regional meeting has facilitated a Spanish track, under the leadership of Bob Priest.

- Officers: We have seen increased diversity among EMS leadership, with nonnative speakers, non-Caucasians, women, and younger leaders serving on the EMS Board. In fact I am finishing my three-year term in 2011 as the first non-Caucasian president of EMS.

We are thankful to the Lord for the diversity among EMS membership and leaders, but we appreciate that there is much room for improvement, as we seek new ways to partner with others.

Both the choice of the theme "diversity" and the selection of contributors from diverse backgrounds are signs that EMS is moving towards diversity. However, it is obvious that though the contributors are diverse in background, this fact did not cause any dissonance; instead it enlarges the circle of participants and enriches the content of this annual monograph of EMS. A glance at the Contents and perusing this volume will verify my point.

I want to take this opportunity to acknowledge the great partnership of members serving on the EMS leadership team in coordinating regional and national conferences. I would also like to express my appreciation to the editors of this EMS monograph, Scott Moreau and Beth Snodderly, for their ministry to EMS, and to you, the reader.

Enoch Wan
president, Evangelical Missiological Society

INTRODUCTION

Not too long ago a glance at just about any text outlining the history of missions would yield some fascinating observations. A person who used them to understand missions could be excused for thinking that the vast bulk of contemporary mission activity originated from Europe and North America and that it was largely (if not exclusively) a male occupation.

This mischaracterization was unfortunate in that it conveyed a picture that the true heroes of the story of mission across our globe were confined to people who share a small set of demographic, economic, educational, and gender characteristics. It was even more unfortunate in that it generated and cemented the idea that the limitation of missional engagement by a small slice of humanity would continue into the foreseeable future.

That this is true is underscored by relative surprise among many American Christians—even those who were globally aware—as shown by sociologist Philip Jenkins, who wrote about the explosive growth and vibrancy of the global church. It is sobering to realize that it took a sociologist in a secular research university to make public what was commonly known in missiological circles—and a reminder that those of us involved in missiological circles are not on the mental maps of many Christians' potential sources of information about the global church.

In reality, the "actors" in God's missional drama (the *missio Dei*) have always been far more diversely imagined by many in Western church circles. Fortunately, given the massive shifts in demographics in the West and easy accessibility to a broader pool of information from everywhere in the world, we no longer are excused from knowing that missional engagement is not confined to a very small slice of God's globally diverse world.

In many respects the mission of the church has always been everywhere to everywhere—albeit not on the scale we see today. Unfortunately, the relatively recent technological, political, and economic dominance on the world stage of Western nations has skewed the picture. We still have a long way to go in the process of straightening this picture out.

This volume is one piece of that picture-straightening process. The authors collectively paint a composite sketch of the mosaic reality of mission today. We have organized their reflections in three sections.

The first section is "Case Studies and Experiments in Diversity." In it our authors offer focused analysis of the numerous ways diversity impacts mission today. How does contemporary social theory help us better grasp diversity in Canadian mission? How are the global immigrants to North America (e.g., Filipino, Ghanaian, and Chinese) engaging in mission? How does a better understanding of generational diversity assist our mobilizing efforts? How are American megachurches engaging mission? All of these are living questions we face and the authors help us better understand our mosaic missional world from a diverse set of disciplinary and personal perspectives.

The second section offers reflections on "The Challenges of Diversity in Teams." Here the authors attend to a variety of ways the increasingly diverse missional laborers have to work through issues in team settings. Leadership, partnership, and member care all need to be rethought when teams are multicultural. Our capstone chapter is a reflection on the reality of multicultural teams in Paul's ministry, a fitting reminder that diversity in mission did not originate recently.

Our concluding section is "Understanding and Facing Diversity." In it our authors explore a variety of ways diversity challenges us in mission even as it helps us engage in God's ongoing redemptive story. How does an agency or institution grow in diversity? In what ways does the biblical call to unity of Christians balance the reality of our God-given ethnic diversity? How can we understand the missional challenges for minority populations who daily face marginalization as part of their heritage? What characterizes age diversity and how does that impact mobilization and member care? We conclude this section—and the book—with an examination of social science perspectives and how they help us think more clearly about diversity in and of mission—giving a metaphoric bookend complementing the sociological framing of the first chapter.

A. Scott Moreau

CONTRIBUTORS

EDITORS

A. Scott Moreau is professor of intercultural studies and missions at Wheaton College. He is editor of *Evangelical Missions Quarterly* and general editor of the *Encountering Mission* series (Baker Books). He has written or edited more than a dozen books and numerous articles in journals, magazines, dictionaries, and websites.

Beth Snodderly is president of William Carey International University (WCIU), vice president of the Southwest Region of the Evangelical Missiological Society, and became editor of the World Christian Foundations degree study program following the death of Ralph D. Winter.

AUTHORS

William Brooks is a PhD candidate in missions at The Southern Baptist Theological Seminary. He is also the pastor of Thompsonville Baptist Church in Springfield, Kentucky, and is a former missionary to East Asia.

George Brown has been involved in international ministry for more than twenty-five years and currently serves as the executive director of the European Christian Mission International–USA.

Ejin Cho is from South Korea, studying at Dallas Theological Seminary for a ThM in Bible Translation.

Donna Downes is currently associate professor of global leadership at Fuller Theological Seminary. She and her husband spent twenty-four years with

OC International, serving in both Kenya and Romania before returning to the US in 2008.

David R. Dunaetz is an assistant professor of psychology at Azusa Pacific University and an adjunct professor at Lithuania Christian College. He was a church planter in France for seventeen years.

Yaw Attah Edu-Bekoe is an ordained, evangelical, and charismatic PCG minister. He is currently a Doctor of Missiology student at Western Seminary in Portland.

Sunny Eunsun Hong serves as an anthropology researcher at the Asia Area Office of SIL headquartered in Manila, Philippines, and is a PhD candidate in Intercultural Studies at Biola University.

Kenhiti Katayama serves as the executive vice president at Crossover, a global mission movement, whose passion is to glorify God by assisting and accelerating church-planting movements among the least reached peoples of the world.

John Kilmarnock serves with Crossover in the United States.

Lisa La George serves in missions mobilization at The Master's College by training vocational teams of students for cross-cultural service, teaching in Intercultural Studies, and discipling international and third-culture students.

Carlos G. Martin serves as professor of world missions and evangelism at Southern Adventist University in Collegedale, Tennessee. In thirty-five years of missionary experience he has travelled many times around the world.

Gil Odendaal, PhD, DMin, serves as global director for PEACE Implementation with Saddleback Church in California and as global director for the HIV/AIDS Initiative under Kay Warren. Previously he served as regional coordinator for Africa with LifeWind.

Rodney Orr is a staff member of Campus Crusade for Christ staff and has served in Kenya, Scotland and Zimbabwe where he helped found a graduate school of leadership called ALMA.

Samuel L. Perry, ThM, MA, is a PhD candidate in the Division of the Social Sciences, University of Chicago.

Narry F. Santos is pastor of Greenhills Christian Fellowship in Toronto and adjunct professor at Tyndale Seminary. He has a PhD from Dallas Seminary (New Testament) and a PhD from University of the Philippines (Philippines Studies).

Dan Sheffield has served with WEC and The Free Methodist Church in Canada, Egypt, and South Africa, and is involved in theological education, church planting, and urban community development. He serves as director of Global and Intercultural Ministries for FMCiC and as an adjunct lecturer at Tyndale Seminary in Toronto.

Sheryl Takagi Silzer is an international multicultural consultant with SIL. She has led multicultural team building workshops in Latin America, the Caribbean, Asia, and the Pacific.

Gabriel B. Tait is a PhD candidate in the Intercultural Studies program at Asbury Theological Seminary. His research focuses on the impact of photography in cross-cultural missions as well as in constructing and representing cultural identities.

Sadiri Joy Tira, DMin, DMiss, is professor of missiology at Alliance Graduate School in Manila, vice president for Diaspora with Advancing Indigenous Missions, and serves as senior associate for Diasporas for the Lausanne Movement.

Enoch Wan is president of Evangelical Missiological Society and director of the Doctor of Missiology Program at Western Seminary. He is the founder/editor of the multilingual online journal www.GlobalMissiology.org.

Chin (John) T. Wang was born in Taiwan and raised in Argentina. He serves as a pastor of First Baptist Church of Flushing, a multiethnic and multi-congregational church in New York City. He is a PhD candidate at Trinity International University.

Dale Wolyniak served as a missionary in the Marshall Islands, Southeast Asia, and with a nonprofit organization in Afghanistan. He is an affiliate faculty with Colorado Christian University and the Nazarene Bible College.

PART I

CASE STUDIES AND EXPERIMENTS IN DIVERSITY

1

CAN MULTICULTURAL SOCIAL THEORY HELP US IN LEADING MULTICULTURAL FAITH COMMUNITIES?

DAN SHEFFIELD

MAKING SENSE OF MULTICULTURAL SOCIAL THEORY

Multiculturalism. We can stop right there. In any gathering of Canadians, the mention of "multiculturalism" will automatically elicit endless talking points, pros and cons, supporters and detractors, and very little satisfactory resolution. Exactly.

Multiculturalism is always a current topic in Canadian public dialogue. On the one hand it appears to have a high level of public support, with 82 percent agreeing that "the preservation and enhancement of the multicultural heritage of Canadians is an objective that the government should support" (Jedwab 2002, 2). On the other it seems to be a festering threat to our social fabric as a nation. A book reviewer for the *Canadian Review of Sociology* (http://onlinelibrary.wiley.com/doi/10.1111/j.1755-618X.2009.01204.x/abstract) commented regarding multiculturalism and alleged hatemongering by the Canadian weekly current affairs magazine, *Maclean's*: "An online search of Maclean's archives in August 2008 turned up 94 headlines, of which the vast majority was cautionary, pessimistic, or downright alarming" (McGregor 2009, 87).

The debate goes something like this:

- Does multiculturalism give too much emphasis to our differences and as a result does it detract from an identification of common values and a strong sense of citizenship?
- Does multiculturalism encourage bonding and/or what is often referred to as "cohesion," which is increasingly deemed essential to societal harmony?
- Is multiculturalism a threat to French identity in Canada?
- Is multiculturalism a threat to aboriginal identity in Canada?
- Does multiculturalism create or remove barriers to full and equal participation in Canadian society?

Let us pause for a moment to define our talking point. In 1971, the prime minister of Canada made the following statement to the House of Commons, in response to the recommendations of the Royal Commission on Bilingualism and Biculturalism, *Book IV, The Cultural Contribution of the Other Ethnic Groups*. By this statement the Canadian government accepted a policy that:

> ... commends itself to the Government as the most suitable means of assuring the cultural freedom of Canadians. Such a policy should help to break down discriminatory attitudes and cultural jealousies. National unity, if it is to mean anything in the deeply personal sense, must be founded on confidence in one's own individual identity; out of this can grow respect for that of others and a willingness to share ideas, attitudes and assumptions. A vigorous policy of multiculturalism will help create this initial confidence. It can form the base of a society which is based on fair play for all. The Government will support and encourage the various cultures and ethnic groups that give structure and vitality to our society. They will be encouraged to share their cultural expressions and values with other Canadians and so contribute to a richer life for all. (Government of Canada 1971)

Thus, the policy of multiculturalism seeks to improve intergroup harmony by:

- Encouraging all ethnic groups in Canada to develop themselves as vital communities, and
- Encouraging their mutual interaction and sharing.

The assumption, which is quite explicit in the policy, "is that such group development will lead to a personal and collective sense of confidence, and this in turn will lead to greater ethnic tolerance" (Berry 1984, 353).

Now almost forty years after that political validation of the worth of all cultures contributing to our collective reality we continue to discuss the practical realities. Recently we have had a debate in Ontario over the acceptance of Sharia law and Quebec's Consultation Commission on Accommodation Practices Related to Cultural Differences (see http://www.accommodements.qc.ca/commission/mandat-en.html). Following the release of the Quebec report, commentator Tahir Aslam Gora wrote this critique in *The Hamilton Spectator:*

> ...in their findings, they have emphasized the importance of Canadians understanding immigrants' cultures rather than urging immigrants to learn about their host country.
>
> The general public's lack of knowledge or interest in this report indicates one more reality—that ordinary people don't feel such solutions work on the ground. Our governments should have understood by now that such reports don't make much sense to the public.
>
> Many citizens have strong negative feelings about some immigrant communities looking for different laws and norms in this country. They especially react to the demands of some fundamental Islamic groups.
>
> The report is full of all the old rhetoric, including granting rights to religious holidays to all immigrant communities, comparing them with traditional Christian holidays.
>
> It looks like some of our multicultural policy makers are trying to turn Canada into an arm of the United Nations. They do not want to see Canada as a country with its own values and norms. They show their pride in turning Canada into a country of hodgepodge laws where some Sikhs are walking to school with their *kirpans* (ceremonial sword) and some Sikhs are asking that Canadian law be overturned so they can wear turbans instead of motorcycle helmets or safety hard hats.

Similarly, feel-good academics, policy-makers and their associated commissions want to present Canada as a role model to the world, a country where one can regularly see veil/burka-wearing Muslim female drivers, delivering a message across the world how great a multicultural society this country is.

Such commissions, fascinated by their own fantasies, do not understand the fragmentation level within those religion-bound immigrant communities.

Rather, these commissions are causing more division. They have no clue that the rights they are advocating in certain communities are already bones of contention within those circles. (Gora 2008)

In the by-line at the conclusion of his rant against multiculturalism, Mr. Gora identifies himself as a Pakistani-Canadian. Exactly.

Have the government and the courts really gone too far to accommodate religious and cultural sensitivities at the price of eroding the equality rights that Canadians hold so dear? Or is this just a simplistic reduction of a complex phenomenon into abstract dichotomies: diversity or cohesion, equality or freedom? Is Canadian multiculturalism a recent postmodern, pluralistic, pragmatic response to our present immigration challenges? Something Pierre Trudeau foisted upon us almost half a century ago? Or is our present story just the continuing emergence of the historic interplay between our everyday lives and our organizing institutions; between our personal experiences with difference and the public arena in which we seek to make sense of those experiences?

Canadian social philosopher, John Ralston Saul, has put forward an intriguing notion in his recent book *A Fair Country: Telling Truths about Canada* (2008). Saul argues that Canada is a Metis nation, heavily influenced and shaped by aboriginal ideas such as: egalitarianism, proper balance between individual and group, and an inclination toward negotiation rather than violence. He says all the important traits we Canadians feel we inherited from Western civilization—tolerance, inclusiveness, and fairness—we have actually learned from Canada's native peoples.

As settlements of immigrants, we profited from the values and practices of the aboriginal peoples we met on the shores of the St. Lawrence River, the

Great Lakes, and Hudson's Bay. We then, in turn, marginalized the peoples who passed those values and practices on to us. The discussion started all over again on the Plains of Abraham—whose values, languages, and practices will triumph? The discussion continued at Confederation—whose values, cultures, and practices will triumph? Aboriginal, French, Scot/English/Irish, Scandinavian/German/Ukrainian, Italian/Portuguese/Greek, Caribbean/Hong Kong, Vietnamese/Cambodian/Sri Lankan, up to the present day, Indian, Filipino, and Chinese?

The geography shaped our responses as well; we just kept shifting around and giving each other enough space so we did not have to assimilate into the group that arrived before us. We begin to see that the choices we have made in constructing our social reality here in Canada, over many generations, are driven as much by psychological predispositions (we are grateful that we were given social/physical space to live according to our cultural practices for as short or as long as we desired), as by pragmatic political motives—whether King George III, Sir John A. McDonald, Brian Mulroney, or Jean Chretien.

The suggestion here is that it is the exploring of relations, rather than underlining of differences that is truly representative of Canadian multiculturalism. People of differing cultures are given the space to express their distinctive identities and in so doing construct and reinforce a cohesive unity that respects, includes, and incorporates. "What appears distinctive about Canadian institutions is their extraordinary capacity to embody conflicting principles within structures ambiguous enough to allow for ad hoc accommodations over time" (Tuohy 1992).

We welcome differences, we reject differences, we talk them out, we argue and state our positions, we crawl along behind an Amish horse and buggy, we get ticked off with a Somali cab driver, we love Chinese food, even if we can't understand our waiter—and perogies are Canadian, aren't they? Exactly.

Queens University professor, Will Kymlicka, helps us navigate the space between the multicultural state and the intercultural citizen. The multicultural state creates constitutions, charters, institutions, and legal structures that fairly allow citizens who are the product of multiple cultures to live together with respect and civility. The individual learns to engage comfortably with the beliefs, values, and behaviors of her neighbor in a manner that ultimately calls for adjustment on all sides. The encounter with difference, with the "other" is transformative; change, adjustment does emerge.

Ideally, these two levels should work together in any conception of citizenship: there should be a "fit" between our model of the multicultural state and our model of the intercultural citizen. The sort of multicultural reforms we seek at the level of the state should help nurture and reinforce the desired forms of intercultural skills and knowledge at the level of individual citizens. Conversely, the intercultural dispositions we encourage within individual citizens should help support and reinforce the institutions of a multicultural state (Kymlicka 2003, 148).

Kymlicka also identifies challenges to living as intercultural citizens in a multicultural state.

- We may be more inclined to be interculturally generous and inquisitive when travelling in southern Mexico than we are with the Mexican migrant workers wandering about our small town in southwestern Ontario on a summer Saturday evening. Local makes it concrete, not just an abstract idea.
- Learning to accept and value the perspective of my "different" neighbor may require levels of mutual understanding for which I am not prepared either with knowledge or skills. The differences may overwhelm. (Kymlicka 2003, 166)

Perhaps it is precisely at this point that we begin to recognize the missing element to this whole discussion. We believe that pieces of this puzzle are held in the intentions of the God who created and sustains humanity.

- The incarnational mission of God calls us to be local, to be concrete. We cannot build a new macro-society; this kingdom stuff is like a mustard seed. We must start in our own communities to be intercultural citizens. (To recoin Oswald J. Smith's motto, if my neighbor has not heard the good news once, why are we sending mission teams to Kenya where they have heard it twice!)
- And the image of God present in my "different" neighbor calls me to learn and develop skills for communicating across the divide that seems overwhelming.

What is missing in our multicultural state are those local spaces where people of different cultures are recognized and accepted—that they have something to contribute to our development as kingdom people. What is missing are kingdom people who persevere through the differences, who acquire knowledge and skills, so that our increasingly diverse congregations are not overwhelmed by the differences.

Over fifteen years ago, one of our preeminent Canadian missiologists, Jonathon Bonk, unequivocally stated, "Trudeau was right and Bibby was wrong" (Bonk 1993, 433). (Reginald Bibby is a Canadian sociologist who wrote *Mosaic Madness: Pluralism without a Cause*.) It is time we bring our internationally acquired knowledge, theological and missiological reflections, and intercultural skill set into this dialogue in the Canadian evangelical community.

MULTICULTURAL SOCIAL THEORY AND THE MISSION

What do our understandings and acquired practices in cross-cultural mission bring to this discussion within the Canadian evangelical community?

We know that language, culture, and personality are the basic building blocks of human identity. We believe that identity is a distorted, broken picture of the image of God. Since culture is a product of the interaction of human beings in a particular place and time, then culture must also reflect something of the image of God as well as the corruptions, the distortions, created by human self-love and disobedience (Newbigin 1989, 185).

God therefore is inextricably involved with the processes of identity and difference. And Volf indicates that "it may not be too much to claim that the future of our world will depend on how we deal with identity and difference" (Volf 1996, 20).

Canadian social philosopher, Charles Taylor, indicates that "what we are asked to recognize is the unique identity of this individual or group, their distinctiveness from everyone else. The idea is that it is precisely this distinctness that has been ignored, glossed over, assimilated to a dominant or majority identity. And this assimilation is the cardinal sin against the ideal of authenticity" (Taylor 1994, 38).

We can find the common ground, and insist on assimilation and superficial accommodations, but what do we do with the damages to individual identity, identity which is rooted in the differences? How does the *missio Dei's* call to shalom and the *missio ekklesia's* call to particularity aid our understanding of this discussion?

By entering into other cultures as learners, some of us have come to find and understand the clues that help us communicate appropriately; we know we have been required to adjust, adapt, and shift both our ways of thinking and our ways of acting. Our identities have been transformed—reframed (Taylor 1994). We who have taken those steps become microcosms of the multicultural, one new humanity; we are becoming Volf's "catholic personality" (Gundry-Volf and Volf 1997). We have learned that wherever the gospel is preached it is preached in a human language, in the language of a particular culture; wherever a Christian community tries to live out the gospel, it emerges in the shape of a particular human culture (Newbigin 1989, 189).

That is the mission given to the church; then we begin to find ways for those particular Jesus-communities to engage with the wider family of the kingdom—and all of a sudden we meet other cultures and other ways of expressing what it means to be a Christian community. We find that we are, in fact, invited to adopt a kingdom identity, which moves us out beyond our own culture, to become aliens and strangers, marginalized in our own cultures. In the second century, Diognetus described Christians this way: "They dwell in their country, but simply as sojourners. As citizens, they share in all things as if foreigners. Every foreign land is to them as their native country and every country of their birth as a land of strangers" (Yaconelli 1989, 212–13).

We are called to begin to recover *shalom* in our actions with Jesus-followers from other cultures. We begin to reimagine what grace-purpose God might have had in mind with the proliferation of languages and cultures from ancient times. We have to decide whether we will commit ourselves to receive correction from "the other."

"The only way in which the gospel can challenge our culturally conditioned interpretations of it is through the witness of those who read the Bible with minds shaped by other cultures ... It is only by being faithful participants in a supranational, multicultural family of churches that we can find the resources to be at the same time faithful sustainers and cherishers of our respective cultures, and also faithful critics of them" (Newbigin 1989, 197).

More than thirty-five years ago, Lesslie Newbigin told us that we need "churches that are open to and rooted in all the cultures of humankind;" churches that correspond to the multiethnic neighborhoods in which they serve as "an increasingly credible sign, instrument and foretaste of God's reign over all nations and all things" (Newbigin 1995, 150).

Decades ago, Karl Barth told us, "The Church exists . . . to set up in the world a new sign which is radically dissimilar to the world's own manner and which contradicts it in a way which is full of promise" (Hauerwas and Willimon 1989, 83).

It was a century ago that Robert Speer, in preparing for the 1910 World Missionary Congress in Edinburgh, argued that "humanity is so great and splendid a thing that its fullness can only be framed out of a world wealth of racial elements, bringing under the glorifying power of the gospel, into the abiding City of God, all those riches which no one race is great enough either to conceive or to attain" (World Missionary Conference 1910, 111). (For a discussion of changing language and understandings of "race" and "culture" in missionary writing see Brian Stanley [2010, 3–10].)

What is the potential, the promise, that we have as multicultural faith communities to be a credible new sign, something different—radically dissimilar—to the popular models of multiculturalism around us? Canada has seen very few of these communities of Jesus-followers where there is profound acceptance and adjustment, mutual critique, and remodeling.

So, what aspects of multicultural social theory can help us as we seek to demonstrate a foretaste of this different reality?

HOW CAN THIS FRAMEWORK HELP US?

Making Sense of Confidence and Acceptance

A key thought in the Canadian government's policy of multiculturalism is that national unity "must be founded on confidence in one's own individual identity; out of this can grow respect for that of others and a willingness to share ideas, attitudes and assumptions" (Government of Canada 1971). This model is the basis for what is commonly called "integration"; where some degree of one's original cultural identity is maintained, while also seeking to selectively adopt behaviors of, and participate fully in, the larger social network. Integration, however, can only be successfully pursued when the dominant society is open and inclusive (accepting) in its orientation towards cultural diversity (Berry 1984, 353; Ward 2003, 195–98).

I believe that Christian leaders in local congregations need to teach and model patterns of interaction with persons of cultures other than their own that demonstrate acceptance of the unique cultural identity of all persons in their faith communities.

It is this acceptance of cultural difference that allows individuals the psychological and spiritual "space" to examine those dimensions of their identity which need to be affirmed, restored, or laid aside as they enter into a transformative relationship with God the Trinity. When cultural identity is *not accepted* in a Christian community—as a valued contribution to the whole—then individuals of cultures that are nondominant in the congregation will identify a need to protect that identity from scrutiny. "If you won't allow my Jamaican identity to factor into how we think and act as a Christian community, then how can I put that aspect of my life on the table for the evaluation, healing, and restoration, that is required for my growth in Christ-likeness?"

At this particular point in time there is fresh discussion about identity that is rooted in the experience of the one-and-a-half and second generation immigrants, those young people living in the in-between world of multiple cultures—same, but different (Lin 2009). Alden Habacon, a Canadian who was born in Manila, says, "Using a new model for cultural identity, or 'schema,' we envision individuals as dynamic identities that move through a complex web of cultures. These 'cultural navigators' see themselves as the product of these networks, available to them through immigration, family roots, and residency in diverse cities all over the world" (Habacon 2007). We will do well to remember that cultural identity is fluid, adding depth and complexity to our work in this area.

Making Sense of Multicultural and Intercultural

In a multicultural society it is the state which should create a framework for appropriate interaction of cultures that recognizes both individual and collective rights; but it is at the level of person-to-person contact that intercultural dialogue and competence become requirements.

I believe that Christian congregations need to intentionally embed values and develop policies that validate the worth of various cultures and their worldviews to the ongoing vision and development of the congregation. Likewise multicultural congregations will develop processes and practices that foster intercultural dialogue and understanding.

Values and policies in Christian communities are most often acquired via various theological frames which are rooted in biblical narratives and didactic passages. There is a need to examine afresh the content of Scripture in order to hear again the God of the universe address particularity from Genesis to

Revelation, to hear that content in our own context, and to let it speak to our uniquely Canadian worldview. Much of the current content available is examining these issues through the particular heritage, social structure ,and worldview of our American friends. In many cases the use of the word, "multicultural," is anathema to them. Let us not let them do our work for us.

In the field of intercultural relations, the *contact-participation* model speaks of the extent to which people value and seek out contact with those outside their own group, and wish to participate in the daily life of the wider, diverse society (Berry 1998, 13). There is a direct connection between contact with other cultures and stress levels. Acculturative stress is a stress reaction in response to life events that are rooted in the experience of encountering cultural difference. When the range of choices includes separation, marginalization, assimilation, or integration, there is a clear pattern of findings suggesting that integration is almost always the least stressful option (Berry 1998, 16).

It is quite possible that Christians are struggling with how to engage their "different" neighbors. Kymlicka suggested the differences may be "overwhelming"—our discipline talks about *acculturative stress,* or *culture shock.* It may be that part of our *shalom, missional* contribution to our neighborhoods is in helping Christians make sense of the differences by their active participation in an *integrating* faith community. Christian congregations can play a unique role in facilitating stress-relieving, healthy culture-contact (processes and practices) in a setting where participants share a foundational set of faith beliefs, experiences, and practices.

Enabling Multicultural Common Spaces

In a recent analysis, researchers identified ten multicultural "common spaces" in the Canadian landscape: "spaces" like metropolitan areas, education centers, workplaces, family units, marketplaces, etc. Religious spaces are completely absent from their list, and the whole discussion; the assumption being that religious spaces may perpetuate separationist differences rather than ameliorate them (Dib and Turcotte 2008, 184).

These common spaces in Canada are defined "as locations in time and space where visible and religious minorities and other Canadians meet and interact; such spaces are the foundation for creating and enhancing a strong Canadian identity (Dib and Turcotte 2008, 162). These are the settings where new combinations of interaction emerge—synergies that are strong enough to lead to a collective national identity. This "common space" approach evokes an image of a town square where people mix in space and time and together produce a new, shared identity for themselves as a community (Dib and Turcotte 2008, 164).

I believe that Christian congregations need to intentionally develop and model patterns of hospitality that allow their physical and social environments to function as multicultural common spaces so that the welcoming of strangers begins to reshape all of us into a clearer picture of the image of God.

The Christian tradition speaks of alien and stranger as particularly significant to our kingdom identity. The Israelites were to offer hospitality to aliens and strangers, as a specific grace-act, to remind themselves of their own previous status, both as slaves in Egypt and captives in Babylon. This motif also encouraged Christians to hold their national (cultural) identity loosely, to remember that they were still sojourners, pilgrims on a journey to the Heavenly City.

In her work on Christian hospitality, Christine Pohl suggests that "hospitality depends on defined communities but, when practiced, presses those communities outward. There is an ever-present tension between maintaining a distinctive identity and welcoming strangers" (Pohl 2006, 97). Parker Palmer indicates that "the Holy City arises in the very process of strangers coming together and bringing the word of life to each other" (1983, 64).

He suggests, "The church could become a kind of halfway house between the comforts of private life and the challenges of diversity—but only if it can stay open to strangeness and help us to experience our differences within the context of a common faith" (Palmer 1983, 28). Pohl emphasizes this caution as well: "When the practice of hospitality to strangers is sustained, fissures and weak spots in the welcoming community are often surfaced, and the presence of strangers becomes a ready explanation for what are in fact preexisting problems" (2006, 97).

In order to do this work of developing multicultural common spaces, we will need to practice hospitality in ways that we may not have done in the past, we will need to acquire skill in facilitating intercultural dialogue, and we will need to be prepared for the "fissures" and dissonance (stress) that will surface because of the presence of difference.

Developing Interculturally Competent Leaders

These multicultural, "common-space" congregations do not emerge naturally. Our natural inclinations lead us to associate with those just like ourselves. This, in fact, is how culture develops and is sustained. Therefore, multicultural congregations with the kind of effective intercultural practices I am advocating will be intentionally led and facilitated by culturally competent leaders—leaders with acquired skills, not naturally occurring ones. There is a growing body of research and professional skills focused in this area of intercultural competence (Bennett 2004, 62–77; Gudykunst and Hammer 1984, 1–10), cultural intelligence (CQ; Early and Peterson 2004, 100–15; Livermore 2009), or global leadership (Caliguiri 2006, 219–28; Mendenhall et al. 2008; Lingenfelter 2008). Global leaders are managers or executives who regularly function in complex, changing, and ambiguous cultural environments. They work with, interact with, and supervise colleagues, clients, and staff from cultures different from their own. Pastors of multiethnic congregations in cities like Toronto, Montreal, Vancouver, or Moose Jaw, will need to become interculturally competent global leaders to effectively oversee their churches. The classic pastoral training skill set is not sufficient.

I believe that the skills and tools of the cross-cultural mission "community of practice" need to be more intentionally shared with denominational leaders responsible for engagement with multiple cultural perspectives and with pastors engaged in leading culturally diverse congregations.

Interculturally competent pastors effectively employ an acquired portfolio of skills that includes adaptability, multiple perspective thinking, intercultural communication, culture-general and culture-specific knowledge, toleration of ambiguity, among other things. They will have acquired this skill set through experience with other cultures. But we should be clear that experience alone is not sufficient to develop competence (Kealey 2001). Experience with persons of other cultures requires reflection and generalized perspective adoption to make sense and produce the adjustment required to develop competence. Normally this will require a combination of formal education in related disciplines, facilitated intensive culture-immersion experiences, application-oriented adult professional development, and ongoing individualized mentoring relationships (Mendenhall 2006, 422–29; Hyatt et al. 2009, 119–20).

At the present moment there still appears to be a disconnection between the academic institutions and the real needs of pastors serving multiethnic congregations. I believe there are two dimensions to this disconnection; on one side is the disregard of pastors in multiethnic congregations for the conceptual and practical skill set associated with developing intercultural competence, and on the other, is the perceived necessity of meeting academic "standards" to deliver appropriate learning opportunities. Many pastors of multiethnic congregations tend to minimize the differences as a pragmatic attempt to build unity and harmony.

In my practice of assessing pastors and ministry leaders of multiethnic congregations using the Intercultural Development Inventory, the majority desire to be "accepting" but just do not have the experience—and reflection on that experience—that is required to move beyond minimization. And it may be that nonformal, experiential learning is the key to passing on the skills of our discipline to our brothers and sisters serving such churches. Can we imagine inviting a pastor to accompany us for two weeks on our next international assignment? This kind of intentional learning and coaching opportunity may be the best thing we have to offer toward the development of an interculturally competent Christian leader.

CONCLUSION

If, as Kymlicka has indicated, we tend to like the "idea" of multiculturalism more than the reality of our Greek neighbor, and if we struggle with the stress of difference, then I would like to suggest that it should be the task of our Christian congregations to help us make sense of our context—which will only continue to become more culturally diverse as we move further into this century.

It is the urgent need of the hour that Christian churches should become so released from their present dependence upon one set of cultural forms that [we] can provide the place wherein we are able to do theology in the only way that it can be done properly—by learning with increasing capacity to confess the one Lord Jesus Christ as alone having absolute authority and therefore recognize the relativity of all the cultural forms within which we try to say who he is (Newbigin 1995, 159).

Our churches need to be released from Western, Eurocentric, cultural dominance—not because that is the multiculturally correct, Canadian thing to do, but because our cultural dominance limits our vision of the God who has chosen to be incarnated in all cultures.

If all truth is God's truth then we can affirm that there are aspects of multicultural social theory with which our discipline of the study of mission is very comfortable. The negative critiques are readily available to us, as well. Our challenge in the Canadian context is that we often hear either a simplistic, Pollyanna-ish representation of multiculturalism, or strident criticism against it. In this presentation, I interacted with some of the more thoughtful formulators of this way of seeing human relationships.

We can learn from multicultural social theory about how recognition and acceptance of cultural identity adds worth and value to people who have been diminished by prejudice, discrimination, and xenophobia. This is a *shalom* issue.

We can learn from multicultural social theory about the accepted meanings and associated usefulness of words and concepts like multicultural and intercultural. How the differences in meaning are not about "PC" subjective uses, but actually add complexity to our understanding of issues that are often simplistically reduced. These differences can help us imagine new policies and practices for our congregations.

We can learn from multicultural social theory that integration occurs in the presence of multicultural common spaces—safe spaces where interaction, inclusion, hospitality, and integration can emerge. Can we reimagine the physical and social spaces of Christian community as centers of welcome, hospitality, and outward orientation?

We can learn from multicultural social theory that interculturally competent leadership is necessary to the facilitation and emergence of hospitable, accepting, and integrating communities. What fresh thinking and resources need to be directed toward the development of such leaders in our Christian communities?

"Our Father in heaven, hallowed be your name, your kingdom come, your will be done, on earth as it is in heaven."

REFERENCES

Bennett, Milton J. 2004. Becoming interculturally competent. In *Toward multiculturalism: A reader in multicultural education*, 2nd ed., ed. J. Wurzel, 62–77. Newton, MA: Intercultural Resource Corporation.

Berry, John W. 1984. Multicultural policy in Canada: A social psychological analysis. *Canadian Journal of Behavioural Science* 16(4): 353–370.

———. 1998. Intercultural relations in plural societies. *Canadian Psychology* 40(1): 12–21.

Bonk, Jonathan J. 1993. Mosaics and melting pots: Canadian grout vs U.S. gravy: A response to Reginald Bibby. *Missiology* 21(4): 431–433.

Caliguiri, Paula. 2006. Developing global leaders. *Human Resources Management Review* 16: 219–28.

Consultation Commission on Accommodation Practices Related to Cultural Differences. 2007. *Accommodation and Differences, Seeking Common Ground: Quebecers Speak Out*, Government of Quebec.

Dib, Kimal, Ian Donaldson, and Brittany Turcotte. 2008. Integration and identity in Canada: The importance of multicultural common spaces. *Canadian Ethnic Studies* 40(1): 161–187.

Early, Christopher, and Randall S. Peterson. 2004. The elusive cultural chameleon: Cultural intelligence as a new approach to intercultural training for the global manager. *Academy of Management Learning and Education* 3(1): 100–15.

Gora, Tahir Aslam. 2008. Report gives Canadian values short shrift. *The Hamilton Spectator*, June 12, A15.

Government of Canada. 1971. Statement to the House by the Prime Minister, October 8.

Gudykunst William B., and Mitchell R. Hammer. 1984. Dimensions of intercultural effectiveness: Culture specific or culture general? *International Journal of Intercultural Relations* 8(1): 1–10.

Gundry-Volf, Judith, and Miroslav Volf. 1997. *A spacious heart: Essays on identity and belonging*. Harrisburg, PA: Trinity Press.

Habacon, Alden E. 2007. Beyond the mosaic: Canada's multiculturalism 2.0. Presentation to Putting Diverse Talents to Work, Couchiching Institute of Public Affairs (CIPA), August 9–12.

Hauerwas, Stanley, and William H. Willimon. 1989. *Resident aliens*. Nashville: Abingdon Press.

Hyatt, L., Leslie A. Evans, and Manhubul Haque. 2009. Leading across cultures: Designing a learning agenda for global praxis. In *Contemporary leadership and intercultural competence: Exploring the cross-cultural dynamics within organizations*, ed. Michael Moodian, 111–124. Thousand Oaks, CA: Sage Publications.

Jedwab, Jack. 2002. Thirty years of multiculturalism in Canada, 1971–2001. Association for Canadian Studies and Environics Research Group, Montreal.

Kealey, Daniel. 2001. *Cross-cultural effectiveness: A study of Canadian technical advisors overseas*. Ottawa: Centre for Intercultural Learning.

Kymlicka, Will. 2003. Multicultural states and intercultural citizens. *Theory and Research in Education* 1(2): 147–169.

Lin, Julia. 2009. Same but different. http//www.schemamag.ca/indepth/2009/09/feature-julialin.php.

Lingenfelter, Sherwood. 2008. *Leading cross-culturally: Covenant relationships for effective Christian leadership*. Grand Rapids: Baker Academic.

Livermore, David. 2009. *Leading with cultural intelligence*. New York: Amacon.

McGregor, Gaile. 2009. Book review. *Canadian Review of Sociology* 46(1): 87–98.

Mendenhall, Mark E. 2006. The elusive, yet critical challenge of developing global leaders. *European Management Journal* 24(6): 422–29.

Mendenhall, Mark E., and J. Osland et al. 2008. *Global leadership: Research, practice and development*. New York: Routledge.

Newbigin, Lesslie. 1989. *The gospel in a pluralist society*. Grand Rapids: Eerdmans.

———. 1995. *The open secret: An introduction to the theology of mission*. Grand Rapids: Eerdmans.

Palmer, Parker. 1983. *The company of strangers*. New York: Crossroad Publishing.

Pohl, Christine. 2006. Responding to strangers: Insights from the Christian tradition. *Studies in Christian Ethics* 19(1): 81–101.

Saul, John Ralston. 2008. *A fair country: Telling truths about Canada*. Toronto: Viking Canada.

Stanley, Brian. 2010. From "the poor heathen" to "the glory and honour of all nations": Vocabularies of race and custom in Protestant missions, 1844–1928. *International Bulletin of Missionary Research* 34(1): 3–10.

Taylor, Charles. 1994. The politics of recognition. In *Multiculturalism: Examining the politics of recognition*, ed. Amy Gutman, 25–73. Princeton: Princeton University Press.

Taylor, Edward W. 1994. Intercultural competency: A transformative learning process. *Adult Education Quarterly* 44(3): 154–174.

Tuohy, Carolyn. 1992. *Policy and politics in Canada: Institutionalized ambivalence.* Philadelphia: Temple University Press.
Volf, Miroslav. 1996. *Exclusion and embrace.* Nashville: Abingdon Press.
Ward, Colleen. 2003. Psychological theories of culture contact and their implications for intercultural training and interventions. *Handbook of intercultural training,* eds. D. Landis, J. Bennett, and M. Bennett, 185–216. Thousand Oaks, NY: Sage Publications.
World Missionary Conference 1910. 1910. Monthly News Sheet 6: 111.
Yaconelli, Mike, ed. 1989. *The Door interviews.* Grand Rapids: Zondervan.

2

MISSION BY THE IMMIGRANT CHURCHES: WHAT ARE THEY DOING?

CHIN (JOHN) T. WANG

Immigration has been a major factor that shaped the religious landscape of United States. The early Protestants from Western and Northern Europe, the later Jewish and Catholic immigrants, and the most recent post-1965 immigrants from Asia, Latin America, and Africa, all brought the religious practices of their home countries and formed new religious groups and ethnic congregations. Recently, there has been an increased interest in exploring the relationship between mission and migration (Escobar 2003, Pohl 2003). The Lausanne Occasional Papers, *The New People Next Door: A Call to Seize the Opportunities* and *Globalization and the Gospel: Rethinking Mission in the Contemporary World* (Lausanne Committee for World Evangelization 2004a, 2004b), include discussion on the topic.

We can identify three foci in the current discussions. The first, on which the majority of researchers focus, explores issues of hospitality and care for the immigrants (Soerens and Hwang 2009, 89; Carroll R. 2008, 129–30; Senior 2008, 29–33; Bevans 2008, 94–95). The second is a focus on to the opportunity given by the immigrants' receptivity to the gospel and stresses evangelistic tasks among them (Su 1991, 3–7; McGavran 1990, 182; Romo 1993, 175–95; Rogers 2006; Conn and Ortiz 2001, 311–39). The third focus explores immigrants and their churches as a new missionary force (Van Engen 2008; Lam 1985, 62–65; Hanciles 2003; Hanciles 2008a; Hanciles 2008b).

In this chapter I will analyze the third focus. It is commonly believed that the immigrant churches have great potential for world mission (Rah 2009, 178–79; Escobar 2003; Hanciles 2008a). However, few researchers have examined what the actual mission practices of these churches are (Nelson 2007; Rogers 2006; Hanciles 2008b; Bongmba 2007). It is important to close the gap between the discussions of the missionary potential of the immigrant churches and the reality of their congregational endeavors.

To do that, I provide preliminary findings of an ongoing research project among the immigrant churches in New York City. Specifically, I report on some of the mission practices from two Chinese churches, two Hispanic churches, and two Anglophone African immigrant churches (Nigerian and Ghanaian).

One Chinese church is affiliated with an American evangelical denomination. It consists of a Cantonese congregation and an English congregation. Most of the members in the Cantonese congregation originated from Hong Kong and Guangdong province of China. The English congregation consists of second- and future-generation American-born Chinese. The second Chinese church is nondenominational and has three services, two offered in Mandarin and Cantonese and one in English. The Mandarin-speaking members consist of mainly first-generation immigrants from Taiwan and China. Most of the Taiwanese members have been living in United States for many years. The members from China are mainly new immigrants who moved to New York during the past ten years. The Cantonese-speaking members are mainly from Hong Kong and other parts of the world. While these first two language groups are people of the first-generation immigrants, the participants for the English service mainly belong to the second generation.

The two Hispanic churches are led by Columbian and Dominican pastors respectively. The congregations are mainly comprised of immigrant families who came from different countries in Latin America. They are first-generation immigrants with bicultural and bilingual children. While the church led by the Columbian pastor is a nondenominational church, the church led by the Dominican pastor belongs to the charismatic/Pentecostal tradition.

Finally, the two African immigrant churches are led by Ghanaian and Nigerian pastors respectively. Both churches are represented by a majority of African immigrants. However, people of other ethnic groups are also present, though in smaller numbers. The Ghanaian immigrant church belongs to an American mainline denomination. In contrast, the Nigerian immigrant church is a local chapter of a Nigerian denomination.

LOCAL MINISTRY

Sang Hyun Lee suggests that the immigrant experience is like a spiritual pilgrimage which implies the willingness "to leave the security of home and strike out into the homeless wilderness in order to become open to the higher purpose of God" (1993, 46). However, if the daily life of an immigrant in America is a pilgrimage, then the ethnic church is a home which meets the needs for belonging. It is a home away from home for the many generations of the immigrant families (Lee 2001, 65; Hertig 2001, 88–114).

In the context of adaptation and assimilation, Pyong Gap Min points out four social functions of Korean immigrant churches: 1) providing fellowship, 2) maintaining tradition, 3) providing social services, and 4) providing social status (1992). Although most of the churches in the study provide fellowship gatherings, evangelistic events, and pastoral counseling services, three community ministries distinguish them from the routine practice of many nonimmigrant churches: English class, home language lessons, and telephone ministry.

With the exception of the English-speaking African churches, the Chinese and Hispanic churches offer English classes which consist of ESL class and citizenship exam preparation for the immigrant community. In one Chinese church, students are charged with a nominal fee of $20 in order to encourage attendance. This amount is refunded to the student if he or she maintains perfect attendance at the end of the term. The teachers, who are all volunteer members of the church, often invite the students to their home for informal gatherings. The classes are divided according to the student's level of English proficiency. It seems that this Chinese church designs the classes less formally with the clear intention of building friendship with the students and eventually reaching out to them with the gospel. In contrast, one Hispanic church offers the English classes through a formal church-sponsored institute. The primary goal is to help the students to learn English and pass the citizenship exam. In addition, the institute also provides preparatory courses for GED exams. The pastor explained that since many Hispanic immigrants came to the United States from places of civil war or social turmoil, many of them did not have a high school diploma. Thus a formal certificate not only promotes self-esteem but also provides practical advantages for future career development. By taking the GED preparatory course, it provides an opportunity for social mobility.

The Chinese and Hispanic churches also provide classes to learn their home language—Chinese and Spanish. However, their targets and purposes differ. One Chinese church offers Chinese classes for its second generation with the goal of preserving their parents' language and tradition. In contrast, the Spanish classes offered by one Hispanic church are targeting first-generation adult immigrants who only received a few years of elementary school education in their home country. That is why the course is called *Clases de Alfabetización*. The pastor believes that while it is important to learn English in America, it is equally important to know Spanish in order to access the resources offered in the Hispanic immigrant community.

The third service is an innovative telephone ministry developed by the Ghanaian immigrant church. This weekday telephone ministry consists of a "prayerline" which is available every day from 10 p.m. to midnight. Through an access code, different people can have simultaneous access to the pastor's prayer in a setting similar to a conference call. The pastor recalled that on one particular Friday there were as many as 146 people from North America and even as far as Europe and Africa who phoned in for intercession and emergency prayer. Since many people from the Ghanaian community work as home healthcare aids and have to work on Sundays, they are not able to attend the church services. Thus the prayerline fills part of their spiritual needs and gives them a sense of being connected to the church. In addition, callers appreciate the anonymity of the prayerline as some do not have proper documents to live in the United States.

The Fujianese Grace Church in Chinatown uses similar technology for its ministry. In this case, the pastor conducts a midnight Bible study with many people who have gone to different parts of the country to work in Chinese restaurants. They often call the dedicated line arranged by the church after a full day of work. He said excitedly, "The greatest blessing is the free minutes provided by the cell phone companies after 9 p.m.!" (Ding 2009).

CHURCH PLANTING

All six churches arose from focused church-planting efforts. The nondenominational Chinese church and the Nigerian church were both founded by their mother church in New York. In other words, they were planted by other immigrant churches.

One of the Hispanic churches started as a ministry of a non-Hispanic American church. The ministry eventually grew and evolved into an independent church. The Ghanaian African churches began with a small gathering of immigrants originally attending American churches. As the group felt increasingly dissatisfied or marginalized, they decided to organize their own church and received facility support through the affiliated denomination.

The Cantonese/English-speaking Chinese church was planted by a group of college students under the leadership of a Hong Kong-born pastor who came to the United States as a student/immigrant. The church joined an evangelical denomination in order to develop its missionary program.

The other Hispanic church began with the arrival of the pastor who identified himself as an immigrant missionary. With the denominational support, he was able to form a cell group which eventually grew to become a church of more than 1,000 members.

All six churches have planted or are in the process of planting a church. The Cantonese/English-speaking church joined church-planting projects through its denomination. The nondenominational Chinese church partnered with its mother church in Chinatown to plant another Chinese church in Long Island. The Ghanaian Church is currently planning to begin a new church in Queens with the expectation of a church building facilitated by the denomination.

The Nigerian church planted fifteen other churches in different areas of the country since its founding. One of its most interesting developments is the recent planting of a Spanish-speaking church among the Hispanic community. Its Nigerian pastor described the divine opportunity of ministering to a Hispanic young man six years ago. As the discipleship commitment deepened, the church eventually asked him to translate sermons into Spanish in order to minister to the Hispanic neighbors who attended the service. While the Hispanic group continued to grow and the differences between African and Hispanic worship styles sharpened, a separate worship service was organized on Sunday afternoons. The pastor indicated that the African leadership gave complete freedom for the Hispanic group to conduct its own worship. After three years of development, the Hispanic church was then formally organized and eventually moved to a separate location. The Nigerian Church continues to provide financial support as well as prayer and fellowship. Similarly, Faith Bible Chinese church in Queens founded a Korean church in addition to the many existing Chinese dialect congregations (Quan 2007).

Some of these immigrant churches support church planting outside of New York through their affiliated denominations. In contrast, one independent Hispanic immigrant church develops its own missionary program by planting churches in different nations in Latin America and Spain. It even collaborated with its daughter church in Chile to plant new churches in Brazil. As the church provides financial and material support to the Brazilian churches, the pastor told me that it was the local Brazilian believers who did the translation of Christian materials provided by the church. There is a high level of outreach partnership between this Hispanic church and its daughter churches in Latin America.

SHORT-TERM MISSIONS

The Chinese churches maintain a traditional mission structure similar to many American churches (Pollard 1988). They have a mission department with a specific budget and hold a mission conference annually. They use the mission budget to support missionaries, mission organizations, short-term mission, and seminary students. The pastor of the nondenominational Chinese church told me that while he was a lay member he joined a short-term mission team organized by the Chinatown mother church to minister to the Chinese diasporic community in Eastern Europe.

As he gradually developed a passion for reaching out to Chinese people in other parts of the world, he was invited to join a teaching team that travels regularly to the mountain region of Myanmar. After his first trip to Myanmar he began theological studies in a Chinese Bible seminary in New York. In the meantime he traveled to Myanmar every summer and taught Bible to the Chinese minorities living in the China-Myanmar border. Currently, he is organizing short-term mission trips to support the Myanmar ministry.

The other Chinese church has organized short-term mission trips annually since the second year of its founding. Each year the church organizes three to five short-term mission trips serving in differing parts of the world, sometimes partnering with the denominational mission agencies.

A different type of short-term mission is organized by a Hispanic church. Because of the numerous churches planted in different countries in Latin America, the church organizes "giras de misión" which consists of pastors and cell leaders making frequent trips to the daughter churches overseas. Typically they visit every daughter church annually; during the trips they consult on the progress of the daughter churches and ministry through revival and other special meetings for the local believers. Their trips thus not only provide ministry to the congregations, they also support and supervise the leaders of the daughter churches.

REACHING OUT TO AMERICANS

All pastors expressed the desire to reach out to people other than their ethnic group. The Chinese churches recognize the enormous challenges of settling in New York City for the first-generation immigrants. Therefore most of their mission/outreach focus is on the Chinese people. The local outreach mainly focuses on the Chinese immigrants from Mainland China. The global ministry is also focused on the Chinese diasporic communities in Myanmar and other parts of the world as it is reflected by the missionaries and mission organizations they support. Their English congregations mainly serve the second generation of the Chinese community. However, a growing number of intermarried couples are attending the English services. The hope is that eventually the English congregations will begin reaching out to the non-Chinese population in their neighborhoods.

Both Hispanic churches work primarily among the first-generation immigrants although they also provide headphone translations into English during the worship services. While a large percentage of the Hispanic second-generation immigrants are becoming bilingual, it appears that the churches are moving toward the inevitable path of language assimilation. Both churches are currently planning to organize their English congregation, and the hope is that the new congregations will be the channel to reach out to non-Hispanic people.

The Ghanaian church currently has two services held in separate locations. One is conducted in its home language and the other is in English. Although the majority of the members in the English congregation are Ghanaian immigrants, there are also some Americans attending the services. The pastor hopes that the congregation will be able to include more Americans without compromising its African distinctiveness.

The Nigerian church conducts its services in English. Similar to the Ghanaian church, the Sunday services are mainly attended by immigrants from Nigeria. However, a small group of people from other parts of Africa, the Caribbean countries, as well as Hispanic residents also attend the church.

The pastor points to the challenges of African accent and worship style that are not always well received by non-Africans.

All three groups expressed their desire to reach out to people beyond their own ethnicity and yet almost all of them put their hope in their own future generations. They believe that their bicultural descendants will have the ability to take the gospel to people beyond their ethnic groups.

CONCLUSIONS

This brief review of the mission practices of the churches among the three immigrant communities demonstrated the distinctive focus and ministry efforts each brings to missional engagement.

The Chinese Christians seem most exclusive in their ministry target (Watts 1999, 231–32). There are several reasons for this concentrated focus. First, Chinese people remain one of the largest unreached people groups in the world (Liu 2007). Even counting on the recent phenomenal growth of Christianity in China, numerically speaking it remains largely unreached. The Chinese Christians believe that due to the difficulties of learning Chinese by Western missionaries, it is their natural responsibility to reach out to the Chinese population, both in China and in diaspora. This is reflected in the community outreach, church planting, short-term mission, and missionary supports. Second, Christianity is not a religion commonly identified by the Chinese. The majority of the global Chinese population practice Daoism, Buddhism, Confucianism, and atheism (Yang 1999, 43–49). Chinese Christians believe that their daily interactions with these religions make them uniquely prepared for the task. Third, the steady increase of Chinese immigrants to New York City makes the group a ready target for ministry (Jue 2009, 126–27). Unlike the African and Hispanic immigrants who come from a Christian tradition, Christianity is still considered a foreign religion for many Chinese immigrants. Thus Chinese people continue to be the main target of both local and global mission work for these Chinese churches.

The Hispanic churches focus strongly on the community ministry. The church assumes responsibility of education and social services. Due to the difficult social conditions of the Hispanic immigrants in United States, church leaders are deeply concerned with the upward mobility of the future generations (Martinez 2008, 80–91). The economic hardship also limits the short-term mission trips making them only available to the pastors and leaders.

Additionally, the church planting efforts can be viewed as an extension of the Pentecostal movement in Latin America. The main role of the Hispanic churches in New York City, in this case, is to provide the financial and material resources to their daughter churches. The Hispanic immigrant churches also target their own people although by nature the population is multiracial.

There may be several reasons to this exclusive emphasis. First, the size of the Hispanic population in America makes it a very visible target. According to recent census results, the Hispanic population exceeded African American population, making it the largest minority group in the United States. New York City has one of the largest concentrations of Hispanic immigrants in the nation. Thus the Hispanic churches assume the responsibility of reaching out to its own people. Second, a large percentage of the Hispanic people live in economically harsh conditions and their social needs are very visible to the church. Third, the widely used Spanish and the development of Spanglish make it a very special group (Ortiz 1993). Many immigrants from Latin America can survive in New York City without the need of speaking English. In fact many public announcements are translated into Spanish. Thus, going to Hispanic churches in New York is like an extension of their Christian practice from Latin American cities. Doing ministry in New York is like doing ministry back home! On the other hand, the popularity of Spanish and the near-official use of the language also reinforce the idea that doing ministry to the Hispanics is indeed doing ministry to the Americans because "the Hispanics are Americans!" The combination of these factors contributes to the continuing focus of ministry to the Hispanic immigrants. Although the pastors expressed their desire to develop an English ministry, the popular use of Spanish in America among the second-generation Hispanics continues to slow down the development of outreach to non-Hispanics.

The African immigrants considered in this study have a short history of immigration in America. Although there is a large concentration in New York City, the community is still relatively small as compared to the Hispanics or African Americans. Because the members of these two churches come primarily from West Africa, English is not a problem for them. Thus social services are organized more informally and there are no language classes offered.

The financial needs in Africa and the financial limitations of the immigrants also make it difficult to develop short-term mission trips as many members continue to send financial support to their mother churches in Africa. Although the churches mainly minister among the African immigrants, the pastors reiterate their strong desire of reaching out to the "Americans."

There are several reasons for such vision. First, the English-speaking African immigrants mainly come from countries like Nigeria and Ghana which have large numbers of Christians. It is not surprising that the majority of the new comers consider themselves Christians (Hanciles 2008a, 324–25). When the limited number of African immigrants in New York City is factored in, it is necessary for the church to look outward for outreach targets. Second, the African immigrants come from churches that have been increasingly critical to the many social and moral debates among different Protestant denominations in America. The sharp difference of values between the two cultures creates a sense of urgency and necessity of converting Americans (Rice 2009). Third, even with heavy African accents, the familiarity with English among West African immigrants makes it possible to share the gospel with the American population (Hanciles 2008a, 366). Fourth, although there may be a sense of competition with the African American community, recently there are also signs of mutual acceptance encouraged by national events such as the election of President Obama. Thus there are fewer barriers of communication and identification among the African immigrants (Robert 2010) than among the other groups.

One interesting observation from the study is the lack of traditional long-term missionary candidates from these immigrant churches. There are many immigrants who have gone to seminary for theological education. However, only two of the six (one Chinese and one Hispanic) churches have seen the emergence of new candidates for traditional long-term mission. Additionally, the few Chinese missionaries who were sent on long-term work were assigned to minister exclusively among the Chinese diasporic communities around the world. Those few pastors who went back to Latin America for church planting projects left partly because they were not able to obtain legal status in the United States. It seems that the United States is considered as the final destination for most of the immigrants' journey. Hopefully more candidates will one day emerge from the one and a half and second generations, though we anticipate this will be rare from the first generation.

For the immigrant churches in New York City, it seems that in the near future, the Chinese churches will continue to concentrate their efforts in reaching out to the worldwide Chinese population. The Hispanic churches will focus on the community outreach and services as the overwhelming demands of the Hispanic community continue to grow. The African immigrant churches will continue to mature and work toward their vision of reaching out to Americans.

As the demographic composition of the American society is becoming increasingly diverse, residents of cities like New York will eventually become more receptive to the different voices and accents of the immigrant churches. Adding to the emerging leaders of the second and future generations, the first generation immigrants' dream of reaching out to the Americans may be realized in the near future.

REFERENCES

Bevans, Stephen. 2008. Mission among migrants, mission of migrants: Mission of the church. In *A promised land, a perilous journey: Theological perspectives on migration*, ed. Daniel G. Groody and Gioacchino Campese, 89–106. Notre Dame: University of Notre Dame Press.,

Bongmba, Elias. 2007. Portable faith: The global mission of African initiated churches. In *African immigrant religions in America*, eds. Jacob K. Olupona and Regina Gemignani, 102–139. New York: New York University Press.

Carroll R., M. Daniel. 2008. *Christians at the Border: Immigration, the church, and the Bible.* Grand Rapids: Baker Academic.

Conn, Harvie M., and Manuel Ortiz. 2001. *Urban ministry: The kingdom, the city and the people of God.* Downers Grove: InterVarsity.

Ding, Matthew. 2009. The flooding of the immigrants, a challenge to the church. Workshop presented in North American Chinese Congress on World Evangelization. December 2, in Mt. Bethel, Pennsylvania.

Escobar, Samuel. 2003. Migration: Avenue and challenge to mission. *Missiology* 31(1): 17–28.

Hanciles, Jehu J. 2003. Migration and mission: Some implications for the twenty-first-century church. *International Bulletin of Missionary Research* 27(4): 146–53.

———. 2008a. *Beyond Christendom: Globalization, African migration, and the transformation of the West.* Maryknoll: Orbis.

———. 2008b. Migration and mission: The religious significance of North-south divide. In *Mission in the 21st century: Exploring the five marks of* *global mission*, ed. Andrew Walls and Cathy Ross, 118–29. London: Darton, Longman, and Todd.

Hertig, Young Lee. 2001. *Cultural tug of war: The Korean immigrant family and church in transition*. Nashville: Abingdon Press.

Jue, Jeffrey K. 2009. Chinese American Protestant Christianity: A history on the margins. In *Globalization and its effects on urban ministry in the 21st century*, ed. Susan S. Baker, 120–37. Pasadena: William Carey Library.

Lam, On Kwok. 1985. *The Chinese church: A bridge to world evangelization* [Chinese]. Hong Kong: China Alliance Press.

Lausanne Committee for World Evangelization. 2004a. *Globalization and the gospel: Rethinking mission in the contemporary world*. Occasional paper No. 30.

———. 2004b. *The new people next door: A call to seize the opportunities*. Occasional paper No. 55.

Lee, Sang Hyun. 1993. Asian-American theology in immigrant perspective: Called to be pilgrim. In *Korean American ministry*, ed. Sang Hyun Lee and John V. Moore, 39–65. Louisville: PC(USA) Distribution Services.

———. 2001. Pilgrimage and home in the wilderness of marginality: Symbols and context in Asian American theology. In *Korean Americas and their religions: Pilgrims and missionaries from a different shore*, ed. Ho-Youn Kwon, Kwang Chung Kim, and R. Stephen Warner, 55–69. University Park, PA: Pennsylvania State University Press.

Liu, Jonathan. 2007. For my fellow countrymen [Chinese]. *Ambassadors Magazine* (September–October), http://www.afcinc.org/cgi-bin/artman/publish/article_308_5.asp.

Martinez, Juan F. 2008. *Walk with the people: Latino ministry in the United States*. Nashville: Abingdon Press.

McGavran, Donald A. 1990. *Understanding church growth*. Grand Rapids: Eerdmans.

Min, Pyong Gap. 1992. The structure and social functions of Korean immigrant churches in the United States. *International Migration Review* 26(4): 1370–94.

Nelson, Dana K. 2007. *Mission and migration: Fifty-two African and Asian congregations in Minnesota*. Minneapolis: Lutheran University Press.

Ortiz, Manuel. 1993. *Hispanic challenge: Opportunities confronting the church*. Downers Grove: InterVarsity.

Pohl, Christine D. 2003. Biblical issues in mission and migration. *Missiology* 31(1): 3–15.

Pollard, Mike. 1988. *Cultivating a missions-active church.* Littleton, CO: Caleb Resources.

Quan, Wei. 2007. First Korean congregation founded by a North American Chinese church [Chinese]. Gospel Herald (January 11), http://www.gospelherald.com.hk/news/gen_851.htm.

Rah, Soong-Chan. 2009. *The next evangelicalism: Freeing the church from Western cultural captivity.* Downers Grove: InterVarsity.

Rice, Andrew. 2009. Missions from Africa. *New York Times*, April 12.

Robert, Dana. 2010. Dana Robert extended interview about reverse mission. "Religious and Ethnics Newsweekly" Public Broadcasting Service (January 8), http://www.pbs.org/wnet/religionandethics/episodes/january-8-2010/dana-robert-extended-interview/5361/.

Rogers, Glenn. 2006. *Evangelizing immigrants: Outreach and ministry among immigrants and their children.* Bedford, TX: Mission and Ministry Resources.

Romo, Oscar I. 1993. *American mosaic: Church planting in ethnic America.* Nashville: Broadman.

Senior, Donald. 2008. Beloved aliens and exiles: New Testament perspectives on migration. In *A promised land, a perilous journey: Theological perspectives on migration,* ed. Daniel G. Groody and Gioacchino Campese, 20–34. Notre Dame: University of Notre Dame Press.

Soerens, Matthew, and Jenny Hwang. 2009. *Welcoming the stranger: Justice, compassion and truth in the immigration debate.* Downers Grove: InterVarsity.

Su, Edwin. 1991. In this historical moment. In *Mainland Chinese in America: An emerging kinship,* ed. Edwin Su, 3–7. Paradise, PA: Ambassador for Christ.

Van Engen, Charles. 2008. Biblical perspectives on the role of immigrants in God's mission. *Journal of Latin American Theology* 2: 15–38.

Watts, Bobby. 1999. Equipping the saints for the work of the ministry: The Overseas Chinese Mission. In *Signs of hope in the city: Ministries of community renewal,* ed. Robert D. Carle and Louis A. DeCaro, Jr., 216–32. Valley Forge, PA: Judson Press.

Yang, Fenggang. 1999. *Chinese Christians in America: Conversion, assimilation, and adhesive identities.* University Park, PA: Pennsylvania State University Press.

3

DIVERSITY OF GHANAIAN DIASPORA IN THE US: MINISTERING TO THE GHANAIAN COMMUNITIES THROUGH GHANAIAN CONGREGATIONS

ENOCH WAN AND YAW ATTAH EDU-BEKOE

INTRODUCTION

In this presentation, the term, "Ghanaian diaspora" refers to Ghanaians scattered and settled in foreign lands. Cultural and generational diversity among the Ghanaian communities in the US cannot be overemphasized. There is a twofold purpose of this paper: first, providing an ethnographic description of the cultural and generational diversities among Ghanaians in the US; second, explaining the missiological implications of ministry to Ghanaian diaspora.

GHANAIAN IMMIGRANTS IN THE UNITED STATES OF AMERICA (USA)

The influx of Ghanaian immigrants to US since the 1960s is due to two major factors. First is the "push" factor in Ghana. Due to sociopolitical instability and poverty, there has been large-scale Ghanaian emigration for decades. Second is the "pull" factor in the US. With the perceived opportunities in the US, Ghanaians feel attracted and pulled. An example is the opening up of "the floodgates" through the Diversity Visa Lottery Program (DVLP).

Moses Biney described the waves of Ghanaian immigrants:

> Ghanaian immigrants in New York . . . first migrated between the 1950s and the early 1990s, whereas the second came after 1990 . . .

> Many Ghanaians in the second group ... came through the Diversity Visa Program, as a recent publication of the New York City Department of City Planning points out. (Biney 2007, 26)

As Biney's statement indicated, there has been an official attempt of the US government to attract Ghanaians for economic reasons since the 1990s. For instance, a Ghana News Agency (GNA) reported,

> The D Visa Lottery programme was instituted by the US Government to give opportunity to non-Americans ... the annual programme had offered opportunities to many people around the world to become American citizens ... in Ghana about 7,000 winners were declared in the previous entry ... a lead in the winning race worldwide. (www.ghanaweb.com)

Consequently, one of the pull factors is favorable immigration conditions in the US which contribute to the massive exile of Ghanaians. However, some problematic immigration issues persist. Calenberg observed:

> There is a serious misconception about life in the USA which makes it appear to be "heaven on earth" ... for diaspora Africans coming to America, major cultural, familial, and spiritual problems lurk ... obligations to family left in Africa are burdensome and as a result, there are Africans who lament having "won the lottery" and long for the simplicity of life at home in Africa. (Calenberg 2010)

Some of the lottery winners became disillusioned due to the harsh socioeconomic conditions they face in the US upon arrival.

GHANAIAN CULTURAL AND ETHNIC DIVERSITIES IN THE USA

Ethnic groupings vary widely in cultural patterns. Selected areas of Ghanaian cultural diversity are discussed in this paper.

Worldview

Robin Horton developed a model (i.e., "intellectualist" or "cognitive") for interpreting religious change in modern Africa (1971, 91–112). According to his theory, there is a two-tier pattern of African cosmology. Level one is microcosmic. In this tier devotion to divinities exists. Activities of adherents are underpinned by localized events and processes. Adherents here often lack formal education. Level two is macrocosmic. Adherents support the idea of the Supreme Being whose relationship with humanity is underpinned by universal events and processes.

With these two levels, a center-periphery analysis was developed. On one hand, at the microcosmic level one, the deities are prominent and are shifted into the center of adherence. The Supreme Being is relegated to the periphery. Deity, ancestral, and natural spirits occupying marine bodies, rocks, trees, and forests operate at this level. On the other hand, at the macrocosmic level two knowledge and adherence to the Supreme Being are highly developed; the Supreme Being is moved to the center while the deities are shifted to the periphery. Adherents include the educated, the socio-economically well-to-do, and urbanized people.

Using this analysis the Akan traditional cosmology can generally be placed in a hierarchical order as illustrated in Figure 1. The composition of the cosmology consists of God as Absolute Reality, mother earth, ancestors, deities, and myriad of spirits. Placed on top, God, the Supreme Being, or the Ultimate Reality is separated in the pantheon. God's attributes cannot be shared by the others. Creator God's transcendence and immanence are very influential in the cosmology. The devil and his agents (demons) exercise influence on every aspect of the natural world. The human being is caught up in the operation of all and is influenced by them. Offering of libation[1] illustrates the Akan cosmology.

God is separated from the capricious evil spirits. Linguistically, the deities or lesser gods are not gods at all. They are called *abosom*. Etymologically,

---

1 Akans use the offering of libation as traditional prayer. It is made up of three major parts: invocation, petition, and doxology. Its invocation and doxology are provided here:

Otumfuo Onyankopon Kwame, nsa (Saturday born Almighty God, a drink);

Asaase Yaa Obeatan, nsa (Thursday born mother earth, a drink);

Yen Nenanom nsamanfo, nsa (our ancestors, a drink);

Abosom ahorow, nsa (etc … various deities, a drink);

Ye dome obiara a ompe yen (anyone who wills this)

Abusua yi ye. Ye fre nananom (family ill is cursed. We call on you)

Nsamanfo, yen abosom, ne (ancestral elders, our gods, and)

Ahonhom se womfa apranaa (spirits to strike such a person)

nkum no (with thunder).

Christians have some caveats with such a traditional prayer. First, after the invocation of the Almighty, Creator, and Providential God, there is no need to call on the others in the pantheon. Second, the doxology is too vindictive. Christians are called to love their enemies and pray for them. In addition forgiveness is one of the greatest virtues and a cornerstone in the Christian faith. To call for the killing of one's enemies with thunder is untenable.

abo means stones and *som* means worship. Thus, those involved with them are worshipping stones and woods, not *Onyankopon*—Almighty God. Only God deserves human worship.

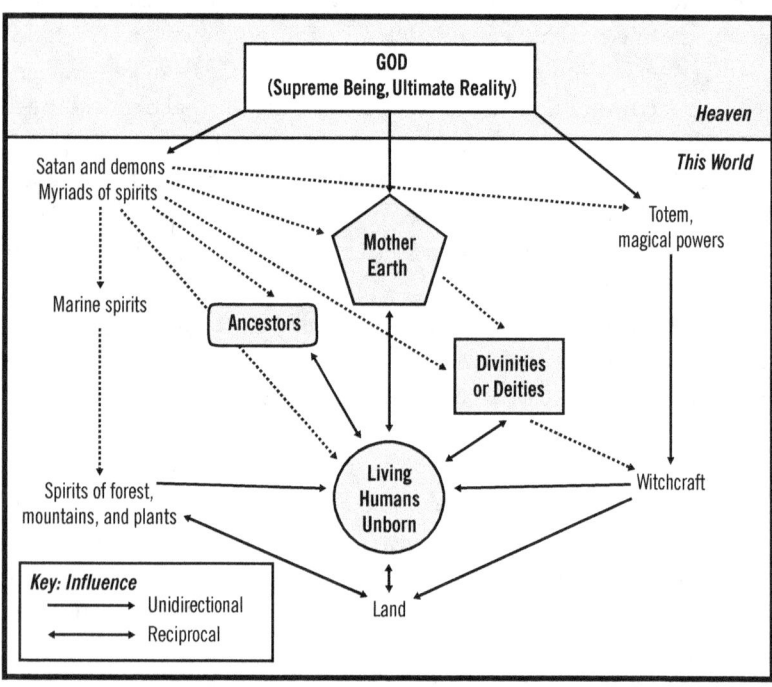

Figure 1: The Akan (Ghanaian) Cosmology and Worldview[2]
(Adapted from Hiebert et al. 1999, 81)

With the Ghanaian worldview above, a comparison between the traditional Ghanaian and Western mind-sets is made in Table 1 with four themes or

---

2 The idea for Figure 1 has been adopted from Paul Hiebert et al. From an *emic* perspective, there are few caveats to note. First, for the *Akan*, God is God—the Ultimate Reality, the incomparable Supreme Being. God's separation is appropriate because of God's exclusive attributes including: *Otumfoo Nyame* (Omnipotent God), *Owo Baabiara Nyame* (Omnipresent God), *Onimde Nyame* (Omniscient God), *Tetekwaforamoa Nyame* (An Ancient to Ancient God), *Ototrobonsu, oboo asu boo awia Nyame* (Creator God who created the rain and sun), *Ahumobo Nyame* (Compassionate God), and *Abawmubuafre Nyame* (God upon whom one calls in one's experience of distress—the dependable God). The evil, capricious, and vengeful others in the cosmology do not share these attributes of God. Second, though the ancestors are living dead, the *Akan* do not lump them with themselves. The ancestors who are venerated are separated from humanity even though they are their nearest and highly influential beings. Third, including the animals, plants, and land in the pantheon is problematic. They are animate and inanimate objects created by God to be respected, tilled, and keep. For the *Akan*, it is the spirits which possess these objects that are part of the pantheon not the physical animals and plants which are used for food and medicines. The land, even though in its created earthly form is next to God, is used for production of food for humanity and serves as the hiding place for human dead bodies.

dispositions, an adaptation from Wan's comparative study (2009) of Chinese and American worldviews.

Table 1: Comparison between Ghanaian Traditional and Western Mind-sets

Ghanaian (Akan)	USA (Western)
Cognition and Emotion	
Conservative: repetitive Emotional: emotional individual life; feelings-expressive Mystical, fantasy, meditative Intuitive and imaginative: mental acceptance and responsive	Dynamic: creative Volitional: individual will-expressive; will-controlled Empirical: details preoccupation Independent: self-sufficiency, self-reliance, self-determination
Individual in Social Organization	
Communal: community-oriented, family, nobody an island Content with and passive to reality Tribal and traditional People-oriented; relationally based	Individualistic; competitive; venturesome; achievement-oriented Causative; rational: always asking "why?" Universalistic: transnational; global perspectives exploitative, discovery, scientific
Socioeconomic Orientation	
Existence: subsistence-oriented Socialism; personality consciousness	Goal: success-oriented, business-oriented Capitalism, time consciousness
Religio-cultural Orientation	
Religion: holistic worldview; related to whole Ontological; person: small part of cosmos, subject to cosmic laws	Dualistic worldview: sacred versus secular Utilitarian; person: controlled object

Comparing the African worldview-controlled mind-set with that of Westerners, the former is more people oriented, conservative, and holistic, whereas the later is individualistic and time oriented.

Religious Multiplicity

The majority of Ghanaians adhere to Christianity (67 percent) and some adhere to Islam (21 percent). However, traditionally, African Traditional Religion (ATR) is to Africa as Hinduism is to India. Relatively speaking, the state-religion separation in the US is nonexistent in the Ghanaian context. Africans live without any separation between religion and socioeconomic life. Peter Sarpong stated, "The African is inseparably religious . . . Religion pervades all areas of African life" (1974, 133–34). Later, Sarpong commented, "For Africans religion is like their skin. They carry it wherever they go . . . Our Western brothers and sisters came to Africa to teach us. Now they should come to Africa to learn" (Ault 2007). Therefore, Ghanaian perception and involvement with religion is generally different from the discerning style in the United States.

Linguistic Diversity

English is the official Ghanaian language—a colonial heritage. However, within the homogeneous Ghanaian culture is heterogeneous linguistic diversity: the Akan speak Twi and Fante, the Ewe speak Ewe, and the Ga speak Ga dialects. The same linguistic stocks also have different dialects. Ruth Benedict expressed linguistic differences as important in understanding cultural diversity, "The numbers of sounds that can be produced by our vocal cords . . . are practically unlimited . . . a great deal of our misunderstanding of languages unrelated to our own has arisen from our attempts to refer alien phonetic systems back to ours as a point of reference" (1989, 23).

Rites of Passage

Generically, rites are closely related to childhood, youth, and adulthood. Birth, puberty, marriage, and death are signposts of human existence. Nevertheless, rites associated with these passage signposts have cultural variety. An example is *obadinto*, the naming ceremony of the Akan, which takes place after the eighth day when the child and mother make their first journey from indoors to outdoors. This "outdooring" rite appears strange when practiced in the US because it is not part of the American culture.

Ethnic Diversity

Several ethnic groupings exist within the Ghanaian diaspora. Table 2 illustrates Ghanaian ethnic diversity, some of whom have migrated into the US.

Contrary to the general assumption of homogeneous Ghanaian culture, ethnicity is an expression of diverse Ghanaian subcultures. In the multiethnic, multicultural-pluralistic US society, various ethnic groups are at various stages of integration and assimilation. Naturally, there is an ongoing dynamic interplay between traditional Ghanaian culture and the influences of dominant US pop culture including thought patterns and lifestyles.

Table 2: Ethnic Distribution of Ghanaians
(2000 Population Census, http://www.ghanaweb.com)

Ethnicity	Population Percentage
Akan	49.1%
Mole-Dagomba	16.5%
Ewe	12.7%
Ga-Adangme	8.0%
Non-Ghanaians	3.7%
Total	100.0%

GHANAIAN GENERATIONAL DIVERSITY IN THE UNITED STATES

Generational diversity within the US population is exemplified by "baby boomers"—a generation born between the late 1940s and early 1960s after the Second World War, and generation-X and generation-Y (or Millennials). Walt Mueller, described generation-Y and its digital attachment:

> Generation Y ... driven by emerging postmodern worldview ... The cries rising out of their deep hunger and thirst are loud, very loud. If we listen, we'll hear it in their music, books and films. We observe it in their choices and behaviors. They long to be "meaningfully connected to life." But the complexities of their world have made it difficult for them to hear the good news—at least in the way the church is now "spreading" it. (Mueller 2006, 18–19)

For Mueller, generation-Y attaches to the computer for "acceptance, understanding, community, meaning, and guidance" (2006, 17) from their online friends. Communication exists in order to obtain individual satisfaction, even with people they never have met.

Characteristically, today's youth are hooked to electronic devices including television and games, computers, mobile phones, iPods and iPhones, and video cameras. Through these vehicles they connect using a variety of social media platforms. Perceiving sexual relationships as institutionalized relationships, they talk, sing, and dance sex. Practices such as "sexting" (sexual texting) are mind boggling. In efforts to keep their bodies pencil slim and sexy, some girls succumb to eating disorders.

Within the Ghanaian diaspora US subculture, there is also generational diversity closely connected with US generational complexities. Generational categorization reveals two main dimensions. Chronologically, there are first, second, and third generations where issues of integration, amalgamation, or assimilation are evident. Additionally, the various Ghanaian generations of immigrants differ in their preservation of traditional Ghanaian culture and adaptation to the US culture.

Figure 2 illustrates readiness and variation of the cultural integration of the overseas born Ghanaians (OBGs) and local born Ghanaians (LBGs) in the US.

Figure 2: Cultural Integration/Variation and Readiness Scale (Source: Wan 1995, 162)

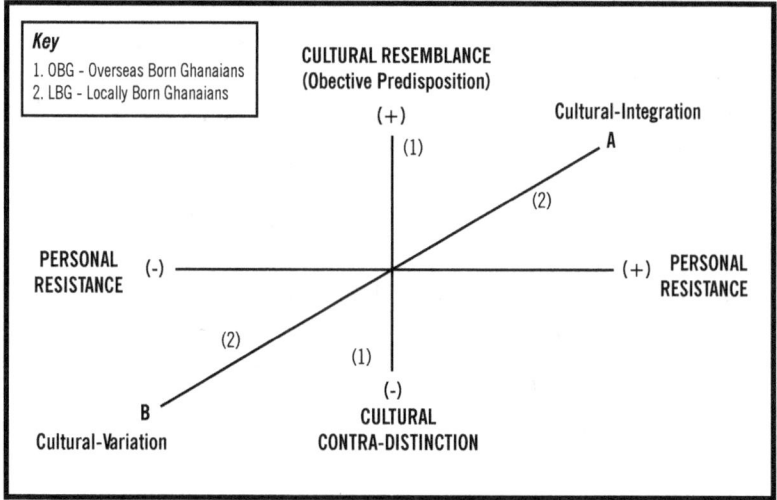

As Enoch Wan explained:

The two major dimensions in the process of cultural integration are: objective predisposition ("the degree of resemblance of an 'OBG/LBG's' own culture to the host culture"), and the subjective preference ("an 'OBG/LBG's' personal choice in terms of motivation, emotion, and volition towards cultural integration"). These two can also be the deterrent factors against cultural integration with resultant cultural variation. [the A-B scale in Figure 2] (1995, 162)

Within the US, generational diversity is the particularity of Ghanaian diaspora generations. The generic values of the OBGs are summarized in comparison with those of LBGs in Figure 2. OBGs retain their cultural values as central, making US culture peripheral. Individualism and assimilation are eschewed.

The second generation constitutes two youthful types. There are those who immigrated with their parents to US (OBG2). These are divided equally between cultural integration and cultural variation (Figure 2). The others are LBG1 and LBG2 who have US citizenship. Ghanaian culture may remain faint at the core of their thinking while US culture is dominant through assimilation and acculturation.

Traditionally, some puberty rites were relevant connections associated with this adolescent generation. However, their physiological and cognitive importance is relatively diverse in various cultures. Formerly, some African puberty rites served to usher in adulthood. Such rites are insignificant in the US. Overall, the technological worldview of the generation LBGs is far different from the OBGs because of globalization, internet technology, computers, and communication drive.

Mueller (2006, 13–14) suggested that the adult generation in the US failed to understand the real worldview of today's youth—a direct reflection of Ghanaian diaspora. The Ghanaian diaspora family, as an institution for socialization, has failed woefully. Attempting to survive the harsh US economy, parents are absentee. Children are virtually abandoned. Therefore, the LBGs are hurting. What then are the challenges and opportunities for Christian ministry?

CHALLENGES AND OPPORTUNITIES OF CULTURAL AND GENERATIONAL DIVERSITIES FOR CHRISTIAN MINISTRY IN THE USA

The following discussion is based on summaries of the challenges and opportunities of ministering to Ghanaian communities through Ghanaian congregations presented in Table 3 and Table 4.

Table 3: Ministering to Ghanaian Diaspora Communities in the USA

Challenges	Opportunities
Communities	
Diverse cultures, worldviews Ethnic churches Similar mainline denominations Pastoral care and counseling Lack of trained leadership Pluralistic environment	Formation and nurturing congregations "Home" from home Operation as community Family values ecclesiology Using cultural values: stories, proverbs, wise sayings, etc.
Generations	
OBGs Widening generational gap Dominant multiculturalism Cultural dislocation: challenging cross-cultural ministry Delineating polychronic-monochronic time Cosmological warfare **LBGs** Linguistic diversity Cultural identity loss Peer pressure Pop-culture assimilation	**OBGs** Mother-tongue gospel; monolingual congregations Meaningful engagement LBGs' care Responsible discipleship **LBGs** LBGs hunger for God Generational-gap as positive evangelization vehicle Youth worship: different times? different congregations?

Table 4: Ministering through Ghanaian Diaspora Congregations in the USA

Challenges	Opportunities
Congregations	
"Colonization": local mainline paternalistic church oversight Challenging employment schedules Long-distance congregational locations Spiritual warfare	Practice: authentic Christians; Africans Functional: satisfying felt needs Self-help; communal support Support for transnational overseas churches Rites of passage celebration Meaningful engagement; toleration and cooperation Responsible discipleship Countering cosmological evil spirits; healing and deliverance Attractive worship for all races, all generations Building bridges among races
Generations	
OBGs LBGs socialization Caring for LBGs LBGs Peer pressures in ministry Difficulties in operating as current members Mother-tongue challenges	OBGs Socializing LBGs through worship Training for LBGs LBGs Teaching mother-tongue through LBG 2 Action ministry: drama, poetry, dancing, etc. Deliverance from "modern day demons"

CHALLENGES OF MINISTERING TO GHANAIAN COMMUNITIES THROUGH GHANAIAN CONGREGATIONS

Worldview Diversity

The scientific and technological worldview found in the US, which is easily adaptable to change, has little connection with the traditional worldview of the OBG. These worldview differences create a wide cultural gap. For both societies, worldview impinges on values, which in turn influences beliefs that control behavior. The challenge for the OBG is fitting into industrialized sociocultural worldview found in the US. Though Ghanaians easily fuse into the dominant culture, the challenge of the OBGs is resistance, avoidance, or rejection of absolute cultural assimilation as they endeavor to eschew individualism. The challenge of the LBGs, on the other hand, is maintaining, preserving, and behaving according to Ghanaian cultural values.

Widening Generational Gap

The generational gap presents a different type of challenge, which boils down to adult and youth cultures. The dominant culture is a serious challenge to the youth. Mueller suggests that in the US-dominant culture, the "'perfect storm, forces, and trends affecting' the youth include the 'rapidly changing, free fall families'" (2007, 39). At the same time youthful independence creates its own protective subculture where "outside influences are shaping teenage values; and changing values are leading to new trends" (2007, 39–76). Essentially, LBGs are in a different world from their parents. Exposed to the US way of liberal life, mostly outside the home, they find it difficult to accept adult conservative views. Table 5 summarizes the differences in values of OBGs and LBGs.

Table 5: OBG and LBG Morality and Values Differences

OBG	LBG
Cognition and Emotion	
Happiness is paramount! Enjoy life Humility: gentle, peaceful, modest Honor: honor wise elders Shame: frown on sin and evil Pain: show no pain—glad to make sacrifices	Success: involving status, wealth, and proficiency Competitive: self-believing ("Toot your own horn; no one else will"), future for youth Honor: behave, speak, and dress American Shame: not of any moral grounds but identifying with the Ghanaian culture Do not be tortured; do not be a masochistic nut
Interpersonal Relationships	
Community: commonality before self Sharing: everything belongs to others Elderly respect; no criticism for elders Universal acceptance: good from all others; despise and chastise the bad Children: gifts from God; shared with others	"Self as number one!" syndrome Ownership: prefer an outhouse over sharing a mansion Critics as good analysts Persuade, convince, and proselytize; be an evangelist/missionary "I'll discipline my own children; do not tell me how to do it."

OBG	LBG
Learning	
Knowledge learning through legends; great past stories Sankofa: "Return to take" old traditional ways and values; they are the best, have been proven Mother-tongue aspirations: cherish own language; speak it	Learning is schooling; get all schooling; cannot be taken from you Look to the future for things new ("Tie your wagon to a star; keep climbing up; up.") You are American; speak English
Religion	
Religion: supreme; relevant; transcends all life's aspects	Individualistic religion
Socioeconomic—Cultural	
Diligence: hard work is sacred Leave things natural Medicinal herbs; God's gifts from mother earth Land is precious: orient self to the land	Live with mind—think intelligently. Show teacher how well you know the answers; be good at books "You should see land when God had it all alone" Synthetic medicines: "Today's laboratories can do anything" Orient yourself to a house, a job

The impact from the host culture, particularly from peer pressure, seems overwhelming to LBGs. As US citizens, they are more inclined to its culture than Ghanaian culture. Honor for them is to speak, dress, learn, and behave like US citizens. Shame is not going against any moral values of the society.

Expectation of a strictly Ghanaian cultural attachment by a different generation seems too much. Such behavior expectations from LBGs—born, socialized, and acculturated in the US by participating in the activities of churches—seem difficult, paternalistic, and overbearing. Urging them to learn the culture of the motherland is problematic. They question the desirability and values of such "outdated" normative traditions. Here is the foundation or basis for OBG-LBG conflict.

Linguistic Diversity

Opposing arguments about mother-tongue aspirations persist among diaspora Ghanaians. On one side is the perception that other overseas-born nationals such as Chinese, Koreans, and Hispanics privately and publicly speak their mother tongue with their children. One of the first social institutions Chinese or Koreans set up in the US is language schools. This is helpful for them to learn their languages. Ghanaians do not do this. To support this argument, an oft-cited instance is the Canadian experience, where the official languages of Quebec are French and English. Quebec laws allow the teaching of Twi, an Akan dialect. Therefore, LBGs in Quebec officially speak three languages, which is helpful.

The other side argues that the perception depends on one's location. Those who live among Whites speak English just as Ghanaians. Meanwhile, related to shame, teasing is the LBG's cognitive challenge. Sometimes it is shameful when peers hear them communicating in their mother tongue. Ironically, speaking Twi, Ga, or Ewe well is a struggle. Linguistically, LBGs are thus psychologically tossed between the two opposing cultures.

Loss of LBG Identity

Assimilation for LBGs is problematic; seen when US OBGs express frustrations in their children's loss of cultural identity. While Christian OBGs are comfortable with their cultural identity, their LBGs are not. This creates problems of identity as well as cultural and intergenerational conflicts. Biney noted:

> People's community life often depends largely on their identification with certain cultural symbols, beliefs and ideas, language, and practices ... This understanding of the relationship between the community and individual is prominent among many Ghanaian immigrants and stands in opposition to the general individualistic ethos of American culture. (2007, 271–72; Department of City Planning 2004)

This is not the case of the LBGs. Coupled with other challenges such as altered cognitive dispositions due to assimilation, lack of parental time and care, and paternalistic adults, the magnitude of LBG identity loss is enormous. This enormity is linked to split personality and cognitive dissonance. Despite their acculturation and assimilation they are neither Ghanaian nor American. Relatively, some LBGs are disjointed and disoriented in terms of their Ghanaian roots.

Delineating Polychronic and Monochronic Orientations

The challenge of African perspectives on time cannot be overemphasized. Two schools of thought have persisted among scholars about so-called African time. On one hand, some scholars call for understanding "African time" on its own terms. Generally, Africans, including diaspora Ghanaians, have a polychronic orientation. Moreau et al. stated:

> Missionaries need to recognize that people in other cultures treat time differently . . . Too often, monochronic missionaries end up communicating that following Christ is a business venture rather than an intimate relationship simply because they do not understand the messages they communicate when they demand that services start on time, that prayer meetings follow prearranged schedule, or that Bible studies end after exactly one hour. (2004, 272–73)

This advice may be relevant for OBG guests and missions in the diaspora. OBG communality makes them start their programs only when appreciable numbers are around. Activities by some congregations never start or close on time. Events scheduled for 10 p.m. could start at 1 a.m. Understanding Africans and rescheduling one's own time to match their sense of time goes a long way to end frustrations and disappointments in ministry.

On the other hand, in all fairness, this issue is problematic in the United States. Western generic perception has a linear monochronic time orientation. Everything is scheduled usually on a pin-point perception of time. Time is essential in all aspects of sociocultural life, including religion. "Time is money."

Diaspora Ghanaians generally are time conscious, diligent, and go to their jobs promptly. They strictly follow the Euro-American monochronic time orientation. However, when it comes to organizing events on their own diaspora, Ghanaians are latecomers. Here, they follow their polychronic time orientation.

Calenberg observed, "A bit strange inclusion . . . is a call for understanding of "African time" on the part of Westerners . . . this seems little forced and indicative of an effort to find . . . a cultural/missiological twist" (Calenberg 2010). Lackadaisical orientation and attitude to time is an anathema. Consequently, calling for diaspora Africans to be understood for their polychronic time orientation is problematic.

OPPORTUNITIES FOR MINISTERING TO GHANAIAN COMMUNITIES THROUGH GHANAIAN CONGREGATIONS

Church Planting: Formation, Mobilization, and Motivation for Multiplication and Development

An undisputed but hardly recognized reality is the creation and nurture of congregations among the African diaspora. They are converting living rooms, garages, defunct warehouses, and dilapidated buildings into imposing chapels in the US to "recaffeinate" some "decaffeinated" US mainline churches. African congregations are reconfiguring and are slowly but surely Africanizing US Christianity. Their existence brings renewal and vitality. African churches are community players which offer spirituality space for worshippers.

Some African churches have transnational operations through contacts with their mother churches back home. There is also double-reverse mission where congregations are set up in the US and then return home to start branches as cooperative ventures. Where are these congregations? How do diaspora Ghanaians use religion as a soothing balm for their psychological, theological, and stressful challenges? The quest for answers is relevant.

Ghanaian churches that have mainline congregations in the US include the Presbyterian Church of Ghana (PCG), Roman Catholics, Methodist Church Ghana, Church of Pentecost (CoP—with over eighty congregations in the US), Assemblies of God, Light House Church, and Apostolic Church of Ghana.

Presbyterians exist in two types: transnationals 1) affiliated with the mainline US Presbyterian Church (PCUSA), and 2) affiliated with the PCG. The former include congregations in Brooklyn and Ogden, New York; Philadelphia; Chicago; Newark; Atlanta; Houston; Arlington, Virginia; Silver Springs, Maryland; and Columbus, Ohio.

Currently nine overseas mission fields (OMF) self-financed congregations and four church plants are affiliated with the PCG with a total membership of more than 1,500. They are responsive to human needs, making them a home away from home. Daniel Wakin explained, "As membership increases, the churches are growing more visible . . . People walk in and find community-friendly African hospitality . . . And second, there's this big emphasis on spiritual power . . . Africans are taking their faith to Africans . . . It is a home away from home for people" (2004, 31).

The type and process of setting up congregations was represented by Enoch Wan in Figure 3 with the observation:

> It is natural and logical, and even expedient . . . to form a monolingual and homogeneous church as in example (4) . . . This is a common practice of OBE . . . Christians . . . The opposite alternative is to form

a multilingual, heterogeneous, and multicongregational church (1) ... The operation of a multilingual and multicultural church (2a) would usually require a lot of mutual respect, careful coordination and Christian love to ensure the health and well-being of such heterogeneous church. (1995, 168)

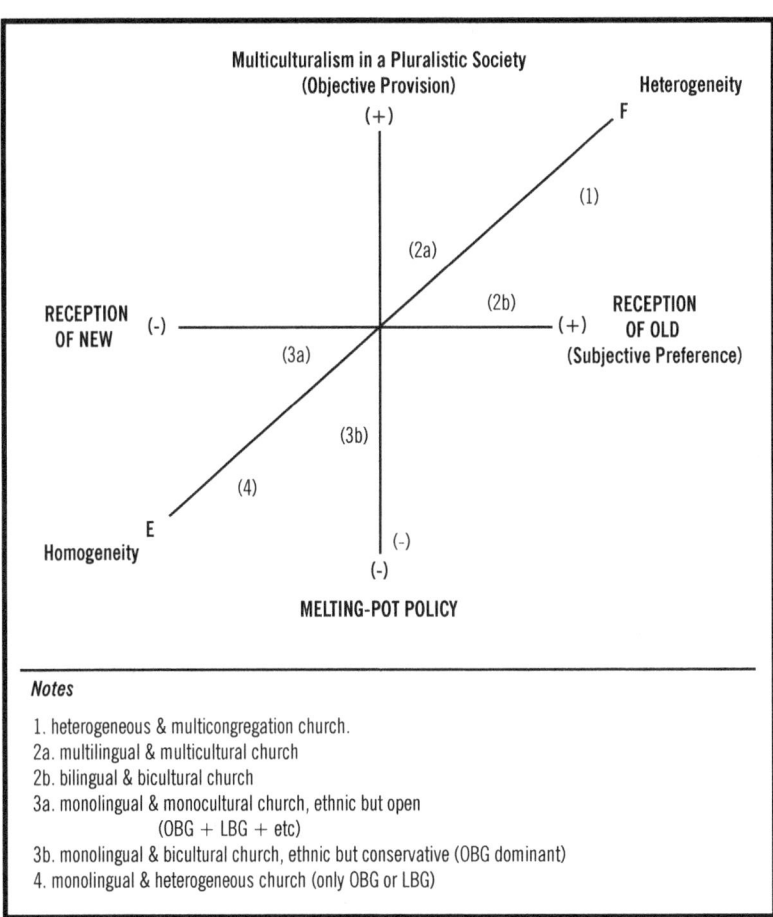

Figure 3: The Congregation Type and Church Planter's Option Scale
(Source: Wan 1995, 167)

OBG congregations are usually set up with the aim of reaching out to non-Ghanaians. The greatest opportunity "is to see churches, reproduce churches" (Patterson and Scoggins 1993, 6). This is an opportunity for the PCG to allow the power of the Holy Spirit to operate for church planting, multiplication, and development.

Linguistic Opportunity

Most of OBGs want to hear the gospel in their mother tongue. Sanneh stated, "In the Christian example the stress on the vernacular brought the religion into profound continuity with mother-tongue aspirations" (1989, 229). Bediako affirmed this when he noted, "Its deeper significance is that God speaks to men and women—always in the vernacular" (1995, 60). Therefore, PCG affiliated congregations are monolingual-homogeneous types which conduct their services mostly in Twi (type 4 in Figure 3). Those PCUSA-affiliated, though made up mostly of Ghanaians, use English first before translating into Twi. Consequently, they are multilingual type 3 in Figure 3. Incidentally, they are not multicultural but monocultural. They also purchase and put on the paraphernalia of the PCG. Nonetheless, they have little or no connections with the PCG.

Wakin wrote, "These churches create a cultural refuge. They are a way for Africans to pass on to their children their African values, particularly for African immigrants who see their children quickly assimilating into African-American culture" (2004, 33). The transmission of cultural values to LBGs is helpful, especially for OBGs who see their children assimilating into US culture.

Authentic Praxis in Practice

Opportunity for ministry comes from the praxis of authentic Christianity within African authenticity. To understand African Christians in the diaspora, arguments between Gerrie ter Haar and Roswith Gerlof about diaspora African Christians in Europe are relevant.

Gerlof argued that Africans in Europe see themselves as Africans. Arguing from her etic viewpoint, to avoid losing their identity, Africans must be categorized as Africans without being labeled as Christians.

From quasi-emic viewpoint, ter Haar (who worships with Ghanaians in Amsterdam), argued that some Africans in Europe see themselves first as Christians before seeing themselves as Africans. She indicates that referring to them as "Africans" in Europe is derisive and demeaning, as it denies them the universality of the faith.

Both scholars are correct. African Christian praxis must be contextualized such that Africans can worship as authentic Christians and authentic Africans. Operating effective mission in African cultural parameters within multicultural US poses a significant challenge. In ministry, Ghanaian congregations need to develop a connection between Ghanaian and biblical worldviews. For instance, there is animosity between God and Satan in the biblical worldview (1 Peter 5:8–9). This resonates well with the African worldview. Other biblical and African worldviews include respect for God's creation, ancestral veneration, subsistence agriculture, community life, strong family ties, and strong moral norms, values, and beliefs that influence behavior.

Worshipping as authentic African Christians is also important. Some categories that can be used to minister through Ghanaian congregations include stories, wise sayings, proverbs, anecdotes, and symbolism. A story and a proverb are used to illustrate: Once, a furious bushfire swept through a village surrounded by grassland. The only thing a mother-hen could do was to gather all its little chicks under her wings while the raging fire drew closer. Eventually, the fire reached them and with swiftness it soon passed over them. All the grass and the mother-hen were totally burnt but the little ones were safe because of their mother's wings that covered them.

This story illustrates Christ's vicarious death (Romans 5:8). No Pauline scholarly theology of Christ's death in place of sinful humanity can explain this better to simple rural people than this story. Akan Proverb: *Abe pe nkwa tenten nti, ode ne ho kowuraa odum yam; na ama wanwu da.* Literally, this proverb means it is because of longevity that the palm tree embedded itself in the belly of the oak tree so that it will never die. In the African tropical rain forest, the oak tree, considered as a forest god by the Akan, can stand for two hundred years if not felled. Periodically farmers and hunters find an oak tree where a palm tree grows in its roots. As a parasite it is believed that the life of such a palm tree depends on the life of the oak tree.

This proverb also illustrates Paul's difficult in grafting as part of Christian life in Romans 11:11–24. In addition, it explains John's concept of Christ's eternal life in 1 John 5:11–13. Such cultural categories resonate well with OBGs in the United States. Christian congregations can take advantage of them to reach out to the unreached among the Ghanaian communities.

Bridge-building among Races

The African diaspora may present a bridge-building opportunity with African-Americans. One misconception is that there is a strong and easy connection between diaspora Africans and African-Americans (Calenberg 2010). The connections are not necessarily natural or easy. Regarding the difficulties of African and African-American relationships, Adeney wrote:

> Sometimes when Africans look at Black Americans they have wondered, "You are the richest black people on earth. Why have you taken so long to come and help us?" For their part, African-Americans have wondered, "Did your ancestors sell mine into slavery?"... Culturally ... African-Americans are quite different from Africans. African-Americans may see "Africans as the face of poverty, disease ... and backwardness." Conversely, immigrants from Africa criticize African-Americans in regard to sexual behavior, work ethic, language, and self-image. (2010, 6)

Even so, Africans in reverse mission are bringing their faith to Africans in the US Wakin suggested:

> As African churches attract increasing numbers of white worshippers, they can serve as a bridge between races ... Like many Pentecostal churches, it is trying to reach beyond ethnic borders ... Maybe the services should be shorter than the usual three or four hours ... or maybe African dress should be discouraged. (Wakin 2004, 32-33)

Such sentiments, describing the CoP in Bronx, are shared by the leadership of some other Ghanaian congregations. They have the potential to serve as bridges to spread the gospel to the unreached among other races and cultures in the US. For instance, the Portland International Church (PIC; Oregon) is multinational. Though Ghanaian-led, among the membership are Ghanaians, Nigerians, Togolese, Cameroonians, Liberians, as well as white, black, and Hispanic Americans. Another example is Victor Seraya's Redeemed Church of Jesus Christ, which meets in the facilities of and enjoys good fellowship with Genesis Community Fellowship, a primarily African American church (Calenberg 2010).

Other opportunities include the exhibition of community, communality, and commonality, family relational values, promotion and operation of self-help, communal support, fraternizing, promotion of Ghanaian culture, socialization and enculturation of children, transmission of financial support for their mother churches back home, and celebration of the rites of passage.

MISSIOLOGICAL IMPLICATIONS: MOTIVATING AND MOBILIZING THE CONGREGATIONS FOR MISSION

Searching for the practical missiological use of US-Ghanaian Christian congregations involves the relational strategies of reaching out to Ghanaian nonbelievers. Mission should strive for the inseparable quantitative and qualitative growth of the congregations. Instead of struggling for unworkable conversion methods care must be taken in strategizing to reach the unreached.

Strategizing to Become Missional in Practice

An important evangelization strategy is meaningful engagement through toleration and cooperation. The popular posture of the unreached is confrontational, defensive, and argumentative. Moreau et al. admonished:

> Tolerance is a term defined in context . . . Scripturally, Christians are called not simply to tolerate, but to go further; they are commanded to love the followers of non-Christian religions . . . the missionary should recognize that cooperating with others is less likely to harm the gospel message than is an intolerant attitude that communicates posture of superiority. (2004, 308–9)

Some non-Christians often open up when they realize that Christians are prepared to listen to them. Ghanaian Christians should eschew their criticisms of and arguments with nonbelievers and instead listen to them. Meaningful dialogue and discussions without coercive or intimidating language or actions are invaluable to win the unreached. Thereafter one can follow a conversation on why Christianity "ticks." In addition, missions in the form of "performing acts of charity whenever appropriate, joining them in working for their benefit when they are oppressed, and demonstrating God's unconditional love for them in all circumstances" (Moreau et al. 2004, 309) are the congregations' nuanced practical strategic mission to win the unreached for Christ.

Second, strongly related to engagement and growth is the function-oriented mission practice of satisfying felt needs. Wakin stated, "What's happening in African churches is largely at the beginning . . . They're very responsive to human needs" (Wakin 2004, 33). Christian anthropologists such as Charles Kraft (2005, 92) and Paul Hiebert employed the "need approach" and functional theories and insisted that different kinds of need have to be addressed among different people groups. However, need-satisfaction should not be the overarching framework for mission practice because it is humanistic without strong theological foundation, reducing missiology to psychology.

Consequently, Enoch Wan proposed a "relational paradigm" (Wan 2006; 2007; 2010a; 2010b) as an alternative to the need-based functionalist approach. Ghanaian culture has a strong relational emphasis, thus the understanding and implementation of "relational paradigm" will be practical and effective when motivating and mobilizing the Ghanaian congregations for mission.

Third, the Great Commission is "to make disciples;" not merely producing religious adherents, nor mere converts, nor to increase church membership. The church is defined as the *ecclesia* (an assembly of God's people) and discipleship (*didache*) requires apprenticeship. A disciple is a follower of Jesus with a Christ-like lifestyle. Bosch suggested, "It is Christ Himself who calls 'Follow Me!' and they follow . . . Following Jesus . . . and sharing His mission thus belong together" (2005, 38). This is a high calling as indicated in James Dunn's question—"Would Jesus have been disappointed with the church?" (1992, 93). Discipleship promotes exemplary character, godly habits, and God-honoring relationships that are absolutely crucial in mission. By the Christian reality of relationally loving one another, the world will know that we are indeed Christ's disciples (John 13:35).

Discipleship should not be isolated and confined to the chapel, but it should also include what happens from Monday to Saturday. If Ghanaian diaspora congregations are not making people relate Scripture to what they do in private, then there is a missing link in discipleship. Notwithstanding the difficulty, meaningful discipleship could revolutionize the Ghanaian diaspora congregations.

Cosmological Warfare Reality

One serious issue in diaspora mission is the African Christology of constant warfare. This resonates well with all Ghanaians as Africans. For Africans, there is no separation between the sacred and the mundane. Most occurrences in human life are attributed to one's perceived and/or real enemies. God is sovereign, eternal, merciful, compassionate, and providential. Conversely, Satan and his demons are devious, capricious, and malignant. Constant warfare between the two forces is a reality. Human beings are caught up in this conflict. Activities of witches and wizards, diviners, occultists, charmers, and malignant ancestors are all directed against Christians to prevent them from enjoying abundant life or fulfilling destiny.

Consequently, salvation is defined as enjoyment of longevity, prosperity, security, and good health. Jenkins stated, "Doctrines of loosing the captives, casting out demons, healing and deliverance, liberating the oppressed and defeating poverty take place against the backdrop of constant spiritual warfare between the Triune God and Satan with his demons" (2007, 149–51).[3] For Ghanaian Christians, Jesus Christ as the Son of God is victorious over all. Christ is the greatest *Osagyefo*, the Supreme Commander-in-Chief who fights to win this constant struggle for a victorious Christian life. Non-Christian Africans are aware of such enemies and Christian mission should use the strategic method of miracles, healing, and deliverance to reach out to them.

Reaching Out to the LBGs

Reaching out to the LBG youth requires ministry strategies that are prayerfully guided by the Holy Spirit and carefully implemented by his faithful followers.

First, the generational gap and language study can be positive factors for evangelization in the US. For example, concerned parents who recognize the reality of the generation gap will gladly come to church-sponsored parenting workshops about raising LBGs in the US. Parents who desire their children to acquire native language will enroll their children in church-sponsored Ghanaian language school. For instance, Fordham University is starting a program of teaching and learning Twi. Mensah-Shalders observed:

> Fordham University will start teaching *Twi* . . . The motivation . . . as a result of the growing number of people who transact business in the Bronx using *Twi* . . . It is amazing to see people communicating in *Twi* . . . The churches . . . The University is proud to undertake this

---

3   Etymologically, *osa* means "war" and *gyefo* means "redeemer," "savior," or "conqueror." *Osagyefo*, therefore, means Redeemer or Conqueror in war.

enterprise as it will help teachers, social workers, and others who will be working in the Bronx communities where *Twi* is spoken ... the course will also look at the various cultural practices of the Akan. (2009)

Young graduates of this program can teach the LBGs Twi in language schools in Ghanaian congregations.

Second, worship is another helpful means to attract LBGs. Ghanaian congregations may have two services: a traditional worship in the native tongue for OBGs and a contemporary style in English for LBGs.

One Ghanaian congregation with two worship services can accommodate both generations and language groups. When teenagers worship with their peers, LBGs vitality, vibrancy, and expressive worship can even attract LBGs non-Ghanaian American youth.

Third, adults in the congregations should care for the LBGs both at home and within "the household of God" (the church; 1 Tim 3:14–16). The younger LBGs should not feel unwelcome; instead they are to be cared for and loved by church leaders who are primarily OBGs. This proposal is not a substitute for parental responsibility but crucial for the health of Ghanaian congregation—our 4/14 Window: "It is crucial that mission efforts be reprioritized and redirected toward 4/14 group worldwide. This requires that we become acutely aware of what is taking place in their lives" (Bush 2009, x).

In one Ghanaian congregation, a group of teenagers were given choices of who they would meet: their teachers, church elders, or parents. Both genders vehemently refused meeting their teachers for the young men complained that their teachers were competing with them over girlfriends. Church elders were refused because they appeared to be too paternalistic. They chose to meet their parents. When a meeting was arranged the teenagers said they needed RAIL at home (RAIL was their acronym for recognition, acceptance, identification, and love). The girls told their parents that because of the lack of love at home, they would fall for anyone outside the home who claimed to love them. Mission through Ghanaian congregations should offer RAIL for its youth as a model for parenting LBGs. The congregations can attempt to help bridge the generational gap and reconcile those who feel hurt and lonely because the church is to be the household of God where healing and help are offered to those in need.

CONCLUSION

The church is a glorious celebration of unity in spite of diversity, including the generational, linguistic, and cultural diversity in Ghanaian congregations. If we all submit to the lordship of Christ within the church (Eph 5:21), then diversity of race, culture, gender, generation, and language are not factors of division.

If all groups, OBGs and LBGs, can live harmoniously together as the spiritual family of God, then it will become a demonstration of the "gospel ... the power of God unto salvation" (Rom 1:27). Diaspora Ghanaian Christian mission, therefore, should apply the recommendation from Moreau et. al.:

> Evangelism is to be given a logical ... priority in the total mission of the church. Mission that does not include evangelism is missing the core ... At the same time; however, mission is more than evangelism. Mission that does not include incorporating those led to Christ into a local body of believers or teaching them to obey all that Christ commanded his followers to be salt and light is, at best, truncated mission. (2004, 88–89)

God's Kingdom Vocation (fulfillment of Christian God-given goal)

=

The Great Commandment of Love
(Deut 6:4, 5; Lev 19:18; Mark 12:25–31)

+

The Great Commission of Witness
(Matt 28:16–20; Mark 16:15–18; Luke 24:45–49; John 20:21; Acts 1:8)

+

The Great Requirement of Humility
(Mic 6:8)

To fulfill this kind of Christian mission, the reminder that Ghanaians are inseparably religious is invaluable. Many diaspora Ghanaians had gone through mission schools, professed Christianity, or are open to the Christian faith. Diaspora Ghanaian Christians should be educated to obey their Christian mandate to reach out to their non-Christian counterparts in love, humility, and embrace. Christian mission should stop its self-praise by not condemning non-Christians but reaching out to them. However, they should not be in-grown in their orientation and effort. Instead, they should reach out beyond their own by obeying the Great Commission and making disciples of all nations.

Ministry to diaspora Ghanaian communities through Ghanaian congregations is only partial ministry; the major solution has to be found for the challenge of reaching out to other races in the US. This is the next and main motif of Christianity—giving mission through and beyond the Ghanaian diaspora.

Diversity is likened to the gorgeous and expensive *Akan kente*—the cloth for pomp and pageantry used by kings and the rich. The threads are in various colors but are useless on their own. However, woven into stoles and hand-woven together, they become a beautifully designed piece of cloth. The designs are in different shapes, but skillfully blended together they become the gorgeous embroidery for royalty.

This is an apt description of Christian diversity of Ghanaian diaspora congregations that minister beyond Ghanaian diaspora in the US. Similarly, the theme for the 2010 North American Mission Leaders Conference (NAMLC) is relevant as explained in the NAMLC flyer:

> A mosaic starts with many pieces of diverse shapes, size, color, texture, depth. Pieces may look random and disorganized—and even ugly spread out. However, the potential is there to put them together into a beautiful design ... Thus, diversity is an apt description of the body of Christ ... yet all held together by the beauty of God's grace and our passion to bring others into relationship with Him. (http://www.crossgloballink.com)

REFERENCES

Adeney, Miriam. 2010. "Colorful Initiatives: North American Cultures in Mission." Paper presented at the Northwest Regional Evangelical Missiological Society (EMS) meeting, March 13, in Portland, OR.

Ault, Jim. 2007. Faces of African Christianity. Documentary film footage filmed in Ghana.

Bediako, Kwame. 1995. *Christianity in Africa: The renewal of a non-Western religion.* Edinburgh: Edinburgh University Press.

Benedict, Ruth. 1989. *Patterns of culture.* Boston: Houghton Mifflin.

Biney, Moses. 2007. "Singing the Lord's song in a foreign land": Spirituality, community, and identity in a Ghanaian immigrant congregation. In *African immigrant religions in America*, eds. Jacob Olupona and Regina Gemignani. New York: New York University Press.

———. 2011. *From Africa to America: Religion and adaptation among Ghanaian immigrants in New York*. New York: New York University Press, 2011.

Bosch, David. 2005. *Transforming mission: Paradigm shifts in theology of mission*. Maryknoll: Orbis.

Bush Luis. 2009. *The 4/14 window: Raising up a new generation to transform the world*. Colorado Springs: Compassion International.

Calenberg, Rick. 2010. Response to paper presented at the Northwest Regional Evangelical Missiological Society (EMS) meeting, March 13, in Portland, OR.

Department of City Planning. 2004. *The newest New Yorkers 2000: Immigrant New York in the millennium*. New York: Department of City Planning.

Dunn, James. 1992. *Jesus' Call to Discipleship*. Cambridge: Cambridge University Press.

Ghana News Agency. 2009. US Embassy Opens DV Visa Lottery. http://www.ghanaweb.com/GhanaHomePage/NewsArchive/artikel.php?ID=170641.

Gibbs, Eddie. 2000. *Church next: Quantum changes in how we do ministry*. Downers Grove: InterVarsity.

Hiebert, Paul G., et al. 1999. Understanding folk religion: A Christian response to popular beliefs and practices. Grand Rapids: Baker.

Horton, Robin. 1971. African conversation. *Africa* 41(2): 91–112.

Jenkins, Philip. 2007. *The next Christendom: The coming of global Christianity*. Oxford: Oxford University Press.

Kraft, Charles. 2005. *Christianity in culture: A study in biblical theologizing in cross-cultural perspective*, rev. 25th Anniversary Edition. Maryknoll: Orbis.

Mensah-Shalders, Ekow. 2009. Fordham University goes Twi. http://www.ghanaweb.com/GhanaHomePage/NewsArchive/artikel.php?ID=172246.

Moreau, A. Scott, Gary Corwin, and Gary McGee. 2004. *Introducing world missions: A biblical, historical, and practical survey*. Grand Rapids: Baker Academic.

Mueller, Walt. 2006. Engaging the soul of youth culture: Bridging teen worldviews and Christian truth. Downers Grove: InterVarsity.

———. 2007. *Youth culture 101*. El Cajon, CA: Youth Specialties Products.

Patterson, George, and Richard Scoggins. 1993. *Church multiplication guide: Helping churches to reproduce locally and abroad*. Pasadena: William Carey Library.

PCG OMF. 2010. Report on proposed overseas presbytery submitted to the 9th General Assembly. August 6–11, in Takoradi.

Sanneh, Lamin. 1989. Translating the message: The missionary impact on culture. Maryknoll: Orbis.

Sarpong, Peter. 1974. *Ghana in retrospect: Some aspects of Ghanaian culture*. Tema: Ghana Publishing Company.

Wakin, Daniel J. 2004. "Where the Gospel Responds in African Tongues" http/www.asu.edu/educ/espl/LPRU/newsarchive.

Wan, Enoch, ed. 1995. Missions within reach: Intercultural ministries in Canada. Vancouver: China Alliance Press.

———. 2006. The paradigm of "relational realism." *Occasional Bulletin* 19 (2): 1–4.

———. 2007. Relational theology and relational missiology. *Occasional Bulletin* 21(1): 1–7.

———. 2009. Understanding Chinese Worldview. *Sino Theology* (unpublished).

———. 2010a. Global people and diaspora missiology. In *Handbook: From Edinburgh 1910 to Tokyo 2010*, edited by Yong J. Cho and David Taylor, 92-100. Pasadena: Tokyo 2010 Global Mission Consultation Planning Committee

———. 2010b. A missio-relational reading of Romans. *Occasional Bulletin* 23(1): 1–8

Wan, Enoch, and Sadiri Joy Tira, eds. 2009. *Missions practice in the 21st Century*. Pasadena: William Carey International University Press.

4

DIASPORA CHURCH PLANTING IN A MULTICULTURAL CITY: A CASE STUDY OF GREENHILLS CHRISTIAN FELLOWSHIP

SADIRI JOY TIRA AND NARRY F. SANTOS

INTRODUCTION

Unprecedented movements of people, hereafter referred to as "diaspora," in larger scale and higher frequency, have clearly set a global trend that has marked the twenty-first century. This global trend caused by multiple factors, both voluntary (e.g., educational, financial advancement, etc.) and involuntary (e.g., natural disasters, war, human trafficking, etc.) is a complex issue that is increasingly changing societies, cultures, economies, and world demography. According to the United Nations Development Program, there are now 214 million international migrants (Human Development Report 2009). Undoubtedly, all nations have been affected by international mass migration.

Experts across disciplines are paying close attention to international migration patterns and its implications on politics, economics, law, religion, and other fields. In particular, missiologists and church planters are monitoring and analyzing the recent mass movements of people. Winter and Koch note, "As history unfolds and global migration increases, more and more people groups are being dispersed throughout the entire globe ... Not many agencies take note of the strategic value of reaching the more accessible fragments of these 'global peoples'" (Winter and Koch 2009, 537).

While it is true that many agencies are responding slowly to the realities of diaspora and their strategic value for reaching the global peoples, we are thankful for congregations who are "reading the times" and are "riding on the wave" of God's movement. Our purpose here is to showcase such a group—the Greenhills Christian Fellowship (hereafter referred to as GCF) in Toronto, Canada. Specifically, we present a model demonstrating the effectiveness of diaspora church planting in arguably the most diverse and multicultural city in the world (http://www.toronto.ca). GCF-Toronto is a local church that has developed its evangelism, discipleship, and missions programs.

The significance of this study, therefore, is that it contributed to the understanding of missions for Filipinos in diaspora and perhaps to other visible minority groups as well as to Christian denominations and parachurch ministries seeking to plant churches among the many diaspora groups in Canada. We chose to organize our material into three parts:

1. Diaspora landscape of Greater Toronto Area to help readers better understand the cultural diversity of the city and the geographical context of Greenhills Christian Fellowship (GCF);
2. A case study of GCF's glocal synchronic and diachronic church-planting strategy; and
3. Missiological analysis and implications for glocal missions.

"Glocal" was originally coined by Robertson (1995, 28) to express a new interweaving of local and global. It is simply "thinking globally and acting locally," as applied in business "glocalization" (Tai and Wong 1998; Rosenau 2003). In recent years, missiologists also borrowed this glocal concept to describe the church and the local congregation's simultaneous ministries in both global and local arenas.

The research methods employed by the writers are case studies and participant observation. The case study approach utilized in this paper is assumed to be the study of a case "over time through detailed, in-depth data collection involving multiple sources of information rich in context" (Creswell 1998, 61). We gathered data from interviews and literature on GCF, including documents from the archives.

Participant observation methodology assumes the complete participation of the observer. This is where the "highest level of involvement . . . probably comes when [the authors] study a situation in which they are already ordinary participants" (Spradley 1980, 61). This methodology is used because one of the authors is the founding pastor of GCF-Toronto and is able to effectively make systematic observations about the birth and development of GCF-Toronto based on firsthand knowledge and familiar relationships with the mother church in Manila, Philippines and the members of the Toronto congregation involved in the past and present activities of GCF-Toronto.

CANADA-WIDE AND GREATER TORONTO AREA DIASPORA LANDSCAPE

Canada is known to be a nation of immigrants—early Canadian Western society was composed of people who originally migrated from Europe. Since early in the twentieth century Canada has opened its doors to diasporas from Asia, Africa, and Latin America. In just the last two decades, Canada has extended its immigration policy to include rising numbers of foreign workers (on work contracts) working from the vineyards of British Columbia to the oil sands of Alberta to the Tim Horton's donut outlets inside the Toronto airport to the fishing boats off New Brunswick. There are also thousands of foreign students from the secondary school level to the colleges and universities across Canada. Also, Canada welcomes asylum seekers and refugees (e.g., political, religious, and climate refugees), who can be found living in high-rise apartments of large cities such as Toronto, Montreal, and Vancouver. Canada is a hospitable country renowned for its multiculturalism.

By December 2008, Canada had: (1) a total of 302,303 foreign workers as temporary migrant workers; (2) granted initial entry to 233,971 foreign students; (3) welcomed 27,956 refugees; and (4) granted 236,758 people permission to make Canada their home as permanent immigrants. Of these, the top ten source countries for permanent immigrants were (in descending order): China, India, Philippines, USA, Pakistan, UK, Iran, South Korea, France, and Colombia (Citizenship and Immigration Canada Facts and Figures 2008; http://www.cic.gc.ca/english/resources/statistics/facts2008/index.asp).

According to Canada's migration experts, visible minorities or non-Caucasian Canadians are predicted to dominate Canada's three megacities (Toronto, Montreal, and Vancouver) by 2017. They will mainly be South Asians and Chinese, adding to the present immigrants who are established members of the Canadian community. They already have their own ghettos (e.g., Little Saigon, Chinatown, Bombay Palaces), places of worship, and cultural associations.

Filipino-Canadians are one of the largest immigrant groups of recent years, particularly in the Greater Toronto Area (http://www40.statcan.gc.ca/l01/cst01/demo24a-eng.htm; also http://www45.statcan.gc.ca/2009/cgco_2009_001-eng.htm). Like other diaspora groups, they have become active participants in shaping the communities of which they have become a part. People of Filipino descent have connected across the country, gathering locally, and branching out to other Filipinos through media and organized meetings, including political, sociocultural, and religious gatherings.

The imagination of a missiologist is boggled by Canada's multiethnic society. The multitudes of people from every corner of the globe—representing all colors, languages, smells, and cultures—are not just a quaint minority in Canada, but are truly Canadians. It is to evangelize and mobilize diaspora peoples for global mission in this Canada that God has called the Canadian disciples of Christ, including the Filipino-Canadian disciples.

GREENHILLS CHRISTIAN FELLOWSHIP: A BRIEF BACKGROUND

Greenhills Christian Fellowship is a thirty-two-year-old Baptist church in Pasig City, Metro Manila, Philippines. GCF was founded and pastored for fifteen years by Rev. David Yount, a Conservative Baptist missionary (Shelley 1971; Davis 2006). Rev. Yount led the church in its growth to more than 600 members through intentional evangelism and discipleship among middle and upper-middle class people in and around Manila. He also guided the church in the purchase of a lot and in the building of a church facility that could accommodate 1,500 people at the worship hall.

After fifteen and a half years, Rev. Yount handed the spiritual leadership of GCF to Dr. Luis Pantoja, Jr., who shepherded the church for the last sixteen and a half years. The ministry of Dr. Pantoja is marked with an emphasis on satellite development (the GCF term for church planting). Aside from its main church in Pasig City (called GCF-Ortigas), GCF has sixteen satellites (or church-plants) in the Philippines and Canada (fourteen in the Philippines and two in Ontario; http://www.gcf.org.ph).

GCF-South Metro: The First GCF Satellite

I (Narry Santos) started ministry at GCF on June 1, 1994. After serving as Christian Education Pastor in GCF-Ortigas for three years, I was assigned to plant the first GCF satellite south of Manila, which is called GCF-South Metro. On January 17, 1997, GCF-South Metro was launched (or birthed). For ten years, I was the resident pastor of this first GCF satellite. On our tenth year, we had 900 people worshipping with us, over 300 students attending our children's Sunday school, and eighty-eight growth groups (or small groups) meeting weekly (http://www.gcfsouth.org).

In 2006, GCF-South Metro was able to buy a lot and to put up its own building that could accommodate 1,500 people and a Christian school that attracted over one hundred students from preschool to high school. GCF-South Metro also spearheaded the launch of three other satellites further south of Manila. These three satellites are GCF-Batangas City (which was launched in 2001 and now has 180 people), GCF-Santa Rosa (which was launched in 2006 and now has 200 people), and GCF-Parañaque (which was launched in 2008 and how has 150 people).

Context for a GCF Diaspora Church-planting Vision

In such a context of growth, the GCF-South Metro leaders have sensed (beginning in 2004) that the Philippines was too small a place to fulfill the Great Commission. We realized that God wanted us to be part in the fulfillment of the global GCF vision: "GCF is one church reaching influencers through satellites in strategic areas worldwide." Our leaders have owned the conviction that the Great Commission is nothing less than global.

However, from 2003 to 2005, a string of five families were preparing to go to Canada as new immigrants. I was getting frustrated with this disappointing development, because after I discipled, trained, and mentored them for years, they would all go to Toronto. I felt that my investment of time and energy was wasted. In fact, the first family that left for Toronto was one of our GCF-South Metro pioneer families, the father of which served as an able Chairman of the Council of Elders.

In hindsight, such an exodus of families was the trigger that solidified our commitment to go outside of the Philippines to help fulfill the Great Commission. These families were to be the catalysts in starting the first international GCF in North America. I began to see them not as losses to

GCF-South Metro but as core leaders of what God was about to do for GCF outside of the Philippines. Thus, my frustration and disappointment turned to hope and anticipation.

These transformed sentiments are expressed in the coffee-table book *Ten Years, Ten Values,* which commemorates GCF-South Metro's tenth anniversary: "As a global paradigm of missions was sweeping GCF South Metro in 2004 and 2005, who would have known that the initial 'losses' of key leaders and members leaving for Canada in the early years would be the very catalyst for bringing the GCF global dream into reality?" (GCF South Metro 2007, 168).

Confirmation for a GCF Diaspora Church-planting Vision

God's confirmation for a GCF *diaspora* church-planting vision came to us from both the new immigrants people in Toronto and the leadership in the Philippines. On their end, the five families took strategic steps to move toward owning a GCF church-planting vision, as seen in these efforts:

> These initial families composed of the Bondocs, the Faliaos, the Geronimos, and the Tes began to conduct informal Bible studies, which became a recognized official GCF Growth Group. As the frequency of fellowship meetings increased to twice a month, Pastor Narry, Elder Peter Corvera and Elder Mark Sosmeña visited the group in 2005 to challenge the Toronto brethren to explore the possibility of launching the first ever global satellite church of GCF. As the fellowship increased, the satellite adopted the Purpose Driven small group model for church-planting and February 2006, the first evangelistic event was conducted ... (It) continued to grow with the addition of several families from the GCF community and from new members drawn from various activities such as the Marriage Enrichment Series and evangelistic services. (GCF South Metro 2007, 168)

Moreover, the new group registered as an official religious entity in Toronto and elected its officers. On its end, the GCF-Ortigas Board of Elders (BOE) approved the request of Pastor Pantoja in his Pastoral Ministry Report at the Board of Elders meeting on April 21, 2006. The request is for a "GCF-Toronto Feasibility Study—the Senior Pastor assigned Pastor Lito Villoria to visit Elder Oddy Bondoc and the GCF core group that intends to organize itself into GCF-Toronto. As an outcome of such visit, Pastor Lito will report to this body and to the deacons the feasibility of launching the first GCF satellite overseas" (Pantoja 2006a).

After the Toronto visit, Pastor Villoria recommended at the June 16, 2006 BOE meeting that:

> GCF proceed with establishing GCF-Toronto as our first GCF overseas satellite and as the parent body, we are asked to provide a fulltime Resident Pastor and to subsidize their annual operating budget. The Senior Pastor intends to ask Pastor Narry Santos to spearhead the project on a minimum two-year assignment as GCF pastor-missionary beginning February 2007. (Pantoja 2006b)

This recommendation was passed as a resolution by the GCF-Ortigas Board of Elders (64th Resolution 2006).

I sensed God's hand in opening the opportunity for my family and me to be part of God's global vision for GCF. However, I realized how difficult it would be for my family to agree with this opportunity. My wife has no relatives in Toronto. My two daughters have many friends in both GCF church and GCF school in Manila. I had a growing ministry among many people whose vision is to reach many more around our strategic area.

The bottom-line question we asked ourselves was: "How can we leave the stability of our 10-year ministry at GCF-South Metro and go as a family to a foreign land and start GCF-Toronto and face all the instability that goes with a new mission work?" Yet, in my heart, I knew and already saw that God could start something totally new and exciting. I saw it when God used GCF-South Metro start GCF-Batangas City in 2001. I saw it when God again used GCF-South Metro to start GCF-Santa Rosa. Even in my absence, God again used GCF-South Metro to start GCF-Parañaque in 2008. Having seen God use us in starting satellites before, I knew in my heart that God could use us again in starting satellites for Filipinos and other different groups in Toronto and beyond.

God sovereignly arranged circumstances so that I was approached by the senior pastor and resident pastors of other satellites on June 14, 2006 and challenged to go to Toronto. The next day (June 15), Pastor Pantoja and Pastor Villoria talked with my wife and me. On June 16, the GCF-Ortigas

BOE approved the request for my family and me to go to Toronto. On June 17, Pastor Pantoja addressed the GCF-South Metro Council about our assignment. With God's grace, the GCF-South Metro leaders agreed to release me for the Canada vision. On June 18, Pastor Pantoja and GCF-South Metro Chairman informed the congregation of my new assignment.

On our tenth anniversary on January 21, 2007, GCF-South Metro commissioned my family and me to be their global missionaries, aside from installing the new pastor for GCF-South Metro. For the rest of January until March, I was asked to speak at ten different GCF satellites to challenge them to pray, give, and refer their friends and family who live in Toronto.

In addition, the GCF-Ortigas BOE approved this motion on March 9, 2007: "Motion prevailed that we officially receive a 'Shower of Blessing' in the form of cash donations for the month of April 2007 as our share in the ministry in Toronto" (31st Resolution 2007). As cited in the Senior Pastor's Pastoral Ministry Report, the "shower of blessing" (i.e., people's designated giving) would "cover the costs of transporting the Santos family and assisting them to settle in Toronto" (Pantoja 2007). On April 9, my family and I left Manila for our new global missions assignment.

Commitment to a Diaspora Church-planting Vision in a Multicultural City

GCF-Toronto was officially launched as the thirteenth GCF satellite on May 6, 2007 at the Centennial Community Centre in Toronto. In its almost three years, GCF-Toronto has moved from a small basement (that could accommodate sixty people) in a North York library, to three adjacent rooms (that could hold 120 people) at a Chinese Cultural Centre in Scarborough, to its current location in a ballroom (that could accommodate 220 people) at the Centennial College Residence and Conference Centre. There is now an average of 150 adults and youth who attend the Sunday worship services at 11 a.m.–12:30 p.m., an average of thirty children who attended Sunday School, and sixteen growth groups that regularly meet throughout the week.

In our first prayer, vision-casting, and planning retreat as a satellite on June 16, 2007, we discussed three issues of prime importance. In our workshop materials on that day, we summarized the three major issues this way:

1. *We Are All Placed in Toronto by God's Providence*—"God is the One who brought us to Canada, whatever be our motivation

or motive in coming here. His sovereign hand took us from the Philippines and placed us in Toronto. It's His idea for you and me, for your family and my family, to be where we are right now" (GCF-Toronto 2007, 1).

2. *We Will Not Be a Filipino Church in Toronto*—"Though almost all of the people who currently attend and serve in GCF-Toronto are Filipinos by ethnic background, GCF-Toronto is not envisioned to be a Filipino church. Being an international church in the most cosmopolitan city in the world means that we are to reach out to the different peoples found in Toronto and beyond. Again, we are not a Filipino church ministering in Canada. Rather, we are a Canadian church (i.e., a church that is sensitive to the effective ways that Canadians can be brought to Christ) ministering to the various ethnic groups that God brings our way" (GCF-Toronto 2007, 5). In addition, I emphasized to the group an important note: "I'm not saying that we lose our being Filipino in order to be a Canadian church. What I'm saying is that we can use our being Filipino to reach to other Filipino Canadians and other Canadians from different backgrounds. To do that, we need the wisdom of God to reach out to them in creative ways (1 Cor 9:19–23)" (GCF-Toronto 2007, 6).

3. *GCF-Toronto Will Be a Church-planting Church*—"Our mandate includes not just the planting of GCF-Toronto, but also the planting of other GCF international churches. In other words, we are a church-planting church. We are to have churches in our 'Jerusalem,' churches in our 'Judea and Samaria,' and churches in our 'remotest part of the earth' (Acts 1:8). We are not to be content in just becoming a big church in the best way we know how. By God's grace, we will be the missional, church-planting church in the best way God will show us how" (GCF-Toronto 2007, 6).

Birth of a GCF-Canada Diaspora Church-Planting Vision

As a result of GCF-Toronto leaders' commitment to a diaspora church-planting vision, the GCF-Canada Triple Vision was born. This triple vision is taken from the Acts 1:8 process of progress. The process begins in Jerusalem, progresses into Judea and Samaria, and peaks at the ends of the earth.

For the first seven-year cycle (2007–2014), we will trust God for this GCF-Canada Strategic Vision: seven GCF satellites in seven years in the four provinces of Canada (i.e., Ontario; British Columbia; Alberta; Manitoba). This is the proposed breakdown of the triple vision per satellite:

GCF-Toronto Triple Vision (2007–2010; God willing, one cycle of satellite triple vision takes three to five years to fulfill, plus one year to pause and pray after the first cycle, and one more year to plan and prepare for the next cycle of satellite triple vision.)

The vision to launch GCF-Toronto in May 2007
(our Jerusalem)
+
The vision to birth GCF-Peel in March 2008
(our Judea and Samaria)
+
The vision to birth GCF-Vancouver in May 2010
(our ends of the earth)

GCF-Peel Triple Vision (2008–2011)

The vision to launch GCF-Peel in March 2008
(our Jerusalem)
+
The vision to birth GCF-Etobicoke in October 2010
(our Judea and Samaria)
+
The vision to birth GCF-Winnipeg in October 2011
(our ends of the earth)

Chapter 4

GCF-Vancouver Triple Vision (2010–2013)

The vision to launch GCF-Vancouver in May 2010 (our Jerusalem)
+
The vision to birth GCF-Surrey in October 2012 (our Judea and Samaria)
+
The vision to birth GCF-Calgary in September 2013
(our ends of the earth).

Once the GCF-Toronto Triple Vision (first cycle) is fulfilled, GCF-Toronto will pause, pray, and plan for its second cycle of its triple vision. God willing, the next GCF-Toronto Triple Vision will be by countries: (1) GCF-Canada as GCF-Toronto's Jerusalem; (2) GCF-USA. as GCF-Toronto's Judea and Samaria; and (3) GCF-New Zealand as GCF-Toronto's ends of the earth.

Seeing the GCF-Canada Triple Vision Gradually Happen

As God confirmed the GCF-Canada Triple Vision in our hearts, God gradually opened doors to make the birthing of these new satellites possible. Three months in our GCF-Toronto launch, we received a request to start GCF-Peel. In response, we started a growth group in Mississauga and then in Brampton. In September 2007, we conducted two preview worship services. From October 2007 onwards, we held weekly services until GCF-Peel was launched on March 27, 2008 (Easter). Just as GCF-Toronto was officially recognized as a religious institution in Ontario in 2006, GCF-Peel was also officially recognized in Ontario in 2009.

In January and February 2008, we challenged a few former GCF members who now live in Vancouver to consider starting GCF-Vancouver. In response, a growth group was born in March, followed by another one later in 2008. These two growth groups became the core team in conducting monthly (and later biweekly) preview services in 2009. With the interim help of Pastor Pantoja in January–April 2010, the GCF-Vancouver began having weekly worship services early that year. On May 2, 2010, this satellite was launched officially, with Pastor Hizon Cua, a resident pastor from Manila, coming that month along with his family to lead GCF-Vancouver in its own Triple Vision on a full-time basis.

We also received a request in January 2009 from Pastor Reymus Cagampan in Winnipeg that GCF-Toronto consider adopting the new church-planting work he initiated in October 2008 to be part of the GCF family of churches. In May 2009, Pastor Cliff Gonzales, a church planter in Calgary, was referred to us by Pastor Pantoja, as a possible partner with GCF. Pastor Gonzales inquired if the new church plant he intended to start in July 2009 could be part of the GCF family.

Initially, we were hesitant about these two requests, because GCF always starts satellite development from scratch. In all the sixteen satellites that were launched by GCF in the past sixteen years, we intentionally initiated the work in different strategic areas. However, in relation to the two requests from Winnipeg and Calgary, we sensed that these requests warrant our prayer and consideration, and that this may be a new and supplementary way to fulfill God's Triple vision for us. We wanted to give such requests much thought and prayer, because they came after we publicly declared by faith that we trusted God to start GCF-Winnipeg and GCF-Calgary.

GCF-Canada Leadership Summit on May 9, 2009

The GCF-Toronto leaders were open to the mode of adopting in satellite development in addition to the birthing approach of church planting, primarily due to the corporate decision at the first biennial GCF-Canada Leadership Summit held at the Immanuel Baptist Church last May 9, 2009. In that leadership summit, sixty-eight delegates from GCF-Toronto, GCF-Peel, and GCF-Vancouver saw the value of GCF-Canada Vision in the context of our multicultural realities in Canada. Three eye-opening talks set the stage for our historic decision: (1) "Leadership in a Missional Church" (by Dr. Brian Craig, leadership development director of the Canadian Baptists of Ontario and Quebec); (2) "Leadership in a Metropolitan Community" (by Mr. Ian Mair, administrative manager of Culture Connexions, a ministry of Serving in Missions (SIM)); and (3) "Leadership in a Multicultural Country" (by Dr. Robert Patterson, the missional director of the Toronto Baptist Ministries and the communications director of CBOQ).

As a result of the summit, we unanimously agreed on this manifesto:

> For the glory of God and the building up of the Church of Jesus Christ, even those whom He has called to be members of GCF-Toronto,

GCF-Peel, and GCF-Vancouver collectively known as GCF-Canada, we the Pastors, leaders, and members assembled for the First Leadership Summit of GCF-Canada held on May 9, 2009 hereby: RESOLVE,

That GCF-Canada shall be missional, metropolitan, and multicultural in its strategy and ministries;

That GCF-Canada shall be one with GCF-Philippines in its fundamental beliefs, mission, and vision but legally, administratively and financially autonomous;

That GCF-Canada shall partner with GCF-Philippines, Canadian Baptists of Ontario and Quebec, and Canadian Baptists of Western Canada in the areas of ministry, missions, leadership development, pastoral training, and other areas of ministry support."

Aside from the GCF-Canada Manifesto, the May 9, 2009 leadership summit also focused on the GCF Vision in both its global and Canadian perspectives, and started the formulation of the GCF-Canada ethos.

GCF-Canada Covenant: The Unifying Document for our Vision

The GCF-Canada Leadership Summit Manifesto catalyzed the formation of the GCF-Canada Covenant, which established the framework of unity and partnership with GCF-Canada. Along with selected GCF-Toronto and GCF-Peel elders, Atty. Bayani Abesamis, a GCF-Peel leader, drafted the GCF-Canada Covenant, and presented it at the joint Council Meeting of the GCF-Toronto and GCF-Peel elders and deacons on June 21, 2009 at the Centennial College Residence and Conference Centre. The final form agreed at the joint council meeting was made available at the GCF-Toronto website, and was ratified at the quarterly business meeting on July 19, 2009.

The ratified GCF-Canada Covenant frames our bases of unity according to four points of agreement; namely: (1) mission; (2) vision; (3) statement of faith; and (4) ethos. These four items are designed to shape the unity of all satellites in Canada and are formulated to serve as the framework for birthing new and adopting potential GCF satellites.

GCF Mission Statement

The GCF Mission Statement, which is the same statement for all sixteen satellites, is as follows: "For the glory of God, we commit ourselves to EVANGELIZE and ENLIST people into our fellowship, to EDIFY and EQUIP them for spiritual maturity and service, and to EXALT God together in worship."

The five "E's" in the GCF Mission Statement refer to our five purposes as a church: (1) *Evangelize* refers to our commitment to be on mission in reaching out to our community (i.e., the people outside the church); (2) *Exalt* refers to our commitment to magnify God in worship among the crowd (i.e., the people who come on Sunday mornings); (3) *Enlist* refers to our commitment to the members in nurturing fellowship among the congregation (i.e., the people joined the satellite as church members); (4) *Edify* is our commitment to be maturing in discipleship with the committed (i.e., the members who desire to follow Jesus as his disciples); and, (5) *Equip* refers to our commitment to equip for ministry those in the core (i.e., the members who volunteer in serving God and God's people). (GCF-Canada adopts the Purpose-Driven Church paradigm of Dr. Rick Warren, Pastor of the Saddleback Church.)

GCF Vision Statement

In addition, the GCF Vision Statement, which is the same for all sixteen satellites, is as follows: "GCF is one church reaching influencers through satellites in strategic areas worldwide." This vision statement is clarified as follows:

1. *GCF is one church*—we affirm our unity as God's people (especially through our mission, vision, statement of faith, and ethos), wherever God desires GCF to go worldwide;
2. *Reaching influencers*—we affirm our ministry toward leaders in society (realizing that leaders are primarily people who greatly influence others to discover and live God's purposes [i.e., 5 E's]);
3. *Through satellites*—we affirm our strategy of intentionally launching, sustaining, and starting other new satellites through the vehicle of growth groups;
4. *In strategic areas*—we affirm our target to locate ourselves in urban centers, where more people can be reached most readily and effectively; and,

5. *Worldwide*—we affirm our scope of missions as to all nations or to the ends of the earth.

GCF Statement of Faith

The GCF Statement of Faith, upheld together by all sixteen satellites, refers to ten doctrinal affirmations on the Bible, God, Jesus Christ, the Holy Spirit, angels, man, salvation, the church, the end times, and civil government, and society.

GCF-Canada Ethos

Aside from the having the same GCF Mission, Vision, and Faith Statements, the GCF-Canada Covenant also upholds our unity in the GCF-Canada Ethos. The GCF-Canada Ethos, expressed in the acronym G.R.E.E.N.H.I.L.L.S., is used to describe the ten quality characteristics, adopted from Christain Schwarz's book, *Natural Church Development*, that we consider as essential in ensuring the spiritual health of each satellite in Canada. (Schwarz lists eight quality characteristics of healthy and growing churches. In GCF-Canada, we added two characteristics that we value; namely: (1) Responsible Stewardship; and (2) Life-Enriching Preaching. The focus of each quality characteristic is not on numerical growth, but on improving the health of the satellites, with the understanding that when the satellites are sufficiently healthy, quantitative growth will follow. The GCF-Canada Ethos is spelled this way:

1. G =Gifts-based Ministry
2. R =Responsible Stewardship
3. E =Effective Structures
4. E =Empowering Leadership
5. N =Needs-oriented Evangelism
6. H =Holistic Growth Groups
7. I =Inspiring Worship
8. L =Loving Relationships
9. L =Life-enriching Preaching
10. S =Sustainable Spirituality

Aside from the four areas of unity, the GCF-Canada Covenant subscribes to three governing perspectives in our satellite development, expressed explicitly at the First GCF-Canada Leadership Summit Manifesto of May 9, 2009.

The Covenant states, "GCF-Canada shall be missional, metropolitan, and multicultural in its strategies and ministries." This is how we describe these three strategies in satellite development:

1. **Missional** Church—the satellites will be intentionally multiplying satellites (through the satellite triple vision) and will incarnationally add value to our communities;
2. **Metropolitan** Community—the satellites will intentionally and strategically minister in the urban centers (i.e., targeting the cities); and
3. **Multicultural** Country—the satellites will intentionally be on mission to the diaspora (i.e., reaching the immigrants in countries that are open to receive different ethnic groups) of "all nations."

Thus, by God's grace and for God's glory, GCF-Canada will be multiplying reproducing missional churches in metropolitan communities in the multicultural country of Canada.

Memorandum of Agreement to Launch GCF-Winnipeg and GCF-Calgary

With the ratified GCF-Canada Covenant at hand, Elder Rick Manguerra (chairman of the GCF-Peel Council), Atty. Abesamis, and I went for an exploratory visit to Winnipeg on July 23–27, 2009. We were sent by GCF-Peel to conduct the exploration, because GCF-Peel owns the Triple Vision of going to Winnipeg for its "ends of the earth" satellite. We met Pastor Cagampan and the core leaders of the new church plant in Winnipeg, presented to them the GCF-Canada Covenant (containing the GCF Mission, Vision, Faith, and Ethos), narrated our GCF-Canada two-year story of satellite development, joined their two small groups sessions and worship service with sixty people.

On their end, Pastor Cagampan and his leaders agreed to bring to their people the option that their new church plant be adopted as GCF-Winnipeg, to pray about it for one month, and to inform us of their group's decision at the end of August 2009. In a month, they informed us of the decision of the whole group to be adopted as GCF-Winnipeg.

To move this decision forward, Pastor Pantoja, Elder Joseph Cachola (chairman of the interim GCF-Canada Board), Elder Manguerra, Atty. Abesamis, and I visited Winnipeg on September 18–20, 2009 to officially sign the Memorandum of Agreement (MOA) between GCF-Canada and the new group, GCF-Winnipeg. We also trained the leaders on how to do satellite development in their target area.

In addition to visiting GCF-Winnipeg, the team also explored the possibilities on September 17–18, 2009 of having the new church plant of Pastor Gonzales and his leaders be adopted as GCF-Calgary. We presented to this leadership group the GCF mission, vision, statement of faith, ethos, and the GCF-Canada Covenant. They asked for two to four weeks to make their decision. In two weeks, they committed to be part of the GCF-Canada family of churches. Elder Manguerra and I returned to Calgary on October 14–18 to conduct satellite development training, to take part in their small group sessions and participate in the worship service with seventy people, and to sign the MOA between GCF-Canada and the new group, GCF-Calgary.

When we asked Pastor Gonzales and his leaders why they chose to be part of the GCF-Canada family of churches—knowing that we are just over two years old then and that we have meager resources to assist them—they replied that they want to be identified with a group that has a clear vision to plant churches in Canada and beyond.

Partnership with CBOQ and CBWC

At the end of our first year as GCF-Toronto, we sensed the need to be affiliated with a family of churches that had similar doctrinal beliefs and a church-planting vision for reaching the whole of Canada for Jesus Christ. We discovered that the Canadian Baptists of Ontario and Quebec (CBOQ) would be that like-minded denomination. So GCF-Toronto went through the process of being recognized as a CBOQ church and I also underwent the procedure of being accredited as an ordained CBOQ minister. As a result, GCF-Toronto and I were officially welcomed as a CBOQ church and as an accredited ordained CBOQ pastor, respectively, at the CBOQ Annual Assembly on June 11–13, 2009.

Such a CBOQ partnership with a big family of churches opened up new doors for us to connect with the Canadian Baptists of Western Canada (CBWC), a sister convention of CBOQ. As we met with CBOQ leaders, we were also introduced to the CBWC leaders. We shared with the CBWC leaders our commitment to be part of the Canadian Baptists, wherever GCF goes, as expressed in the GCF-Canada Leadership Summit Manifesto and in Section 9.3 of the GCF-Canada Covenant: "GCF-Canada shall be affiliated with the Canadian Baptists of Ontario and Quebec, the Canadian Baptists of Western Canada, the Canadian Baptists of Atlantic Canada, and the Canadian Baptists of French Canada and such other groups and associations as the Board may decide" (GCF-Covenant 2009, 7).

Currently, we are processing the membership of GCF-Vancouver, GCF-Calgary, and GCF-Winnipeg with CBWC, through the help of Pastor Tom Lavigne, the CBWC church-planting director. In addition, Atty. Abesamis is helping out in the process of having GCF-Vancouver, GCF-Calgary, and GCF-Winnipeg officially recognized as religious institutions in their respective provinces. Pastor Lavigne has budgeted for 2010 a specified amount to support the satellite development of each of the three GCF satellites in Western Canada. Moreover, Pastor Lavigne and Pastor Rob Ogilvie (CBWC British Columbia director) plan to represent CBWC at the launch of GCF-Vancouver on May 2, 2010. Pastor Lavigne and Pastor Dennis Stone (CBWC Alberta director) also have expressed their commitment to be present at the launch of GCF-Calgary on May 16, 2010. Pastor Lavigne and Pastor Ken Thiessen (CBWC Manitoba director) are also scheduled to grace the launch of GCF-Winnipeg on October 3, 2010.

In addition, CBOQ has committed to partially support for three years (2009–2011) GCF-Peel's satellite development of GCF-Etobicoke (which is GCF-Peel's Judea and Samaria satellite). We are currently in communication with Vision 360 in Toronto through Mt. Andrew Lamme, the Vision 360 Toronto City Catalyst, to explore the possibilities of GCF-Etobicoke being financially supported by this new church-planting movement in Toronto. God willing, we will have that arrangement in place for 2011–2013. For now, there is one growth group in Etobicoke, and one other growth group will be started in April 2010. By faith, GCF-Etobicoke will be launched on 10-10-10 (or October 10, 2010), which will be attended by CBOQ leaders as well.

CBOQ has also been extending their services, training, resources, and assistance to us in tangible ways—speaking at GCF-Toronto and GCF-Peel as guest preachers; giving training sessions at our leadership summit; extending training subsidies to me as pastor (e.g., Church-Planting Congress; Natural

Church Development; Axiom training with Forge); facilitating the processing of government documents (e.g., my Ontario license to officiate weddings). We are blessed to be part of a bigger family that comes to our side and assists us in times of need.

Continuing Partnership with GCF-Philippines

God willing, in its three years of being on mission, GCF-Canada may be able to see six launched satellites by the end of 2010: (1) GCF-Toronto (May 6, 2007); (2) GCF-Peel (March 23, 2008); (3) GCF-Vancouver (May 2, 2010); (4) GCF0-Calgary (May 16, 2010); (5) GCF-Winnipeg (October 3, 2010); and (6) GCF-Etobicoke (October 10, 2010). However, with such growth in the number of satellites comes the challenge of producing and reproducing spiritual leaders who will shepherd the GCF-Canada satellites. So far, I am the only full-time pastor, serving full-time in GCF-Toronto and part-time in GCF-Peel. In the first two years, I would shuttle back and forth Toronto and Peel to preach in the two satellites (i.e., 9:30 a.m. at GCF-Peel and 11 a.m. at GCF-Toronto).

GCF-Ortigas has been a continuing help in providing pastoral assistance to the GCF-Canada churches. Aside from providing pastoral assistance to GCF-Toronto by assigning me as resident pastor, GCF-Ortigas has been financially supporting GCF-Toronto since 2007 and will continue to do so in decreasing amounts until the end of 1012. Additionally, GCF-Ortigas released Pastor Hizon Cua (formerly the resident pastor of GCF-Northwest in the northwest portion of Manila) to be the Resident Pastor of GCF-Vancouver. He and his family are scheduled to arrive in Vancouver on April 22, 2010, in time for the GCF-Vancouver launch on May 2, 2010.

In addition, in his retirement years starting January 2010, Pastor Pantoja is tasked to give interim pastoral leadership in places where his ministry is needed. For January–April 2010, he is interim Pastor of GCF-Vancouver, and he will be functioning in the same interim capacity at GCF-Peel for May–July 2010, until a permanent resident pastor arrives.

Though there is willingness to help from GCF-Philippines, there is a limit to the number of pastors who can be sent to Canada. Strategically, it may not even be helpful in the long run to get a pastor in the Philippines to minister in Canada. In fact, it may be wiser to raise new leaders in Canada or look for like-minded pastors from Canada. We see the need to look for or raise new pastors who will have the heart and skills to start and build intentionally intercultural churches in order to fulfill God's mission to GCF.

Initial Initiatives to our Missional and Multicultural Mandate

As GCF-Canada, we are forced to answer these two questions: "How will we raise new spiritual leaders who will lead our satellites in the future? How can we as churches learn the skills of becoming intentionally intercultural in order to fulfill God's mission for us?"

In answer to the first question, GCF-Toronto has taken the following seven baby steps in order to move toward being an intentionally intercultural:

1. At the May 2009 Leadership Summit, the three satellites of GCF-Toronto, GCF-Peel, and GCF-Vancouver decided to abide by the three ministry approaches: (1) missional (i.e., going to the community through satellite development and incarnational acts of service); (2) metropolitan (i.e., targeting the urban centers or cities where people of different groups flock); and (3) multicultural (i.e., reaching out to the different diaspora groups or people on the move).

2. Since 2008, GCF-Toronto has contracted the part-time services of Mr. Eric Hart as our Youth Ministry Worker. Mr. Hart was born and raised in Toronto, and his parents originally came from Trinidad and Tobago.

3. There were fifteen church leaders who attended the SUBS (School for Urban Biblical Studies) class called "Preparing Leaders for Intercultural Ministry," which was taught by Pastor Robert Cousins for eight Monday evenings in October and November 2009. Pastor Cousins is the director of the TIM (Tyndale Intercultural Ministries) Centre and is missionary with the AIM (Africa Inland Mission).

4. Pastor Cousins has made himself available to help and coach us for ten hours every week starting September 2009 toward becoming intentionally intercultural (including preaching at GCF-Toronto and GCF-Peel on missional and multicultural themes).

5. All our fifteen growth groups served in different volunteer capacities in our community during the "Better Together" spiritual growth campaign of November–December 2009.

6. We formed one multicultural growth group in May 2009. This growth group is composed of church members who originally came from Burma, India, Ireland, Canada, and the Philippines.

7. We started celebrating Multicultural Sunday in March 2010. This special Sunday featured Pastor Cousins' sermon "Does God Love Diversity?" and two song numbers from forty Karen people from Burma.

The second question was, "How will we raise new spiritual leaders who will lead our satellites in the future?" In answer, we have two students who are currently enrolled at Tyndale Seminary (one from GCF-Toronto and one from GCF-Peel), and our part-time youth staff is studying at Master's Bible College. A new immigrant who serves as an elder in GCF-Toronto will also take a master's degree at Tyndale Seminary.

Moreover, we are consulting with Dr. Brian Craig, the CBOQ leadership development director, to explore the possibilities of taking a specified number of courses that CBOQ can recognize, so that our leaders who take these courses can work toward being accredited part-time CBOQ pastors. Hopefully, we can also partner with Pastor Cousins and the TIM Centre through the Life-Long Learning program to make such leadership development possible.

Two Realities and Realizations toward Integrative and Incarnational Initiatives

In light of our missional mandate to start and reproduce GCF-Canada satellites and to add value to our communities, we have discovered two realities and two realizations toward integrative and incarnational initiatives. Our desire is that these two sets of realities and realizations would move us forward in seeking to become multicultural and missional GCF satellites.

Our primary reality is this: "Our outreach events have been intentional, but have been focused on the attractional approach." We thank God for the specific times we were able to share the gospel through evangelistic events in church (e.g., Valentine's Day, Easter Sunday; Mothers' Day; Anniversary Sunday; Philippine Day; Christmas). We know that God has used the attractional approach in proclaiming the good news to pre-Christians. However, the reality is that we are having difficulty in bringing more people to church.

On the other hand, we have occasionally tried the incarnational approach through acts of kindness and community service (e.g., giving bottled water;

volunteering in homes for the homeless; hosting garage sales; donating in times of crisis). Though this approach is commendable, our acts of service have been few and far between. In other words, they have been part of a church campaign, not of the church culture.

In light of this reality, we have seen the value of realization number one: "To be healthy in our church outreach, we need to focus on loving our neighbor." Though we need to keep proclaiming the gospel to those who would hear, we now realize that we are to be more intentional in going more often to our community and in serving continually our neighborhood (Mark 9:35; 10:43–45). We now know that we must integrate our efforts to share the gospel of grace with our efforts to serve the people as a gracious expression of love that comes from the gospel (Mark 12:31).

In addition, we learned Reality #2: "Our new church recently moved to a new area, but the area has many churches around it already." GCF-Toronto has moved from a basement of a library in North York to a Chinese cultural center, and now to a college residence and conference center in Scarborough. Our current location is bigger than the other two sites, and has potential for expansion in it. However, this location is surrounded by a good number of other churches (including a big church near us).

In relation to this second reality, we now understand better Realization #5: "To reach out better to the people in and around our current location, we need to know our neighborhood and help meet the needs of the people there." For now, God has providentially placed us where we are—right at the heart of the Centennial College Residence and Conference Centre. Is it not part of God's divine appointment (Acts 16:9–10) that we are here now in order to reach the college students?

Aside from the students, our church has been able to reach the new Filipino immigrants. It seems that as immigrants ourselves, we are naturally being used by God to reach other immigrants in our area. If that is part of God's sovereign plan for us (i.e., as immigrants, God wants us to reach other immigrants), can we intentionally know the needs of the new immigrants (not just Filipinos but also the other groups) in our neighborhood and seek to help meet their needs? Of course, it will be helpful to not just understand the demographics of our area, but to also appreciate the way God sovereignly placed us among them to reach out to them.

What four steps are we taking to equip and connect us to our neighborhood?

1. CBOQ has sponsored my missional training through the five-day (once a month) Axiom sessions with Forge Canada from February—June 2010.

2. Pastor David Devadason, who is passionate in reaching Hindus and Muslims, equipped the GCF-Toronto people on Friendship Evangelism for three Sundays afternoons beginning April 18, 2010.

3. Pastor Cousins is seeking to connect GCF-Toronto to a parachurch ministry focusing on student ministries (e.g., Power to Change) and to a church with passion to serve the community (e.g., Salvation Army), so we can partner in reaching our neighborhood.

4. Mie Tha Lah, a host program worker for Karen Youth in Toronto, who is a GCF-Toronto member and who joins our Multicultural Growth Group, is planning to introduce our church volunteers be part of a Host Program for new immigrants (i.e., two hours/week for six months of interaction time [e.g., shopping; theatre; English practice] with assigned new immigrant(s) to volunteer(s)[either individually or as a family]) to intentionally build relationships with people.

We realize that these are baby steps to seek to connect with our neighborhood and to serve our neighbors. May God honor such steps, so that GCF-Canada satellites will not simply plant churches, but seek to serve the communities where God sovereignly places us.

MISSIOLOGICAL ANALYSIS AND IMPLICATIONS TO DIASPORA GLOCAL MISSIONS

The church plant that is GCF-Toronto is now ministering in partnership with a network of Canadian churches, and we anticipate the ripple effects of her glocal ministry. The data provided in the previous section will now be analyzed through the lens of missions history and sociology in order to provide transferable concepts for other diaspora congregations.

Legacy of Colonial Missions Forces

Protestant mission in the Philippines began at the dawn of the twentieth century when the United States of America took possession of the Philippines from the Spaniards (1556–1898) at the Treaty of Paris in 1898. Today, adherents of the Roman Catholic and Protestant churches make up approximately 95 percent (see *Operation World*, "The Philippines") of the Philippine population. Due to this fact, the Philippines is considered to be the most Christian nation in Asia. Indeed, the Philippine Church is growing and the evangelicals are advancing.

However, when is a country or a nation considered reached or evangelized? There is an ongoing debate among mission practitioners about the moratorium of missions to what they call a reached country. Some mission pundits say that it is when there is a vibrant or mature national church that is fully self-supporting, self-governing, and self-propagating. If we use this measurement of success, then the Philippines is an evangelized nation. Consequently, foreign missionaries are no longer needed in the Philippines.

GCF, as described in the preceding section of this paper, is a legacy of American Conservative Baptist missionary work through the ministry of Rev. (and Mrs.) David Yount. The Baptists began their work in the Philippines in 1900. The Younts were deployed to the Philippines in 1967. However, it must be noted that at the time of the founding of GCF in 1978, the debate on moratorium was at its height. In fact, just a few years before, respected Filipino theologian, Emerito P. Nacpil, then president of Union Seminary in Manila, proclaimed that:

> Cooperation between Asian and Western Christians can only be a partnership between the weak and the strong. And that means the continued dependence of the weak upon the strong and the continued dominance of the strong . . . In other words, the most missionary service a missionary under the present system can do today in Asia is to go home. (1971)

Had the Conservative Baptists followed the Pied Piper and succumbed to the trend of withdrawing foreign missionaries from the Philippines, and had the Younts not responded to the call of Christ to minister in the Philippines, one can only imagine the outcome of their decisions. We praise God for his providence and attribute the growth of GCF to Western missionaries such as the Younts and the many others who spent years of faithful service in foreign missions.

Yet, there remains the unfinished task of the Great Commission. For now, however, we give glory to God and celebrate the colonial missionaries who evangelized the Filipinos.

Filipino Global Scattering

Scattered: The Filipino Global Presence (Pantoja, Tira, and Wan 2004) is a compendium describing the global scattering of the Filipino people. In their seminal work, the contributors agreed that the Filipinos are widely scattered (in over 210 countries) for a divine purpose. The Filipino diaspora is caused mainly by economic and political reasons. However, Filipino missiologists noted that many Christian Filipinos in the diaspora are actively witnessing for Christ and planting churches. Migrant Filipino workers are found in the 10/40 window, particularly in the Buddhist, Islamic, Hindu, and Jewish worlds (Pantoja, Tira, and Wan 2004). They also can be found in the Western world, particularly in North America.

Evidently, their Filipino global presence (even on the oceans as seafarers) is an act of God. They are a providentially dispersed nation, destined to be heralds of the gospel. While many of them became born-again Christians while working abroad, many also have lived out their faith wherever they are. This is the case of many Filipino immigrants in GTA who have become members of GCF-Toronto.

Diaspora Filipinos, therefore, are not only subjects of evangelism but can be mobilized to help fulfill the *missio Dei*! Revisiting the topic of moratorium and global partnerships for missions, one is amazed at the providence of God in raising Filipinos to partner with the whole church in bringing the whole gospel to the whole world.

GCF, specifically GCF-Toronto's, glocal vision and mission is to become a missional congregation—ministering both globally and locally simultaneously. It is important to nurture their vision and support their mission in order for them to reach other diasporas in Canada. We appeal for practical partnerships with like-minded individuals and organizations for kingdom advance. Reaching the diasporas in GTA requires healthy partnerships.

Glocal Missions: GCF-Toronto Agenda and Ripple Effects

Andrew Walls, a former missionary to Sierra Leone and Nigeria and founder of the Centre for the Study of Christianity in the non-Western World at the University of Edinburgh seems prophetic in his description of the new reality of diasporas and Christianity. In his unpublished paper, "The Future of Musicology: Musicology as Vocation" presented at the University of Aarhus in Denmark, Dr. Walls summarizes:

Another people movement began, as thousands upon thousands from Africa and Asia and Latin America came to Europe and North America. All the evidence suggests that this process will continue for the foreseeable future . . . It has brought Latin America to North America with immense force. It has made Hinduism and Sikhism and Islam into Western religions, and it has brought vast numbers of Christians of non-Western origin, to Europe and North America, often bringing with them expressions of Christian faith and practice new to the host societies in the West. (January 2010)

GCF-Toronto is but one example of this process. Diaspora congregations in Canada are on the rise as the flow of migration continues. However, GCF-Toronto seeks to be different, and while her ties to the homeland and her hub are evident as indicated by her choice of name "Greenhills Christian Fellowship" and affiliation with fifteen other GCF satellites, GCF-Toronto endeavors to be purposely missional, metropolitan, and multicultural in the city where God has placed her.

Seeking to be international and not Filipino by definition, GCF-Toronto seeks to bring people of diverse cultural backgrounds together, as Dr. Walls envisions, to "cohere, live, and learn together, all functioning as necessary organs in the Body of Christ; hearing each other's stories, getting an inner realization of . . . the stories of others who live under the Cross."

It is our hope that the GCF-Toronto model will inspire many other diaspora congregations to join in this movement of reaching beyond cultural borders, and partnering for the *missio Dei*. May there be a ripple effect of diaspora church plants across the country, and even around the world, cropping up as quickly as the waves of migration and God's providence take them.

CONCLUSIONS

The church-planting strategy of GCF and GCF-Toronto is an exemplary case study of diversity in evangelical missions. It is also a model of diaspora missions in action as outlined by Evangelical Missiological Society President, Enoch Wan (2007), in that it is conceptually deterritorialized and multidirectional and that, in contrast to traditional missions strategies of sending and receiving, GCF moves providentially where God places people spatially and spiritually.

Chapter 4

In diaspora missions and for GCF, every person outside the kingdom of God is priority, and these persons are everywhere. GCF, specifically GCF-Toronto, remembers that it is God who determines where people will live at certain times, so that wherever they are in the universe, they can call upon God and find God (Acts 17:26–28).

It is evident that GCF-Toronto is a product of a providential history, from the early missions initiatives of the colonial period in the Philippines to the great scattering of the Filipino peoples of the last three decades. In August 2007, Dr. Mary Wilder of Western Seminary said of the Filipinos, "100 years ago, the Filipinos were a mission field. Now, they are moving out to take their place in missions, reaching around the world in very creative ways!" Indeed, we affirm GCF-Toronto's role as a diaspora church reaching the world in our diverse nation. May her model be emulated by diaspora congregations in Canada and everywhere around the globe.

REFERENCES

31st Resolution. 2007. Minutes of the GCF BOE Meeting, March 9.

64th Resolution. 2006. Minutes of the GCF BOE Meeting, June 16.

Davis, Jim. 2006. From carryall beginnings to crossing borders: A 50-year journey of Conservative Baptist ministries in the Philippines. Manila: LifeChange Publishing.

GCF-Covenant. 2009. Section 9.3, ratified on July 19.

GCF-South Metro. 2007. Ten years, ten values. Las Piñas, Metro Manila, Philippines: GCF South Metro.

GCF-Toronto. 2007. Global vision workshop materials at the GCF-Toronto prayer, vision-casting, and leadership retreat, June 16, in Greater Toronto.

Human Development Report. 2009. United Nations Development Program, http://hdr.undp.org/en/reports/global/hdr2009/.

Pantoja, Luis. 2006a. Pastoral Ministry Report, Minutes of the GCF BOE Meeting, April 21.

———. 2006b. Pastoral Ministry Report, Minutes of the GCF BOE Meeting, June 16.

———. 2007. Pastoral Ministry Report, Minutes of the GCF BOE Meeting, March 9.

Pantoja Jr., Luis, Sadiri Tira, and Enoch Wan, eds. 2004. *Scattered: The Filipino global presence*. Manila, Philippines: LifeChange Publishing Inc.

Robertson, Roland. 1995. Glocalization: Time-space and homogeneity-heterogeneity. In *Global modernities*, eds. M. Featherstone, S. Lash, and R. Robertson, 27–44. London: Sage.

Rosenau, James N. 2003. *Distant proximities: Dynamics beyond globalization*. Princeton: Princeton University.

Shelley, Bruce. 1971. *A history of Conservative Baptists*. Wheaton: Conservative Baptist Press.

Spradley, James P. 1979. *The ethnographic interview*. New York: Hold, Rinehart and Winston.

Tai, Susan H. C., and Y. H. Wong. 1998. Advertising decision making in Asia: 'Glocal' versus 'regcal' approach. *Journal of Managerial Issues*, 10(3): 318–29.

Walls, Andrew. 2010. "The future of missiology: Missiology as vocation." Unpublished paper presented at the University of Aarhus in Denmark.

Wan, Enoch. 2007. Diaspora missiology. *EMS occasional bulletin* 20(2): 3–7.

Winter, Ralph D., and Bruce A. Koch. 2009. Finishing the task: The unreached peoples challenge. In *Perspectives on the world Christian movement: A reader*, ed. Ralph D. Winter and Steven C. Hawthorne, 531–546. Pasadena: William Carey Library.

5

"KIDS THESE DAYS!" GENERATIONAL ISSUES IN MISSIONS MOBILIZATION

LISA LA GEORGE

The mobilization of college-age students to missions involvement has long been a part of the fabric of mission history, from the 1806 Haystack Prayer Meeting to the Student Volunteer Movement founded in 1888 to the triennial Urbana Missions Conference inaugurated in 1946. I have spent the last two decades on college campuses in Pennsylvania, Alaska, South Carolina, and California, first as a student, then as a missionary, and now as a professor, and my passion is for college students to know that God's desire is for men and women everywhere to be reconciled to himself, and that God intends to utilize his people as his ambassadors. As the generations change, I have to keep asking, "How can more students catch a vision to participate long-term in the global outreach of the kingdom of God?"

Recently, I began to investigate how mission mobilizers (mission agency representatives, professors, pastors, parents) might connect more effectively with undergraduate students. In addition to interviewing representatives about their experiences in mobilization, I sponsored a round table discussion during the fall of 2009 with fifteen missionary representatives and pastors. I have also conducted extensive participant observation and survey research with students. Insights from these sources will be woven throughout the following generational profile, and this exploration will conclude with recommendations for greater effectiveness in mobilizing college students to live a life of enduring impact for the global kingdom of God.

THE GENERATION DEFINED AND DESCRIBED

For the past decade, Beloit College has released a "Mindset List," an annual attempt to describe to educators the world of the incoming undergraduate freshman class in North American colleges. The 2009 list included mundane references to blue Jello, Kevin Costner, and Avon, but it also reminded educators that the freshmen have "never used a card catalog to find a book," that "the KGB has never officially existed," and that they have always been able "to watch wars, coups, and police arrests unfold on television in real time." These are the young people who require our attention if we are to recruit the next generation of missionaries.

Students born between the years of 1985 and 2000 have been called the "Net Generation" (Cheese 2008), "Mosaics" (Barna 2008), and "Emerging Adults" (Smith and Snell 2009). Another descriptor assigned to this current generation is "Millennials" (Pew 2010), and this is the nomenclature which will appear most often in this study.

When I moved to Alaska to serve as a missionary, I encountered a different language, wardrobe, and worldview. Reaching across generational bounds in North America is much like reaching across cultures: the one crossing the boundaries must understand a different context and worldview. I will provide a brief examination of three critical characteristics of today's college students who, God willing, are the missionaries of tomorrow. We will note that these Millennials are overprotected, digitally native, and highly mobile.

OVER-PROTECTED

Millennials have grown up in an age which views knitting needles, four ounces of shampoo, and shoes as potential weapons. These students were in elementary school when New York's Twin Towers fell at the hands of terrorists, and crime was at an abysmal level nationwide. An anxious society has slapped warning labels on everyday items from coffee cups ("Caution: This beverage is hot!") to baby strollers ("Remove child before folding."). College students have grown up in a world that is fearful.

A fear-filled world influences parenting styles. Nancy Gibbs describes the driving force behind parents with these words: "Fear is a kind of parenting fungus: invisible, insidious, perfectly designed to decompose your peace of mind. Fear of physical danger is at least subject to rational argument; fear of failure is harder to hose down" (2009, 55). Gone are the days when children just play. Gibbs describes how parents can drive their children's achievements as if the child was an industrial product in development. Preschoolers start intensive music lessons; kindergarteners have handwriting tutors; high school students have multiple after-school extracurricular commitments daily. Even if the job market were more favorable, few high-schoolers would have time to work between soccer, debate, orchestra, and tutoring.

The effects of intensive, overprotective parenting are observable among students of every level, including college students. Recent higher education student-development literature describes rise of the "Helicopter Parent" who, after delivering forgotten homework and lunches for years to primary and middle school, is now calling the college professor to inquire about grades and complain about the cafeteria. A parent recently called the student dean's office to ask someone to order a pizza for her daughter. Another concerned mother worried on the phone that her freshman daughter's choice of bedspread might not match her roommate's décor. Similarly, professors have encountered increasing numbers of students who arrive at their academic advising meetings with a parent in tow.

Student-development colleagues have observed a number of results from this overprotection. Many students are unacquainted with common household chores, including basic cleaning and laundry. Students carry credit cards and cell phones, but don't understand compounding interest and budgeting minutes. Many undergraduates have never had a job and possess little understanding of a dedicated work ethic. The array of cultural complexities, academic options, extracurricular events, and even church selection proves to be paralyzing to students who are unaccustomed to making choices under their own power.

DIGITALLY NATIVE

This generation of college students is more than technologically proficient—technology is their birthright. Using the motif of citizenship and cross-cultural adaptation, Marc Prensky coined the phrase, "Digital Native" (2001), to describe this generation of students who move with ease through various forms of technology. Today, the majority of young people between the ages of eight and eighteen own an iPod/MP3 player (76 percent), cell phone (66 percent), and handheld video gaming device (59 percent). The homes they live in have

TVs (99 percent), computers (93 percent), and Internet access (84 percent) (Rideout, Foehr, and Roberts 2010, 9). While students can use their familiarity with media to their advantage, they have never lived without it. Even a brief electrical or network outage can cause huge disruptions for students.

These digital natives spend more than a third of their waking hours connected to some form of media. In 2009, the Kaiser Family Foundation replicated a 2004 study surveying eight to eighteen-year-old North American youth regarding their possession and use of technology and media. In 2009, the average youth engaged in hours of media use daily, including TV content, music/audio, computer, video games, print, and movies. When the multitasking use of technology was considered, using more than one medium at a time, these young people racked up ten hours and forty-five minutes of media usage daily (Rideout et al. 2010, 11). Technology is not just a part of Millennials' waking hours. A recently released Pew Research study reported that 83 percent of Millennials sleep with their cell phones close at hand (2010, para. 26).

Social networking sites are increasingly popular with many age demographics, especially among Millennials. The Kaiser study of youth media consumption reported that young people spend an average of one hour and twenty-nine minutes on a computer daily, not including homework or job usage, with one-third of that time spent in social networking sites (Rideout et al. 2010, 20). A recent survey of college students on The Master's College campus indicated that the majority of students would now rather be contacted by text message or Facebook than by e-mail.

Relational connections are greatly impacted by the Millennials' familiarity with technology. Robert Putnam's text, *Bowling Alone*, describes the disintegration of America's social connections as PTAs, community groups, and bowling leagues (Putnam, 2000). While Putnam's research included the generations older than the Millennials, he demonstrates how the stage was set for the disjointed sense of societal interaction now characteristic of many college students. Few Millennials are actively engaged with community organizations or civil activity. However, Smith and Snell describe, "They can be said to be extremely socially engaged in quite a different way: they are deeply invested in social life beyond their immediate selves primarily through their interpersonal relationships . . . Much of their lives appear to be centered on creating and maintaining personal relationships" (2009, 73). Not surprisingly, much of this relational communion is managed through technology: texting, Facebook, cell phones, and iMing. Nancy Gibbs suggests that the Millennials "are more likely than any generation to think technology unites people rather than isolates them, that it is primarily a means of connection, not competition" (2010, 72).

The generations who have gone before the Millennials may shy away from technology either because the learning curve is frustrating or because of the uncertain dangers that may accompany new forms of electronic communication. In the summer of 2009, John Piper wrote a few thoughts about social media:

> I see two kinds of response to social Internet media like blogging, MySpace, Facebook, Twitter, and others.
>
> One says: These media tend to shorten attention spans, weaken discursive reasoning, lure people away from Scripture and prayer, disembody relationships, feed the fires of narcissism, cater to the craving for attention, fill the world with drivel, shrink the soul's capacity for greatness, and make us second-handers who comment on life when we ought to be living it. So boycott them and write books (not blogs) about the problem.
>
> The other response says: Yes, there is truth in all of that, but instead of boycotting, try to fill these media with as many provocative, reasonable, Bible-saturated, prayerful, relational, Christ-exalting, truth-driven, serious, creative pointers to true greatness as you can. (2009 Piper)

The Millennials' ease of using media is a challenge to older generations. Technological advances in computing and communication systems have permitted instantaneous electronic exchange worldwide, and those advances have contributed to the development of rapidly shifting communication and community among college students.

HIGHLY MOBILE

Millennials are vocationally, geographically, and missionaly more mobile than any previous generation. Generational attitudes regarding jobs and vocation have shifted from a loyal corporate longevity to a pragmatic individualistic mobility from one job to another. International travel has become an acceptable part of life for many Millennials, and the transitory nature of both jobs and location contribute significantly to Christian college students' understanding of the role they play in mission.

One word which describes the world of Millennials, these emerging adults, is the word *transition* (Smith 2009, 34), and many Millennials hop from one job to another. Their understanding of vocation and employment is simply as temporary means to an end—a job provides money which helps buy the items and experiences necessary for happiness. Smith's survey of American Millennials demonstrated that the consensus position, regardless of religious conviction, concerning materialism is this: "As long as people can afford it, they may buy and consume whatever they happen to want without limit. There is nothing problematic with America's consumer-driven socioeconomic system (2009, 67)." Work is not a calling, but a financial transaction.

Millennials are also geographically mobile. When I received my first passport nearly thirty years ago, I was one of two students in my K–12 school who had one, and the other student was my brother. Many of my teachers and classmates had never left the state. Travel was prohibitively expensive, and international travel was almost unheard of in small-town America. However, a more fluid airline industry and a comfortable economic situation in North America have contributed to expanded travel and greater ease for travelers (Zehner 2008, 187). For better or for worse, the majority of all current Christian college students have traveled out of the country, often on a short-term missions (STM) trip. This is a relatively new phenomenon, for as one mission agency recruiter told me, "My parents' generation went [to the mission field] because of a mandate, not a vision trip."

Priest and Priest (2005) conducted an assessment of STM participation among seminary and Christian college students, and they found that 51 percent of all Masters of Divinity students who responded to their survey had participated on one or more STM trips outside of the US. Their sample of the Christian college students was almost identical to the reporting of the seminary students. The conservative, evangelical schools all had STM participation in the upper ranges of the study, between 63 percent and 77 percent (Priest and Priest 2005, 12).

Students at my institution, The Master's College, show similar rates of STM participation. Since 2003, each entering student has submitted an institutionally designed Student Growth Inventory to the Student Life Department in which the student self-reports previous experience in areas of service, church involvement, and spiritual development. In 2003, 210 or 71 percent of the entering class had participated in at least one cross-cultural STM trip before they came to college. Although that number has declined slightly to 62 percent STM involvement prior to entrance in 2008, this generation of college students is still participating in more travel and STM activity than any other time in history.

A thorough exploration and critique of STM has been addressed elsewhere (La George 2009), but a few elements of STM must be included in this discussion. The current format of STM is attractive to this generation of mobile college students. Edwin Zehner's assessment of STM among North Americans examines the rhetorical appeals of STM and notes that motivations for missions in general among the evangelical community in general have shifted dramatically in the past half century. STM, he states, has absorbed, and perhaps promoted, these changes as well:

> The growth of STM parallels broader developments in North America, including the growth of international tourism, high school community service, college study-abroad and service-learning program, and humanitarian volunteer programs. Among evangelicals, motives for mission have likewise shifted. Though most still focus on evangelism or evangelistic support, many evangelicals have adopted a broader definition of mission that includes humanitarian concerns. This shift is amply expressed in STM. (Zehner 2008, 187)

Students' motivations for STM participation are often difficult to parse. Some students may participate because they see the STM opportunity as a time to mature personally and to prove themselves worthy of respect and responsibility. Priest, Dischinger, Rassmussen, and Brown suggest that the environment created by STM can be compared with rites of passage:

> Like pilgrimages, these trips are rituals of intensification where one temporarily leaves the ordinary, compulsory routine life "at home" and experiences an extraordinary, voluntary, sacred experience "away from home": in a luminal space where sacred goals are pursued, physical and

spiritual tests are faced, normal structures are dissolved, *communitas* is experienced, and personal transformation occurs (2006, 433–34).

Is it possible that the desire for escape from an overprotected life and an increased acceptance of mobility may have led to a sanctified novelty of STM? In his excellent critique of STM, *Serving with Eyes Wide Open*, Livermore notes that STM appeals to participants' sense of adventure, and that STM agencies cater to this desire for adventure:

> Some organizations aren't subtle at all about the role of adventure and fun in motivating people to participate in short-term missions. For example, Teen Mania, a youth organization based in Texas, ... [recently ran a] full-page advertisement in a magazine for youth workers [which] featured this huge headline: "Missions Should Be Fun!" (2006, 51)

Such STM structures facilitate participants' travel in spite of egocentric motivations, negligible culture and language skills, and incompetent leadership. Some trips result in little more than braided hair, pictures of participants with dark-skinned children, and comical stories of strange foods and unfortunate bathroom facilities.

Millennials have traveled through STM—a lot. In their 2008 study of evangelicals' participation in STM, the Barna Group describes any participant who has participated in five or more STM trips as a "service-trip enthusiast" (para. 10). One STM trip participant recently described himself to me as a "STM Junkie" (name withheld, personal communication, October 26, 2006), a term which has also been used in missiological circles to describe the group that Barna graciously calls the "enthusiast." Ironically, the term *mission junkie* has been used recently by an anthropologist to describe international aid workers who travel from site to site: "those who simply go from crisis to crisis, drawn to the adrenalin, the pay, the danger, the morality, and the freedom allowed under such start-up, emergency conditions" (Coles 2007, 24).

What good might come of this global wandering? Perhaps Millennials are more likely to be unhindered by ethnic and lifestyle divisions their previous generations. The Barna Group has christened the Millennials as "Mosaics" because of their "eclectic lifestyle and diversity" (2008, para. 10). In comparing

Millennials to earlier generations, the Barna report notes, "Mosaics are globally aware and cause-oriented. They relish risk, stimulation, and diverse experiences. And they are more sensitive to issues related to justice and poverty" (para. 10). Likewise, Pew Center research found that "the public—young and old alike—thinks the younger generation is more racially tolerant than their elders" (2010, para 29). While the study emphasizes that "acceptance does not in all cases translate into outright approval" (para. 32), Millennials seem to be more tolerant with other diverse populations, including immigrants, people with various sexual orientations, and nontraditional families.

Mobilizers and mission educators must work to see this forbearance translate to thoughtful engagement of that diversity for the sake of the kingdom. We must help students understand the role they have in living and speaking the gospel. They must recognize that missions is not just a tool of the church or what they did on their summer vacation, but is the very identity of the Christian who pursues people because God pursues reconciliation with man through Jesus Christ. Globalization and tolerance is not as simple as monitoring the world situation on a Twitter feed.

IMPLICATIONS FOR MISSIONS RECRUITERS

So what would all of this mean for a mission representative who wants to reach out to college students? How do we call students to an ambassadorial, pilgrim life? As I have interviewed agency mobilizers over the last years, a few key reps have modeled what it means to care for and pursue Millennials. I have learned from them a number of simple strategies which help to challenge students to consider God's call to long-term missions work.

Text, Friend, Tweet

All three of these are used as verbs here. Become accustomed to working through different types of media to reach and remain connected with students. Some of the recruiters who have visited the campus admittedly go for weeks without checking their email, but one savvy recruiter at the roundtable emphasized the critical nature of technology, "If you are not on Facebook, you are invisible." And brace yourselves for the next wave of technology, because it is coming. To quote Piper, "Can you magnify Christ with a thimble full of letters?" (Piper 2009).

Visit

Don't be a stranger. Visit a campus more than just during the missions conference. Go multiple times a year, and if a campus permits it, stay in the residence hall with students. Provide a multigenerational model of relationship to Millennials. Become acquainted with professors who are sympathetic to missions mobilization. In addition to Bible and Intercultural Studies professors, many educators across campus, including those in the fields of medicine, communications, and business, would be willing to have representatives take a few minutes of class to discuss ministry opportunities. Develop partnerships with missions pastors in local churches. Take students to coffee—often!

Care

Pursue the international community. It can be a key factor in mobilizing the campus. My college has over one hundred students who grew up in a country other than the United States. Half of those students are third culture kids, half are international students, and any of them would love to talk with someone who is interested in their home and how they could serve there more effectively. Just as the international community can benefit from the mobilizer's challenge, so domestic students can learn from internationals, and both populations can begin to recognize international realities and to care for people outside of their own cultural realm.

Mentor

Students crave discipleship, especially from someone who has walked the path they are on. Build relationships over the long term with students. Arrange to travel with students on an STM trip or on a visit to the home office. Sponsor a weekend on campus to focus on missions. Investigate the theology of vocation and calling. Study the Scriptures with students and pray with and for them.

Challenge

Tell the students that serving Jesus cross-culturally over the long haul will cost them their lives. Do not be afraid to call them to step up. The culture has aided and abetted Millennials in prolonging their adolescence, but missions mobilizers can call these students to commit to mature cross-cultural ministry for the sake of the magnification of Jesus. In a recent study of the religious life of American teenagers, Kendra Dean reminds readers where the call of mission begins:

The God of the Bible traffics in life and death, not niceness, and calls for sacrificial love, not benign whatever-ism. If the God Jesus Christ is a missionary God who crosses every boundary—life and death and space and time—to win us, then following Jesus is bound to be anything but convenient. Jesus Christ doesn't tinker; he tears down walls, draws up new plans, makes demands; "Have no other gods before me. Love one another as I have loved you. Leave your nets, and follow me." (2010, 37)

CONCLUSION

Missions mobilization among the Millennial generation is not for the faint of heart. Mobilizers encounter overinvolved parents, dramatic technology, and a dizzying movement among students. Mobilizing Millennials is in itself a cross-cultural ministry to call young people to cross cultures for Jesus' sake. William Borden, Lilias Trotter, Eric Liddel, and Jim Elliot were used mightily by God even while they were students, and although culture has shifted, God's call to his people's vocational identity of reconciliation and mission have not changed. Through the power of the Holy Spirit and submission to his Word, this generation of students has no less capacity for passionately serving God in cross-cultural ministry.

REFERENCES

Barna Group. 2008. Despite benefits, few Americans have experienced short term missions trips. http://www.barna.org/FlexPage.aspx?Page=BarnaUpdateNarrowPreview&BarnaUpdateID=318.
Beloit College. 2009. Beloit College mindset list. www.beloit.edu/mindset/2013.php.
Cheese, Peter. 2008. Netting the net generation. *Business Week*, March, 13.
Dean, Kenda Creasy. 2010. *Almost Christian: What the faith of our teenagers is telling the American church*. New York: Oxford University Press.
Gibbs, Nancy. 2009. Can these parents be saved? *Time Magazine*, November 30.
———. 2010. Generation next. *Time Magazine*, March 22.
La George, Lisa. 2009. Short-term missions at The Master's College: An experiential education. PhD diss., Biola University.

Livermore, David A. 2006. *Serving with eyes wide open: Doing short-term missions with cultural intelligence.* Grand Rapids: Baker Books.

Pew Research Center. 2010. The Millennials: Confident. Connected. Open to change. http://pewresearch.org/pubs/1501/millennials-new-survey-generational-personality-upbeat-open-new-ideas-technology-bound.

Prensky, Marc. 2001. Digital natives, digital immigrants. *On the Horizon* 9 (5): 1–6.

Piper, John. 2009. Why and how I am tweeting. http://www.facebook.com/note.php?note_id=102186034469&comments.

Priest, R. J., T. Dischinger, S. Rassmussen, and C. M. Brown. 2006. Researching the short term missionary movement. *Missiology* 34(4): 431–50.

Priest, R. J. and J. P. Priest. 2007. They see everything and understand nothing: Short-term mission and service learning. Paper presented at the meeting of the Evangelical Missiological Society, October, in Minneapolis, MN.

Rideout, Victoria J., Ulla G. Foehr, and Donald F. Roberts. 2010. *Generation M2: Media in the lives of 8- to 18-Year-Olds.* Menlo Park, CA: Kaiser Family Foundation.

Smith, Christian, and Patricia Snell. 2009. Souls in transition: The religious and spiritual lives of emerging adults. New York: Oxford University Press.

Zehner, Edwin. 2008. On the rhetoric of short-term missions appeals, with suggestions for team leaders. In *Effective engagement in short-term missions: Doing it right!*, ed. R. J. Priest, 185–208. Pasadena: William Carey Library.

6

FROM KITCHEN TABLE TO BOARDROOM TABLE: DIVERSITY ISSUES IN GLOBAL MISSION LEADERSHIP

GIL ODENDAAL

The efforts of Saddleback Church and the PEACE plan (www.thepeaceplan.com) in Rwanda under the leadership of pastor Rick Warren is relatively well known and has been widely reported in the secular and religious press since its inception in 2005. Likewise the phenomena of short term missions going forth from Saddleback Church (more than a thousand STMers to Rwanda alone) has also been the subject of much discussion.

However, there is a story within the story, a story of trial and error. A new kind of partnership is in the process of being forged, a partnership in which the partners are striving to honor diversity and wrestling with the reality of globalization and what appropriate models of leadership can look like that will enable the church to fulfill the Great Commission and the Great Commandment. It is the unfolding story of the integration of national aspiration using cultural appropriateness calibrated by the biblical mandate of being the body of Christ where every member needs the other.

And in this process ethnic, generational, and socioeconomical diversity, as well as doctrinal and theological diversity is at play as more than eighty denominations and the leadership from Saddleback Church pioneer new ways to work together. This is a process in which the principles that Walls articulates in *The Cross-cultural Process in Christian History* (2007) plays out on a daily basis. It is the story of how the rich and the poor, the perceived powerful members of the Global North and the less powerful partners from the Global South are learning from their mistakes, while growing in their understanding and dedication to ensure that the emerging model conforms to biblical norms resulting in an empowered church.

It is the story of how partners began to meet around the "kitchen table" for years, drinking gallons of tea and listening to one another and are now slowly moving to the "boardroom table" painstakingly nurturing an emerging model of partnership that could transform church and community in Rwanda and beyond. They are slowly moving from the kitchen table that represents informal fellowship to the boardroom table that represents true partnership with equality for all, towards a place in which meaningful decisions are made because of a common vision, calling, and burden. It is the story that portrays the excitement and confusion that manifests when diverse partners discover they are producing new wine together—trying to design new wineskins that have to be put in place while the subliminal message (that old wine is better) remains.

It is the story of an unfolding "new hermeneutic," to use Sherwood Lingenfelter's words:

> . . . a redefinition, a reintegration of the lives of God's people (the church) within the system in which they find themselves living and working. Jesus said, 'My Kingdom is not of this world' (John 18:36). He thus denied the existence of a Christian sociopolitical system but called for the transformation of his disciples' thinking and social relationships with others. (Lingenfelter 2009, 123)

I have been intimately involved in most of this process and have spent four to five months a year in Rwanda for the past four years as a participant observer with a deep commitment to see the church become more effective in its mission. To facilitate this process I have been using a qualitative research approach.

I will concentrate on the leadership and diversity issues relating to the Western Province where the Western Rwanda HIV/AIDS Healthcare Initiative was formally launched in May of 2007 with the signing of the first official Memo of Understanding between the national government of Rwanda (Health Department), the local government (Western Province, Karongi District), the Steering Committee representing about eighty denominations in Rwanda, and Saddleback Church.

Chapter 6

HOW IT STARTED

In 2004 President Kagame of Rwanda called Pastor Rick Warren. Kagame had just read *The Purpose Drive Life* and wanted to know if Warren thought a nation could become a Purpose Driven Nation. He invited Warren to implement Warren's newly-announced PEACE (**P**romote Reconciliation, **E**quip Servant Leaders, **A**ssist The Poor, **C**are For The Sick, and **E**ducate the Next Generation) plan (www.thepeaceplan.com) in Rwanda.

The vision behind the PEACE Plan is to mobilize Christians ("ordinary people") everywhere to address the world's five giant problems: 1) Spiritual emptiness; 2) Corrupt leadership; 3) Extreme poverty; 4) Pandemic disease; and 5) Rampant illiteracy. Each component of PEACE is distinct and works with the others as a "holistic" unit. As the expression of Christ and the world's largest distribution network, the ideal is that local churches globally will provide the leadership and ownership of all PEACEworks (a designation we use to identify the uniqueness of the integrated projects that are emerging) carried out to create sustainable and reproducible physical and spiritual community transformation.

From the beginning, Saddleback considered it nonnegotiable that the local churches in Rwanda had to lead in unity. The first years of Saddleback's involvement in Rwanda were spent investing time in facilitating the creation of a Steering Committee (SC) representing the more than eighty Christian denominations in Rwanda. Although the details were yet to be fleshed out, the main idea of the church in Rwanda leading the efforts was firmly embedded in the strategy from the beginning.

Through trial and error in our efforts in the Western Province, a three-level approach (Table 6) emerged as a possible framework for how PEACE could be implemented. Table 6 was designed primarily to educate enthusiastic Saddleback Valley Community Church (SVCC) members with rich professional backgrounds and newly awakened to the needs of the Global South who were preparing to go on short-term mission trips. It was an effort to educate them as to the place of outside resources and its application in a developmental approach that will be sustainable and would help the poor rather than hurt them (Corbett and Fikkert 2009). The various blocks were filled in with suggested tasks and activities which the Steering Committee found helpful as they continued to position themselves to lead with implementation of the PEACE Plan in Rwanda rather than to simply be passive recipients of the goodwill of donors in the Global North.

Table 6: The PEACE Plan

Planting Churches/ Reconciliation	Equipping Servant Leaders	Assisting the Poor	Caring for the Sick	Educating the Next Generation
Tertiary				
Seminary trained, pastors, government (reconciliation) global expansion	Seminaries, universities, government	Medium and large business development	Hospitals (doctors and full services)	Universities (equipping professionals)
Secondary				
Denominational church plants nation wide	Seminars (professional speakers)	Small business development	Clinic building and professional	High schools/ vocational schools specialized training ESL, computer literacy
Primary				
House churches, CPM, 40 DOP	PDC, PDL	IGA, micro enterprise	Preventive and primary healthcare (CDT)	Elementary, (reading writing, basic math) literacy training

Primary: Simplest, most reproducible efforts, requiring no outside resources and easily taught to virtually anyone. Unless this level is firmly established there will not be ownership or sustainability. (This is where local churches will be able to mobilize the greatest number of its members.)

Secondary: Some expertise required as well as outside resources to initiate.

Tertiary: The greatest expertise and care provided, requiring the greatest amount of resources to initiate and maintain.

Chapter 6

We experienced the truth of Miriam Adeney's provocative short story as we slowly moved forward:

"Would you like to know what it is like to do mission with Americans? Let me tell you a story," said David Coulibaly, a ministry leader in Mali, West Africa. Elephant and Mouse were best friends. One day Elephant said, "Mouse, let's have a party!" Animals gathered from far and near. They ate, and drank, and sang, and danced. And nobody celebrated more exuberantly than the Elephant.

After it was over, Elephant exclaimed, "Mouse, did you ever go to a better party? What a blast!" But Mouse didn't answer. "Where are you?" Elephant called. Then he shrank back in horror. There at his feet lay the Mouse, his body ground into the dirt—smashed by the exuberance of his friend, the Elephant.

"Sometimes that is what it is like to do mission with you Americans," the African storyteller concluded. "It is like dancing with an Elephant." (2000)

This delicate dance has been going on now for more than five years as short-term mission teams led by church members constantly adjusted their field strategies under the tutelage and direction of the Global PEACE staff of SVCC, learning from mistakes as well as successes. Directly and indirectly we constantly wrestled with the issues of power and influence in the delicate context of ethnicity. Engel and Dyrness accurately and provocatively note the heart of this challenge:

While the modern development of missions was associated with centers of power and influence, today those places are not important centers of Christianity, and the most vital Christian communities are found in areas of limited political and economic power. What this means, in no uncertain terms, is that past practices cannot continue to be the model for the future of the missions. Our dilemma then can be put in these terms: while our mission structures and attitudes have been formed by a particular historical and cultural situation, missions must now be carried out in a wholly different situation. Here is where our reflection . . . on Jesus' instructions and practice of the early church takes on renewed importance. (2000, 47–48)

What they do not address sufficiently in this otherwise excellent book is the role of ethnicity as the church in North America seeks to play a more active role in global missions in this age of post-postmodernity. I believe churches will not only severely limit their effectiveness in the twenty-first century but also run the risk of engaging in partnerships that are not based on biblical principles unless they are willing to confront adjust to the challenges of the realities of post-postmodernity. That is why we have been seeking unity built on diversity, and globalism built on localism (Hiebert 2003, 2).

Glocalism demands that we seek truth together and come as equals to the table of negotiation. More and more we have to learn how to share the gospel and resources with others so they can be empowered to make their own decisions in their situations. The periphery and center of missions are becoming interchangeable (2003, 2) and we have been committed to seek new ways of partnering in mission outreach.

Two years ago Archbishop Kolini of the Anglican Church in Rwanda, elected as the chairman of the SC by his peers, commented that working with SVCC is indeed a new experience for them. Not only do they feel empowered but he also said that if SVCC would leave Rwanda it would still have accomplished its purpose. He noted that this was because for the first time in the history of Rwanda, all the denominations were working together, not only in various evangelical subgroups but truly as the body of Christ. They had never convened in this fashion and were growing in their appreciation for one another as fellow servants of Christ in spite of some doctrinal differences.

HOW IT UNFOLDED

One of the first decisions the SC made, in cooperation with the Department of Health of Rwanda, was to direct SVCC to implement the Healthcare Initiative in the Western Province. This was based on the fact that it was the most underserved area in the country and also one of the regions that have been hardest hit by the genocide of 1994.

The Healthcare Initiative was implemented through a two-pronged approach. We initiated working with three hospitals and twenty-one clinics in the region (tertiary level, see Table 6.1) to build capacity of healthcare professionals, assess needs, and redesign the care for those living with the HIV virus, as well as identify a delivery system for their medication. At the same time we also started a bottom-up approach (primary level of Table 6) to mobilize the more than five hundred churches in the region as providers of basic preventative healthcare though holistic ministry.

The plan was (and remains) for Karongi District to be a laboratory to produce a model for integrated ministry. The principles would then be extrapolated and used to build a country footprint for PEACE implementation, which in turn can be used continent-wide and potentially worldwide through appropriate contextualization. It is intended that this implementation will take place fully recognizing that the world is "moving toward greater homogenization. On the one hand, ethnographies reveal increasing growth of ethnic, national and tribal identities in many parts of the world. On the other hand, locals are increasingly participating in global agendas" (Hiebert 2008, 249).

More importantly, I wanted to ensure that the churches owned the entire work and were recognized as owning it by the government and outsiders—not only in theory but in reality. We did this through an integrated approach known as Community Health Evangelism, a strategy I had used for many years with Medical Ambassadors International. However there was one major difference—this would be an attempt to work exclusively *through* the church and not just *with* the church with the goal that the church will embrace and execute the project as their own.

"Church-based" and "Church-owned" Defined

It is important to define church-*based* and church-*owned* and the distinction I make between working *with* the church and *through* it. They are fundamentally different approaches and strategies with proverbial "continental divide" outcomes.

Through implementing community development and particularly Community Health Evangelism programs globally, it occurred to me that most programs that are faith based are also only church based. Most of the times an individual or organization in the Global North will develop a ministry plan and then shop for a partner in the Global South with whom to execute the plan. The Global North partner will convene some church leaders, or simply approach a local church and explain to them the program, asking if they could do it "in their church." Inevitably the answer would be "Yes"; the recipients anticipating that this program will come with an influx of funds. Their belief is rewarded when the "donor partner" funds positions to make the program functional, but ultimately resulting in very little if any local ownership. Sadly, after an average of two years, grants usually run out or donor fatigue sets in and the program closes down sometimes leaving the intended beneficiaries in the church and community worse off than before the program started. The main reason this happens is the lack of local ownership. It is simply an outside program "based" in a church with very little or no chance for sustainability and possible scalability.

Church-owned, however, refers to a process in which local pastors and leaders catch and own the vision of what God wants to do through them and their churches. They grow in their own convictions of the biblical imperatives of holistic ministry. For example, they may come to understand God's heart for orphans in a new way and determine that they will address it—with or without any outside help. They initiate interventions in which their churches play the primary role. Outsiders may or may not join them in their efforts. The sustainability that is built into such an approach is obvious as well as the possible scalability depending on the availability of resources.

Working through the Church Defined

Working *through* the church implies making it a priority to mobilize the local church leadership and membership for the tasks they have identified as well as working through existing distribution channels and with the local church personnel. Not following this route could be perceived as disrespect. For the church to move forward in partnerships to the extent that God intended it, prejudice has to be faced for what it is. As we embrace a post-postmodernist approach we have to embrace ethnic equality as God given and be open to hear God speak through voices other than those of the Global North. Saayman give us a very harsh warning:

> Personally I think that the experience of slavery and colonialism, with everything this implied in terms of brutal dehumanization and degradation is still at work today in Africans' perception of not being taken seriously as mature Christians. Yet it also cannot be denied that African theologians and church leaders are indeed not

taken seriously as they deserve by first world theologians and church leaders. (2003, 64)

Working *through* the church is an expression of respect and validation of our Global South partners' ability to lead.

Stage One: Not Church-based but Church-owned

In light of this, our primary concern as we started this initiative was to make every effort to work through and not with the church. It had to be a process and ministry that was owned by the church since without local ownership sustainability, scalability, and reproducibility would be impossible. To accomplish this I started with a two-day "Vision Seminar" for pastors in one sector (in Rwanda there are five provinces—every province is divided into districts and every district is divided into sectors) in the Western province, Bwishyura, with a population of around 30,000 people.

Saddleback Church, under the direction of the national SC, was in the process of building the capacity of 200 pastors on a national level who were identified by the SC using the Purpose Driven curriculum. Three of the pastors that attended the training in September of 2007 were from Bwhishyura Sector. Together with them I planned the first Vision Seminar for pastors in that region.

During the two-day Vision Seminar I dealt with worldview, the biblical imperative of integrating the Great Commission and the Great Commandment, the difference between relief and development, and what it means to be church-owned. The entire seminar is based on using the LePSAS training system. LePSAS is an acronym (Le = Learner, P = Problem posing, S = Self-discovery, A = Action oriented and S = Spirit directed) defining the participatory training approach which focuses on the learner, not the trainer, with an emphasis on empowering rather than instructing. The intent is to involve the participants in the discovery/learning process through skits, sketches, or "starters" which pose a problem without giving any answer. The "starter" fosters discussion. Many times the larger group is broken into smaller groups for discussion questions. Then each group reports back what they have found or observed.

Through the use of participatory learning activities and Participatory Rural appraisal techniques (Bradshaw 2002, 240), the pastors were exposed to the entire Initiative and what it would mean to be partners in this venture. By the end of day two and after some frank discussions regarding the fact that it will have to be a volunteer church-led movement, the pastors were given a two-week window to decide whether or not they wanted their churches to participate. We wanted them to "consider the cost of the tower." If they chose to participate, each pastor could send two leaders from their respective churches to be trained through a six-month process. All thirteen churches opted to participate and were represented by two leaders from their churches.

The training process has profoundly impacted the community. Training of Trainers sessions I, II, and III were conducted, with appropriate field work in between. Healthy home standards were adopted, seed projects completed, churches worked together, and the government asked if their community health workers could also be included in future trainings. Upon completion of the TOT III, the pastors and the trainers from their churches worked together to select 225 church members to be trained by the newly graduated trainers to serve their church and community. The training of the Community PEACE Volunteers went very well (now Rwandese training Rwandese) and soon each one was assigned seven homes to visit twice a month with a physical health lesson (as agreed upon by the local health officials) and a Bible lesson.

The program grew rapidly. By the end of 2010, 124 Community PEACE Trainers (CPTs) in five sectors had trained around 2,000 Community PEACE Volunteers (CPVs). The CPTs became the chief implementers and facilitators for the visiting short-term teams from SVCC and partner churches that joined the effort. Based on the information gathering exercises and various participatory activities, the church leaders identified assets and needs and incorporated outside resources appropriately, keenly aware of the challenges unique to the African context (Calderisi 2006, 35–56).

A fledging clean water ministry developed and funding for a hundred wells were received, with the result that the first fifty went in very fast. The need of a technical school was identified by the interchurch council. This could provide employability for a growing number of young men and women (including street children) who were caught in the cycle of poverty. The idea was quickly developed by short-termers. It included site plans and land acquisition strategies. However, the pastors were only *informed* of these after the fact.

At this time an English as Foreign Language (EFL) school and computer literacy classes were established in the facilities used by the Community PEACE

Trainers. All of these were launched in response to participatory learning activities conducted with and by the CPTs. A number of medical teams also came in the name of the initiative as part of the PEACE Plan. They had very effective ministries working with the local hospitals. At the same time the HIV/AIDS capacity building component, developed in partnership with a leading US university, gained traction and visibility.

On the surface things looked excellent. A growing number of NGOs and government affiliated organizations visited the work and were extremely complimentary and eager to learn what the principles were that resulted in this visible transformation of the communities and the very low attrition rate with volunteers.

Then I discovered a flaw that has gone unnoticed: the initiative was only a church-*informed* initiative, not a church-*owned* effort. In spite of my efforts and thinking that we are doing this in "partnership" with the church as a church-*owned* effort and preventing the seven most common pitfalls (Guthrie 2000, 123–4), the national leaders experienced it differently.

Stage Two: From Church-*informed* to Church-*owned* Ministry

In hindsight I realized that the work at the primary community level (see Table 6) was not the focus point in the initial planning for the Steering Committee or SVCC since most attention was on the tertiary level. Yet, it has been the primary level (Table 6) of the PEACE Initiative in the Western Province that grew exponentially as church members and leaders were empowered and took full ownership of their destiny while the pastors and the Steering Committee were only watching from the sidelines. The more the lay leaders and members realized who they were in Christ and that they could do things to immediately and significantly change their environment, the faster the work grew. They were demonstrating a "true community-ownership approach" in the fullest sense as described by those doing community-based health research (Blumenthal and DiClemente 2004, 71). This was fueled by the visiting short-term missions teams who, despite tedious preparation prior to leaving the US, moved faster than the local churches could themselves incorporate and own.

Neither the national Steering Committee nor the local Interchurch Council representing the churches in Karongi were prepared for this. Concepts they approved in principle and ideas they verbalized suddenly became a reality—and they did not feel part of the process. Lingenfelter and Mayers observed, "In cultures in which prestige is ascribed, such prestige tends to be permanent" while in other culture where prestige must be achieved, such as the US, "respect is given to success that is current and continuing" (Lingenfelter and Mayers 2003, 94). In this situation the cultural respect given to church hierarchies and the prestige connected to being a pastor trumped any success the lay leaders and members had. The perceived result was that the real leadership did not emanate from the pastors but from others (the lay Rwandese as empowered by the short-termers). While Africa is stereotyped as having a "big man syndrome" (Moss 2007, 37–45), this was not the case here after numerous encounters with key pastors involved. Rather, it was a genuine desire of pastors to take control of their own destiny in a culturally appropriate way—without which sustainability will never be accomplished.

The pastors and Steering Committee members felt they were only *informed* of what happened after the fact. Thus, when the Steering Committee scheduled a planning retreat in Karongi district in September 2009, they were surprised by the tremendous progress but also alarmed by the apparent lack of influence the local pastors had on the overall direction and implementation of the work. This led to a reorganization of the leadership structure, a structure that is strongly centralized but bespeaks the need for gaining ownership of what had transpired. More importantly, this signaled that the national leadership felt empowered and was willing to speak into a rather delicate situation assertively. However, they established a control structure that itself had problems. Within five months a number of pastors began to express great reservations about the new leadership structure and accompanying decision making process, fearing that it would become too much like an NGO. The key criticisms were that it inhibited scalability and reproducibility and diminished the role of the local church because the leadership structure was outside of it.

Two factors were important. First, the church leaders felt they were only informed of new ministries coming. While they liked these new ministries, they were not in control of them and thus lacked ownership. A result was that they overcorrected by implementing a rigid structure. Second, this highlights how easy it is to assume that you are empowering churches which are initiating ministries even though the reality is that the church is "informed" of the activity and does not have genuine ownership. Though feeling disrespected, the pastors also felt empowered enough to speak up. This appears to be a direct result of the participatory processes that had previously been utilized.

ATTEMPTING TO UNDERSTAND THE UNFOLDING STORY AND KEY LESSONS LEARNED

Using Pedagogical Principles to Navigate through Post-post-modern Diversity Issues in Leadership

I often hear church leaders or mission executives say, "We are on a learning curve," in reference to their partnerships with churches in the Global South. Few if any apply a pedagogical framework against their efforts or insight to advance more rapidly and make the required changes to establish biblical and functioning partnership models. I propose that to effect the necessary changes to accomplish this we have to proactively "create new ways of talking about the global scene" (Rutt 2009, 61) and interpret the past as well as charting the future in terms of pedagogical dimensions.

Importance of Internalization of Information

My personal research concern has included the pedagogical aspects of effective HIV and AIDS ministry. I deeply believe how we communicate is as important as what we communicate. However, it never occurred to me that the same principles are applicable to organizational growth and leadership diversity issues in this age of globalization. In a study on the responses of churches to HIV/AIDS in South Africa, Parry concluded, "The national level of awareness on HIV/AIDS is generally high but the gap is wide between *awareness* and *internalization* of the messages that would result in effective changes in the norms of society" (Parry 2005, 29). I believe this is equally true in the case of partnerships and diversity issues. The literature regarding cross-cultural leadership and partnership is exponentially growing and theoretical models of the ideal kind of partnerships proliferate and yet the gap between *awareness* and *internalization* remains wide. As we were implementing the Western Rwanda Initiative, we thought we were aware of the issues yet we discovered a gap between our awareness and internalization of the truths we held.

Incorporating Nonformal Educational Principles

In situations of high HIV/AIDS incidence rates, formal and informal education and the acceptance of new information are rarely (if ever) effective in breaking taboos and changing worldviews (Kraft 2003, 389). A similar situation exists in relation to cross-cultural leadership models. Here, as with HIV/AIDS, in Africa there are deep cultural beliefs as well as deep wounds associated with colonial and postcolonial practices. Kraft is correct in noting that people have to be convinced of the need and solution if they are to accept change (2003, 388).

The same is true for change in understanding partnerships no matter what part of the world you come from. Although my team and I were more than willing to change, at first we did not see the need for change. It took a "disorienting dilemma" (Mezirow 1991, 168–69) to make me aware of the gap between what I believed we were doing and what our partners saw us as doing. The disorientation happened for me when the Steering Committee implemented the new leadership structure, aided by the perceptive and culturally skillful way Mark Affleck, executive director for PEACE, led us through it. The challenges that we have experienced on this journey towards partnership with the Church of Rwanda have highlighted the importance and role of nonformal education to address diversity issues.

Concerning nonformal education, Ted Ward states, "There are some educational activities that do not fall neatly into the informal or the formal sectors. They are not a part of socialization, or of schooling. They are a category apart, which we might label "other." Much of instruction in religion has historically been done in the "other" realm (Ward 1987, 7). The goal is to facilitate change in a nondirective way. I am increasingly convicted that it is a critical component of the engagement pathway towards meaningful partnership based on mutual respect in this post-postmodern era of missions. This is also the methodology followed by most Global South societies as part of initiation ceremonies (Kraft 2003, 276). Indeed, it is the way that most education that is transforming happens around the world (2003, 277).

Self-discovery: Learning to Change

To accomplish real change, Kraft also suggests that the focus of change must be identified, which he believes is the mind (2003, 366). Culture does not change, it is changed and "when it is changed it is changed by people who change their behavior, sometimes following, sometimes preceding a change of mind. Culture is rooted in mind change" (2003, 366). This is also a critical point for Bradshaw who maintains that "explanations do not always provide an adequate basis for transformation; people can understand the causes of a problem without finding the solution (Bradshaw 2002, 175). This concept has been the foundation for all the Training of Trainers seminars I implemented, and I believe the foundation for the success we are experiencing, yet I failed to apply the same principles consistently to leadership issues.

These pedagogical principles must be adhered to in order to move a ministry form being church-informed to being church-owned. Freire argues that dialogue is more important than curricula (2000, 122), or (as I see it) agendas. He argues against the common "banking" educational model, which is that education is simply depositing information in the minds of people without application (2000, 71–74). In this model, "Education becomes the act of depositing in which the students are the depositories and the teacher is the depositor" (Freire 2000, 72). This model presupposes that the teacher knows everything and the students know nothing; the teacher chooses the program content and the students adapt to it; and the teacher is the subject of the learning process, while the students are the objects (Freire 2000, 73). He argues for a problem-posing educational model which "breaks the vertical patterns characteristic of banking education" (2000, 80). As I am beginning to intentionally apply these same principles to the history of our Initiative leadership practices and how we can move forward, the insights are profound. For example, they illustrate why our Rwandese colleagues adapted the new leadership structure and rejected the old one.

Kraft (2003, 402) and others (Taylor and Taylor 2002, 63) point out that the refusal of groups to accept "guided change" is often the fault of the sponsoring organization rather than the recipients. It is critical and nonnegotiable that the local community must be fully engaged if we hope to effect lasting change. Only when the local community grows in confidence of their own abilities and they decide what their real problems are will real change take place. This is the critical turning point for a ministry to move from being a church-informed ministry to a church-owned ministry. In this the educator is a "midwife" rather than "father" (since that is "bastardization"). We too had to adopt the role of midwife, a position strongly promoted and endorsed by Rick Warren and now incrementally adopted and implemented under the skillful guidance of the executive direct for Global PEACE, Mark Affleck.

Elmers' Learning Cycle: Roadmap to Understanding.
Few things are as frustrating to me as having driven for a day on rough roads thinking I know where I am going only to discover that I am lost. This is why I still love roadmaps—they enable me to see the big picture and to orient myself. Understanding where and why I made a wrong turn and where I am now on the journey is liberating in itself. Similarly, I've used the learning model described by Duane and Muriel Elmer as a *Learning Cycle* (Elmer and Elmer 1999; see Figure 4) as a "roadmap." I have used it to orient myself as I navigate through the diversity issues on the way towards a meaningful partnership with our Rwandese friends. It provides me with a framework to interpret what has taken place as well as what the potential next steps may be as we take this journey together. It has been a critical resource connected to the nonformal educational process (the "how" of our journey).

Figure 4: Elmer Learning Cycle

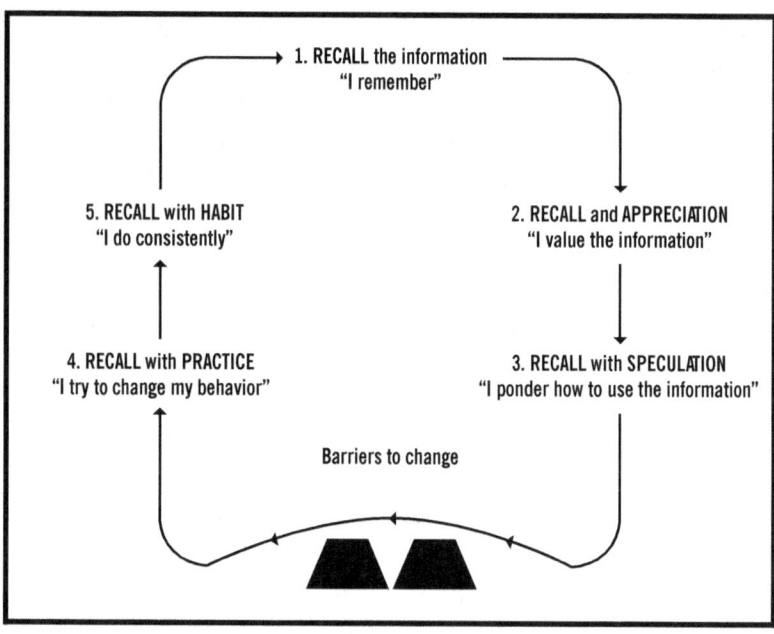

As Figure 4 illustrates, the learning cycle consists of five phases. The learner must participate and take ownership at every point in the cycle or learning is jeopardized. Not doing this is the reason that potential partnerships are too often aborted before they even have a chance to develop.

Like Freire, Elmer and Elmer strongly believe that dialogue is critical and must accompany every phase of the learning process. The first phase in the learning circle is *Recall the Information* phase, which focuses on remembering accurately without yet engaging in critical thinking. The second phase is *Recall and Appreciation,* where the individuals begin to value the information. This is followed by *Recall with Speculation,* where the participants begin to consider how to use the information as well as the types of barriers that can stall or stop the process of putting the information into practice. I believe we and our Rwanda friends are currently in this phase. The fourth phase is *Recall with Practice,* which naturally progresses into the fifth and final phase, *Recall with Habit.* This five-phase process has so far proven to be of great value as we intentionally deal with diversity issues in strengthening our partnership.

CONCLUDING REMARKS

The next chapter of this story is being written at a retreat center one hour south of Kigali, which happens to be where I am writing this reflection. Ten Rwandese church leaders, representing over eighty denominations, and three senior staff members of Saddleback have been meeting around the kitchen table drinking gallons of tea and reflecting on what God has accomplished through the PEACE Plan over the past couple of years. More importantly, we are also "recalling with speculation" what we have learned from our joint leadership efforts and the myriad diversity issues through which we are navigating. We are identifying the barriers to change that have to be overcome in order for us to function in partnership as the body of Christ where eye, hand, head, and feet all realize they need each other (1 Cor 12:21.) Barriers once removed and overcome will make it possible for a governance structure to emerge that is biblically motivated rather than determined by financial wealth, political correctness, or cultural appropriateness. Our prayer is that this will be a partnership where "there is neither Jew nor Greek, slave nor free, male nor female because all are on in Christ Jesus" (Gal 3:28); one in which Jesus' prayer "that all of them may be one, Father . . . so that the world may believe that you have sent me" (John 17:21) becomes a reality.

Our partnership is slowly moving from the kitchen table to the boardroom table because it is a partnership based on spiritual giftedness and a shared call from God to fulfill the Great Commission and the Great Commandment. Strength emanates from the diversity of perspectives we bring. This diversity is embraced as God's gifting to God's body for the purpose of seeing God's kingdom purposes fulfilled on earth. We are moving from the kitchen table to the boardroom table because we are also sitting around the communion table.

The journey is a slow one, sometimes painful but always rewarding. It is journey towards honoring diversity while wrestling with the reality of globalization and what appropriate models of leadership can look like that will enable the church to fulfill the Great Commission and the Great Commandment. It is a journey towards a partnership that integrates national aspiration with cultural appropriateness while calibrated against the biblical mandate of being the body of Christ where each member needs the other.

It is a journey worth traveling because one day the boardroom table will be replaced by a wedding banquet table and diversity celebrated as voices representing every culture and language will shout, *"Hallelujah! For the Lord God Almighty reigns. Let us rejoice and be glad and give him glory! For the wedding of the Lamb has come and his bride has made herself ready"* (Rev 19:6–7).

REFERENCES

Adeney, Miriam. 2000. When elephants dance: Thoughts on short term missions. Mission Mobilizer, http://home.snu.edu/~hculbert/dance.htm.

Blumenthal, Daniel, and Ralph DiClemente. 2004. *Community-based health research: Issues and methods.* New York: Springer Publishing Company.

Bradshaw, Bruce. 2002. *Change across cultures: A narrative approach to social transformation.* Grand Rapids: Baker Academic.

Calderisi, Robert. 2006. *The trouble with Africa: Why foreign aid isn't working.* New York: Palgrave Macmillan.

Corbett, Steve, and Brian Fikkert. 2009. *When helping hurts: How to alleviate poverty without hurting the poor and yourself.* Chicago: Moody Publishers.

Earl, Riggins R. Jr. 1993. *Dark symbols, obscure signs.* Maryknoll: Orbis.

Elmer, Duane, and Muriel Elmer. 1999. The learning circle. Unpublished.

Engel, James F., and William A. Dyrness. 2000. *Changing the mind of missions: Where have we gone wrong?* Downers Grove: InterVarsity.

Freire, Paulo. 2000 [1970]. *Pedagogy of the oppressed.* New York: Continuum.

———. 2002. *Education for critical consciousness.* New York: Continuum.

Guthrie, Stan. 2000. *Missions in the third millennium: 21 key trends for the 21st century.* Colorado Springs: Paternoster Press.

Hastings, Adrian. 1979. *A history of African Christianity 1950–1975*. London: Cambridge University Press.

Hiebert, Paul. 2003. Doing glocal theology. Unpublished paper.

———. 2008. *Transforming worldviews: An anthropological understanding of how people change*. Grand Rapids: Baker Academic.

Kraft, Charles H. 2003. *Anthropology for Christian witness*. Maryknoll: Orbis.

Lingenfelter, Sherwood. 2008. *Leading cross-culturally: Covenant relationships for effective Christian leadership*. Grand Rapids: Baker Academic.

———. 2009. Prisons, pilgrims and transformation: Understanding your cultural captivity. In *Global mission handbook: A guide for cross-cultural service*; ed., Steve Hoke and Bill Taylor, 122–124. Downers Grove: InterVarsity.

Lingenfelter, Sherwood, and Marvin K. Mayers. 2003 [1986]. *Ministering cross-culturally: An incarnational model for personal relationships*. Grand Rapids: Baker Academic.

Mezirow, Jack. 1991. *Transformative dimensions of adult learning*. San Francisco: Jossey-Bass.

Moss, Todd J. 2007. *African development: Making sense of the issues and actors*. London: Lynne Rienner Publishers.

Parry, Sue. 2005. *Responses of the churches to HIV and AIDS in South Africa*. Unpublished report prepared for the World council of Churches Ecumenical HIV/AIDS initiative in Africa

Rickett, Daniel. 2002. *Making your partnership work*. Enumclaw: Winepress Publishing.

Rutt, Douglas L. 2009. Global mission partnership: Missiological reflections after ten years of experience. In *Missions from the Majority World: Progress, Challenges and Case Studies;* ed. Enoch Wan and Michael Pocock, 59–73. Pasadena: William Carey Library.

Saayman, Willem A. 2003. "Ex Africa Semper Aliquid Novi": Some random reflections on challenges to Christian mission arising in Africa in the twenty-first century. *Mission Studies* 20: 57–81.

Taylor-Ide, Daniel, and Carl Taylor. 2002. *Just and lasting change: When communities own their futures*. Baltimore: Johns Hopkins University.

Walls, Andrew F. 2007. *The cross-cultural process in Christian history: Studies in the transmission and appropriation of faith*. Maryknoll: Orbis.

Ward, Ted. 1987. Putting non-formal education to work. *Together* (July–September) 7–8.

PART II
THE CHALLENGES OF DIVERSITY IN TEAMS

7

THE MULTIFACETED JOURNEY TOWARD GLOBALIZATION IN MISSION: LESSONS IN FLEXIBILITY, HUMILITY, AND COMMUNITY

DONNA DOWNES

A PERSONAL JOURNEY

In November of 1984, my husband and I left for our first term as career missionaries to Kenya, East Africa, to be involved in leadership development with OC International. We were both armed with graduate degrees in communications and cross-cultural studies, ten years of business and teaching experience, and plenty of short-term mission exposure. Our hearts were full of enthusiasm and anticipation and a sense that we had prepared well for this very moment.

Even better, we believed we were part of the best and most progressive missionary organization we'd ever encountered to that point. We joined eleven other enthusiastic first-term missionaries who all arrived in Kenya within our first year there. Two of the couples were from Kenya originally, two other men (one single, one married) were from Ethiopia, and the remaining seven were from various geographic regions and denominational backgrounds in the United States. Our leader was an older Kenyan man who, together with his wife, had ministered many years in their home country and were respected leaders in their local Kenyan church. All thirteen of us had been trained either at seminaries or universities in the United States. We were part of an experimental multicultural team that our mission hoped would become a stellar model of new efforts to internationalize its missionary force.

Everyone on the team went through a two-month-long field training program at our US headquarters where we heard the same teaching about the priority our mission placed on family and team relationships and about the mission's commitment to leadership development, to equality in gender roles, and to partnership in ministry. We also learned together about organizational policy issues (like vacation time, salaries, insurance, retirement, etc.). Everyone on the team was to be considered equal in terms of missionary status. Finances were shared so that everyone received essentially the same salary each month regardless of how much donors gave. The idea was that those with more funding would share with those who had less.

My husband and I thought our missionary life would be as good as it gets short of heaven! We'd be working with eleven other people who loved the Lord and wanted to dedicate their lives to serve the Lord and the Lord's church in Kenya. We all eagerly anticipated the wonderful possibilities of Christian community that the word "team" conjured up. And our multicultural mix just added to the excitement as we dreamed about being living examples of the outworking of God's multicultural harvest force through which God would expand God's eternal kingdom!

Within the first three years of our arrival, several disturbing events occurred:

- One cross-cultural couple was asked to leave the field and the mission because of infidelity and family violence. What was greatly disturbing is that no one on the team had any idea that there was a problem. Even more puzzling was the fact that a few teammates felt the mission had overstepped its boundaries by questioning how husbands treat their wives. Such issues were culturally determined, in their opinion, and should not be subject to organizational scrutiny.
- Housing, salaries, cars, children's schooling, and finances became major issues of contention as teammates argued over what constituted an appropriate missionary lifestyle for the context we were in.
- Everyone on the team was questioning organizational policies and priorities. In fact, our Kenyan field leader was ready to resign

from the mission accusing the organization of imperialism, prejudice and unfair leadership and management practices.
- And basically, conflict instead of unity became the norm.

Interestingly enough, OC's ministries in Kenya were growing and prospering during this time. Externally we looked like a "dream team." Internally, however, we were a mess! What happened to our Kenya "dream team" to cause us to move so rapidly from being a positive model of internationalization in mission to a negative one? Could our organization and our team have been better prepared for ministry together? Were our problems all a matter of sinful attitudes and actions? Was there something else happening in our team and our organization that led to some of the difficult circumstances we were facing?

MY ORGANIZATION'S JOURNEY

Within eight years of beginning OC's work in Kenya, several of the Africans on our team had left the mission, many of the Americans remained hurt, bewildered, perhaps even angry, and the mission as a whole went into a multi-year process of reexamining where its internationalization strategy had gone wrong and what must be changed to be able to embrace the growing diversity in the global harvest force. In addition to the challenges encountered on the Kenya team, OC International was facing similar challenges to its efforts in other regions of the world

Suffice it to say here that the solutions to our Kenya team problems were multifaceted. Aside from the family and marital situations that required professional counseling, there were problems that required paradigm shifts in our theology of mission and in our understanding of leadership, servanthood, and partnership. There were historical, social, and political issues that plagued our relationships—problems that we as a team were ill prepared at the time to handle. There were management issues that required changes in organizational dynamics. Spiritual warfare definitely played a role, but so did a host of organizational policies and team dynamics that were insensitive to cultural realities. As a whole, OC remained dedicated to the process of internationalization, although the model they used became significantly different over the next fifteen years.

RESEARCHING THE CHALLENGES OF GLOBALIZATION IN MISSION

In the mid-1990s, as our Kenya team and our entire mission were still reeling from various challenging experiments with internationalization around the globe, I began a doctoral program at Biola University with the specific goal of studying cross-cultural leadership and organizational dynamics to see if I could better understand our team dynamics and possibly help our mission to address some of the problems that led to the breakdown of our "Kenya dream team." In the process, I discovered that many North American-based mission organizations were going through similar struggles. My studies culminated in two key research projects.

Corporate Values and Personal Cultures: The Anthropology of Social Organizations

First, I investigated the role that culture and ethnicity played in both team and organizational dynamics. Using a model of social organizations developed by Mary Douglas (1982) and expanded by Christian anthropologist Sherwood Lingenfelter (1996, 1998), I explored how several key cultural values affected the attitudes and behaviors of our teammates toward one another as well as toward the international organization as a whole. (The results of this study, in an abbreviated form, are contained as a case study of "Union Ltd." in Sherwood Lingenfelter's *Agents of Transformation* [1996].)

Differences in team members' attitudes toward authority in the family and community, toward property, labor and productivity, gift giving and generosity, and toward communication protocol and methods of conflict resolution loomed large in the problems that arose in our Kenya team. Each infraction of the other's cultural rules (whether intended or unintended) eroded the possibility of building a trust bond among team members. A key discovery from this study was that although OC had worked hard to communicate and prepare its recruits to understand and minister through the grid of the organization's mission, vision, and values, all of those value statements eventually were interpreted through each person's cultural lenses. Values from one's personal and ethnic culture always seemed to trump the organizational culture—especially in times of conflict or pressure.

Some examples of cultural value differences and their effect on organizational behavior include the following:

Family Values: One of OC's stated values has always been to place a high priority on the health and welfare of the family. For the Americans on our team, that meant the nuclear family (the husband, wife, and children who were present on the mission field); for our Kenyan coworkers, the health and welfare of the family included a host of extended family members for which and to which they were responsible financially, socially, spiritually, and sometimes even politically.

Team Relationships: Furthermore, OC placed a high stated value on healthy team relationships. However, because of traditional and historic feuds, our African teammates found that their tribal and national affiliations interfered with the establishment of healthy relationships between them. Neither of the two Ethiopian teammates nor the two Kenyan families developed deep trust bonds together, let alone with members from non-African cultures.

Leadership style: In addition, leadership style became problematic as the egalitarian Americans looked at our Kenyan team leader as an equal among equals who was expected to help the team reach consensus on major decisions. We Americans were not prepared for the high-context, power-distance culture within which our African colleagues seemed comfortable to work. While the Americans were comfortable with open-team discussions and "creative conflict," our African teammates often interpreted these sessions as offensive and disrespectful. In addition, policies about health insurance, housing costs, salaries, taxes, cars, children's schooling, and vacations all became suspect as organizational "perks" favoring American citizens. The list of cultural minefields became extensive.

As missionaries, we had prepared ourselves to face adjustments to the local cultures outside our OC team. However, we had NOT prepared ourselves well for the cultural adjustment that had to take place within our multicultural team! It is interesting to note here that international corporate management experts such as Geert and Gert Jan Hofstede (2005), Fons Trompenaars and Charles Hampden-Turner (1998), Robert Moran and Philip Harris (2007), House (2004), and others had been researching and writing about these very problems since the 1970s and had produced a wealth of literature on the subject, yet discussions about that literature were virtually nonexistent in missionary circles.

Creating Organizational Cultures that Value and Leverage Diversity

A second area of research culminated in my doctoral dissertation, the purpose of which was to "explore and document how US-based international mission agencies [were] practically responding to the issue of globalization in missions; to analyze selected organizational approaches to globalization; and to identify, explain and suggest strategies to address the problems organizations may face as they work toward globalization in their own agencies" (Downes 2004, 17). The study was divided into several phases.

Phase One: Survey of Mission Organizations with Non-North American Staff

First, I conducted a mail survey of 367 US-based mission organizations that had indicated they had non-North American personnel on their staff as listed in the 2001–2003 edition of the *Missions Handbook* (Siewert and Welliver 2000). This list also included the largest 116 mission agencies in terms of the size of their missionary staff. The 367 agencies surveyed represented over 90 percent of all missionary personnel sent from or through US-based mission organizations at that time (Downes 2004, 82–84).

My purpose in conducting this survey was to determine the percentage of non-North American missionary personnel serving in strategic leadership positions at the regional level or above based on the following assumption: If globalization of the missionary harvest force was occurring in North American-based agencies, we would see a significant percentage of non-North Americans in key international leadership positions, on governing boards and in regional leadership posts. We would also see major efforts being made to recruit non-North Americans at all levels: local, regional, and international.

This first phase of the research, however, yielded several surprising results:

- While 86 percent of the responding organizations had some non-North Americans on their full-time missionary staff, the vast majority worked at field or regional levels. In fact, fewer than a third of the agencies had non-North Americans ministering in international management positions, and the numbers of those managers were small. In other words, the transition of strategic decision-making roles from Americans to non-North Americans had not yet taken place.

- In the same vein, just 13 percent of the organizations with governing boards (or nineteen agencies out of 148) indicated that one-third or more of their board members were non-North American.
- Denominational mission agencies had far fewer non-North Americans in international management or board positions than nondenominational agencies, which was surprising to this author since denominational agencies had such long histories of church planting and leadership development in various areas of the world. In fact, out of the nineteen agencies that reported having non-North American members serving on their governing boards, only one was denominationally based.
- Smaller, newer agencies (established after 1970) showed considerably more international diversity in their missionary staff at all leadership levels than did the older, larger, more established agencies.

Phase Two: In-depth Case Studies of Globalization Efforts

The second phase of this research was to conduct eight in-depth case studies of mission organizations that had evidenced significant efforts in globalization "to determine how their strategies, management cultures, structures, and historical processes might serve as models for other agencies attempting to globalize their missionaries forces" (Downes 2004, Abstract, np).

This part of the research revealed that several of the organizations had traveled through various stages toward globalization. These stages were first identified in missions literature by J. David Lundy (1999), who differentiated between internationalization and globalization—the former being quite common in missions since the 1970s. He describes "internationalization" as a process whereby mission agencies have added a wealth of national workers to their staffs in various nations and, therefore, consider their organization as being highly diversified. "Globalization of mission, on the other hand," he writes, "means all that internationalization does, plus incorporates structural and attitudinal components" that invite people from any culture to feel at home in that organization, to be involved in key global leadership roles, and to champion "local diversity while maintaining a universal purpose" (Lundy 1999: 147–48). A globalized organization would be one where key strategic leadership goes beyond national or regional boundaries.

From the case study interviews, it also became apparent that while the organizational journeys usually began with a commitment to internationalization (as Lundy described it), regionalization of leadership was often a second step as organizations and denominations looked to Asian, African, Hispanic, or European leaders to lead in their respective regions. Very few organizations could be described as fully global where personal and management practices and policies encouraged shared partnership and leadership which Escobar (2003) describes as being "from everywhere to everyone." In other words, it was very rare to find Asian or African mission leaders serving in international-level strategic leadership roles outside of their respective regions. One mission leader explained the situation by saying that Western European, British, and American educational systems train people to be more globally aware and less parochial in their interests so that they make more objective decisions. I laughed at this response thinking the leader most certainly was poking fun at the thought that historically global mission policies and strategies were somehow objective and nonparochial. Unfortunately, I learned that he was serious!

This phase of the research revealed a multitude of models for globalization of mission too numerous to fully explain in this article. However, very broadly speaking, these models of globalization included: 1) many types of long- and short-term partnerships based on sharing personnel, finances, technical expertise, equipment, and other resources; 2) independent regional and national franchises in which regionally based mission agencies are structurally and financially independent, but they share a common ministry goal or expertise that ties them to a corporate name (e.g., MAF International); 3) global alliances where organizations are decentralized nationally and/or regionally but are tied together through their commitment to the mission, vision, and values set by and monitored through a globally representative board (OC International, World Vision, for example); 4) mergers or acquisitions where locally based organizations are subsumed under a larger global entity; 5) financial investment in national or regional missionaries and mission movements without deployment of personnel; and, 6) standard membership models where all personnel are somehow connected to a North American-based headquarters. Each model, of course, comes with its own challenges of recruitment, training, deployment, financial, and personnel management.

Phase Three: Comparison of Case Study Results with Best Practices
In phase three of this research, the results from these case studies were then compared to the "best practices" in international management and missions literature to identify the key factors that seemed to contribute positively to globalization. Since that study, my continuing research has confirmed and elaborated on these six categories:

1. A strong commitment to globalization by mission leadership. Over and over again, both international business leaders and the respondents to my own research indicated that if organizational leaders are committed to diversity and globalization, then the adjustments necessary to make globalization work will more likely be viewed as positive and necessary. Key writers on diversity management, all emphasizing the importance of leadership commitment to cross-cultural organizational diversity, include Taylor Cox (2001), Robert T. Moran et al. (1996), and Fons Trompenaars and Charles Hampden-Turner (1998).
2. A positive attitude toward diversity must be cultivated at all levels of the organization. Members of the organization must see global diversity as a necessary, good, and helpful goal that is part of God's plan for his worldwide church rather than as a difficult challenge that achieves political correctness at the expense of efficiency and effectiveness. Learning to hear and embrace the voices of diversity in global mission has been a process fraught with uncertainty as well as celebration. Historical and missiological perspectives are particularly helpful in tracing the global missionary movement and the response of Western Christianity to the new global harvest force. These perspectives are provided by Andrew F. Walls (2002), Lamin Sanneh (2008), Dana Robert (2009), Jehu Hanciles (2008), and Samuel Escobar (2003). One of the early pioneers to write about this subject was Ralph Winter in his seminal article that first appeared in 1981 on sodalities and modalities: "The Two Structures of God's Redemptive Mission" (1999).
3. Organizations must adjust their personnel and leadership development policies to help globalization happen. If the organization

does not specifically and proactively emphasize international recruiting, training, and development for non-US personnel, then globalization will remain more of a missiological dream than a practical reality. This includes creating multinational leadership development programs and purposefully selecting and preparing non-Western personnel to sit on executive international and regional boards. Disengaging leadership selection practices from Western-based values is critically important. Furthermore, training must be internationalized and should include an emphasis on multicultural teams and how organizational culture is affected and adjusted by personal cultural values. One of the first authors to recognize a need for missionary training beyond Western approaches was William D. Taylor of the World Evangelical Fellowship (1991). While the literature on this subject remains small, several excellent recent case study articles appeared in the January 2008 edition of *Missiology*, including: "Training the Trainers: A Latin American Case Study" (Brynjolfson 2008) and "Training Cross-Cultural Missionaries from the Asian Context" (Tai-Woong Lee 2008). In addition, Taylor wrote an overview article, "Global and Personal Reflections on Training/Equipping for Cross-Cultural Ministry Today" (2008).

4. Restructuring and policy changes usually must take place for diversity to flourish. For example, such changes may include shifting policy making, recruiting, training, deployment, strategic decisions, and financing to regional centers, demoting the historically privileged position of North American headquarters to one regional center equal to other regional centers. Strategic decision-making then is not based on finances or historic power but on the ability to bring diverse and creative ideas to the table. In addition, organizations should encourage languages other than English to be used in meetings, in organizational literature and on websites so that the skillful use of English is not seen as a prerequisite for one's voice being acknowledged and heard.

Also, organizations should work at facilitating frequent networking, communications, learning, and problem solving across cultural groups within the agency. E-mail, Skype, and other electronic forms of communication make such international meetings possible at much less cost than a decade ago. And the benefit of such international idea exchange is priceless. Such networking encourages appreciation for the creativity that a diversity of voices can bring to the global missionary task.

It is important to note here that restructuring for globalization can take many viable forms including mergers, partnerships, franchises, regionalization, and support of or subordination to national movements, among others.

5. Adjustments in financial policies are essential if globalization is to work well. First, systems must be established that allow and can account for funds raised in multiple locations and currencies. Furthermore, health and life insurance programs and other benefit plans must take into consideration the availability of national health care systems in many countries. Realistic support levels must be set commensurate with local economies, and there must be flexibility according to individual needs and situations. A "one size fits all" financial policy simply will not work in the global mission context in which we find ourselves today.

Recent authors that have written on finances, mission structures, and the encouragement of diversity in mission include Jonathan Ingleby (2006), Steve Sang-Cheol Moon (2008), Gene Daniels (2009), Mary M. Lederleitner (2009), and Sherwood Lingenfelter (2008).

6. Organizations must leave behind the idea of financial independence and self-sufficiency as a sign of ministry viability. Financial independence should not be seen as the golden standard of success for missionary deployment in ministry. Rather, we should replace this value with a sense of interdependence where resources are shared across nations as a positive sign of God's delight in international unity and partnership in the building up of God's kingdom. Those who have more resources should delight in sharing those resources without the strings of dependency attached. For a fascinating, but somewhat controversial, treatment of this subject see John Rowell (2007). Further perspective is provided by Lederleitner (2010).

REINITIATING THE JOURNEY TOWARD GLOBALIZATION IN OC INTERNATIONAL

My own mission organization has changed and grown tremendously over the last fifteen years since my husband and I were in Kenya. OC has established a new structure called the "OC Global Alliance" to encourage and facilitate global diversity in its missionary force and to rectify some of the mistakes it made in the past with regard to partnership, power, and money. It is now possible within OC to be recruited, trained, supported, and sent out from various parts of the world without ever having passed through what used to be known as OC's "US Headquarters." The former "headquarters" is now called the US Mobilization Center and is primarily responsible for recruitment, training, and deployment of US missionary staff. The US center, at least in theory, is equal to and not greater than the ten other mobilization centers worldwide. All funds, spiritual counseling, strategic planning, deployment decisions, and ongoing support services now come through one or more of OC's worldwide mobilization centers.

One of our teams in Spain, for example, is comprised almost entirely of Latin American missionaries prepared by, sent, and supported through various Latin American Mobilization Centers and funded through a variety of church and parachurch groups throughout Latin America. Funding levels and lifestyles vary on this team, but the inequities do not seem to be causing major problems at this point. An American recently joined this team, so it remains to be seen how her addition may change team dynamics.

OC's teams in Asia have members from Taiwan, Korea, the Philippines, Singapore, and North America and soon there will be Brazilians joining one or more these teams as several of the Brazilian churches have recently joined efforts and set a goal to send 100 missionaries to Asia in the next few years. OC's president reported that, as of January 2010, more than 50 percent of OC's missionary force is now comprised of non-US citizens and the numbers are growing rapidly as God continues to build and mature God's church around the world and as he calls and sends his people from every nation (Gripentrog 2010).

But challenges remain, not the least of which are issues with accepting and processing multiple currencies, leadership of missionaries on the field, occasional ethnic rivalries and power struggles, and confusion over health coverage, vacation policies, employee benefits, etc. And probably the most pressing challenge will continue to be how an organization of multinational and multiregional alliances can truly minister in accordance with a united goal.

It is encouraging to note that OC is just one example of an increasing number of mission organizations that have been making major shifts in their structures and policies to accommodate and embrace new global realities. Some are forming strategic global partnerships, others are involved in mergers, and still others are encouraging the establishment of "Great Commission companies" and "businesses as mission" as they look for creative ways to bring God's good news to the nations.

For a good overview of new strategic practices and structures in missions see Michael Pocock et al. (2005) and C. Neal Johnson and Steven Rundle (2009). Indeed, the multifaceted journey toward globalization defies a single definition or path. What each journey DOES have in common, however, is the necessity to learn how: 1) to relinquish power and to work in partnership; 2) to incorporate cross-cultural sensitivity in organizational policies, finances, member recruiting, training, and leadership development; and, 3) to be immensely flexible in structures for and approaches to ministry while still retaining a central unifying purpose and set of values.

CONCLUSIONS AND CHALLENGES FOR FURTHER STUDY

Around the world today, people everywhere are answering God's call to make disciples of all nations. We've read and heard about the shift of the center of Christianity from the Global North to the Global South and the dramatic rise in the number of missionaries being sent from the majority world. Still, my research shows that we have a long way to go until we see the majority of North American mission organizations rejoicing in and facilitating diversity in mission not only in their harvest force but in their mission leadership.

Progress has been made for sure, but we must ask ourselves: What needs to change or improve in North American mission agencies so that we can be better partners in mission and not merely power-brokers and principal strategists in world evangelization? What leadership profiles do we prefer in North America that might exclude many leaders who operate with a different cultural leadership paradigm? What methods and best practices in missions globalization can we share with one another to help us partner more effectively? Are there cross-disciplinary lessons mission leaders can learn from the multicultural corporate world? Furthermore, as church and parachurch organizations are established in the majority world, how might they benefit from assistance and support to enable their growth and proliferation without losing the vision and momentum for missions in and from North America? Steve Sang-Cheol Moon, executive director of the Korea Research Institute for Missions, recently asked this question about the Korean missionary movement (2008).

May we be inspired and prepared to explore these questions further to the glory of God and to the establishment of his church among all peoples, even to the uttermost parts of the earth.

REFERENCES

Brynjolfson, Rob. 2008. Training the trainers: A Latin American case study. *Missiology* 36: 17-31

Cox, Taylor, Jr. 2001. *Creating the multicultural organization*. San Francisco: Jossey-Bass.

Daniels, Gene. 2009. Decoupling missionary advance from Western culture. *Evangelical Missions Quarterly* (October), http://www.emisdirect.com/emq/issue-309/2343.

Douglas, Mary. 1982. Cultural Bias. In *In the active voice*. London: Routledge and Kegan Paul.

Downes, Donna R. 2004. The globalization of mission: Missiological dream or management nightmare. PhD diss., Biola University.

Escobar, Samuel. 2003. *The new global mission: The gospel from everywhere to everyone*. Downers Grove: InterVarsity.

Gripentrog, Greg. 2010. January 2010: The beginning of a new decade. Letter from the president of OC International to the constituency.

Hanciles, Jehu. 2008. *Beyond Christendom: Globalization, African migration and the transformation of the West*. Maryknoll: Orbis.

Hofstede, Geert, and Gert Jan Hofstede. 1991. *Cultures and organizations: Software of the mind*. New York: McGraw-Hill.

House, Robert J., et al. 2004. *Cultures, leadership and organizations: GLOBE study of 62 societies*. Thousand Oaks, CA: Sage.

Ingleby, Jonathan. 2006. Globalisation, glocalisation and mission. *Transformation* 23: 49–53.

Johnson, C. Neal, and Steven Rundle. 2009. *Business as mission: A comprehensive guide to theory and practice*. Downers Grove: InterVarsity.

Kim, Hansung. 2009. Rereading Acts 6:1-7: Lessons for multicultural mission organizations. *Evangelical Missions Quarterly* (January), http://www.emisdirect.com/emq/issue-306/2213.

Lederleitner, Mary M. 2009. Funding kingdom work by building financial capacity in national organizations. *Evangelical Missions Quarterly* (July), http://www.emisdirect.com/emq/issue-308/2310.

———. 2010. *Cross-cultural partnerships: Navigating the complexities of money and mission.* Downers Grove: InterVarsity.

Lee, David Tai-Woong. 2008. Training cross-cultural missionaries from the Asian context. *Missiology* 36: 111–30.

Lewis, Richard G. 2009. How cultures work: A roadmap for intercultural understanding in the workplace. *Evangelical Missions Quarterly* (January), http://www.emisdirect.com/emq/issue-306/2211.

Lingenfelter, Sherwood. 1996. *Agents of transformation.* Grand Rapids: Baker.

———. 1998. *Transforming culture.* Grand Rapids: Baker.

———. 2008. *Leading Cross-Culturally.* Grand Rapids: Baker.

Lundy, J. David. 1999. Moving beyond internationalizing the mission force. *International Journal of Frontier Missions* 16: 147–55.

Moon, Steve Sang-Cheol. 2008. The protestant missionary movement in Korea: Current growth and development. *International Bulletin of Missionary Research* 32: 59–62, 64.

Moran, Robert T., Philip R. Harris, and Sarah V. Moran. 1996. *Managing cultural differences*, 4th ed. Burlington, MA: Butterworth-Heinemann.

Pocock, Michael, Gailyn VanRheenen, and Douglas McConnell. 2005. *The changing face of world missions.* Grand Rapids: Baker.

Robert, Dana. 2009. *Christian mission: How Christianity became a global religion.* Malden, MA: Wiley-Blackwell.

Rowell, John. 2007. *To give or not to give: Rethinking dependency, restoring generosity, and redefining sustainability.* Atlanta: Authentic.

Sanneh, Lamin. 2008. *Disciples of all nations: Pillars of world Christianity.* New York: Oxford.

Siewert, John, and Dotsey Welliver, eds. 2000. *Missions handbook, 2001–2003.* Wheaton: Evangelism and Missions Information Service.

Taylor, William D. 1991. *Internationalising missionary training.* Grand Rapids: Baker.

———. 2008. Global and personal reflections on training/equipping for cross-cultural ministry today. *Missiology* 36: 76–86.

Trompenaars, Fons, and Charles Hampden-Turner. 1998. *Riding the waves of culture: Understanding diversity in global business*, 2nd ed. New York: McGraw-Hill.

Walls, Andrew. 2002. *The cross-cultural process in Christian history*. Maryknoll: Orbis.

Winter, Ralph. 1999. The two structures of God's redemptive mission. In *Perspectives on the world Christian movement: A reader*, 4th ed., eds. Ralph D. Winter and Steven C. Hawthorne, 244–53. Pasadena: William Carey Library.

8

EFFECTIVE CROSS-CULTURAL MINISTRY TEAMS

GEORGE BROWN

INTRODUCTION

I emerged a bit frustrated from the general assembly of the church plant in France where we were serving. My American, task-oriented temperament expected that we would have at least decided something about how we would move forward. Instead a national's comment struck me when she said, "Wasn't that a great meeting. Everyone got to share their opinion." At that moment I knew I had come face-to-face with a cross-cultural experience.

Not only did I have to come to grips with cross-cultural differences within the church plant, I found myself working on a church planting team made up of two American couples including ourselves, one from the "builder generation" (those born before 1945) and one from the "boomer generation" (those born between 1946 and 1964), and a couple in which the husband was Canadian and the wife French. At that time I did not completely understand the cross-cultural dynamics that came to play in our ability to work together. In addition, the church board was made up of French, Martiniquais, Americans, and a few other nationalities. We were a team, but our cultures informed and influenced how we related to each other, and how we understood and responded to the issues that the church faced.

Nearly twenty-five years later, I find myself serving another organization made up of more than twenty nationalities all focused on one thing: establishing and developing reproducing churches that evangelize and disciple the peoples of Europe. Today I am struck by the beauty and diversity of these teams that I observe and work on. Some of these teams work very well together. Others struggle to overcome their own cultural diversity: not only the diversity that exists between the team members, but also between the members and the cultures they are trying to reach.

All of these examples have led me to wonder how God accomplishes his work with such cultural diversity. What are the critical biblical and anthropological elements for effective cross-cultural teams? How do we overcome the challenges that such teams face? Is it worth it? Can we be more intentional in creating environments that encourage effective cross-cultural teams?

Cross-cultural teams can exist at different levels of an organization. Effective and God-honoring ministry takes place when Christian unity is displayed in these teams. I will examine three components of effective cross-cultural teams, the development of which may help us better steward the relationships and results of these teams. They are:

1. Key elements of effective cross-cultural teams.
2. Common challenges and possible solutions that exist for cross-cultural teams.
3. Benefits that come from working with cross-cultural teams.

In addition to understanding biblical and practical elements of cross-cultural ministry teams, I will also examine potentially applicable concepts that emerge from business and secular literature.

DEFINITIONS

Three key terms need clarification for the purpose of developing a coherent understanding of what it means to have effective cross-cultural teams. I will not use a great deal of space discussing the merits of various definitions, but I will state or use definitions that I find helpful in developing this subject.

Teams

John Katzenbach and Douglas Smith develop this definition of team: "A small number of people with complementary skills who are committed to a common purpose, set of performance goals, and approach for which they hold themselves mutually accountable" (Katzenbach and Smith 2005, 162).

Such definitions are often contrasted with those of groups, committees, or communities. For the purposes of this reflection, I will adopt Katzenbach's and Smith's understandings because of the emphasis on common purpose, goals, accountability, and relationships. In terms of what "a small number" means, Katzenbach's and Smith's study demonstrates that an ideal team size is ten or less. These teams can be as small as two, but probably should not be larger than twenty-five (Katzenbach and Smith 2005, 167).

The kinds of teams we are talking about exist in ministry organizations at multiple levels. Often these teams focus either on operational matters and goals, or they focus on the completion of a project that has a beginning and an end. A church-planting team, for example, would be considered a project team (assuming that there is a beginning and an end to the planting phase of a church). That is not to say that a planted church has no team. The process of establishing a church would include the development of an oversight or governance team (elders, deacons, etc.) which takes on an operational role.

In churches and ministry organizations, operational teams exist at the field, regional, and international leadership levels of the organization. They give emphasis to the overall strategy, direction, and management of the ministry. Within each domain of responsibility, projects often arise that need singular focus. The formation of project teams at these levels can also take place.

Cross-cultural

Lianne Roembke understands cross-cultural or multicultural teams as those teams made up of missionaries from more than one ethnic or cultural background working together in one location (Roembke 2000, 3). While this is certainly one application of a multicultural team, I would broaden that definition in our virtual world to include teams connected across continents and around the world through email, audio, and video conferencing.

The term "cross-cultural" would imply that two or more cultures come together to form an experience that differs from a monocultural experience. If we understand "culture" to mean "the totality of socially transmitted behavior patterns, arts, beliefs, institutions, and all other products of human work and thought characteristic of a community or population" (*American Heritage Dictionary*), then a cross-cultural experience exists when two or more cultures come together. That experience can highlight similarities and differences between the cultures. The differences between cultures often become the source of confusion, misunderstanding, and conflict.

Duane Elmer offers this insight into the biblical nature of cross-cultural interaction:

> There are sound theological reasons for committing ourselves to understanding other cultures and appreciating them wherever possible. Making that commitment will unfold for us new and wonderful dimensions of God's character, for our God can be properly revealed only through diversity. When God had finished creating the world, he looked at the "vast array" (Gen 2:1) and announced that "it was very good" (Gen 1:31). To celebrate creation is to celebrate diversity, including diversities of people. And we cannot celebrate out of ignorance. Genuine celebration comes from genuine appreciation. This requires learning and understanding, and these are incompatible with egocentrism and superiority. (Elmer 1993, 13)

Some would argue that overcoming the challenges of engaging cross-cultural teams is just not worth the effort. Yet, the overwhelming body of biblical evidence suggests that cross-cultural unity and working together plays a major role in our Christian witness and testimony. Jesus' team was composed of several Jewish subcultures including fishermen and tax collectors. The book of Acts and the epistles illustrate multiple teams consisting of multiple cultures.

Effective
Defining the term "effective" is perhaps more precarious than the other two. Immediately I understand that my North American culture biases me in that regard. Coming from a capitalist and results-oriented society pushes me to define "effective" in terms of results. Added to that is my results-oriented temperament. But effectiveness is more accurately defined around several components that include relational and performance dimensions. Blanchard, Carew, and Parisi-Carew put forth seven characteristics of high performing teams. They use the acronym PERFORM to highlight those characteristics:

- **Purpose:** People know what they have to do and the team's goals are clear.
- **Empowerment:** Everyone has adequate training, resources, and responsibility for accomplishing their role.

- **R**elationships and Communication: Team members listen to and respect what others have to say.
- **F**lexibility: Members are adaptable and willing to explore various ideas and approaches to issues.
- **O**ptimal Performance: The team is producing quality results through effective decision making and problem solving.
- **R**ecognition and Appreciation: Members feel respected, appreciated and supported by others.
- **M**orale: Team members enjoy working together and have fun (Blanchard et al. 1990, 20–23).

An effective cross-cultural team then is a small group of people with a common purpose and set of goals whose members represent a diversity of backgrounds and cultures, who appreciate the gifts and abilities that each member brings to the team, who respect and appreciate the cultures that each member comes from, who are equipped and resourced to get the job done, who develop skills in listening to one another, who mutually agree to methods for problem solving and decision making, and who enjoy working and being together.

KEY ELEMENTS IN FORMING MULTICULTURAL TEAMS

The above attempt at coming up with a concise definition of this subject immediately reveals its complexity. While the definition may not be completely adequate, I attempt to consider its implications for Christian ministry.

In my straw poll of international missionaries with the agency I represent, the following list of key elements emerged from their responses, representing several different nationalities. Interestingly enough, these closely parallel Roembke's thorough research in which she identifies a similar set of critical elements related to cross-cultural or multicultural teams (Roembke 2000, 13–49):

- Leadership: Competent leadership with international experience
- Expectations
- Clearly articulated goals, purposes, and expectations
- Clear job descriptions
- Team member commitment

- Resources
- Adequate resourcing and training
- Variety of gifts and abilities for getting the job done
- Mutual care or member care
- Communication
- Regular and consistent two-way communication among team members
- Strategies for conflict resolution
- Regular meetings
- Culture
- Knowledge of team member cultures
- Knowledge of culture where work is taking place
- Use of local language.

COMMON CHALLENGES

The challenging dynamics of cross-cultural teams usually arise from different perspectives and understandings of the topics listed above. When not adequately addressed they manifest themselves as pitfalls or "booby traps" in the following ways:

- Lack of leadership training
- Lack of long-term commitment
- Lack of team unity
- Failure to value the team members
- Disparity of personal resources between team members and between team members and the local culture
- Inadequate and ineffective communication
- Inadequate cultural knowledge
- Insensitivity to the cultures one is working with and working in
- Expressions of nationalism
- No strategies for conflict resolution
- Different understandings of the role of women (Allen 1991).

These problems not only arise in cross-cultural teams, but they can easily manifest themselves in a so-called monocultural environment. The solutions for many of these issues rest with appropriate attention to the selection, training, and team formation processes (Roembke 2000, 197).

SELECTION

Selection requires the utmost attention in discerning the spiritual and emotional maturity of the individual and his or her gifting and calling as it relates to the roles that need to be filled on the mission field or in the ministry. Articulating in written form the purpose and goals of the team will allow proper attention to defining the roles that need to be filled, the gifts and abilities needed for those roles, and the resources needed to support those roles.

When recruiting for missionary service, agencies typically look at a candidate's character, experience, training, temperament, and gifting. If everything looks good, we often accept them without a clear understanding of how they will fit in the agency or on the field. We want warm bodies because the need is so great and there are so few workers.

The selection process is a precursor to placement and team formation. Field leadership should continually develop and refine objectives and goals for the various fields. Included with those goals and objectives should be the matrix of spiritual gifts and abilities that the teams have and need.

TRAINING

Training involves a variety of disciplines from cross-cultural orientation before and after arriving on the field that involve cultural adjustment, language acquisition, personal conflict management, spiritual development, skills development, leadership training, and others. I would like to look at three areas of training and development that contribute to effective cross-cultural teams: cultural intelligence, conflict resolution, and leadership development.

Cultural Intelligence

As a relatively new discipline of study, Cultural Intelligence, or CQ, needs consideration in the selection and training of team members.

> Cultural intelligence is related to emotional intelligence, but it picks up where emotional intelligence leaves off. A person with high emotional intelligence grasps what makes us human and at the same time what makes each of us different from one another. A person with high

cultural intelligence can somehow tease out of a person's or group's behavior those features that would be true of all people and all groups, those peculiar to this person or this group, and those that are neither universal nor idiosyncratic. The vast realm between those two poles is culture. (Early and Mosakowski 2004, 139–40)

Earley and Mosakowski also give us a tool whereby one can determine one's CQ. This tool examines a person's cognitive (head), physical (body), and emotional or motivational (heart) perceptions and flexibility (2004, 139–40). They provide a scoring system from one (strongly disagree) to five (strongly agree) in response to several statements. An average score less than three would indicate a need for improvement, while an average score of four to five reflects a strong cultural intelligence. Here are the following statements that they use to evaluate one's CQ.

Cognitive CQ Statements
___ Before I interact with people from a new culture, I ask myself what I hope to achieve.
___ If I encounter something unexpected while working in a new culture, I use this experience to figure out new ways to approach other cultures in the future.
___ I plan how I'm going to relate to people from a different culture before I meet them.
___ When I come into a new cultural situation, I can immediately sense whether something is going well or something is wrong.
___ TOTAL ÷ 4 = _____ Cognitive CQ

Physical CQ Statements
___ It's easy for me to change my body language (for example, eye contact or posture) to suit people from a different culture.
___ I can alter my expression when a cultural encounter requires it.
___ I modify my speech style (for example, accent or tone) to suit people from a different culture.

___ I easily change the way I act when a cross-cultural encounter seems to require it.
___ TOTAL ÷ 4 = _____ Physical CQ

Emotional/Motivational CQ Statements
___ I have confidence that I can deal well with people from a different culture.
___ I am certain that I can befriend people whose cultural backgrounds are different from mine.
___ I can adapt to the lifestyle of a different culture with relative ease.
___ I am confident that I can deal with a cultural situation that's unfamiliar.
___ TOTAL ÷ 4 = _____ Emotional/Motivational CQ (Early and Mosakowski 2004, 139–40).

They conclude, "Unlike other aspects of personality, cultural intelligence can be developed in psychologically healthy and professionally competent people" (Early and Mosakowski 2004, 146). They also provide a six-step framework (146) that one might apply in developing this aspect of a person's arsenal of skills that could easily be made part of cross-cultural training before and after arriving on the field:

1. Identify CQ strengths and weaknesses. For example, I scored high on emotional/motivational CQ, but low on physical CQ. That was no surprise to me as I tend to wear my emotions on my sleeve.
2. Find some training that focuses on his or her weaknesses. They suggested someone like me with a low physical CQ might enroll in acting classes to master body language control. A homiletics or public speaking class might also help.
3. Apply training in incremental and targeted fashion. For example, if I had scored low on motivational CQ, I might take my training by mastering simple activities. One of the most intimidating activities for me in France was going to the post office and communicating in French with someone behind a one-inch-thick plate glass window. Mastering that activity

could have gone a long way to helping me feel more confident in that culture.
4. Be intentional in scheduling time and resources devoted to CQ enhancement. This means that support schedules for missionaries might include funds targeted for this ongoing type of training.
5. Coordinate training with others that allows for group dynamic in exercising strengths and evaluation of an event. I recall going to one of the famous fried food restaurant bars in Madrid with our leadership team. Ordering, eating, interacting with the locals, and paying for our meal was indeed a cross-cultural experience. Eating the fried squid sandwiches was as well. This type of environment could allow for having each person assume responsibility for one or more elements of the experience. After a good night's sleep the group could then debrief on how they did.
6. Make sure there is a review process that includes 360-degree feedback from colleagues who are able to observe the person's behavior. Out of that process one can then discern progress that has been made and any additional training that might be needed.

Conflict Resolution
One of the most challenging and difficult parts of working on a cross-cultural team involves overcoming cultural norms and perceptions which distort how we see others interacting with us. While sin and sinful behavior lead to conflict, culture and values lead to conflict more often than sin and sinful behavior.

Anthropological research has shown that such challenges often result from national culture barriers that arise in areas such as differing styles of communication: direct versus indirect communication, trouble with accents and fluency, differing attitudes toward hierarchy and authority, and conflicting norms for decision making (Brett et al. 2006, 86).

Those differences may not be adequate in and of themselves for helping us to understand root causes of cross-cultural conflict. Values-driven differences also exist: time orientation versus event orientation, dichotomistic thinking versus holistic thinking, crisis orientation versus noncrisis orientation, task orientation versus person orientation, status focus versus achievement focus, and concealment of vulnerability versus willingness to expose vulnerability (Mackin 1992).

Richard Tiplady (2003) cites the research of several experts in this domain of national culture. Included are Hofstede's five dimensions of culture, Hampden-Turner and Trompenaar's six dimensions, and Richard Lewis' three types of cultures (Tiplady 2003, 102–4). All of these categories enrich our understanding of culture and why cultures act and respond the way they do.

Most of our conflict arises from a lack of awareness and understanding of these differences. For example, an American might ask a simple series of questions to another nationality like, "How are you?" and "What's your favorite style of music?" because he or she wants to get to know a person. Someone from another nationality might become defensive as though he or she is being interrogated (Roembke 2000, 105–6). Two different national styles of communication can easily lead to this avoidable type of misunderstanding.

James Plueddemann (2009) does an excellent job of helping us move from cultural norms and understandings of leadership to a biblical view of leadership in light of cultural differences. He takes the research described above and moves us toward a biblical application of leadership, taking into account those cultural differences. As he says:

> Researchers in the business world have spent lifetimes and astounding amounts of money to discover the differences in cultural values. It makes good sense for leaders in the global church to pay attention to these studies to learn how God might have designed cultural differences in believers from every nation, tribe, people and language. (Plueddemann 2009, 61)

A Romans 12:3 assessment of ourselves is called for: "Do not think of yourself more highly than you ought." Training should include tools that help individuals discern their own tendencies and the tendencies of those they work with. Instead of waiting for one culture to adapt to "my way" of doing things, both cultures should attempt to move closer to the other culture's way of doing things.

Awareness alone will not necessarily address the issues that arise from conflict. Matthew 5:23, 24, and Matthew 18:15–18 give us a solid framework in dealing with conflict and sin in the body of Christ. But often we need simple tools that help us have those crucial or breakthrough conversations. These are conversations where opinions and perspectives vary, the stakes are high and emotions run strong (Patterson et al. 2002, 1–2). We typically handle these conversations in one of three ways: we avoid them; we address and handle them poorly; or we address them and handle them well (Patterson et al. 2002, 3).

Failure to arrive at a pool of shared meaning and understanding lies at the heart of cross-cultural conflict. An environment of safety is required for us to tackle critical subjects and dialogue about them. We need to avoid the "fight" or "flight" defense mechanisms that often lead to abandonment by one and dominance by another. How we respond to issues comes from our personal stories which are informed by our past, temperament, culture, education, and relationships. Mastering one's story and understanding the story of the other party(ies) becomes critical to a successful outcome. Training should include tools that are offered in books like *Crucial Conversations* and *Crucial Confrontations* (Patterson et al. 2005).

While cross-cultural misunderstanding often arises on the mission field, it can also arise at the international leadership level. Often it is a question of removing barriers of trust (Thrall 1999, 26). Cultivating relationships of grace and creating forums for the safe and frank exchange of ideas is absolutely necessary. Tensions that develop between countries that send missionaries and those receiving missionaries serve as one example that I have now experienced in two different agencies.

As I sit around the table with my Australian, British, Brazilian, Dutch, French, Irish, and Spanish colleagues who mobilize missionaries and resources for missions, each of us faces multiple challenges related to the changing dynamics in each of our sending countries and in the national churches of those countries. Across the table from us sit eighteen to twenty field leaders from as many different nationalities who find themselves trying to define the needs of their countries in terms of workers and needed resources. The classic tension arises between what the sending countries feel they can provide and what the receiving fields feel they need. Providing forums and think tanks for dialogue on these matters become absolutely essential. Leadership of such teams and forums then becomes absolutely critical for creating the environment where win-win solutions are developed.

Leadership Development

Jim Plueddemann rightly assesses the challenge of leadership development this way when he says:

Chapter 8

Missionaries are going from everywhere to everywhere. But the globalization of the church also presents dangerous possibilities for cross-cultural tensions, especially regarding leadership values. Church leaders must learn to cooperate with people who have radically different assumptions about leadership. (Plueddemann 2009, 11)

An organization is only as good as the leadership it models and develops. Sherwood Lingenfelter has done a thorough job of developing the role and issues of leadership in a cross-cultural context. He defines it this way, "Leading cross-culturally, then, is inspiring people who come from two or more cultural traditions to participate with you (the leader or the leadership team) in building a biblical community of trust and then to follow you and be empowered by you to achieve a compelling vision of faith" (Lingenfelter 2008, 21).

Roembke reminds us that irrespective of cultural tendencies toward various leadership styles, biblical injunctions for leaders are binding on all cultures. Leadership development should always include character development. She cites Richard Foster's seven marks of creative power found in leaders and team members alike (Roembke 2000, 36–37):

1. Love for the other expels the egotism in power.
2. Humility is power under discipline.
3. Self-limitation that refrains from doing some things out of respect for the individual.
4. Joy that is not insincere frivolity.
5. Vulnerability that leads from weakness, does not dominate, but patiently waits.
6. Submission to the ways of God that allows us to receive from others.
7. Freedom that does not bind or crush people of their hopes, but allows them to be what God created them to be.

She concludes:

The cultural backgrounds of the team members will determine how they perceive the leadership. Everyone will tend to look at the exercise of leadership through their own cultural glasses. They should be quick to observe and slow to judge. And they should be wise enough to call their own cultural values into question. In summary, power and its use is a fact of life. The decision of how people groups and organizations use power is crucial: creatively for the good of others, or destructively, for their own selfish purposes and the detriment of others. Because of human fallenness, building in checks and balances of power is healthy and wise. (Roembke 2000, 37–38)

Lingenfelter goes on to develop the tasks and tools needed to lead cross-culturally. These elements should also be part of leadership development: how to inspire people, build trust, and empower people of differing cultures. "The true measure of effective leadership is whether the team does the hard work of loving one another in the midst of disagreement and then pulls together to accomplish the will and purpose of God" (Lingenfelter 2008, 66).

He focuses on the importance of developing covenant relationships in the context of team. The key to developing those relationships is learning and understanding the social games that people and cultures tend to play. He develops four categories of games that he describes as the bureaucratic, corporate, individual, and collectivist games. They fall into one of four quadrants of a grid defined by the vertical importance of role and rule, and the horizontal importance of group interests versus individual interest (Lingenfelter 2008, 74; see Figure 5).

Figure 5: The Prototype Social Games
(Source: Lingenfelter 2008, 74)

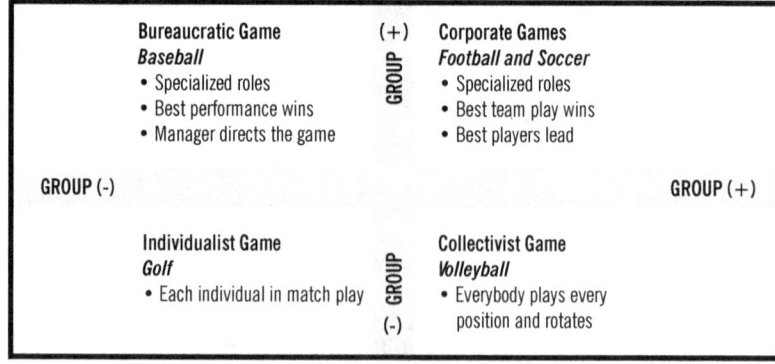

Critical to effective teams is the leader's ability to learn and understand the various social/cultural games that take place in any group. Leadership development needs to include training that helps leaders ask and answer the right questions which inform him or her of the games that are being played. With that knowledge comes the ability to address a situation effectively.

Developing a covenant community alternative assumes that every multicultural team has or will have a proper theological understanding as the foundation of its relationships. Team leaders must commit to teaching and practicing these principles. Lingenfelter identifies eight principles of biblical teaching that lead to a covenant community (Lingenfelter 2008, 76):

1. Identity in Christ as God's chosen people
2. Presence of the Holy Spirit
3. Love one another
4. One body—serving in diversity
5. One body—working together in unity
6. Submitting to one another
7. Speaking graciously
8. Restoring mercifully

First priority must be given to the formation of a community of trust and the hard work of creating that community and trust. After that, attention needs to be paid to making sure skill or technical training is given to attaining the goals of the project or team. These cannot be mutually exclusive, but ultimate success will hinge on the relationships, values, and behaviors that come from a covenant community.

Finally, the task of leadership development must include the components of empowerment and mentoring. Empowerment is not simply the delegation of a task, but empowerment evaluates where a leader and members are in terms of spiritual and emotional maturity and skill development. Too often leaders and team members are set up for failure because of inadequate evaluation of the individual and the task requirements.

The "Situational Leadership" model (Blanchard et al. 1985, 46–50) in the context of teamwork provides a framework for contracting with leaders and followers whereby the individual's competence and confidence are evaluated against task requirements (see Figure 6). The leader or supervisor then determines if the person needs a directive, coaching, supportive, or delegating style of leadership. By not providing this assessment leaders and their followers are set up for failure. The evaluation process often gets skipped over and delegation becomes the default mode and results in abdication of responsibility on the part of the leader.

Figure 6: Situational Leadership Model
(Source: Blanchard et al. 1990, 79)

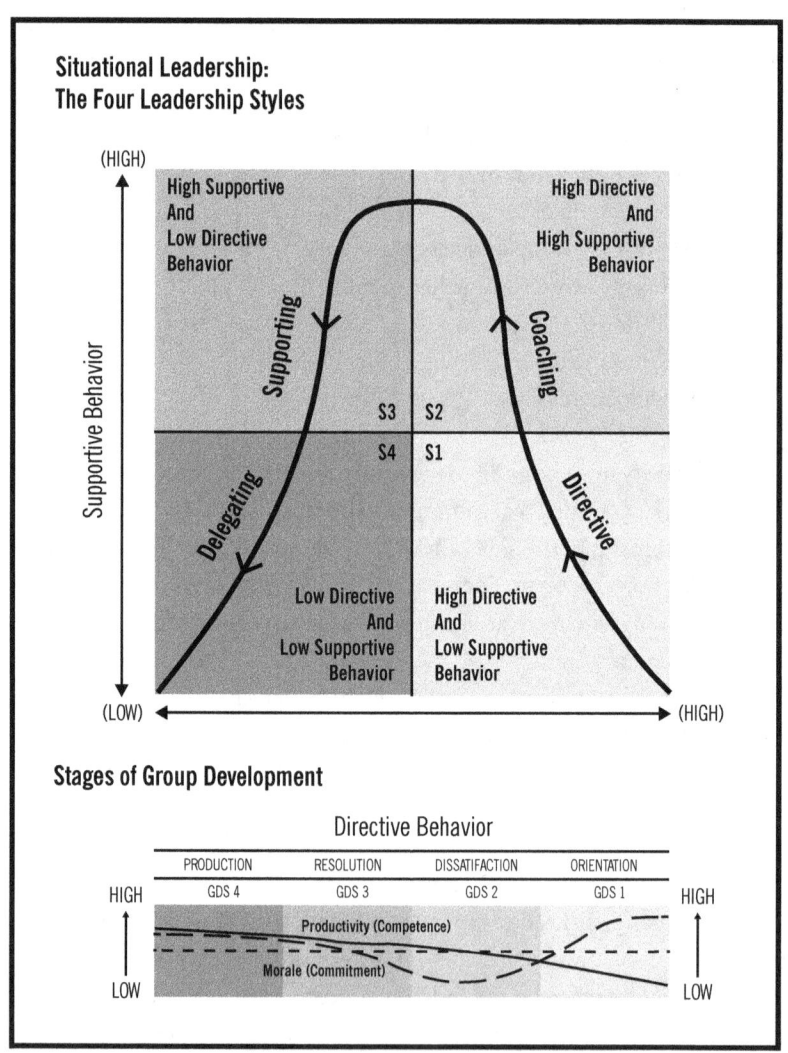

This model empowers team members to do their job by providing them with the correct management style and resources for getting the job done. This fits well with Lingenfelter's covenant community because it requires agreement between the leader and team member on what style of leadership is needed. Lingenfelter says, "One of the most important principles of empowerment is to release people to do the work, always within a context of discipling them, and at the same time to resist the temptation to intervene to assure the correct results" (Lingenfelter 2008, 123).

In examining the common challenges related to cross-cultural teams, focus needs to be given to areas of training in cross-cultural intelligence, conflict resolution, and leadership development in the context of covenant communities.

BENEFITS OF DIVERSE TEAMS

Industry has long argued for a culturally diverse workplace, but they, like Christian organizations, often struggle to reap the full benefits for a number of reasons. For a long time, the argument for diversity was made from a *discrimination and fairness paradigm*. This paradigm operates from the assumption that we are all the same or that we aspire to be the same. The *access and legitimacy paradigm* assumes that diversity will allow us to better serve a diverse constituency. It's not just about being fair, it's about good business.

Emerging from the workplace research is a different paradigm demonstrating that diversity actually produces a synergy of perspectives. The *connecting diversity to work perspectives paradigm* leads not just to fairness, or a better connection to constituents, but actually to better decision making related to markets, products, strategies, missions, business practices, and even cultures.

> This new model for managing diversity lets the organization internalize differences among employees so that it learns and grows because of them. Indeed, with the model fully in place, members of the organization can say, "We are all on the same team, *with* our differences—not *despite* them." (Thomas and Ely 1996, 86)

Terence Brake explains:

> Existing intellectual capital is not enough. New ideas and knowledge must be created to generate internal breakthroughs in how the business operates and external breakthroughs in finding and working with new partners. A workforce with diverse perspectives provides a rich resource for creativity. New ideas will not be enough for success. It requires the inventiveness and resourcefulness of all employees to transform intellectual capital and ideas into viable products and solutions. Where will this inventiveness come from? From a diverse workforce whose contrasting perspectives can generate a competitive edge. (Tiplady 2003, 95)

Interestingly this sounds like the paradigm that emerges from the chapters of the New Testament in describing how the body of Christ is to work. From the pages of Scripture we know that in diversity:

Our unity incarnates the gospel to the culture (John 17).
We utilize a variety of gifts, abilities, and perspectives (1 Cor 12–14).
We reach better decisions in problem solving (Acts 6:1–7).
We develop a greater appreciation of others (Rom 12:9–13).

In *Doing Member Care Well* a multicultural team of authors has this to say:

> Multicultural teams have a built-in, heightened sensitivity as to what is biblical and what is cultural about themselves. They help their members to see themselves and the host culture from outside their individual cultures. Diverse cultural backgrounds provide perspective and help the team, as a unit, to respond appropriately. (Greenlee et al. 2002, 400)

Other benefits could be listed and developed as well. Stetzer highlights three advantages of a multicultural team (Stetzer 2003):

1. Decreased suspicions of any cultural imperialist motives.

2. Experience that comes from a diversity of cultures and opinions.
3. Modeling that reflects true biblical community.

In addition to our biblical and experiential insights related to the benefits and blessings of effective cross-cultural teams, we would be well served to note some pragmatic organizational culture and environmental factors that could help us achieve these benefits as observed by Thomas and Ely (1996):

1. The leadership must understand that a diverse workforce will embody different perspectives and approaches to work, and must truly value variety of opinion and insight.
2. The leadership must recognize both the learning opportunities and the challenges that the expression of different perspectives present for an organization.
3. The organizational culture must create an expectation of high standards of performance from everyone.
4. The organizational culture must stimulate personal development.
5. The organizational culture must encourage openness.
6. The culture must make workers feel valued.
7. The organization must have a well-articulated and widely understood mission.
8. The organization must have a relatively egalitarian, nonbureaucratic structure.

Combining our biblical understanding of the benefits of cultural diversity on teams with tools at our disposal should help us to increase the effectiveness of our teams.

CONCLUSION

Effective cross-cultural teams possess some common strengths, challenges, and benefits. As mission leaders, all of us want to see teams modeling the body of Christ in ways that attract others to the Savior. We have a job to get done, that of reaching the world for Christ. In increasingly connected and global societies, the task of getting the job done will not rest on the shoulders of any one nation or culture; it will rest on the global Christian community. What would be better than to model the unity of John 17 through cross-cultural teams working effectively together in covenant communities? Given the power of the Holy Spirit and proper relationships of humility and grace, we have the tools to get the job done.

REFERENCES

Allen, Frank W. 1991. Your church-planting team can be booby-trapped. *EMQ* (July), http://www.emisdirect.com/emq/issue-138/584.

Blanchard, Kenneth, Donald Carew, and Eunice Parisi-Carew. 1990. *The one minute manager builds high performing teams.* Escondido: Blanchard Training and Development, Inc.

Blanchard, Kenneth, Patricia Zigarmi, and Drea Zigarmi. 1985. *Leadership and the one minute manager.* New York: William Morrow and Company.

Brett, Jeanne, Kristin Behfar, and Mary C. Kern. 2006. Managing multicultural teams. *Harvard Business Review* (November): 86.

Early, P. Christopher, and Elaine Mosakowski. 2004. Cultural intelligence. *Harvard Business Review* (October), 139–40.

Elmer, Duane. 1993. *Cross-cultural conflict: Building relationships for effective ministry.* Downers Grove: InterVarsity.

Greenlee, David, Yong Joong Cho, and Abraham Thulare. 2002. The potential and pitfalls of multicultural mission teams. In *Doing member care well: Perspectives and practices from around the world,* ed. Kelley O'Donnell, 400. Pasadena: William Carey Library.

Katzenbach, John R., and Douglas K. Smith. 2005. The discipline of teams: What makes the difference between a team that performs and one that doesn't? *Harvard Business Review* (July–August): 162.

Lingenfelter, Sherwood G. 2008. *Leading cross-culturally: Covenant relationships for effective Christian leadership.* Grand Rapids: Baker Academic.

Mackin, Sandra L. 1992. Multinational teams: Smooth as silk or rough as rawhide? *EMQ* (April), http://www.emisdirect.com/emq/issue-243/1388.

Patterson, Kerry, Joseph Grenny, Ron McMillan, and Al Switzler. 2002. *Crucial conversations: Tools for talking when stakes are high.* New York: McGraw-Hill.

———. 2005. *Crucial confrontations: Tools for resolving broken promises, violated expectations and bad behavior.* New York: McGraw-Hill.

Plueddemann, James E. 2009. *Leading across cultures: Effective ministry and mission in the global church.* Downers Grove: InterVarsity Academic.

Roembke, Lianne. 2000. *Building credible multicultural teams.* Pasadena: William Carey Library.

Stetzer, Ed. 2003. Multi-cultural teams in church planting. *EMQ* (October), http://www.emisdirect.com/emq/issue-279/1762.

Thomas, David A., and Robin J. Ely. 1996. Making differences matter: A new paradigm for managing diversity. *Harvard Business Review* (September–October), 86.

Thrall, Bill, Bruce McNicol, and Ken McElrath. 1999. The ascent of a leader: How ordinary relationships develop extraordinary character and influence. San Francisco: Jossey-Bass.

Tiplady, Richard. 2003. World of Difference. http://www.tiplady.org.uk/pdfs/WorldofDifference.pdf, 102–04.

9

MISSIONARY MEMBER CARE IN A CULTURALLY DIVERSE MINISTRY TEAM

EJIN CHO

In the changing era of missions from modernity to postmodernity, from the West to the Third World, and from the local to the global, mission agencies and missiologists reflect on this history of missions since Christ commanded the Great Commission (Matt 28:19–20) and prepare to fulfill the final task which remains within their stewardship. The need for more effective use of human and material resources stimulates examination of the detailed reasons why missionaries often leave the field prematurely, and the significance of the role of member care is emphasized now.

An examination of missionary member care reveals hidden—or neglected—issues of *how to do it* rather than *what to do* in member care. As Kelly O'Donnell says, "Our relationship with Christ is fundamental to our well-being and work effectiveness. Member care resources strengthen our relationship to the Lord and help us to encourage others in the Lord" (O'Donnell 2002, 16). To provide good member care, it is necessary to examine the quality of missionary life and relationships in the changing context of missions.

Communication and relationships are important factors for retention of South Korean missionaries in the context of a culturally diverse ministry team. Two recent extensive research projects related to missionary attrition and retention and an interview of a member care staff member in a South Korean mission's agency provide the background for this study.

First I will examine the purpose, process, and quantitative results of the two research projects, focusing on the issues of South Korean missionaries. Specific cases which recently occurred with South Korean missionaries in culturally diverse teams on the mission field, as reported in an interview, will shed further light on the significance of communication and interpersonal relationship for missionary retention and enhanced member care.

BACKGROUND STUDY

Missionary Attrition and the First Research Project (ReMAP I)

The term *attrition* is used to describe all forms of "departure from the field service by missionaries" (Taylor 1997, xvi–xvii). From the viewpoint of effectiveness in the mission field, departure causes the loss of workers from the field as well as ineffective use of resources—human and material—in the mission enterprise.

Attrition is not a simple matter, however, since many cases of attrition are related to God's master plan for God's kingdom. For example, general statistics of attrition include unpreventable departure from the field such as retirement, completion of a contract, medical leave, and a "legitimate call to another service" (Taylor 1997, xvi–xvii). Many who have dedicated themselves as long-term field missionaries fall into the category of "attrition," even though they may be serving as missiologists, mission administrators, related with the mission in some way, or, at least, continuing in ministry in extension of God's kingdom (McKaughan 1997, 15). On the other hand, it is certain that there are many cases of attrition which could have been prevented.

Reducing Missionary Attrition Project (henceforth, ReMAP I) (Taylor 1997) is the project which was commissioned by the Missions Commission in the World Evangelical Alliance in the early 1990s to deal with the matter of missionary attrition. In ReMAP I, the focus is on the causes of preventable attrition as well as how to reduce preventable attrition. ReMAP I reveals various reasons for attrition, which can be divided as unpreventable and preventable, and concludes that two-thirds of all missionary attrition could have possibly been avoided (Rob et al. 2007, 13).

The purpose of the project was based on stewardship "to reduce undesirable attrition in the long-term missionary body and thus increase the effectiveness of the global mission task force" (Taylor 1997, 4). In fact, the result of the survey in fourteen nations and the conclusions from it are not just used to point out what was going wrong in the mission fields, that is, *what makes missionaries leave mission fields*, but the project went further to raise valuable questions about what can be provided further for missionaries, that is, *what prevents missionaries from leaving the mission field.* In the process, the reality of member care correlated with attrition proves that the attrition factors are closely related with the reality of member care system of the mission agency. Each stage of member care such as candidate selection, prefield training, personal care, leadership, and supervision on the field has correlated areas for reducing attrition.

Second ReMAP: Missionary Retention and Member Care
Eight years after ReMAP I, a follow-up research was conducted, named ReMAP II. The same acronym stands for a different title of the project, which is Retaining Missionaries, Agency Practices (henceforth, ReMAP II) (Hay et al. 2007). Like the name suggests, ReMAP II focused on missionary retention and the contribution of member care, especially in overall areas such as candidate selection, vision and purpose, leadership, communication, personal support, member care, ministry, ministry outcomes, continuous training, finance, and home office operations. ReMAP I had focused on the attrition factors themselves, pointing out the importance of member care. Consequently, ReMAP II, conducted in twenty-two nations, proves a clear positive correlation between missionary retention and member care given by mission agencies. It shows the characteristics of mission agencies that have high retention rates, such as the following:

1. They expect well-trained mission candidates and apply careful candidate selection.
2. They have effective leadership with good interaction with their missionaries and a lean quality administration with a servant attitude and flexible structures.
3. They provide their missionaries opportunities for continuous training and development of new gifts.
4. They encourage their missionaries to actively work towards the continuous improvement of their ministries and their agency's operations and structures. This is even more important as many mission agencies are presently undergoing extensive structural changes to adjust to current needs.
5. Good practice agencies do not impose these changes from the top, driven by external advice.

6. They utilize the expertise and insight of their missionaries.
7. These agencies understand and value synergy and work in partnership with other agencies to maximize resources. They do not look at their own success but for the global kingdom of God (Blocher 2004, 23).

ReMAP II promotes good practice in detail, and, therefore, suggests a detailed blueprint for what mission agencies should do to devise their member care strategy for serving their missionaries. Even though ReMAP II has limitations in its quantitative research by focusing on *what to do* as better practice in member care, it is important that it gives room for the further research on the next step forward to *how to do it* as a qualitative approach.

REMAP IN SOUTH KOREA: PROBLEMS

The missionary movement in Korea has grown astonishingly since the early 1980s. In 2008, 18,035 South Korean missionaries were working in 177 nations in the world, making this the third largest group of a nationality in the mission field, following the Unites States and India (Moon 2009). The number of missionaries has continued to increase by about 10 percent every year since 2000 (Moon 2009). In spite of those positive statistics, however, two ReMAP projects diagnosed issues and problems in the reality of South Korean missionaries in which improvement is needed. First of all, in the survey, ReMAP provided systemized details of member care process and missionary life, some of which had been ignored or overlooked in the Korean context. For example, South Korean mission agencies have been known for their strength in their candidate selection, but ReMAP II showed that they relatively overlooked personality of candidates and character references (Kim 2004, 69). In addition, statistics show that South Korean agencies tend to put less emphasis on leadership, supervision, and personal care on the field than on candidate selection and prefield training (Kim 2004, 68–69).

Two ironic issues can be found in the ReMAP results concerning South Korean missionary attrition and retention. On the one hand, poor interpersonal relationships with colleagues can be found at the top of the list of reasons for attrition of South Korean missionaries. In ReMAP I, the most-weighed reason for leaving missionary service in South Korea was "problems with peers," (Brierley 1997, 94) which is not so highly weighed in any other sending nations except for Costa Rica. On the other hand, Kim explains that "(South) Korean agencies build more on personal relationships than formal structure," when he interprets the data showing that South Korean agencies put less emphasis on clear plans and job descriptions, or on leadership and structure for organizational communication and documentation (Kim 2004, 69).

Apparently interpersonal relationships and organizational relationships in leadership and supervision are not clearly separate for South Korean missionaries and agencies. In that case, we can assume several problems. First, if South Korean missionaries depend on their personal relationships as their organizational structure, their personal relationships will likely be reflected in the organizational leadership and supervision. That means poor personal relationship can lead to poor organizational structure. Secondly, due to the weakness of the formal organizational system, if interpersonal conflicts occur, they cannot be handled properly or in a timely way.

These problems become far more complex when the ministry is conducted by a multinational ministry team. When there were a few South Korean missionaries on the field twenty years ago, cultural difference among the colleagues and adjustment to their cultures—mostly, Western cultures—could be the simple key to their retention in multinational ministry teams. Nowadays, however, since South Korean missionaries are no longer a minority on the field, and some of them even function as leaders or supervisors in the multinational teams, measures for prevention of the problems caused by interpersonal and organizational communication is urgently needed.

SOUTH KOREAN CASE STUDIES ON COMMUNICATION IN MULTINATIONAL MINISTRY TEAMS

Case studies were conducted based on an interview with a member care staff member in a South Korean agency, which is one of the oldest and largest missions agencies in South Korea, founded in 1985. In 2009, 191 long-term missionaries were serving as members, and among them, the number of missionaries in cross-cultural fields is 135. Most of them (90 percent) are serving as Bible translators or literacy experts in culturally diverse ministry teams.

Case Study 1:
Success in Cultural Difference but Failure in Cultural Similarity

As a result of the emphasis on cross-cultural differences and various academic and practical approaches to multinational ministries in the period of the shift of the missions paradigm to the Third World, the mind-set and behavior of missionaries has been improved much by cross-cultural training as a mandatory prefield or on-field training in many missions agencies. Nowadays on the mission field, missionaries seem to prefer working in a multicultural team rather than a monocultural one, since multinational ministry teamwork proved to be beneficial and synergetic for the ministry as well as spiritually life-enhancing for the individual on a spiritual basis (Roembke 2000, 109–10).

In the context of success in understanding cultural differences, however, relationships with members of the same nationality raises a new teamwork issue.

Three years ago, a South Korean missions agency prepared a training program for their Korean missionary candidates on a field in Southeast Asia. Since there were many international missionaries, including South Koreans, near the training spot, many of them were invited to the training program as visitors for a panel discussion. South Korean staff decided to follow the practice of international agencies—inviting missionaries to sign up in advance and pay for their own meals at the training event. The staff had no problem when they notified the missionaries from other nations of the procedure for meal registration, but they needed to spend more time to find a proper and polite way to help South Korean missionaries understand their decision. They should consider Korean cultural codes before letting them know the arrangements which could look quite impolite to Koreans at first, even though the South Korean missionaries there were accustomed to the international custom of serving food. (In the Korean culture, it is virtuous for the host to prepare bountiful food which looks overflowing and to offer it again and again even though the guest is already full. Preparing only enough food for the number of guests, or making them pay for the food is considered as ungenerous.)

Thus, the staff informed Korean visitors individually of the reason why they wanted them to sign up and pay for meals. They made individual phone calls to them and explained that sign-up was needed because they were not able to prepare food generously at the training location and that payment was needed in order to afford to purchase sufficient food. The clarification of the reasons worked and Korean visitors were not offended.

The interviewee said that the lowest retention rate is shown among South Korean missionaries who work in a team comprised of South Koreans only, rather than those who work with nationals or in a multinational team. He added that it was hard to find a ministry team comprised of only South Koreans nowadays, and it is the only form of deployment which is not recommended in his agency.

Prefield and on-field training of communication skills based on cross-cultural preparation and training must not be optional for South Korean missionaries, who hardly have a chance to learn interactive communication skills through their formal school education which is conducted in one direction, from the top down.

How to communicate with others should be the more important question in cross-cultural studies and training, rather than learning about another culture or language. The purpose of cross-cultural training is not just for cross-cultural adjustment, but also for enhancing interpersonal communication skills, since the work of the missions is not merely about the task but about people and God.

Case Study 2:
Language Ability versus Communication Skills
The most interesting thing the interviewee pointed out was that South Korean missionaries confess to each other that they sometimes behave as opportunists in multinational teams. It means that when there are choices between a Westernized way of thinking and a Korean way, they choose the way which is favorable to them on a case-by-case basis. For the cultural majority in the team, it is not easy to distinguish between personality and culture in a team member who is in the cultural minority. If you are the only one of your nationality in a multinational team, it is hard for your team members to know if your (different) way of thinking and living comes from your personality or from your cultural background (Roembke 2000, 109–10).

When there were relatively few South Korean missionaries on the field, it was common that only one South Korean member existed in some multinational teams. At that time, South Korean missionaries suffered from loneliness due to other members' confusion between personality and culture. But since then, Korean missionaries have been using a unique strategy to make the situation favorable to them, namely, they acquired the strategy of making cultural excuses for their personal faults. For example, when a South Korean missionary makes a mistake in trying to follow the principles of his team, he makes excuses that he is not used to doing it in that way. On the other hand, when he fails while trying to do something in his preferred way, he makes excuses that it is not his fault, but rather that the way of his culture does not work in the situation.

When Koreans are not in the minority on multinational ministry teams, the strategies above do not work any longer. Rather, if there are Korean colleagues on their team, their excuses can hurt their personal relationship with their peers of the same nationality. These cultural excuses can also hurt the interpersonal trust in peers of a different nationality as well, since peers of other nationalities will work with more than one South Korean missionary and it becomes easier for them to distinguish between personality and culture of Korean missionaries.

Traditionally the biggest problem related to communication seems to be the problem of language. Thirty years ago, Nicholls claimed that Third World missionaries had to understand one more culture than Western missionaries. In addition to understanding the culture of the Bible, their own culture, and local cultures of the field, they also had to understand "that of the Western missionary who first brought the gospel" (Nicholls 1979, 72). Nowadays, due to the decrease of the number of Western missionaries and the existence of a variety of nationalities in ministry teams, the use of a local language on the field as a lingua franca in the ministry tends to be encouraged, although English is still used as a lingua franca in many multinational ministry teams on the field. Though the disadvantage that the lingua franca other than a local language in the ministry team is not their mother tongue still exists, however, it does not seem to be a significant factor affecting missionary attrition. That is supported by the result of ReMAP I, showing that the attrition rate of international agencies was lower than that of South Korean local agencies. The advantage from systematic prefield training and expertise in member care in international agencies can offset the disadvantage of using English (Moon 1997, 136).

On the contrary, many cases of poor communication skills come from two cultural issues. First, the Korean culture of saving face causes communication problems in a multinational ministry team. Secondly, Korean missionaries' strong conviction of their ministry goal sometimes leads them to communicate to each other as well as to others in undesirable ways.

Because of their culture of saving face, South Korean missionaries have a tendency not to ask questions about what they do not understand well. Most South Koreans are not accustomed to asking questions and participating in discussions, since they have grown up in a culture where asking questions is considered as showing their ignorance to others. When they communicate with their coworkers in their accustomed way, various cases of misunderstanding occur both among the South Korean missionaries who make rough guesses among themselves as to what should be done, and with the colleagues who thought that they were understood at that moment but realize later that they were not. Missionaries in the older generation frequently have this tendency.

Marjory Foyle maintains that the primary rule in relationships between missionary coworkers is "when you don't understand, ask for clarification" (Foyle 2001, 111). That is the most important but frequently lacking communication skill in South Korean missionaries.

In addition, as a personal factor, South Korean missionaries are not good at expressing their thoughts and beliefs properly because of their strong convictions of their own calling and vision. Most of them take thorough prefield training courses, including formal theological and missiological training, and they are ordained before they become missionary candidates (Beattie 2007, 116).

Since South Korean missionaries usually have strong conviction about their ministries, they easily show dominating attitudes and use words that tend to imply that "one among all is the right way, and the others are not" rather than compromising with other opinions from other colleagues. The interviewee pointed out that since South Korean missionaries tend to consider that training for interpersonal relationships and communication skills are of little importance for their actual ministry for the missions, many of them suffer from interpersonal problems caused by miscommunication with coworkers on the field.

Some problems in interpersonal relationships can be prevented only through careful candidate selection. Strong conviction with clear calling and vision is one of the most important retention factors, but, at the same time, too strong of a sense of conviction can be an indication of lack of flexibility. In addition, developing good communication skills must not be an optional step in prefield training for South Korean missionaries. Good communication skills can help prevent interpersonal problems, which is the most important reason for attrition among South Korean missionaries.

Case Study 3:
Confusion in Authority: Social Aspects

South Korean mission agency executives consider "problems with peer missionaries" as the most serious reason for South Korean missionary attrition (Moon 1997, 136). Moon adds that the most typical cases of problems with peers are conflicts between a senior missionary and a newly arrived one, pointing out problems in leadership and supervision.

First, age is a crucial cultural and social factor for South Korean missionaries, which causes leadership problems. In the Korean culture, the most important cultural code is age. Korean language is very sensitive to age difference both with a complex calling system to call each other and with grammar including a complex honorific system. Since language is age sensitive, if a person who is senior is younger than the newly arrived, it is possible for both of them to have troubles when they start their formal relationship in the workplace as well as their personal relationship.

This difficulty often occurs in a multinational team setting. South Korean missionaries usually arrive at the field for the first time when they are relatively older than missionaries from other nations, because of the two-year mandatory military service and longer and stricter prefield training including internship in the local churches for ordination. When they are placed under the leadership and supervision of a younger team leader on the field, it takes time for them to accept her or his authority and in the time of adjustment, misunderstanding can occur between them and the younger team leader who cannot understand their confusing behaviors.

Secondly, South Korean missionaries' mindset of strict distinction between ordained and lay missionaries causes problems in leadership as well. Since strong denominational structures in South Korean Christianity make ordination one of the important factors in candidate selection and prefield training, many missionaries are ordained seminary graduates with an MDiv degree. Ordained South Korean missionaries can have difficulty when they are under the leadership of a lay missionary, and South Korean lay missionaries can have difficulty when they have to supervise ordained missionaries. Those difficulties are apparently projected in the relationship with colleagues in a multinational team as well as nationals on the field.

Thirdly, confusion of personal relationship and organizational structure causes difficulties in leadership as well as in personal relationship. Since the number of South Korean leaders has recently increased in multicultural ministry teams on the field, this is a newly raised issue which must be dealt with.

When South Korean missionaries first arrived on the field, they experienced Western senior missionaries' strict distinction between official and personal matters, which made them feel uncomfortable. That is because Western missionaries tended to be kind and flexible in personal matters to help new missionaries adjust to the field and the team, but principled and somewhat inflexible at work, it was confusing to South Korean missionaries and it was hard for them to work within that setting.

When South Korean missionaries who have had that kind of experience become a senior and leader in the team, they are very sympathetic and show maximum flexibility to the newly arrived, even in the formal organizational areas. That affects their team ministry positively for the stage of settlement of the newly arrived missionaries. Later on, however, that kindness usually turns out to be a disaster to the teamwork, because the friendly personal relationship which was good at the beginning becomes less friendly due to accumulated tension and misunderstanding. Documentation of policies, clear job descriptions, and conflict resolution processes are important factors which affect missionary retention (Hay et al. 2007, 251–56), but are weaknesses of South Korean missions leadership and supervision (Kim 2004, 69).

Leadership and supervision are important in member care because leaders and supervisors are responsible for keeping the balance between the well-being of the members on the field and the quality of the ministry of the team in the community (Roembke 2000, 110). Therefore, leadership training and trainings for administrative skills are not a waste of time on the field or during the furlough.

CONCLUSION

As an English proverb shows, "Prevention is better than cure." The role of member care is getting larger and wider for finishing the final task of the Great Commission. It does not mean mechanical administration for efficiency to complete the work, but care for the people in need with love of God.

Missionaries are the people in need, with very special and specific needs. They are not just people who are sent to meet others' needs. Thus, they need a team to be with and a support to help them be themselves before God and other people. We must not forget that "teams can be a source of conflict, but are also a source of support" (Hay et al. 2007, 177). Christ also ministered with a team, whose members caused a lot of troubles and hurt each other, but he also met his relational needs through them.

The need for good relationships can be found under the surface of all the issues of the South Korean missionaries mentioned here. Member care should help them to build healthy interpersonal relationships to provide proper guidance and training for the glory of God because the peoples who they serve will see God's glory through their lives as well as their work.

REFERENCES

Beattie, Stroma. 2007. Enhancing member care in the Singapore context: Towards good practice and the resolution of problematic issues. In *Missions matrix: Navigating 21st century missiological issues*, ed. Florence P. L. Tan, 103–34. Singapore: Singapore Bible College.

Blocher, Detlef. 2004. Good agency practices: Lessons from ReMAP II. *Connections* 3 (June): 12–25.

Brierley, Peter W. 1997. Missionary attrition: The ReMAP research report. In *Too valuable to lose: Exploring the causes and cures of missionary attrition*, ed. William D. Taylor, 85–103 Pasadena: William Carey Library.

Foyle, Marjory F. 2001. *Honorably wounded: Stress among Christian workers*, rev. ed. Mill Hill, London: Monarch Books.

Hay, Rob, Valerie Lim, Detlef Blocher, Jaap Ketelaar, and Sara Hay. 2007. *Worth keeping: Global perspectives on best practice in missionary retention.* Pasadena: William Carey Library.

Kim, Dong-hwa. 2004. National Report: Korea. *Connections* 3 (June): 68–70.

McKaughan, Paul. 1997. Missionary attrition: Defining the problem. In *Too valuable to lose: Exploring the causes and cures of missionary attrition*, ed. William D. Taylor, 15–24. Pasadena: William Carey Library.

Moon, Steve Sang-Cheol. 1997. Missionary attrition in Korea: Opinions of agency executives. In *Too valuable to lose: Exploring the causes and cures of missionary attrition*, ed. William D. Taylor, 129–42. Pasadena: William Carey Library.

———, ed. 2009. *Korean missions handbook 2007–2008*. Seoul, Korea: Global Missions Fellowship Press, CD-ROM.

Nicholls, Bruce J. 1979. *Contextualization: A theology of gospel and culture*. Downers Grove: InterVarsity.

O'Donnell, Kelly. 2002. Going global: A member care model for best practice. In *Doing member care well*, ed. Kelly O'Donnell, 13–22. Pasadena: William Carey Library.

Roembke, Lianne. 2000. *Building credible multicultural teams*. Pasadena: William Carey Library.

Taylor, William D., ed. 1997. *Too valuable to lose: Exploring the causes and cures of missionary attrition*. Pasadena: William Carey Library.

10

GLOBAL LEADERSHIP IN MISSIONS: REFLECTIONS ON THE ISSUES FACING A GLOBAL LEADER IN A MULTICULTURAL MISSION ORGANIZATION

SUNNY EUNSUN HONG

God uses people to accomplish God's mission. Some of those God used were multicultural (global) leaders like Abraham, Joseph, Moses, Daniel, Nehemiah, and Paul. They were used in extraordinary ways to bridge different cultures in their time. Paul, with the multicultural Antioch church, overcame Jewish-centered Christianity in the first century and laid the foundation for the gospel to be universal. He truly became all things to all people in order to win them over to the gospel (1 Cor 9:19–23).

With modern transportation and technology reaching all parts of the globe, the twenty-first century is more multicultural than the times described in the Bible. The whole world has become a global village made up of different cultures and languages (Sookhdeo 1994, 50), making it necessary for the people God uses today to be more multicultural.

Thirty years ago, mission initiatives tended to move directionally from the West to the Global South. Today, however, there is no "from and to" in missions geographically. There is "from everywhere to everyone" (Escobar 2003). Thirty years ago, cultural issues arose in crossing from the missionary's home culture to the field culture. Today's missionaries must not only cross from their home country culture to that of the field, but also to the cultures of colleagues who may come from many different countries. Lundy questioned this issue: "Great skill in cross-cultural communication of the Gospel is needed but what about intercultural skills with your own missionary colleagues?" (1999, 148). Dynamics among missionaries have changed as multicultural teams have been formed, bringing new demands on leadership.

It has been assumed by mission organizations that once a person has worked cross-culturally, he or she has gained the insights necessary to be an effective leader in a multicultural setting. Leadership in a globalized world, however, requires a different set of skills than field ministry (Charan, Drotter, and Noel 2001). Global leaders must be able to function effectively in a multicultural setting, as well as help their multicultural team function effectively. Effective global leadership appears to be a key factor in the success of a multicultural team.

The purpose of this presentation is to understand the issues facing a global leader in a multicultural mission organization in order to discover how to energize cultural strengths among multicultural members working together to move the gospel forward. I will examine current trends of missionaries and hindrances to the internationalization of an international mission organization facing global leadership issues. I will also provide some practical recommendations for global leadership issues.

There are at least four interchangeable terms used in literature to identify leaders of multicultural teams: cross-cultural leader, multicultural leader, transnational leader, and global leader. The term *cross-cultural* has been widely used to refer to the adjustment to a field culture. The term *multicultural* has often been used to describe the "melting pot" or "salad bar" make-up of the United States and Canada. *Transnational* is a relatively new term, commonly used in the business sector to denote a multinational company. *Global* has been used more frequently in the business sector to include more than just cultural issues. To make it possible to embrace the many different aspects of leadership in mission organizations, the term *global leader* was chosen for this paper.

MISSIONARIES FROM THE GLOBAL SOUTH

In *The Next Christendom,* Jenkins cites statistics to compare the Global North to the Global South to help his readers understand new happenings within the church around the world in the twenty-first century (2002).

According to the statistical tables produced by the respected Center for the Study of Global Christianity, some 2.1 billion Christians were alive in 2005, about one-third of the planetary population. The largest single bloc, some 531 million people, is still to be found in Europe. Latin America, though, is already close behind with 511 million, Africa has 389 million, and 344 million Asians profess Christianity. North America claims about 226 million believers. If we extrapolate these figures to the year 2025, the Southern predominance becomes still more marked. Assuming no great gains or losses through conversion, then there would be around 2.6 billion Christians, of whom 595 million would live in Africa, 623 million in Latin America, and 498 million in Asia. Europe, with 513 million, would have slipped to third place (Johnson and Ross 2009, 2–3).

Not only is the number of Christians in the Global South important, but so is the significant number of missionaries from the Global South. According to the *Atlas of Global Christianity*, in 1910, among 62,000 missionaries, 60,550 were from the Global North and 1,450 (about 2 percent) were from the Global South. In 2010, among 400,000 missionaries, 272,800 were from the Global North and 127,200 were from the Global South (Johnson and Ross 2009, 261). That means over 31 percent of missionaries were from the Global South in 2010, which is a significant increase when compared to the 2 percent of missionaries sent from the Global South in 1910.

Missionaries fall into two different groups, national or international, based on the organizations they join. Churches in the Global South have often built mission organizations independently from international organizations. If a national mission organization works independently from an international organization, their need for cross-cultural understanding may be limited to the understanding of the field in which they are working. However, national mission organizations may choose to partner with international organizations. Once a national organization partners with an international organization, then the cultural understanding of the national organization will need to be expanded in order to understand people in the international organization from other cultures. Another possible scenario is that missionaries from the Global South might join an international organization that is predominantly Western. If a missionary from the Global South joins a Western international organization, their understanding of Western culture becomes a critical issue for their membership. International organizations with many different nationalities represented face critical issues with their multicultural team and global leadership.

HINDRANCES

Due to the significant number of missionaries from the Global South, we can suspect that cultural diversity will be rampant in an international organization, which may be both a blessing and a potential disaster. This section examines the various hindrances that may emerge from different cultural expectations, cultural fatigue, inadequate cultural training, composition of leadership teams, ethnocentrism, and language issues that global leaders and organizations are facing.

Different Cultural Expectations about Leaders and Followers

People are influenced by their culture, and missionaries are not exceptions. "All Christian leaders, regardless of their cultural background, carry their personal histories and cultural biases with them wherever they serve" (Lingenfelter 2008, 15). Depending on their cultural background, people's expectations for leaders and followers within a varied group will differ.

Both leaders and followers have implicit and explicit images of what a leader ought to be and do. Leadership expectations are shaped by cultural backgrounds. In cross-cultural situations where leader expectations do not align with follower expectations, leadership dissonance may occur (Crow 2000, 185).

Mary Douglas' grid and group theory is useful for comparing expectations of leaders with followers. Grid indicates the degree of explicitly defined roles and rules for social relationships. High grid society distinguishes distinctive differences in social status, age, education, and so on. The group defines cohesiveness or collectiveness of members in a society. High group society values the desire of the group more than that of individuals. There are four cultural types: bureaucratic, hierarchical, individualistic, and egalitarian cultures based upon grid and group theory. *Bureaucratic* is high grid and low group; *hierarchical* is high grid and high group; *individualistic* is low group and low grid; and *egalitarian* is high group and low grid (Lingenfelter, 1998).

Expectations of Bureaucratic Cultures (High Grid, Low Group)

In a bureaucratic culture good leaders are expected to motivate people to follow and to make good decisions but not necessarily to have close relationships with people working under them. Mikhail Grachev et al. report on a Russian leader as following:

> The profile of an effective business leader in Russia is based on administrative competence and the capability of serious decision-making. He or she is able to motivate followers in order to meet performance targets, work in teams, and integrate efforts. However, there is no serious caring about humane motivation and modesty in personal behavior. Universal characteristics such as Charismatic/Value-based leadership and Team Oriented leadership are considered as contributors to outstanding leadership in Russia, however at a lower level when compared to most of the other countries. Participative and Humane Orientation have only limited impact in Russia. (Grachev 2007, 829)

Followers in a bureaucratic culture have a tendency to look for an authority figure with charisma as a leader. The followers do not want to know much about the leader's personal life and keep their distance from the leader. Because of the distance between the followers and leaders, it may seem leaders do not care for people. In a bureaucratic culture, the best follower keeps the rules and follows orders without many questions.

Expectations of Hierarchical Cultures (High Grid, High Group)

An ideal leader in a hierarchical society has high status and can play the role of a good patron. A good leader makes decisions after listening to a group. The followers are happy to follow the leader if their collective desire is reflected in the decision-making or the leader gives clear direction. An ideal follower in a hierarchical society is loyal to the leader and group and follows well under the leader's direction. If people do not like the leader, they will create social pressure—using gossip or hinting by body language—to communicate their desires. If indirect communication is not successful, then the leader may be removed by the group. Lorraine Dierck's research on Thai culture presents well the expectation of the hierarch's mind-set of a leader.

> Thais regarded the best leader as one with access to financial resources and power... This implies that Thais expect leaders to exhibit a blend of authoritarianism and benevolence towards their followers. The two strands woven into the leader's mantle are called *phradet* (authority) and *phrakhun* (benevolent patronage). A leader who finds the right balance between these two factors has *baramee*, that is, power and strength derived from respect and loyalty. (2007, 149, 153)

Expectations of Individualistic Cultures (Low Grid, Low Group)

In an individualistic culture, a competent leader listens to an individual's opinions to make things happen. A leader does not need a prominent social/family background. A quality follower is independent and can do his or her work well and express opinions well. Michael Hoppe and Rabi Bhagat report ten major characteristics of an American leader:

> Stand out through their individual achievements. Inspire through their optimism, can-do mentality, and energy. Stand up for their beliefs. Focus their efforts. Strive for excellence in their and others' performance. Seek change. Act quickly. Promote team spirit. Encourage participation. Care about people. (2007, 525–26)

Expectations of Egalitarian Cultures (Low Grid, High Group)

A genuine leader in an egalitarian society does not necessarily stand out as a leader and consciously makes himself or herself equal with the followers. People usually do not want to be a leader. They hold the concept of a tall poppy syndrome. The expression "a nail that sticks out gets pounded" describes the tall poppy syndrome well. If someone makes progress and becomes taller than others, someone else knocks him or her down to make everybody equal. The expectation of a leader is to be very low key. Neal Ashkanasy describes his research on the Australian concept of a leader as follows:

> Australians are proud of their egalitarian culture, but at the same time also value rewards for high achievers. Its leaders are expected to inspire high levels of performance, but must do so without giving the impression of self-sacrifice or of not being anything more than "one of the boys."... The strong leveling tendency among Australians based on their egalitarian and meritocratic heritage has promoted a cynicism about promoting personalities to the status of heroes. (2007, 311, 329)

Misunderstandings Caused by Different Expectations

Misunderstandings caused by the different expectations of leaders and followers in a multicultural environment are unavoidable.

Perceptions of a Bureaucratic Culture (High Grid, Low Group)

People from a bureaucratic cultural background will be disturbed by people from an individualistic cultural background when they question the rules or leaders, even if their intention is to improve the system or to give suggestions to the leaders. People from a bureaucratic cultural background are not pleased by people coming from the hierarchical background when they create social pressure to make a change or to challenge a leader. People from a bureaucratic cultural background consider egalitarian leadership disrespectful.

Perceptions of a Hierarchical Culture (High Grid, High Group)

People coming from a hierarchical cultural background regard individual and egalitarian leadership as offensive and disrespectful. They also do not understand the fact that people from a bureaucratic background do not have cohesiveness as followers. Followers coming from a hierarchical background are disappointed if a leader does not show benevolence to them as a good patron. For example, "Thai team members often regarded the missionary or the expatriate team leader as a high-status patron with the obligation to provide for his or her followers" (Dierck 2007, 101).

Followers coming from a hierarchical background would place everyone in the "right place" based upon status, without knowing they are doing it. The factors that inform status are a mixture of seniority in ministry, age, country of origin, gender, family background, ministry experiences, academic degrees, and so on. Hierarchs know who is in what place. If someone is trying to step forward, the hierarchs may be displeased with those individuals who are making personal progress without group consent. They will use social pressure to push the person down. People coming from a hierarchical background have a hard time understanding people from an individualistic culture, especially when they recognize and accept praise without also sharing it with the group. They will think the individualists are very arrogant.

Perceptions of an Individualistic Culture (Low Grid, Low Group)

People coming from individualistic cultures may not understand why people from a hierarchical or egalitarian background cannot make a decision based upon what an individual wants, but always have to follow the group's opinion. They cannot understand why people from hierarchical and egalitarian backgrounds cannot accept individual recognition or credit but pass that to others. They may think people from hierarchical and egalitarian backgrounds are hypocrites or do not understand what they deserve. They also do not understand why people cannot be creative and cannot make a change in the system by presenting logical solutions individually. Individualists do not understand why people from bureaucratic and hierarchical backgrounds blindly follow a leader without questioning.

Perceptions of an Egalitarian Culture (Low Grid, Low Group)
People coming from an egalitarian background have difficulty in understanding that people coming from hierarchical and bureaucratic cultures respect and follow a leader, even if a leader does something wrong. Among the followers, people coming from an egalitarian culture will not understand how people are placed according to status and may find themselves in trouble by misplacing or simply not placing themselves on that status scale. They may also have difficulty with the individualist when the individualist shares their accomplishment and stands out from the group.

Cultural Fatigue
As reviewed above, the concept of leader and follower based upon four different cultural types creates very different expectations and consequent misunderstandings. If other cultural aspects are examined—decision-making, concept of time, task/people orientation, relationships, family life, cosmology, personal property, life goals, communication styles, and so on—the complexity deepens. It is clear that cultural expectations and misunderstandings must be dealt with in an international mission organization to build a healthy multicultural organization and global leaders.

In an international mission organization, many layers of cultures exist: the missionary's national culture, organizational culture, host country culture, and the target or people group culture where missionaries are working. The layers of the many cultures make personal relationships, including the relationship between leaders and followers, very complex. Luzbetak describes the potential problems of multicultural team members if they are unable to adjust to the cultures around them. They may be "constantly perplexed, disappointed, irritated, frustrated, fearful, apprehensive, bored, disgusted, depressed, homesick, psychologically exhausted and even physically ill" (Dierck, 2007, 43).

If there is any chance to avoid the layers of culture, people unintentionally do so because of cultural fatigue. Western missionaries have the tendency of identifying their home culture with the organizational culture due to the dominant make-up of the membership. For example, more than 50 percent of the members in SIL are Western members, with the majority of them from North America. Therefore, it is possible that half of the membership in every branch might be North American. After working in the field and expending energy to appropriately relate to the people in the field according to their culture, North American members who come to the branch office or centers and see many other North American members may want the freedom to be themselves culturally, without even realizing it. Therefore, sometimes the branch culture could tend to be North American due to homesickness and cultural fatigue. North Americans, however, often seem to forget that non-Western coworkers' cultures are more similar to the field culture than North American culture. Asian missionaries who work on other fields in Asia are usually fairly comfortable with the field culture even though they need to adjust to specific cultural differences. They may find a bigger cultural gap, to which they must adjust, when they come to a branch that tends toward North American culture.

Cultural fatigue can hinder one from making the effort to understand members coming from other cultures. Missionaries may view their work as being with the people on the field and relegate secondary priority to relating with other members in their organization, especially those from a different cultural background. People can choose their friends in the branch as they wish. Nobody wants to unnecessarily add another cultural stress to friendships because relating to coworkers is a choice, not an obligation. With staffing options as they are, it is unavoidable that such culturally fatigued leaders would still have to lead the culturally tired followers in international mission organizations.

Inadequacy in Cultural Training

Donna Downes reviewed literature in missiology and concluded that current cross-cultural training has predominantly been for Westerners to adjust to the Global South in a field situation and that there is a lack of training mission leaders in global management (2004, 58). Most of the cross-cultural materials in missions have a clear direction: from the West to the Global South. Lundy provides an example with Operation Mobilization (OM). When 48 percent of the membership of OM was from the Global South in 1999, OM's cultural training was a Western type of training (1999, 148). Cross-cultural training on how non-Western members can adjust in another non-Western culture is seldom available, and resources for how non-Western members can adjust to their Western colleagues have also been sadly lacking. Few resources can be found for how Western members can adjust to members from the Global South. There have been very few resources on multicultural team work, and those existing materials include only the Westerner's view point. The training that has been done has been limited in scope so global leaders have not been fully prepared for the multicultural situations they face.

For example, if Asian members working in Asia received training with the training materials geared for the Westerner who is adjusting to Asian culture, Asian members cannot comprehend the content, since it is coming from the Western mind-set. Due to the mind-set of the training materials, Asian members need to understand Western culture in order to understand the presentations. Also if a trainer is a Westerner who cannot comprehend the implications of the multicultural formation of the organization's membership, the training would be in one direction: from the West to the Global South. If a non-Western trainer uses the materials written by a Westerner which do not cover multiculturalism, the content of the training might not be useful to non-Westerners. Multiculturalism in membership brings cross-cultural training issues to a different level.

The learning curve of missionaries from the Global South is very steep, not so much with the field culture, but more so with the culture of their Western coworkers and the organizational culture. Because of the lack of proper cross-cultural training, non-Westerners have to be "Westernized" in order to function as members of an international organization while Western members do not have to be 'non-Westernized' to function as members. Lundy pointed out this very issue: "OM is still very Anglo-Saxon in orientation ... with very few Westerns becoming like Indians, although they [the Indians serving in OM] are becoming like us" (1999, 148). Therefore, a non-Westerner has to learn how to be a "Westerner" first to understand the content of the training. This is an example of how a global leader in missions might handle multicultural leadership issues without much training with followers who also lack multicultural training.

Composition of the Leadership Team

In recent years several researchers have focused on the composition of leadership teams and related issues. According to Bishop's research in 2004, leadership of YWAM was dominated and controlled by mostly Westerners, important leadership positions were not given to non-Westerners, and the issues that the Westerners consider important were not regarded important by the non-Westerners.

Western leaders coming from the North American or European-Australasian cohorts depict the challenges as a series of hurdles to overcome with respect to gender inclusion, age, authoritarianism, and the need for a strong biblical model. Likewise, non-Western leaders also discuss obstacles to conquer but they have different faces: organizational politics, a predominantly American style of leadership, and lack of genuine inclusion (Bishop 2004, 203).

The case of YWAM points out two problems: the formation of the leadership and different issues raised by different perspectives.

Downes researched six international mission organizations to see how much effort they place in being globalized or internationalized. She focused on the number of non-Western people on their boards. She noted that six organizations were internationalized by the increase in numbers of non-Westerners on their boards over the years. However, internationalization or globalization issues require a look beyond the formation of the board to the cultural implications that non-Western board members may bring. Most non-Western cultures are nondirective and more collective. Unless the non-Western board members begin to give voice to their concerns, having non-Western members on the board will not solve the problem of internationalization. Even worse is when the non-Western board member has a colonial mind-set or client/patron mind-set and only goes along with the Western members' opinion.

Another issue is the way meetings are conducted. If the meeting is conducted in a Western way, by making necessary presentations and then asking that a decision be made on the spot by raising hands, how is a non-Western member to be effective in comprehending all the issues in a second language and arrive at a sound judgment? Most non-Western members are not comfortable enough to vote by raising hands when everybody is watching. The way of conducting a meeting is an issue to ponder when considering the internationalization of leadership. Therefore, global leadership in missions needs to go deeper than the number of non-Western people in leadership positions, even though putting non-Westerners on a board might be a very sincere first attempt.

On the other hand, it should not be simply judged that an organization is not internationalized unless there are a number of non-Western people in leadership positions. People who are truly multicultural and understand multiculturalism, regardless of their race, could be a channel for making an international organization truly international. Internationalization of an organization is not a simple issue.

Ethnocentrism

Ethnocentrism resides within each culture. Some Christians place their national identity ahead of their Christian identity without even recognizing it (Lingenfelter 2008, 47). Throughout the history of missions, Protestant missions have been influenced by anthropological theories like cultural relativism, social structuralism, cognitive theory, symbolism and so on. "On the negative side, the theory of cultural evolution has affirmed Western arrogance, ethnocentrism, racism, and colonialism" (Hiebert 2009, 85). Due to the influence of anthropological theories, missions in its pioneering stage elevated ethnocentrism. Ethnocentrism is one of the hindrances to building up global leadership. Lundy recognizes ethnocentrism as sin that hinders the internationalization or globalization of a mission organization.

> Ethnocentrism will increasingly be identified and dealt with in a globalized organization ... Moreover, it is argued here that ethnocentrism is essentially a spiritual problem, and so unless addressed on that level, will not essentially be rooted out as this paradigm shift from West/North to East/South in missions transpires. (Lundy 1999, 147)

There are different phenomena which exemplify ethnocentrism in an international mission organization. First, running an organization is usually done the Western way. Let us not be guilty of insisting that national missionaries be converted to our way of doing missions. That is one more way we demonstrate we have been blinded by the spirit of pride which is at the root of ethnocentrism (Lundy 1999, 154)!

If non-Western members are to be considered as leaders in an international organization, they will undoubtedly have to understand the worldview of the West to be on par with Western members. Non-Western members cannot avoid this learning curve. Members from the Global South have to adjust to more cultures than members from the West, which means members from the Global South have more burdens on their shoulders. There is no simple solution on how to run a multicultural organization; however, ethnocentrism should not be embedded in the organizational structure.

Second, leadership must be given to a person who is qualified for the position regardless of their ethnicity. Passing the work to a national or a non-Western member from a Western member, will require an intentional effort or ethnocentrism might cause the transition of leadership to fail.

While this type of collaboration may seem ideal, Jim Reapsome, former editor of *Evangelical Missions Quarterly*, says that North American mission agencies have always been reluctant to pass the baton of leadership to people of other cultures. In comparison to the international corporate world where qualified non-North Americans have been holding significant management positions for years, Reapsome says that mission agencies are "way behind in empowering nationals to run things. They are behind in nominating national church leaders to sit on their boards" (Downes 2004, 10).

Third, ethnocentrism should be examined from all directions. Sometimes people from the Global South, who have a colonial mind-set or strong grid concept, can work against people whom they think have a lower status due to race while lifting the Westerners unnecessarily higher.

Language
There must be a common language to communicate in international mission organizations. With few exceptions, that language is English. People whose mother tongue is not English have a disadvantage in communication. Unless they can overcome difficulty in mastering English, they might not be considered a leader even though they may have all the other qualifications. The nonnative English speakers themselves might not even try to see themselves as leaders due to their deficiency in speaking English.

Language is not simply a code in communication. The assertion of the "Sapir-Whorf hypothesis" is that language is not just a neutral medium through which we express our ideas but a powerful structure that shapes all that we think, say, and do. Most of what we see and understand is filtered through language (Adeney 1995, 125).

Rebecca Piekkari stated that "each language is a window into a specific view of life and a general frame of reference that is culturally bound to its speakers" (2008, 240). Therefore, a nonnative-English-speaker has not only to learn one more language but also has to understand the worldview English brings.

There are only twelve countries in the world that have English as their first language and it so happens that most of these are in the Western world. The fact of the matter is that language norms in the English-speaking world have to do with national identity and pride (Lundy 1999, 152)!

Another issue language brings is power. Team members who are fluent in the common language are likely to dominate discussion, hindering the exposition of the perspectives of members who are less able or less willing to express their opinions in a language that is not their primary language. Thus, the choice of the team's lingua franca will enfranchise some team members and disenfranchise others (Janssens and Brett 2006, 133).

Native English speakers have more potential power for controlling an organization, or at least in giving more input to the organization. Therefore, language can be another hindrance to making international organizations internationalized and to producing global leaders.

RECOMMENDATIONS

The internationalization of the international mission organization is not only a knowledge issue but also a heart-level issue. Lingenfelter pointed out that building trust is one of the core issues in building the leadership of a multicultural team. "The complexity of leading cross-culturally lies in the challenge of building a community of trust among people who come from two or more cultural traditions that provoke a clash of worldviews" (2008, 20). Leading multicultural teams requires many different aspects of endeavor to irrigate the organizational culture. Here are some suggestions to help that endeavor.

Enable the Whole Team to Understand Multicultural Issues

The Bible confirms multiculturalism as God's design. John Lee researched this issue in the Bible and concluded the following:

> In this passage [Acts 17:26–27], Paul refers to the human race as made from one man or of one blood and states that times and boundaries of their habitation were appointed or determined for every nation. This passage implies that ethnicity was part of God's original intent and that the times and places for every ethnic group were determined even before creation. (2005, 102)

Therefore, the very first requirement for a leader in a multicultural organization is to understand different cultural expectations and to know how to lead and communicate with diverse cultures. Besides the leaders, the members of the organization should also have an understanding of different cultural expectations. It takes the whole team, not only the leaders, to make an international organization truly international. "But even more importantly, this vision must be tested in the community of the body of Christ, refined by the participation of the body in shaping it, and then mobilized by the body in prayer and action" (Lingenfelter 2008, 32).

One way of promoting a grass-roots level of understanding multicultural issues is to have a cultural coach system. People from different cultural backgrounds could be on the cultural coach team to promote an increased understanding of different cultures within a particular branch. People could consult a cultural coach to obtain advice for their cultural issues. Cultural coaches could provide improved understanding and promote diversity intentionally.

Multiculturalism can be used positively by using strengths of different cultures to bring together different viewpoints. For example, missionaries from the Global South can relate more easily to the field culture than Western missionaries, as previously mentioned. This means that missionaries from the Global South may be able to function as a bridge between the field and Western missionaries. By considering cultural aspects, missionaries from the Global South may be able to find a better way to approach field projects.

Cultural differences can help personnel resources and cultural resources be used more wisely. "Culture is no longer an obstacle to be overcome. Rather, it is a critical lever for competitive advantage" (Rosen and Digh, 2001, 74). Bureaucrats can help other cultural types in bringing orderliness and in having a more systematic approach to the work. Hierarchs can help other cultural types in bringing more respect and togetherness in the interactions of all the members. Individualists can help other cultural types to develop more independence. Egalitarians can help other cultural types in bringing equality for members from all cultures.

Acceptance of cultural differences must follow understanding. There should be a safe environment in which to be different. This concept might be very hard for people from the collectivistic society to accept. They need to learn how to separate different from wrong, because conformity in their culture means being right, while being different is considered wrong. Everyone should feel at home as a member of an international organization, regardless of their race. The international mission organizational culture should be as such:

> Whether one is a Korean or an American, the missionary will feel at home in the mission agency anywhere that it works in the world. For this to happen, international organizations that have their origins in the Western world will need to retool resourcing patterns, structures, and values so that true partnership and synergy can emerge between the diverse sides of the worldwide Church in the task of completing the Great Commissions. (Lundy 1999, 147)

Global leadership is one of the key factors in making all these things happen.

Reduce Cultural Fatigue

Lingenfelter and Mayers suggested a cross-cultural worker should be a 150 percent person, having 75 percent of their own culture and 75 percent of the field culture (1986, 24–25). That concept only works in a context with two cultures. As you go in and out of two cultures, you can put on 75 percent of you, according to the culture in which you need to function. However, in the multicultural setting, there is no way to be a multiple of 75 percent of all the cultures. Also, it is not possible to go in and out of many cultures. Multiple cultures are there at the same time. In whichever cultural setting one functions, one may offend another type of culture in the group and that is what makes the multicultural setting very difficult and different from a bicultural setting. That is why grace must cover all these situations.

There should be efforts to reduce cultural fatigue by celebrating cultural differences and providing cultural space. For example, praying in one's mother tongue could be encouraged, seminars on understanding different cultures in the branch could be arranged, and cultural days could be held to experience the various colleagues' culture.

Revise Training to Reflect Multicultural Backgrounds of Workers

Current cross-cultural training must be revised to reflect the changes in the missionaries' cultural backgrounds. This is another area for research that needs attention. It needs to include all-directional cultural training so that the training helps to stimulate the understanding of cultural differences. The target of the multicultural training should focus on all the members of a mission organization so that the new way of thinking in a multicultural team and in global leadership can be implemented on every level of the organization (Rosen and Digh 2001). From the multicultural team, a global leader could then emerge naturally. The purpose of the training should provide a safe environment for all races to work together for the kingdom.

Choose Multicultural Leaders from a Variety of Cultural Backgrounds

Another way of internationalizing mission agencies is to accept leaders from a variety of cultural backgrounds who are multicultural. Leaders can be drawn from multicultural people like seasoned missionaries and diaspora people who truly have become multicultural or at least bicultural. "A growing number of missionaries are in-betweeners who stand between different worlds, seeking to build bridges of understanding, mediate relationships, and negotiate partnerships in ministry" (Hiebert 2009, 179). Mission organizations will need to make an intentional plan to put people in leadership who will champion the idea of making the organization internationalized.

Intentionally Seek Unity, Not Uniformity

There is a supracultural aspect to the gospel that unites Christians beyond cultural differences. The gospel both critiques and affirms every culture. Unity does not require uniformity. The tension between diversity and equality must be maintained in mission activity in order to do justice to who God is and how God wants God's people to live. As we take the gospel to unreached people groups, we must intentionalize what it means interracially to be united and equal, that we are part of one catholic global church (Lundy 1999, 154).

There needs to be constant and intentional efforts in bringing the unity spoken of in John 17, because we are bound first to Jesus, the giver of our identity, as opposed to being bound to culture. The cross is the place every culture should meet to confess their sins, to forgive each other, and to embrace each other (Lingenfelter 2008).

Be Creative in Dealing with Language Issues

There is no easy solution to deal with the language issue. There has been an effort in the business world to use a neutral language—everyone's second language—to avoid dominance (Janssens and Brett 2006, 147). Some fields have tried to use a national language of the field as a common language, which brings different issues in an international organization since there still is need for an international language to communicate to the headquarters or to the other fields. Another way might be to use a common-language cluster approach to communicate to specific sublanguage groups with a translation to the greater team.

If English stays as a common language of an organization, there must be intentional efforts to lessen the burden of the nonnative speakers of English. Cultural coaches could remind the native English speakers to speak in simple English and avoid using idioms, or if idioms are used, to explain them. Nonnative English speakers will not be able to express all they want to communicate in English. This is an area where the native English speakers will need to exercise grace and seek to understand the other's intention and heart rather than only the language they hear or read.

CONCLUSION

We talk about cultural change or a transformed worldview on the mission field as one of the main outcomes of introducing the gospel. What about the change in the workers bringing the gospel? Could the workers experience the cultural change first in the midst of their work among the culturally diverse team with whom they work? We need a paradigm shift in international missions so that they become truly international in attitude and administration. Intentional effort to learn the strengths of other cultures must be promoted by global leadership. The Antioch church provides a model and an inspiration for us in overcoming cultural issues of our time.

Revelation chapters five and seven clearly picture the multiculturalism in God's kingdom. When the church is multicultural, we express the kingdom better than when the church is monocultural. Therefore, by working together, the true worldwide body of Christ can bolster the cultural weakness of one with the cultural strength of another, and in so doing, help to expand God's glorious kingdom. This is a true celebration of God's diverse creation and the universality of the gospel. As multiculturalism is embraced by mission organizations, its members from each culture can bring cultural, missiological, and theological strengths so that the whole gospel is preached to the whole world by the whole church.

REFERENCES

Adeney, Bernard T. 1995. *Strange virtues: Ethics in a multicultural world.* Downers Grove: InterVarsity.

Ashkanasy, Neal M. 2007. The Australian enigma. In *Culture and leadership across the world: The GLOBE book of in-depth studies of 25 societies*, ed. Jagdeep S. Chhokar, Felix C. Brodbeck, and Robert J. House, 299–333. Mahwah, NY: Lawrence Erlbaum Associates, Publishers.

Bishop, Camille F. 2004. Generational cohorts and cultural identity as factors affecting leadership transition in organization. PhD diss., Trinity Evangelical Divinity School.

Crow, Michael D. 2000. Spiritual authority across cultures: The cultural contours of pneumatic leadership, East and West. PhD diss., Fuller Seminary.

Dierck, Lorraine Wendy. 2007. Teams that work: Leadership, power and decision-making in multicultural teams in Thailand. PhD diss., Biola University.

Downes, Donna R. 2004. The globalization of mission: Missiological dream or management nightmare? PhD diss., Biola University.

Escobar, Samuel. 2003. *The new global mission: The gospel from everywhere to everyone.* Downers Grove: InterVarsity.

Grachev, Mikhail V., Nikolai G. Rogovsky, and Boris V. Rakitski. 2007. Leadership and culture in Russia: The case of transitional economy. In *Culture and leadership across the world: The GLOBE book of in-depth studies of 25 societies*, ed. Jagdeep S. Chhokar, Felix C. Brodbeck, and Robert J. House, 803–31. Mahwah, NY: Lawrence Erlbaum Associates, Publishers.

Hiebert, Paul G. 2009. *The gospel in human contexts: Anthropological explorations for contemporary missions.* Grand Rapids: Baker Academic.

Hoppe, Michael H., and Rabi S. Bhagat. 2007. Leadership in the United States of America: The leader as cultural hero. In *Culture and leadership across the world: The GLOBE book of in-depth studies of 25 societies*, ed. Jagdeep S. Chhokar, Felix C. Brodbeck, and Robert J. House, 475–543. Mahwah, NY: Lawrence Erlbaum Associates, Publishers.

Janssens, M., and Jeanne M. Brett. 2006. Cultural intelligence in global teams: A fusion model of collaboration. *Group and Organization Management*, 31(1), 124–53.

Jenkins, Philip. 2002. *The next Christendom: The coming of global Christianity*. Oxford: Oxford University Press.

Johnson, Todd M. and Kenneth R. Ross, eds. 2009. *Atlas of global Christianity*. Edinburgh, UK: Edinburgh University Press.

Lee, John J. 2005. An investigation into multicultural/intercultural competence of leaders in Southern California's multicultural/intercultural churches. PhD diss., Biola University.

Lingenfelter, Sherwood. 1998. *Transforming culture: A challenge for Christian mission*. Grand Rapids: Baker Books.

———. 2008. *Leading cross-culturally: Covenant relationships for effective Christian leadership*. Grand Rapids: Baker Academic.

Lingenfelter, Sherwood, and Marvin Mayers. 1986. *Ministering cross-culturally: An incarnational model for personal relationships*. Grand Rapids: Baker Books.

Lundy, David J. 1999. Moving beyond internationalizing the mission force. *International Journal of Frontier Missions* 3: 147–55.

Piekkari, Rebecca. 2008. Language issues in multicultural management. In *21st century management: A reference handbook*, vol. 1, ed. Charles Wankel. Los Angeles, CA: Sage Publications.

Plueddemann, James E. 2009. *Leading across cultures: Effective ministry and mission in the global church*. Downers Grove: InterVarsity Academic.

Rosen, R., and P. Digh. 2001. Developing globally literate leaders. *TD* 55: 71–81.

Sookhdeo, Patrick. 1994. Cultural issues in partnership in mission. In *Kingdom partnerships for synergy in missions*, ed. William Taylor, 49–66. Pasadena: William Carey Library.

11

A MULTICULTURAL TEAM-BUILDING WORKSHOP

SHERYL TAKAGI SILZER

As a number of papers in this volume have indicated, there is a critical need for multicultural team training. Although cultural differences are apparent, the reasons why cultures are different are often unknown or unrecognized. This misunderstanding leads to ongoing, long-term conflicts and unresolved issues.

For the past five years I have run a five- to six-day "Multicultural Team Building" workshop for SIL International in a number of its field locations. This workshop helps SIL associates discover their own culture so that they will be able to work more effectively with team members from other cultures.

At present SIL has more than sixty nationalities working in more than thirty countries around the world. Some locations have team members from as many as twenty foreign nationalities as well as local citizens from different local language groups. In spite of a shared desired to be involved in the work of Bible translation, there are often misunderstandings and conflicts that arise from their different cultural assumptions.

The multicultural team-building workshop provides a series of cultural self-discovery activities designed to help participants discover how their cultural practices were first formed in their childhood home. Mary Douglas' theory of culture presents the concept of "Culture based Judging System" (CbJS) whereby an individual maintains their preferred cultural way of doing things (Douglas 1992, 6). Once participants have discovered their cultural type, they can examine their responses to cultural differences to understand whether they are culturally or biblically based. The workshop concludes with suggestions for applying biblical truth to cultural differences.

I will briefly describe the workshop's development, its design and implementation, and its successes and remaining challenges.

THE WORKSHOP'S DEVELOPMENT

A major factor in the development of the workshop was my own multicultural background. I am Japanese American; my grandparents immigrated to the United States in the early 1900s. Although I was raised in South California, there were not many other Japanese Americans where I lived and all my friends were white Caucasian. I considered myself a white American, particularly compared to African Americans and Hispanics. I really did not sense that I was an ethnic minority until I went to college and met other Japanese Americans.

I later met and married a German/British/Irish American and served in language projects with SIL for twenty-five years in Latin America, the Pacific, and Indonesia. When I came home for an extended home assignment in 1992, I was very stressed out. In the midst of my stress I began a study program in Intercultural Studies at Biola University.

In 1993 I learned that I had breast cancer. At first I questioned why God allowed me to have cancer after serving God for so many years. I assumed I must have done something wrong and that God was displeased with me. I also reflected on the stress I had faced as a woman (wife, mother, household manager) over the years of cross-cultural living. Eventually I learned that stress and cancer go hand in hand and that my cultural ideal regarding work had contributed to my cancer.

At Biola I studied culture and learned that cultures have different underlying beliefs or worldviews. These beliefs are maintained by the way things are done on a regular basis. People make decisions based on their cultural ideals and thus cultures make decisions in different ways.

An example of a way people of different cultures make different decisions is in how they meet their need for housing. In one of my classes I compared the floor plan of my childhood home with the home of a woman from a country where I had served. When I saw her house floor plan, I began to understand why I had experienced so much stress living in her culture. I realized how much culture was reflected in the house floor plan and how useful the house floor plan was to understand cultural differences. The process of going room-by-room to discuss activities helped me see how I had used my own Culture based Judging System (CbJS) to maintain my cultural values and how I had unintentionally followed my cultural way of doing things instead of following biblical truth.

As part of a study program I began to develop a course addressing cross-cultural stress using the concept of the image of God and Mary Douglas' theory of culture (Douglas 1982) along with two ethnographic tools—a family tree and house floor plan. As I worked through the lessons myself, God helped me to understand that my cross-cultural stress was caused by the culturally shaped false beliefs I held about who God was as well as who I was. I used my cross-cultural stress as a starting point to help others recognize that their own cultural beliefs are a potential source of stress and misunderstanding when working with others of different cultural backgrounds. Douglas' theory of culture helped me understand how many American values I had, as well as the Asian values I followed. As I began to process the stress I had felt living in Indonesian and Latin cultures, I saw how a house floor plan could be used as a tool to discuss the childhood practices such as visiting, eating, working, resting, and cleaning and that reflecting on my present day responses to cultural differences would help me understand how my CbJS worked. If this process helped me, perhaps it could help others.

The Workshop
Although the title of the workshop, "Biblical Multicultural Teams," appears somewhat authoritative, it was chosen to emphasize the differences between cultural values and biblical truth. I found that I was not the only person who believed my way of doing things was right; so did many other people. When I discovered that my normal reactions to cross-cultural stress was culturally shaped, I became more aware of how my Culture based Judging System (CbJS) distorted the image of God.

The Content
The Multicultural Team-building workshop is based on an unpublished manuscript "Biblical Multicultural Teams: Applying Biblical Truth to Cultural Differences," and a fifty-page workbook. The workbook helps participants discover how their CbJS can distort the image of God and gives suggestions for applying biblical truth to cultural differences.

The workshop material first presents a concept of the image of God as it relates to the Trinity and shows how, like the Trinity, the image of God can be reflected through our decision making (our will compared to God the

Father's authority), our thinking and our responsibility for creation (our mind compared to God the Son as Truth), and our relationships with others (our heart compared to God the Holy Spirit as our guide into Truth).

Secondly, Mary Douglas' model of four types of culture is presented showing how each type uses a different kind of decision making (will), thinking and responsibility for creation (mind), and relationships or social responsibility (heart). Each type is maintained by a Culture based Judging System (CbJS) that justifies the preferred way of doing things. The CbJS is evident in our responses to cultural differences in what we say and do in regard to cultural differences. A child learns right from wrong through the nurturing and discipline they receive and this shapes their CbJS.

Two anthropological tools are used to help with cultural self-discovery—a family tree and a house floor plan. The family tree helps explore family structure, relationships, and characteristics. Childhood experiences are compared with present day conflicts and misunderstandings.

The last portion of the workshop provides an opportunity for participants to share what they learned about their Culture based Judging System (CbJS) and how it has distorted the image of God. Forgiveness and reconciliation are discussed and depending on the response of the group, the workshop may conclude with an extended time of forgiveness and reconciliation.

Each workshop topic contains Scripture, examples from the four types of cultures, questions about childhood activities that reveal the CbJS, and reflective prayer exercises to apply biblical truth to cultural differences. As participants discover their CbJS, they become aware of how they distort God's image. The final chapter shows how typical sins of each cultural type prevent the application of biblical truth to cultural differences. Participants then consider the next steps God wants them to take both individually and as a group.

Although the workshop material presents resource materials about the underlying cultural ideals for a variety of countries, each person is encouraged to discover their own type by identifying their personal responses in each of the topics.

WORKSHOP DESIGN AND IMPLEMENTATION

The workshop is an interactive experience based on adult learning principles in which participants learn not only from the facilitators but also from each other. The optimal workshop involves participants from the same work group to help them learn how they and their coworkers have been culturally shaped and to help them consider how to address misunderstandings in the workplace. Each topic is explored through small group discussion around the tables of four to six participants. A number of varied activities, including dramas and panel discussions, help participants recall how things were done in their childhood home.

The major topics of the workshop are:

Day 1: Image of God and Model of Culture
Day 2: Nurturing and Discipline and Family Structure
Day 3: House Floor Plan and Visiting Practices
Day 4: Eating and Working Practices
Day 5: Resting and Cleaning Practices
Day 6: Applying Biblical Truth to Cultural Differences, Evaluation, and Next Step.

Cultural differences are highlighted each day. Participants are welcomed and take leave using a different greeting (e.g., handshakes, bowing, and rubbing foreheads). A facilitator opens in prayer using different cultural ways of praying (sitting, standing, raising one's hands, all praying at once, etc.). A simple chorus (e.g., "This is the Day") is sung in a different language each day. If possible, participants are asked to provide a cultural mid-morning or afternoon snack along with a brief explanation of the foods, how they are served, etc. This can range from the proper way of making British tea with scones, to Argentina mate tea with sweet cake, to Mennonite Sunday afternoon tea, to Korean tea with sweets, etc.

SUCCESSES OF THE WORKSHOP

The success of the workshop has been in part due to the interactive nature of this workshop compared to SIL workshops in other subjects. One participant stated, "This has been the most beneficial, thought-provoking, challenging, paradigm-adjusting SIL course I have ever attended. Absolutely brilliant!"

Participants' suggestions have also helped to improve the workshop. A sampling of participants' comments is listed below in four areas: content, design, facilitator, and self-discovery. Most comments relate to the workshop question: "What was most helpful about the workshop?" or "What is one reason you thought the workshop was successful?"

Content

Although a number of people had previous training in cultural studies and even in Mary Douglas' grid and group theory, a number commented that they understand the theory of culture better now and prefer terms "structure and community" to "grid and group."

- I studied Grid and Group theory before but understand it much better now. I like the terms structure and community rather than grid and group.
- Community/structure grid was very helpful for understanding myself, my culture, and others.

A number of participants mentioned that the model of culture help them understand themselves as well as other cultures better.

- Learning a general tool to see cultures. Learning about my own culture.
- The multicultural course taught me not just how people from other cultures do things but, more importantly, why.
- I've always thought of myself as pretty sorted! As we say in the UK, "I'm comfortable in my skin." But the course structure and content really helped me see more! And to look outside of myself more.

Design

Participants liked different aspects of the workshop. Comments on each section are as follows:

1) Devotionals and Scripture
- Having devotions about each topic—seeing the biblical view.
- I liked it that it was based on the Bible. I didn't know that the Bible had to say that much about this topic.

2) Multicultural Mix
- Having a variety of people from different cultures made our discussion times interesting and informative.

- Through interaction with each other I could learn other cultures by real people, not by only books.
- Good to have us working together with people from other cultures.

3) Learning from the Group
- The most valuable times were hearing other members talk.
- Hearing what others are learning and processing. How they process it.
- One of the biggest things for me was hearing and learning from my colleagues about their own culture and seeing differences. It also helped me understand how my culture influenced me in my own life.
- The balance of examining my own background with other cultural types was brilliant!

4) Adult Learning Styles
- Interacting together as a class and also at table groups.
- Using illustrations like the house floor plan brought the issues to life.
- I think for me what was helpful was to be able to have different topics to consider and then think about individually and also together as a group—to learn about myself and how it impacted me and then to hear others reactions to the same circumstance.
- Being guided through very practical things to think about my own culture and family background as a source of reasons to my behavior now.
- I also really appreciated the variety of changing the seating arrangement each day and half day—it was good to mix us up and get us a bit uncomfortable.
- The skits were also an effective teaching/learning method for me.

5) Multicultural Breaks
- The "tastes" of other cultures at breaks was fun.
- Perfect fill in of the breaks with different snacks from different cultures!

6) Facilitator
- The facilitator's background was a factor, because she came from a multicultural background herself, so she had her own revelation of the difference culture makes in a person's expectations and outlook.
- The facilitator's life experiences (which she freely shared) give her great credibility. Her journey to a better understanding of this topic and its impact on her life encourages us (students) to listen and be willing to let God change us.
- The facilitator's openness and honestly really helped us to share with each other and be honest about our own cultural judging.

7) Self-discovery
- I learned that we all judge others based on our own cultural norms/values.
- It's helpful to remind myself that people are generally acting with the best of intentions, even when they offend me!
- I think the workshop was successful because it was moderated (guided), not "taught" (driven or information—"dispensed") which allowed for self-discovery. In my case, it was valuable because I was already asking some of the questions, rather than because it was required.
- I began to be more aware about me being from an institutional culture, and that others are from other cultures, and the implications of this. I want others to take rules as seriously as I do, because it is what we agreed upon, and the agreement is holy, going by it is what makes things work. I trust in rules. In the national culture, people trust in charismatic leaders, rules are things on paper, or agreements of the moment, that you can change. Americans seem to take agreements of meetings seriously, but see them as very provisional, things that you are very flexible to change quickly.
- The assumptions of others have become clearer to me through the workshop and later thinking about it, it helps my understanding and my expectations of the other cultures I am involved with.

- The breaking down the presentations into small chunks that explored the individual, cultural/formative pieces of the puzzle that make up the whole "me" was done so sensitively—in a way that didn't threaten or challenge too deeply—and really helped the process of self-revelation or awareness.
- I don't want to just serve to "translate" the Word, but rather "live" the translated Word among my colleagues and those we're trying to reach.

REMAINING CHALLENGES

Many of the challenges for the workshop arise from the history and development of SIL mainly as an American organization. SIL International and its sister organization, Wycliffe Bible Translators, were both initially incorporated in the United States and subjected to US corporate laws particularly in regards to finances. Additionally, 53 percent of its field membership and 34 percent of its administrators are from the USA. As a result, SIL's greatest challenge is for its majority members to recognize how American cultural values permeate its organizational structure, policies, and processes, creating misunderstandings and difficulties for members from other countries. This challenge includes how to make SIL structures, policies, and processes more welcoming for the twenty-first century global world. The focus of SIL and WBT's mission Vision 2025 is to begin translation work in each of the languages that need it by 2025 and more recently discussion on reinventing SIL's organizational structure to work more effectively in the twenty-first century.

American Individualism

The main American value that is a challenge for multicultural team building is individualism or the individual as the cultural ideal. This perspective has unintended consequences, including how an individual is socialized to relate to others. Wilkins and Sanford addressing individualism: "When I claim to be the primary reality in the universe, this requires that I see others either as a tool for maintaining my status or as a competitor for my place at the center" (2009, 42).

American individualism minimizes the need to learn about other cultures. People from a majority culture do not deal with cultural misunderstandings on a daily basis. It is difficult for them to understand what others are going through. Non-American participants said:

- Would appreciate more emphasis on application as a member of a minority culture understanding other cultures goes part of the way toward building healthy teams, knowing how to deal with always having to live within a different culture would be helpful. Do you choose your fights, ignore your needs, submit, or try to make a difference? I still don't know where to go with what I learned.
- I personally have felt like I am struggling to live in this community where many of the minority cultures are being snuffed out by the majority culture (American). I believe mostly because of a lack of understanding in applying biblical truth in our cultural settings.

Leadership Buy-in

The cultural ideal of individualism affects leaders who are already busy and may view multicultural training as important for others but not necessarily for themselves. In the five years I have conducted these workshops, no one from senior leadership has participated. However, several regional directors have taken the course. At the same time, the participants in each of the workshops have recommended that their administrators (directors, associate directors, and managers) take the workshop in order to understand them better. Comments from workshop participants include:

- As a group it could help having some of our authorities in the workshop.
- I would love to have the department managers and assistant managers and those in directorship to have this workshop because this will help them to understand people better.
- Personnel from leadership position should attend this kind of workshop.

In a number of locations participants have made a list of recommendations and given them to the administration but the administration has been slow to take action. This is very discouraging to the minority participants in particular.

- This is a wonderful workshop. I'm really enjoying it. But if only we put them into practice and help each other understand each other's culture better.

- More nationals must attend this workshop. Could this workshop material be translated into the national language? I would like to attend if there would be another workshop. I want to teach this to nationals.
- If our group could hold this workshop every year at least other members could get a chance to learn about each other.

American Focus on Time

The American emphasis on time presents another challenge for the workshop. The first time the workshop was offered, only two half days were made available. The nationals in particular were upset because they felt like an opportunity had been put in front of them for foreigners to understand them better and then not able to help them make changes. More recent workshops have been given five days and participants still feel there is not enough time.

- It would have been more helpful to me if the workshop was for a bit longer—like two weeks.
- I needed time on my own to reflect and digest what was impacting my head and my heart—so I would have preferred mornings only for more days.
- A less intense schedule spread out over a longer time. There is so much to process in each session, but no time, especially as the mother of small children!
- Maybe I'm processing more slowly than other people but often it is hard for me to know after each session what God is teaching me and also to share and pray with people that I don't know well.

One American participant said that it was good to learn about other cultures and hear that they value relationships, but the participant concluded they do not have enough time to both do their job and develop relationships.

Fear of Criticism

Another challenge in regard to Americans taking a multicultural team-building workshop is that some Americans are reluctant to attend because they are afraid they will get "bashed." Evidently when cultural discussions came up in the past, non-Americans criticized Americans for the way they do things. Therefore some Americans are reluctant to expose themselves to this kind of treatment. One non-American participant expressed this view:

- I'm sorry but I don't think Americans can be Christians!

This multicultural team-building workshop is one of the ways that cultural differences are being addressed. Although there are a number of challenges, particularly in an American-based organization and with American culture, these challenges are not insurmountable. However, if the top leadership is behind the need for multicultural training, and strategies and policies are in place, changes will occur more quickly (Cox 2001, 31).

CONCLUSIONS

In light of the critical need for multicultural training in SIL and in other agencies, the multicultural team-building workshop described in this article has proven to be an effective tool to help people to discover the source of their ongoing cross-cultural stress and to address it appropriately. The workshop, by taking participants back to their childhood homes, enables participants to discover how their Culture based Judging System (CbJS) reinforces their cultural type and how their ongoing stress distorts the image of God. SIL needs to address a number of challenges, however, to minimize the continuing impact of American individualism on future iterations of this training. To be more effective, future multicultural training in SIL will require more buy-in from senior leadership, recognition that the workshop requires adequate time away from other work duties, and proactive steps to address the American fear of criticism.

REFERENCES

Cox, Taylor Jr. 2001. *Creating the multicultural organization: A strategy for capturing the power of diversity.* San Francisco: Jossey-Bass.

Douglas, Mary. 1982. Cultural Bias. In *In the Active Voice.* London: Routledge and Kegan Paul.

———. 1992. *Risk and blame: Essays in cultural theory.* London: Routledge.

Wilkins, Steve, and Mark L. Sanford. 2009. *Hidden worldviews: Eight cultural stories that shape our lives.* Downers Grove: InterVarsity.

12

A BIBLICAL UNDERSTANDING OF THE DIVERSITY OF PAUL'S MISSIONARY COWORKERS

WILLIAM BROOKS

INTRODUCTION

Paul was not a loner. He developed deep, long-lasting relationships by mentoring others and training them for ministry. Paul revealed his love for the believers and his commitment to training future church leaders and missionaries when he mentioned the names of coworkers and contacts. The book of Acts and the Epistles mention one hundred different people associated with the Apostle Paul, thirty-eight of whom were coworkers (Earle 1970–71, 437–39; Schnabel 2008, 248; Michael 1995, 48). Many of these coworkers were converted by Paul and subsequently recruited out of the churches he planted (Schnabel, 255). Paul's letters reveal a man who was profoundly committed to investing in and working with others. While Paul's network of coworkers has been well documented (Ellis 1970–71; Kane 1976, 83; Schnabel 2002, 1426), the diversity of these ministry partners has not received adequate attention. I will show that Paul's coworkers were diverse in ethnicity, in gender, and in socioeconomic background. After surveying these three areas, I will make contemporary applications from the principles discovered from this study of Paul's ministry.

Two presuppositions need to be made clear before starting. First, Paul should be understood as our example in missions. Paul described himself as a "master builder" of the church (1 Cor 3:10). In commenting on this verse

Little writes, "Anyone who desires to engage in cross-cultural mission should therefore be willing to learn and benefit from [Paul's] strategy. To be unwilling to do so would imply the claim to know more about how to effectively spread the Christian message than Paul did" (Little 2005, 97). Studying Paul's life and letters serves to inform contemporary missions strategies; therefore, several applications from this study will be made in the conclusion of the paper.

Second, it must be noted that the New Testament documents do not directly address the question of Paul's coworkers. While Luke sometimes records those traveling with Paul, and Paul himself often references others in his letters, the issue of who traveled with Paul and what work they did is never explicitly stated. The information in this paper has been garnered from a study of the names of people associated with Paul and the limited information given about them in Acts and in Paul's letters.

THE ETHNIC DIVERSITY OF PAUL'S COWORKERS

The list of Paul's coworkers displays an intricate blending of people from numerous locations (See Table 7 in the chapter Appendix) (Schnabel 2002, 1426). Barnabas is from Cyprus. Silas and John Mark are from Jerusalem. Timothy is from Lystra. Luke is from Antioch. Aquila and Priscilla are from Pontus and have lived in Rome. Tychicus is from Asia. Achaicus, Fortunatus, and Stephanas are from Corinth. Apphia, Archippus, Epaphras, Onesimus, and Philemon are from Colossae. Apollos is from Alexandria. Aristarchus is from Thessalonike. Clemens, Euodia, and Syntyche are from Philippi. Phoebe is from Cenchrae. Trophimus is from Ephesus. In terms of geographic regions, this list includes people from Palestine, Galatia, Syria, Pontus, Italy, Asia, Achaia, Egypt, and Macedonia.

It is not surprising that Paul would have recruited coworkers from so many different geographical regions since the leadership of his sending church was equally diverse. In Acts 13:1 Luke explains that the leadership team of the church at Antioch, whom he calls "prophets and teachers," is comprised of five men (Bock 2007, 439). Barnabas is a Jew from Jerusalem. Saul is a Jew from Tarsus. Lucius and Simeon are from North Africa. Simeon is a black man. Manean was raised with Herod and would have had high social standing and influence with government officials. The diversity of this group laid the foundation for the diversity of Paul's future missionary coworkers.

Not only does the list of Paul's coworkers include people from numerous geographical regions, but perhaps more importantly, it reveals people from several ethnic backgrounds. Luke and Paul tend to categorize people into two ethnic groups: Jews and Gentiles. Although it is difficult to determine ethnicity from name alone (Schreiner 1998, 792), certainty of ethnicity can be gained for 70 percent of Paul's coworkers. Of that 70 percent, 48 percent are Jewish, and 48 percent are Gentile. Timothy is an exception since his mother was Jewish and his father was a Gentile.

It is important to note that Paul did not recruit people for his team because of ethnic similarity. Paul was born in Tarsus and was educated in Jerusalem under the most renowned teachers of his day (Acts 22:3). While he certainly had experience among both Jews and Gentiles because of his background, and while he certainly felt called to reach Gentiles (Rom 1:13; 11:13; 15:16–18; Gal 1:16; 2:8; Eph 3:8; 1 Tim 2:7), Paul's missionary strategy included going first to the Jewish synagogue (Acts 13:5, 14; 14:1; 17:1, 10, 17; 18:5, 19). It might seem safe to assume that when Paul trained other coworkers, he would train them to implement the same type of strategy. Since there is no New Testament evidence of a Gentile leading a Jew to Christ (Schnabel 2002, 1432), one might likewise assume that Paul would primarily recruit Jewish Christians to be part of his work. The evidence, however, strongly contradicts this second assumption. Paul did not recruit coworkers based on ethnicity but for their commitment to Christ and their willingness to do anything to see Christ's name proclaimed in unreached areas.

One example of Paul's flexibility in working with others is seen in Galatians 2:1–3. Paul was traveling with both Barnabas and Titus. Barnabas was Jewish. He became a Christian in Jerusalem either on or shortly after Pentecost, and he sold land he owned and donated the money to the church. Titus, on the other hand, was a Gentile who was possibly converted under Paul's ministry in Syria. These two believers stand in stark contrast to each other yet they were both traveling and ministering with Paul during this early period of his ministry.

While some scholars argue that Galatians 2:1–3 relates to Paul's visit during the Jerusalem council (Merkle 2005, 56; Lea and Griffin 1992, 272–73) and that Paul took Titus along as a test case, it is more likely that Galatians 2:1–3 relates to Acts 11:30 and Paul's famine visit to Jerusalem (Longenecker 1990, 46; Schnabel 2002, 1430–31). If Galatians 2:1–3 is Paul's famine visit to Jerusalem, then Paul is not taking Titus along as a test case but simply because these three men are doing ministry together. The picture is a powerful one for how the gospel can overcome ethnic barriers: Jews lead a Gentile to Christ. That Gentile becomes concerned for a church of Jews experiencing a time of famine. He then works alongside two Jews to gather a collection of money to alleviate the suffering of that Jewish church.

While Paul often traveled with others, in some cases, he worked with people in their native regions. According to Philippians 4:2–3, Paul worked with Clemens, Euodia, and Syntyche in their hometown of Philippi. He also worked with Archippus in his hometown of Colossae (Col 4:17). In addition, Paul sent coworkers back to their hometowns to complete specific ministry objectives. Tychicus is one of Paul's companions on the third missionary journey. During that time, Paul sends Tychicus back to his native region in order to deliver the letters to the Ephesians, Colossians, and Philemon (Moo 2008, 335–36; Lea and Griffin 1992, 253). Paul tells the Ephesians that Tychicus will "encourage your hearts" (Eph 6:22), which reveals that Tychicus' task is more than simply to deliver a letter. Epaphras was most likely converted during Paul's ministry in Ephesus and subsequently returned to his hometown of Colossae as a missionary (Moo 2008, 414; Schnabel 2002, 1432). Epaphras then planted a church among his own people, to whom Paul eventually wrote Colossians.

At times, though, Paul sent coworkers to minister among people of different ethnicity. Barnabas and Silas accompanied Paul on the first and second missionary journeys, respectively. Both Barnabas and Silas were Jewish and had spent most of their lives in Jerusalem among people of similar ethnic descent, but while traveling with Paul they spent a significant amount of time ministering to Gentiles.

Another example of a cross-cultural minister is Timothy. Since Timothy was the child of a mixed marriage, he had never been circumcised. Paul had Timothy circumcised (Acts 16:1) to help him gain a hearing among Jewish audiences (Bock 2007, 521–22). In later years, however, Paul sent Timothy to Ephesus, and since Ephesians is primarily written to address Gentile Christians (Lincoln 1990, lxxvi; O'Brien 1999, 50), it is safe to assume that Timothy engaged in a considerable amount of cross-cultural ministry. Likewise, Titus and Apollos both ministered in Corinth. Titus was a Gentile, and Apollos was an Alexandrian Jew. Since the church in Corinth contained a mixture of Jews and Gentiles (Garland 2003, 19; Thieselton 2000, 25; Garland 1999,

25-26), both Titus and Apollos would have ministered to those of different ethnic backgrounds.

Paul's words in Galatians 3:28 provide an apt summary of his approach to working with and reaching people of other ethnicities when he writes, "There is neither Jew nor Greek . . . for you are all one in Christ Jesus." While Paul certainly did not mean to cancel out ethnic distinctions, Schreiner is correct to note, "The decisive reality for Paul is whether one belongs to Jesus Christ" (Schreiner 2001, 401). As a result, Paul often utilized the connections and understanding that locals would have in reaching their own communities. At the same time, though, he was not afraid to send coworkers to minister among different ethnic groups in places they had never been.

THE GENDER DIVERSITY OF PAUL'S COWORKERS

Not only does the list of Paul's coworkers reveal ethnic diversity, but gender diversity is clearly present. In fact, a considerable number of Paul's coworkers were women. While women certainly did not travel with Paul, one scholar has estimated that 18 percent of those connected to Paul's mission were women (Köstenberger 2000, 225; Schnabel 2008, 251). In Table 7, 26 percent of the coworkers listed are female. These statistics make it clear that Paul was not afraid to utilize women in reaching the nations for Christ.

At the same time, however, one must not go overboard in evaluating the role women played. While 18–26 percent is a considerable amount of female involvement for the Early Church period, this calculation also means that most of Paul's coworkers were men (Köstenberger 2000, 225). To better understand the gender diversity in Paul's missionary work, it is best to start by looking at some of the women Paul references in his letters and describe the roles they played.

One of the ways that Paul utilized women was by putting them to work in reaching their communities as gospel proclaimers. In Philippians 4:2–3 Paul refers to Euodia and Syntyche as colaborers in the gospel. Although these women are engaged in some bitter disagreement that threatens the livelihood of the church, at one time they worked together with Paul in seeing the gospel proclaimed in their community. The diversity of this evangelistic group becomes clear when Paul writes that he, Euodia, Syntyche, and a man named Clement all ministered "side by side" (4:3). There is no reason to assume, though, that these two women violated cultural standards by proclaiming the gospel to men. Based on Paul's other teachings (Tit 2:3–5), it is safe to assume that these women primarily shared the gospel with other women while Paul and Clement shared with men.

Another of Paul's female coworkers was a single woman named Phoebe. Paul commends Phoebe to the church in Rome in Romans 16:1. Most scholars conclude from this commendation that Phoebe was the bearer of the letter to the Romans (Mounce 1995, 272; Schreiner 1998, 786; Jewett 2007, 943). In this commendation, Paul refers to her as a "deacon" of the church. While it is not likely that she served as the leader of the church in Cenchrae (Harrison and Hagner 2008, 226), it is highly possible that she served Paul as a missionary patron (16:2) (Schnabel 2002, 1435) or that she served the church by either ministering to the needy (Köstenberger 2000, 229) or by leading evangelistic endeavors to other women. Once again, though, there is no evidence in Romans 16:1–2 that Phoebe served in a position of authority over the entire church (Köstenberger 2000, 229).

In the same way that Paul worked with single women, he also worked alongside married women. The married woman whom Paul mentions more than any other is Priscilla (Acts 18:2, 18, 26; Rom 16:3; 1 Cor 16:19; 1 Tim 4:19). Priscilla and her husband, Aquila, were Jewish Christians and were forced to leave Rome in AD 49 when Emperor Claudius' edict commanded all Jews to leave Rome because of a disturbance concerning Christ (Acts 18:1–2) (Thieselton 2000, 1347). The couple met Paul in Corinth, where they worked as tentmakers. With Paul, they served as missionaries who planted churches, hosted house church meetings, and discipled believers everywhere they went (Köstenberger 2000, 228; Lea and Griffin 1992, 259; Schreiner 1998, 795).

What is interesting about Priscilla is that in four of the six places in the New Testament where she and her husband are mentioned, Priscilla's name is mentioned first (Acts 18:18, 26; Rom 16:3; 2 Tim 4:19; cf. Acts 18:2; 1 Cor 16:19). While some scholars interpret this to mean that Priscilla was of a higher social status than Aquila (Dunn 1988, 892; Jewett 2007, 956), it is more likely that she held greater prominence because of her Christian service (Polhill 1992, 382; Harrison and Hagner 2008, 228). There is no doubt that Priscilla played an important role in Paul's missionary work and that she was as involved in the work as her husband (Schreiner 1998, 795).

Paul also mentions a number of other female coworkers in the last chapter of Romans. In fact, of the individuals that Paul mentions by name in Romans 16, 32 percent are female. In addition to Phoebe and Priscilla, Paul also sends greetings to female coworkers named Mary, Junia, Tryphaena, Tryphosa, Persis. In describing Mary's and Persis' ministries, Paul uses the term, "worked hard," which he also uses to explain his own ministry to the churches he planted (1 Cor 4:12; Phil 2:16; Col 1:29) (Dunn 1988, 893–94). It is a hermeneutical fallacy, though, to conclude that the similar terminology means that these women had the exact same ministry as Paul did (Köstenberger 2000, 226). Paul uses the term to show that these women extended tremendous effort and made considerable sacrifices in order to minister to others (Köstenberger 2000, 232).

One of the women mentioned in Romans 16 is Junia, who is mentioned along with her husband Andronicus. Paul describes them as "outstanding among the apostles." The easiest way to understand what Paul means by this phrase is that this couple is an esteemed traveling missionary team (Köstenberger 2000, 231). While it is likely that Junia's role in their ministry was focused primarily on reaching other women (Schnabel 2002, 1432–33; Schreiner 1998, 797; Schreiner 2001, 401), there is no way to know the specifics of her ministry with any certainty.

Paul's utilization of both single and married women in missionary efforts speaks of the social revolution implemented by Christians in the first century (Jewett 2007, 961). It was revolutionary for women to play any role at all in Paul's missionary work since women "had no public rights or influence but were entirely under the *potestas* [power] of their husbands" (Green 1970, 118). Despite their lack of power and influence, though, women clearly played a significant role in Paul's missionary enterprise.

At the same time, there is no reason to assume, as some scholars do, that these women assumed leadership roles contrary to 1 Timothy 2:11–15 (Dunn 1988, 900; Jewett 2007, 961). While women played a crucial role in the spread of the gospel during the Early Church period, no evidence exists in the New Testament that women ever pursued ministries in contradiction with Paul's teachings in his letters. Köstenberger helpfully notes that for Paul "equality in worth and dignity does not mean equality in function in role" (Köstenberger 2000, 237). Nonetheless, the diversity of Paul's coworkers is seen in the fact that women did play a vital role as they worked with Paul to advance God's kingdom.

THE SOCIOECONOMIC DIVERSITY OF PAUL'S COWORKERS

As the list of Paul's coworkers reveals ethnic and gender diversity, it also reveals a socioeconomic diversity. Paul's coworkers were from a wide range of backgrounds: a doctor, an entrepreneurial couple, a city treasurer, several others displaying high social status, a number of freed slaves, and at least one current slave. This diversity shows that when Paul recruited coworkers, he did not distinguish between the various social classes of society. He was willing to work with anyone who was committed to advancing God's kingdom.

One person who displays the socioeconomic diversity of Paul's coworkers is Luke. Luke is best known as the author of the Gospel of Luke and of Acts. Since Luke does not name himself in either work, little is known about his background (Melick 1991, 30). Some information can be pieced together from the "we" passages in Acts (Acts 16:8–17; 20:5–15; 21:1–18; 27:1–28:16), where Luke lets the reader know that he is traveling with Paul. Most of what is known about Luke, though, comes from Colossians 4:14 where Paul explains that Luke is both a Gentile and a doctor (Moo 2008, 347). To write such an expansive work and to perform his tasks as a doctor proves that Luke clearly was an educated man. The extent of the "we" passages conveys that he traveled abundantly with Paul and played an important role in Paul's ministry.

The missionary couple, Aquila and Priscilla, likewise displays socioeconomic diversity. Based on their names, they were most likely former slaves who, once freed, developed their own leather and tentmaking business (Acts 18:3) (Thieselton 2000, 1343). Their ability to relocate for the sake of mission means that they were well-to-do business owners, and quite possibly the founders of the church in Ephesus (Murphy-O'Connor 1996, 171; Garland 2003, 772; Dunn 1988, 892).

Another coworker of Paul's who was of high social standing was Erastus. In Romans 16:32 Paul describes Erastus as the city treasurer of Corinth. Erastus is also mentioned in Acts 19:22 and 2 Timothy 4:20, which indicates that he traveled with Paul and ministered with him in Macedonia. Schnabel notes that the evidence indicates that Erastus was quite wealthy (Schnabel 2002, 1432). If so, Erastus likely helped Paul by both ministering at his side and funding his work.

In contrast to the economic status of the workers already considered, the majority of Paul's coworkers were freed slaves. In the greetings of Romans 16, most of the names are common among slaves and former slaves (Dunn 1988, 900). Dunn notes, "This gives a fairly clear picture of the extent to which the first Christian groups in Rome drew their strength from the lower strata of Roman society" (Dunn 1988, 900). Of those in Table 7, whose background is certain, 47 percent are former slaves. The abundance of former slaves, most of whom would have still been considered lower class, reveals the socioeconomic diversity of Paul's team.

One final coworker to consider is Onesimus. Onesimus was a runaway slave who was led to Christ under Paul's ministry (Moo 2008, 368–69; O'Brien 1999, 266; Schreiner 2001, 435). The belief of the day was that Phrygian slaves were unreliable and unfaithful, and as Philemon's slave, Onesimus personified those negative traits (O'Brien 1999, 292). The change he experienced when he came to Christ, though, was nothing short of miraculous. Paul explains this transformation with a wordplay: while he was once "useless," he is now "useful" (Phlm 11) (Moo 2008, 409; O'Brien 1999, 292). Despite Paul's desire to continue utilizing the runaway's services, for the sake of the gospel he knows he must send Onesimus back to Philemon (Melick 1991, 362–63). Paul's commendation of and work with a runaway slave displays the socioeconomic diversity that characterized his ministry.

Paul did not solely work or communicate with those who were most apt to help his ministry financially or politically, but he worked with all those committed to the spread of the gospel, even those of the lowest strata of society. Rich or poor, slave or free, if someone was willing to labor to see Christ's name exalted in a dying, lost world, Paul would work with them.

CONCLUSION AND APPLICATIONS

Now that the lives of Paul's coworkers have been considered in some detail, it is necessary to make some contemporary applications.

Missionary Work is Done Best in a Team Context

First, because Paul's missionary work was conducted in the context of a team, contemporary missionaries should recognize the value of team structures. With the exception of Athens (even while there Luke writes in Acts 17:16 that Paul was waiting for others), Paul always traveled with and ministered alongside other believers. The reality of this practice has ramifications for how missionary organizations send people to the field and for how they organize the work done on the field. Implementing Paul's team-driven approach means that there would be no more "See you in six months" types of supervisor-personnel relationships, but supervisors would see other personnel as younger team members in need of discipling. Nor would missionary personnel be so isolated that they end up burned out and headed home, but they would be organized for maximum encouragement and accountability.

Equip Indigenous Leaders to Reach Their Own Communities

Second, since Paul utilized existing relationships by sending converts to minister among their native regions, contemporary missionaries ought to seek to equip and empower national leaders to reach their own communities. In sending Epaphras back to Colossae, Paul took advantage of Epaphras' emic perspective of Colossian culture. He also made use of the existing network of relationships that Epaphras naturally had as a member of that society. Before sending Epaphras, though, Paul certainly spent countless hours preparing him for the task ahead.

Train Leaders for Both Evangelism and Theology

Third, and along the same lines, today's missionaries must also be freed to train national leaders practically, evangelistically, and theologically. If indigenous leaders are going to reach their own communities in Epaphras-style missions, missionaries must expend the time and energy to train them both for evangelistic effectiveness and theological fidelity. Missionaries must teach national leaders to read and interpret Scripture in a way in which they are able to apply biblical truth to their own cultural contexts. (I am aware of the difficulties in reaching and training oral learners. While there are a number of positive short-term approaches to reaching and teaching oral learners, for the long-term health of the church, leaders must be taught to read so that they interact with the fullness of revelation in the written word.) The most helpful model for this process is Paul Hiebert's critical contextualization in which the missionary and the indigenous church work together to examine cultural practices in light of biblical teaching (Hiebert 1985, 186–90).

Cross-cultural as Well as Indigenous Workers Are Essential

Fourth, the fact that Paul sent coworkers to minister in cross-cultural settings likewise has ramifications for contemporary missions. The fact that some Western missions organizations say to believers in the West, "We want your money but not your people," is not revolutionary, but both foolish and nearsighted. Completion of the Great Commission will require both Epaphras-type indigenous missionaries and Timothy/Titus-type cross-cultural missionaries. As God calls some to shepherd their own people through pastoral leadership and some to evangelize their own people through itinerant missionary work, God also calls some to cross-cultural ministries.

Moreover, missionaries must recognize that God may convert some through their ministries who are called to minister cross-culturally. Paul never grew so concerned for the work in one area that he stopped thinking about the unreached areas of his world (Rom 15:20). As a result he recognized that while many of his converts would become advocates for the gospel among their own people, some would be called out to share the gospel with other peoples. Missionaries, then, must encourage even young national churches to begin considering whom God might be calling out to take the name of Jesus to peoples who have never heard it.

One Ethnicity Is Not of Greater Value Than Another

Fifth, since Paul did not consider one ethnicity of greater value in reaching the nations than any other, contemporary missionaries should not either. The implications being made by one missionary strategist who said, "All the teams effectively reaching their people in this area have Asians on them," are dangerous. (Although it may seem from the quote that this missionary was simply stating what he had observed, in our conversation he made this statement as evidence for why he was only recruiting Asians for his team.) Paul did not single out those of Jewish faith who were more familiar with the Scriptures, but he ministered alongside anyone whom God gifted and impassioned for the task.

Carefully Consider the Role of Women in Missions

Sixth, Paul's willingness to utilize single and married women in his missionary work means that contemporary missiologists must continue to support women missionaries, and they must celebrate the long-lasting legacy of faithful missionary women. From Ann Judson to Lottie Moon to Elisabeth Elliot, the list of women missionary heroes is a long one. For the sake of the next generation of women missionaries, missiologists must continue to celebrate the faithful work done years ago by women committed to the cause of Christ.

At the same, though, contemporary missionary leaders must take caution that we do not let the praxis of utilizing women workers take priority over the biblical theology of women in ministry. Two of the pressing missiological issues of the day are the lack of young male missionaries in some parts of the world and the lack of male leadership in many national churches. The inherent theological difficulty is that women missionaries and indigenous leaders are often forced to make difficult decisions about whether to conduct ministries in violation of 1 Timothy 2 or allow the work to be undone. I believe mission leaders must allow a biblical understanding of women's ministry to guide the roles that women play in reaching the world.

Multiple Socioeconomic Levels Must Be Represented

Seventh, since Paul valued and utilized the work of people from numerous social classes, contemporary missionaries must do the same. While students of missions have often debated the top-down approach of Alexander Duff and the bottom-up approach of Rufus Anderson (Beaver 1967), Paul targeted both the lower and upper classes. Not only did he target them in evangelistic endeavors, but he also worked with both in the continuing work of missions. While targeting one socioeconomic segment can often be an effective church-planting tool, missionaries must not limit themselves to one segment of society, but they must ultimately seek to connect with multiple individuals on multiple socioeconomic levels.

Paul's missionary team was a diverse team. Diversity was the outcome of what it means to be reconciled to God through Christ Jesus. Paul explains this truth in Ephesians 2:15 when he speaks of Jesus who "made us both one and has broken down in his flesh the dividing wall of hostility." In Jesus, believers are not only reconciled to God but to those of other ethnicities, genders, and socioeconomic classes from whom they were formerly separated.

Galatians 3:28 is again a helpful reminder where Paul writes, "There is neither Jew nor Greek, there is neither slave nor free, there is neither male nor female, for you are all one in Christ Jesus." Ethnic, socioeconomic, and gender diversity happens as a result of being united in Christ. Paul did not seek diversity for diversity's sake alone, but for the purpose of exalting Christ. The goal of his ministry was the exaltation of Christ, and Christ is greatly exalted when the sound of his praise is echoed in more and more places by more and more peoples in more and more tongues for the glory of his name.

APPENDIX

The sections of Table 7 with information concerning name, hometown, and location of missionary work are taken from Schnabel 2002, 1426. The line after Tychicus indicates that the first eight coworkers are mentioned more frequently than those listed in numbers 9–38.

Table 7: Information on Paul's Coworkers

Coworker	Hometown	Gender	Ethnicity	Strata	Location of Missionary Work
1. Barnabas	Jerusalem	Male	Jewish	?	Antioch, Cyprus, Galatia
2. Timothy	Lystra	Male	Mixed	?	Macedonia, Achaia, Thessalonike, Ephesus, Corinth
3. Luke	Antioch (?)	Male	Gentile	Doctor	Antioch (?), Macedonia, Philippi
4. Aquila	Rome	Male	Jewish	Business owner	Corinth, Ephesus, house church in Rome
5. Priscilla	Rome	Female	Jewish	Business owner	Corinth, Ephesus, house church in Rome
6. Silas	Jerusalem	Male	Jewish	High (Roman citizen)	Macedonia, Achaia
7. Titus	?	Male	Gentile	?	Antioch, Corinth, Crete, Dalmatia
8. Tychicus	Asia	Male	Gentile	?	Colossae, Ephesus, Crete
9. Achaicus	Corinth	Male	Gentile	Freed slave	Ephesus (1 Cor 16:17)
10. Andronicus	?	Male	Jewish	Freed slave	?, then Rome (1 Cor 16:17)
11. Apphia	Colossae	Female	?	?	see Philemon (Phlm 2)
12. Apollos	Alexandria	Male	Jewish	High (well educated)	Achaia, Corinth, Ephesus, Crete
13. Archippus	Colossae	Male	?	?	Colossae (Col 4:17)

Coworker	Hometown	Gender	Ethnicity	Strata	Location of Missionary Work
14. Aristarchus	Thessalonike	Male	Jewish	?	Ephesus, Jerusalem, Caesarea
15. Clement	Philippi	Male	?	?	? (Phil 4:3)
16. Crescens	?	Male	?	?	Rome, Galatia or Gaul (2 Tim 4:10)
17. Demas	?	Male	?	?	Rome (Col 4:14; Phlm 24; 2 Tim 4:10)
18. Epaphras	Colossae	Male	Jewish	?	Ephesus, Colossae, Laodikeia, Hierapolis
19. Epaphroditus	Philippi	Male	Gentile	?	Rome (Phil 2:25–30)
20. Erastus	Corinth	Male	Gentile	City Treasurer	Ephesus, Macedonia (Acts 19:22)
21. Euodia	Philippi	Female	?	?	Philippi (Phil 4:2–3)
22. Fortunatus	Corinth	Male	Gentile	Freed slave?	Ephesus (1 Cor 16:1)
23. Junia	?	Female	Jewish	Freed slave	?, then Rome (Rom 16:7)
24. Jesus Justus	?	Male	Jewish	?	? (Col 4:11)
25. John Mark	Jerusalem	Male	Jewish	?	Antioch, Cyprus, Rome
26. Mary	?	Female	Jewish	Freed slave?	?, then Rome (Rom 16:6)
27. Onesimus	Colossae	Male	Gentile	Slave	? (Philem 13)
28. Quartus	?	Male	?	?	Corinth (Rom 16:23)
29. Persis	?	Female	?	Freed slave	?, then Rome (Rom 16:12)
30. Philemon	Colossae	Male	Gentile		Laodikeia ? (Philem 1)

Coworker	Hometown	Gender	Ethnicity	Strata	Location of Missionary Work
31. Phoebe	Cenchreae	Female	Gentile	High standing	Corinth, Rome (Rom 16:1)
32. Sosthenes	?	Male	?	?	Ephesus (1 Cor 1:1)
33. Stephanas	Corinth	Male	Gentile	High standing	Achaia, Corinth, Ephesus (1 Cor 16:15, 17)
34. Syntyche	Philippi	Female	?	?	Philippi (Phil 4:2–3)
35. Trophimus	Ephesus	Male	Gentile	?	Macedonia, Achaia, Asia
36. Tryphaena	?	Female	?	Freed slave	?, then Rome (Rom 16:12)
37. Tryphosa	?	Female	?	Freed slave	?, then Rome (Rom 16:12)
38. Urbanus	?	Male	?	?	?, then Rome (Rom 16:9)

REFERENCES

Beaver, R. Pierce. 1967. Introduction: Rufus Anderson, grand strategist of American missions. In *To advance the gospel: Selections from the writings of Rufus Anderson*, ed. R. Pierce Beaver. Grand Rapids: Eerdmans.

Bock, Darrell L. 2007. *Acts*. Baker Exegetical Commentary on the New Testament. Ed. Robert Yarbrough and Robert H. Stein. Grand Rapids: Baker Academic.

Dunn, James D. G. 1988. *Romans 9–16. Word Biblical Commentary*, vol. 38b. Ed. David A. Hubbard and Glenn W. Barker. Dallas: Word.

Ellis, E. Earle. 1970–71. Paul and his coworkers. *New Testament Studies* 17: 437–39.

Garland, David E. 1999. *2 Corinthians. The New American Commentary Series*, vol. 29. Ed. E. Ray Clendenen. Nashville: B&H.

———. 2003. *1 Corinthians*. Baker Exegetical Commentary on the New Testament. Ed. Robert Yarbrough and Robert H. Stein. Grand Rapids: Baker Academic.

Green, Michael. 1970. *Evangelism in the Early Church*. Grand Rapids: Eerdmans.

Harrison, Everett F., and Donald A. Hagner. 2008. *Romans. The Expositors Bible Commentary: Romans—Galatians*, vol. 11. Ed. Tremper Longman III and David E. Garland. Grand Rapids: Zondervan.

Hesselgrave, David J. 2000. *Planting churches cross-culturally: North America and beyond*, 2d ed. Grand Rapids: Baker Academic.

———. 2005. *Paradigms in conflict: 10 key questions in Christian missions today*. Grand Rapids: Kregel.

Hiebert, Paul. 1985. *Anthropological insights for missionaries*. Grand Rapids: Baker.

Jewett, Robert. 2007. *Romans. Hermeneia*, ed. Eldon Jay Epp. Minneapolis: Fortress.

Kane, J. Herbert. 1976. *Christian missions in biblical perspective*. Grand Rapids: Baker, 1976.

Köstenberger, Andreas J. 2000. Women in the Pauline mission. In *The gospel to the nations: Perspectives on Paul's mission*, ed. Peter Bolt and Mark Thompson, 221–47. Downers Grove: InterVarsity.

Lea, Thomas D., and Hayne P. Griffin Jr. 1992. *1, 2 Timothy, Titus. The New American Commentary Series*, vol. 34. Ed. David S. Dockery. Nashville: Broadman.

Lincoln, Andrew T. 1990. *Ephesians*. Dallas: Word.

Little, Christopher R. 2005. Mission in the way of Paul: Biblical mission for the Church in the twenty-first century. *Studies in Biblical Literature*, vol. 80. New York: Peter Lang.

Longenecker, Richard N. 1990. *Galatians. Word Biblical Commentary*, vol. 41. Ed. Bruce M. Metzger, David A. Hubbard, and Glen W. Barker. Nashville: Thomas Nelson.

Marshall, I. Howard. 2000. Luke's portrait of the Pauline mission. In *The gospel to the nations: Perspectives on Paul's mission*, ed. Peter Bolt and Mark Thompson, 99–113. Downers Grove: InterVarsity.

Martin, D. Michael. 1995. *1, 2 Thessalonians. The New American Commentary Series*, vol. 33. Ed. E. Ray Clendenen. Nashville: B&H.

Melick, Richard R. Jr. 1991. *Philippians Colossians Philemon. The New American Commentary Series*, vol. 32. Ed. David S. Dockery. Nashville: Broadman.

Merkle, Benjamin L. 2005. The need for theological education in missions: Lessons learned from the Church's greatest missionary. *The Southern Baptist Journal of Theology* 9: 56.

Moo, Douglas. 2008. *The letters to the Colossians and to Philemon.* The Pillar New Testament Commentary. Ed. D. A. Carson. Grand Rapids: Eerdmans.

Mounce, Robert H. 1995. *Romans. The New American Commentary Series,* vol. 27. Ed. E. Ray Clendenen. Nashville: B&H.

Murphy-O'Connor, Jerome. 1996. *Paul: A critical life.* New York: Oxford University Press.

O'Brien, Peter T. 1999. *The letter to the Ephesians. The Pillar New Testament Commentary.* Ed. D. A. Carson. Grand Rapids: Eerdmans.

Polhill, John B. 1992. *Acts. The New American Commentary Series,* vol. 26. Ed. David S. Dockery. Nashville: B&H.

Schnabel, Eckhard J. 2002. *Early Christian mission.* Downers Grove: InterVarsity.

———. 2008. *Paul the missionary: Realities, strategies and methods.* Downers Grove: InterVarsity.

Schreiner, Thomas R. 1998. *Romans. Baker Exegetical Commentary on the New Testament.* Ed. Moises Silva. Grand Rapids: Baker Academic.

———. 2001. *Paul, apostle of God's glory in Christ: A Pauline theology.* Downers Grove: InterVarsity.

Thieselton, Anthony C. 2000. *The first epistle to the Corinthians: A commentary on the Greek text.* The New International Greek Testament Commentary. Ed. I. Howard Marshall and Donald A. Hagner. Grand Rapids: Eerdmans.

PART III

UNDERSTANDING AND FACING DIVERSITY

13

DIFFERENT FOR GOD'S GREATER GLORY: BENEFITS OF AND BARRIERS TO EMBRACING ETHNIC AND GENERATIONAL DIVERSITY IN MISSION LEADERSHIP

KENHITI KATAYAMA AND JOHN KILMARNOCK

God is glorified when those God has redeemed from among peoples all over the earth work together for the advancement God's kingdom among all nations. Scripture recognizes diversity among the members of Christ's body, but glories in the fact that this diversity finds unity in Christ (Eph 2, 4). Unity in diversity shows Jesus to be Lord over all cultures and ethnicities and shouts to the world that following Jesus is not simply a tribal affinity, but that God's kingdom transcends all others and breaks down any barriers that purpose to divide those who belong to him (John 17:13–26).

The Lausanne movement's call to action for "the whole Church to take the whole gospel to the whole world" (http://www.lausanne.org/global-conversation/whole-gospel-whole-church-whole-world.html) speaks to the issue of diversity in mission leadership. It is God's mission and God's desires, and one day, God will have worshippers from every tribe tongue and nation. Every believer must find where they fit in God's mission for God's glory through which all the peoples of the earth will be blessed.

If participating in the Great Commission is nonnegotiable for all who come to follow Christ then we should naturally expect to see leaders emerge from every people in which the gospel takes root and the church grows. Also, Jesus exhorted his followers to unity (John 17:13–26) and Paul repeatedly makes the case that we are parts of one body, and that we are one in Christ

Jesus (Eph 4; Col 3). Certainly the unity that our Lord and the apostles had in mind was more than the mere ability to get along with one another without quarreling. The parts of a body do far more than peacefully coexist, they function together, being interdependent parts of the same organism. This necessitates on our part an intentional effort to work together within the universal church in a way that maximizes our strengths and makes the fullest use of the broad range of knowledge, skills, abilities, resources, and gifts that are found distributed throughout the body of Christ covering the earth. It is toward a global view of mission leadership and diversity at the decision-making table that this paper aims.

This paper focuses on a global mission movement and the example of one leader who serves in a key leadership role within that movement whose story illustrates the movement's approach to both ethnic and generational diversity. This study examines how the vision and values of this movement work themselves out into diversity in leadership. It also looks at what factors exist within the movement that prevent barriers to diversity in mission leadership and those that encourage this diversity. Furthermore, it examines the barriers to and the benefits of generational and ethnic diversity as experienced by this movement.

THE STORY OF A YOUNG GLOBAL MISSION MOVEMENT

This organization uses the term "movement" to describe itself. It sees itself as being more of a movement than an institution. The distinction here speaks to the way in which an organization structures itself. For our purposes, a movement is typified by being organized around a common vision, has leaders that share common goals, is highly relational in nature, and thus spreads based on its relational network, has a relatively "flat" leadership structure, is team oriented, and tends toward empowering, rather than managing its members. This description of the qualities of a movement is contrasted with that of a more institutional structure that tends toward being organized around by-laws and ground rules, has more elaborate and formalized policies and procedures, is more bureaucratic and compartmentalized, relies more on procedure and process, has a more "top-down" system of leadership, formalized methods for organizational growth, focuses on managing rather than empowering, and while personal relationships may exist between leaders they are not a key basis for binding the organization together.

(For a helpful discussion on this topic see Tim Keller's discussion of this subject at http://christianresearchnetwork.com/?p=17772.)

The movement we are looking at was formed in the late 1980s by two North Americans. From its inception the movement had the goal of seeing churches planted among unreached people groups. The first area that the movement focused on was the countries of the former Soviet Union in Eastern Europe. Around the same time one of the cofounders went to South America to mobilize believers in a specific country on that continent. Over the last few years the movement has grown to include four "sending bases," parts of the movement based in specific geographic locations that focus on sending workers from reached people groups to unreached people groups. Each sending base is a national corporation with its own legal name and board. They have the autonomy to function independently, so the structure is less like a hierarchy and more like a spider web. In order to keep the movement moving forward together with the same values and vision, an International Leadership Team was created. The team is comprised of key leaders from the sending bases and the field as well as board members. This team meets every eighteen months to help guide the movement.

The movement goes beyond empowering national leaders, to viewing ministry together as a partnership from the outset as leaders emerge or are drawn to the movement. This movement exists not as four independent mission agencies working together in close partnership, but because they are bound so closely by a common vision, values, strategy, and strong relational ties among the leadership; the movement functions like a single organism. As one leader within the movement described it, "We are a very tightly integrated movement."

The leadership of the movement is not dominated by North Americans either. A good example is the leader who is tasked with a position best described as the chief operating officer for the North American office, who is a thirty-year-old South American of Japanese descent. This leader initially served in the South American sending base of the movement for six years before moving to North America and serving in that office for the last five years.

AN ENVIRONMENT OF ETHNIC AND GENERATIONAL DIVERSITY IN LEADERSHIP

So, what conditions exist within this movement that have created an environment where ethnic and generational diversity in leadership have become a reality? This is a relatively young movement and two elements in particular have had a big impact on how this movement views and practices ethnic and generational diversity from the start.

From the Reached to the Unreached

The first key element has to do with how the movement expresses the way in which the gospel travels; not from the West to the rest, but rather from the reached to the unreached. The movement's founders believe that diversity of leadership is inherent in this concept. If those who reach a given people group focus on multiplication of leaders, are very relational, and work to impart a passion for God's glory among all nations to this newly reached group, as leaders emerge, partnerships will be formed. Being structured as a movement as opposed to a more rigid hierarchical organization helps in this regard. There are fewer issues of territory and control, but rather than relying on the bonds of common vision, values, strong interpersonal relationship, and trust, the focus is shifted to how the strengths, resources, gifts, and abilities of all parties involved can be combined in order to reach others with the good news.

For a period of its history, this movement focused on church planting in Eastern Europe. When the first successful church plant was realized, the leaders began to impart this "From the Reached to the Unreached" philosophy. Early on, the movement leaders wanted this church not only to multiply but to think cross-culturally, to help the new, growing church see how it fits in the task of taking the gospel to the ends of the earth as opposed to regarding those who brought the gospel to them as the "real missionaries." Eventually more churches were planted and leaders within this people group began to emerge. The movement helped to develop leadership training and formed partnerships with national leaders, which eventually led to the formation of an autonomous branch of the movement being formed in this country.

In the early stages of growth of the movement, this "From the Reached to the Unreached" philosophy and the resulting value placed on diversity in leadership worked itself out in other tangible ways as well. As the movement saw fruit in the mobilization ministry in which it was engaging in South America, a South American leader was invited to join the North American board of the movement, even before the South American portion of the movement developed its own board. This showed in a practical way the movement's commitment to ethnic diversity in its leadership.

Second, as we mentioned earlier, as the movement grew further, leaders identified the need for the formation of an International Leadership Team. This team would seek to guide the movement by giving a forum to discuss specific ministry initiatives that the various parts of the movement could partner together to accomplish. The International Leadership Team also provides a means of continued relational contact as well as serving to strengthen movement-wide commitment to the common vision and values. Even though the movement was founded by two North Americans and, at that stage in the movement's history, the majority of those involved in leadership of the movement were North Americans, a leader from South America was chosen to head the International Leadership Team for the first two years of its existence. Again, this affirmed in practice what the leaders were committed to in principle.

Multiplying Leaders

The second key element has to do with the way in which the movement seeks to multiply leaders. Raising up the next generation of leaders is seen as strategic for the growth of the movement, and more importantly for carrying out the Great Commission. In talking with key leaders within the movement, all of them placed very high priority on mentoring young leaders. The agency values youthfulness so that the movement carries on. This is not to say that the movement values youthfulness over and above or to the exclusion of leaders above an arbitrarily set age limit. Rather the movement seeks to identify and develop young, emerging leaders so as to insure capable, dynamic leadership in the future. The qualifying factor here is maturity, not simply age. This practice finds its roots early in the movement's history. One of the cofounders was nineteen years old when he was invited to help lay the foundation for the movement almost twenty-five years ago. Years later this same leader was instrumental in mentoring, coaching, and training the young South American leader who currently serves in a key leadership role in the North American office.

The movement is team focused, so the emphasis is not on raising up the "Next Great Leader" to guide the movement, but rather the "Next Generation of Leaders" that will guide and expand the movement and in turn identify the following generation of potential young leaders and mentor and empower them as they emerge (2 Tim 2:2).

BENEFITS OF DIVERSITY IN LEADERSHIP

The "From the Reached to the Unreached" philosophy and the desire to raise the next generation of leaders permeates the culture of the movement, greatly increasing the likelihood that these values will be continually passed on beyond those who are currently responsible for leadership. It is worth noting that the movement's network of leaders has grown by multiplying leaders from within the movement as well as by the addition of those who, while already involved in God's mission, join the movement because they see value in the vision of the movement and its network of relationships. So what benefits does this movement realize from having ethnically and generationally diverse leadership? Four main areas of benefit came to the forefront in the interviews with leaders.

Thinking More Clearly about Culture

By having leaders with a broader range of ages and ethnicities guiding the movement, the leadership team can "see" better. Diversity gives the leadership team a wider base of experiences, as well as varied cultural and generational perspectives to draw from when making decisions or crafting ministry strategy in a given area. As long as good team dynamics are employed in the process, all other things being equal, a more diverse leadership team results in stronger decisions with broader support among the leaders and throughout the movement.

Related to this is that the diversity represented in the movement's leadership makes the movement as a whole, and its individual members, more sensitive to culture in general. Because the leadership is constantly working with a multicultural dynamic internally, it makes the movement more sensitive to cultural issues in planning and carrying out ministry strategy. In short, it helps the movement think more clearly about culture.

Team Unity

Having a diverse leadership team also serves to increase unity within the movement. At first this may seem counterintuitive, but in practice this benefit becomes visible. Because diversity allows a wider variety of viewpoints and concerns to be voiced in the decision-making process, it guards against an "Us against Them" mentality. Because the movement is guided by the "From the Reached to the Unreached" philosophy and leadership is comprised of people from various ethnicities, it is clear to all parties that everyone in the movement is "us" and all of "us" are trying to reach "them" with the message of Jesus Christ so that God may be glorified.

Also, because younger emerging leaders are empowered to lead while being mentored, they do not feel stifled or ignored because they play a vital role in guiding the work that is being done. At the same time the younger leaders are more willing to receive guidance from the older, more experienced leaders because they see that their input is valued. This does not mean that differences of ethnic and cultural background or age simply disappear, but because the leadership is not monoethnic or heavily weighted to one end of the age spectrum, everyone stays keenly aware that they are all quite literally on the same team.

Confidence in a Biblical Approach to Leadership

Another benefit derived from an ethnically and generationally diverse leadership team is confidence, in that diversity of leadership in these areas is biblical. Surely Paul's words to Timothy regarding the training of other men who would in turn train others also (2 Tim 2:2) apply to mission leadership. Timothy was not an old man by any standard and was heavily engaged in ministry and emerging as a leader when Paul penned these words to him.

Also, no convincing argument can be made against ethnic diversity in mission leadership on the basis of Scripture. Ethnocentric leadership cannot be chosen as the lesser of two perceived "evils," the other being loss of control. The desire to move forward biblically must outweigh pragmatic concerns that seek to avoid being "slowed down" by the issues that are inherent in culturally and ethnically diverse leadership teams. Surely the Lord who will receive glory for all eternity from redeemed worshippers coming from every tribe, tongue, and nation, also receives glory here and now when ethnically diverse leaders work side-by-side for the advance of the kingdom and the glory of the King.

OVERCOMING DIFFICULTIES IN DIVERSE LEADERSHIP TEAMS

What then are the difficulties in opting for greater diversity? To be sure there are choices to be made and some barriers that must be overcome for diversity of any type to develop and bear fruit within a mission leadership team.

Leadership Structure

The first observation regarding possible barriers from studying this movement is that leadership structure impacts leadership diversity. One of the choices this movement made early on was to function *as a movement*, thus choosing greater plurality of leadership as it grew rather than creating a hierarchy and being paternalistic. To be sure, they worked through their own issues in this regard, but as the movement spread, a region that at first received workers began to see churches planted and then began to send out workers. The movement not only empowered and encouraged these new national leaders, but treated the newly created sending base in that country as standing on equal footing; as a new partner rather than as a subordinate. Because they view diversity as a way to maximize the strengths of the various parts of the movement by working together in a complementary way, the fact that the various partners all come to the table with a different mix of resources is viewed as a contribution not a deficiency.

Young, Emerging Leaders

Plugging young, emerging leaders into leadership and helping them find their best fit by giving them freedom to lead and learn, while providing guidance to grow and develop, allows this movement to reap the benefits of young eyes and minds. The young leader that we focused on in this case study mentioned that he felt that this movement was a good fit for him because he could actually engage in what he felt called to do. He knew he was being mentored, but did not feel micromanaged.

Trust

Also, trust is essential for any leadership structure to function well and a lack of trust can be an insurmountable obstacle to any group of people working together. Every leader within this movement that we talked with credited the highly relational culture of the movement with creating an atmosphere of trust and goodwill within the movement's International Leadership Team, as well as between individual leaders.

Good Communication

The movement's leaders also place a high value on communication. This seems like an obvious choice, but with the number of languages and cultures involved, communication, and thus perceived progress, happens more slowly.

The movement adopted English as their working language for meetings because it had the most universal overlap among the leaders. For some of the leaders involved, English is their second or even third language. As a result, it takes more time to be sure everyone has truly had a chance to hear and to be heard, to understand and to be understood.

This pace can be trying, especially for team members with a "Let's get it done!" attitude, but as we mentioned earlier, the resulting decisions are stronger and have broader support across the movement, so patience is required, and it pays off. Also, different members of the International Leadership Team have very different personalities and leadership styles. It has been important, especially early on, not to let one leader dominate because they are the strongest personality, or to let one culture dominate the discussion simply because they are the majority voice.

Finances

Another area that has potential for difficulty in diverse mission leadership is that of finances. One can hardly imagine a discussion of mission work today that does not at some point address the topic of money. Much has been written in recent years discussing and debating the role and proper use of financial resources in furthering kingdom work; a full treatment of this subject is beyond the scope of this paper. For an excellent discussion of these issues see the chapter, "The Changing Uses of Money: From Self-Support to International Partnership," in *The Changing Face of World Missions* (Pocock et al. 2005). It is helpful to note, however, that beyond the issues of financial dependency and control there are other areas related to finances that affect the function of multiethnic, cross-cultural mission leadership teams.

In the movement we studied, the leaders who comprise the International Leadership Team represent a wide range of economic demographics and live in cultures with different economic standards of living. A middle-income North American is exponentially wealthier than his middle-income counterpart from most other parts of the world. It is imperative that there is sensitivity to this fact in the leaders' interaction with one another. Without careful consideration of this area, there is potential for insensitivity to genuine needs on one hand, and potential for behavior that, although well intentioned, would risk being condescending or arrogant on the other. When movement leaders from around the globe spend extended time together for planning, what do they do during free time together between meetings? What may be a normal leisure activity for the leader from one culture might seem a great extravagance for others. Even a heartfelt personal gift could be misunderstood. Again, strong relationships, communication, and trust help reduce the risk of misunderstanding, but the potential for misperception is there.

THE FUTURE: REMAINING ETHNICALLY AND GENERATIONALLY DIVERSE

One leader interviewed voiced the necessity for the movement to remain intentional about bringing ethnically and generationally diverse leaders to the table as the movement grows. Tim Keller, senior pastor of Redeemer Presbyterian Church in New York City, notes that movements have a propensity to become more institutionalized as they grow, and a small measure of this is necessary.

> We may try to stay very informal, non-codified, and non-centralized. But part of what makes a movement dynamic is a unified vision, and that requires some codification and control. [A gospel movement must] strike the dynamic energy-producing balance between being an organization and an organism— it must be an "organized organism" so that the structure always serves the cause and truth, not the other way around ... It means that first, the vision of the movement attracts people with leadership potential, and, secondly, that the work of the movement naturally reveals emerging leaders through real-life experience and prepares them for the next level of leadership in the movement." (Keller 2009)

If the leaders of this movement want to continue reaping the benefits of diversity of leadership, it must continue to not only adhere to its own vision and values, but those values must also continue to work themselves out into a diverse range of leaders coming to the table. If the structure of the movement becomes too static the movement will lose its ability to raise and empower diverse emerging leaders and to form partnerships with a broad spectrum of leaders coming from outside of the movement.

Lest anyone raise the concern that the desire for diversity in leadership is an accommodation of current demands for political correctness, all of the leaders we interviewed made it clear that regardless of age or ethnicity, a leader must have gifts and abilities, as well as a Christian attitude that qualifies them for leadership. Diversity simply for the sake of diversity is not the issue. Humility, maturity, and teachability are supracultural and their importance as qualities for a leader are not lessened by a desire for greater diversity in mission leadership. The leader we focused on for this study was considered by others to be qualified to lead entirely apart from his ethnicity or age.

We should note that both of the authors are part of the movement examined here and view this movement from an insider's perspective. Someone with a more critical eye from the outside may well notice other issues within this movement related to diversity in leadership or recognize other struggles that are likely to be met because of structure or philosophy. Certainly there are other ways to structure mission leadership that would have different effects on how an organization would experience diversity in leadership, and these effects may be positive or negative. We believe, however, that the primary point remains the same. If we desire to bring the full resources of the universal church to bear on the task of world evangelization, we must realize that mission leadership teams comprised of ethnically and generationally diverse leaders are biblically faithful and, if the barriers and concerns are properly addressed, they can allow a mission organization to enjoy the unique benefits that this diversity brings to the decision-making table.

REFERENCES

Keller, Timothy. 2009. Being a gospel movement. Redeemer Leaders Training (September).

Pocock, Michael, Gailyn Van Rheenen, and Douglas McConnell. 2005. *The changing face of world missions: Engaging contemporary issues and trends.* Grand Rapids: Baker Academic.

14

UNDERSTANDING THE IMPORTANCE OF DIVERSITY IN MISSIONS: AN AFRICAN AMERICAN PERSPECTIVE

GABRIEL B. TAIT

Much of the current writing about missions and mission theory boils down to the discussion of the motives for missions—a kind of psychoanalysis of the motivation of missionaries, mission boards, and sending churches. This self-analysis may clean house for the new patterns of missionary endeavor that will replace some methods of the past that are no longer useful; but it must not be confused with the solutions of the problem. A bold new plan is needed in missions (Wold, 1968).

INTRODUCTION

In the book of Revelation, John, the revelator, paints a vivid picture of the eschaton as elders worship and praise the Lamb of God (Jesus) for paying the ultimate sacrifice for humanity. During this time of praise they note that Jesus' blood was shed to purchase "(wo)men for God from every tribe and language and people and nation," for the specific purpose of service for the kingdom of God. As followers of Christ, we have come to reflect on this passage for its inclusive significance. It reminds us, it was God who authored human diversity (Elmer 1993, 23). Every person regardless of his or her race, creed, or ethnicity will participate in the festivities of God's church around the throne. The joy in knowing that one's distinctiveness will be celebrated in the last days should encourage and motivate every believer to embrace their part in the Great Commission as instructed by Jesus (Matt 28:19–20).

Unfortunately the hope that John illustrates does not warn us (the church) about the work that will be necessary to fulfill this goal: unification of a diverse population in heaven. Freddy James Clark, pastor and founder of Shalom Church (City Of Peace)—a predominately African American church in Florissant, Missouri—reminds believers that, "The church can never understand itself in isolation, it can only understand its roles and functions, its meaning and mission in relationship to others" (Clark 2007, 39). If we are going to accomplish this task practitioners will need to embrace rigorous training, sound research methods, educational and theological reflection, community relationships, and self-sacrifice with others different than themselves. It will be a daunting task. But this task is not insurmountable. In fact, the Christian gospel challenges believers to seek new ways to engage old issues that hinder pre-Christians from becoming followers of Christ. As we move forward in this calling let us not be naïve that there are no divisions in the church and in missions.

One such issue is the perceived lack of involvement of African Americans in cross-cultural mission whether short or long term. The question, "Where are all the African Americans in missions?," is often presented by non-African Americans. Why is this important? Does the traditional mission community miss the contributions of African Americans? Or does the traditional mission community miss the factors that forced African Americans to retreat to their own fields?

I explore what I call the collision of the question. It seeks to offer a corrective to this negative perception that exists about African Americans' involvement in mission service. It also looks for a common ground for us to begin dialogue on how to involve more African Americans in mission organizations and theological institutions. Finally, it affirms for the mission community that diversity does in fact include theological and practical contributions from the African American community.[1]

This "essentializes" the concept that African Americans can bring a unique historical and bicultural (especially in the Western context of North America) approach to God's kingdom service to seek and save the lost. Marvin Mayers reflects that, "Each society (person) is nevertheless functioning as a system

---

1   I am sure the whole African American community does not necessarily share my thoughts. Therefore I attempt to offer useful insight grounded in theological, missiological, and anthropological reflections.

and must be regarded as such although it may be a vastly different system from that to which we are accustomed" (Mayers 1974, 344).

Despite this, the proverbial elephant in the room of cross-cultural missions is the issue of diversity in missions. We highlight the benefits of diversity but we often teach and reflect on text and models that are not incorporating the very people we hope to reach. Miriam Adeney stresses the importance of understanding diversity from the Chinese context noting: "Fifty years from now Chinese may lead the world church" (Adeney 2009, 48). Adeney offers a great insight that should force each follower of Christ to check his or her ethnocentric attitudes about others. How will the church and mission communities respond if/when this comes to fruition? Will we employ our methods from the past or will we neglect the communities we are seeking to reach?

We have an opportunity to get ahead of the curve. To do this it will take diverse people aligning themselves to the *missio Dei*. Robert Priest rightly suggests that if this is to happen, "We need anthropology's ability to help us develop experience-near understandings of diverse people, bringing experience-near understandings into meaningful relationship with experience-distant ones, both anthropological and theological" (Priest 2006, 185). Anthropology provides the space for humanity to see the value and traditions of a culture, while theology affirms the culture's understanding and experiences of how they come to know and reflect on God. These two pieces provide a much needed bridge in building respect for one another's understanding and practice of God's mission.

The traditional mission community must seek ways to engage and appreciate the unique possibilities that are present through African American involvement in mission. As the need to reach more diverse populations increases, the traditional mission community will benefit from the realization that methods and strategies employed by diverse communities expand the reach of God's mission. Of course God is already working in communities around the world. But the way in which these diverse hermeneutical communities come to reflect on the challenges within a culture is often different. The experiences and sociological struggles are often understood differently. It is imperative for the Christian community to seek and embrace a more diverse community.

In the previous paragraphs we acknowledged a need for a more diverse missional community. We noted that the work of diversifying the mission community will be a daunting task that some may not desire. We also highlighted the unique perspective and theological reflection a diverse missional community brings to the table. In the next section we will redirect our focus back to African American involvement in missions. More specifically, the question we are most often faced with is, "Where are all the African American missionaries?"

WHERE HAVE YOU ALL BEEN?

In 2006, waiting for dinner at the Mayfield Guest House in Nairobi, Kenya, my family and I were asked by a visiting missionary from East Africa, "Where have you all been?" I paused, trying to figure out the context. We didn't know the person. I looked at my wife—she paused. It was as if time had stopped, as we continued to process . . . (*Where is this conversation going? What does she mean?*). We looked at one another, eyebrows raised, and braced ourselves for the next question. The unidentified lady then said, "I don't see very many Americans (African Americans) in the mission field. I was wondering where have you all been?" By now the table had stopped passing the food and was waiting for our response. I obliged the crowd. "Ma'am, my family and I will have just finished our assignment in Cheptebo, Kenya," I calmly stated. She then said, "Oh, it is good to see you all here. I hope more of you come back to Africa." I nodded in acknowledgement and she walked away.

I wish I could say this was the first time we have been asked about African American involvement with international missions, but it is not. Each time we head to the field there is someone (generally not African American) that asks about our involvement with international missions.

While this question is valid and has been explored by numerous communities (African American missionaries, mobilizers, pastors, and our white counterparts), there is an inherent cultural bias. I do not think it properly reveals all the issues that underlie the African American missional experience. It also assumes African Americans serving locally, regionally, or nationally do not hold the same calling as international missionaries. David Emmanuel Goatley, executive secretary-treasurer of Lott Carey Foreign Mission Convention, argues this "assumption presumes a normativity of missions that I would question. Who says what is normative and on what grounds?" (Goatley 2010).

To establish a useful foundation to Goatley's question of so-called normative missions for the remainder of this paper we will use Charles Van Engen's definition of missions as:

> The people of God intentionally crossing barriers from the church to non-church, faith to non-faith, to proclaim by word and deed the coming of the kingdom of God in Jesus Christ; this task is achieved by means of the church's participation in God's mission of reconciling people to God, to themselves, to each other, and to the world, and gathering them into the church through repentance and faith in Jesus Christ by the work of the Holy Spirit with a view to the transformation of the world as a sign of the coming of the kingdom in Jesus Christ. (Van Engen 1996, 26–27)

This definition reveals the importance of following God (regardless of color) and the intentionality of crossing cultural, ethnic, racial, economic, and religious barriers for the sake of proclaiming a risen Savior, lover of all humanity (John 3:16). As we move forward in this discussion it is important that we look back at the history of African Americans in cross-cultural missions. I will do this in two segments: the first will look at the "numbers" and the second will address the possible reasons for the low African American participation in international missions.

THE NUMBERS

Work has been done on African American missionary history. Unfortunately, these contributions have been largely overshadowed by an apparent lack of involvement in international missions. One must pause when we consider the disparities between the African American population and its noted absence in the mission field. For example, in 2000, African Americans accounted for about 34 million or 12.06 percent of the United States population (CensusScope 2010), yet they accounted for fewer than 500 missionaries serving internationally (Sutherland 2004, 1). If accurate, this represents about one percent of the estimated 43,000 Protestant missionaries serving from the Unites States (Sutherland 2004, 1).

Current interviews with several mission agencies unfortunately present a similar picture. Paul Gazan of African Inland Mission notes that they currently have nine African Americans who are full-time members. The Mission Society, according to Richard Coleman, currently has one African American. David Cornelius of the International Mission Board (Southern Baptist) reports that presently they have approximately fifty-five African American missionaries in the field. Cornelius notes, "The majority of them are not on the continent of Africa. They are literally all over the globe" (Cornelius 2010b). We believe that the numbers from other mission agencies would largely parallel the three noted here.

It is important to note that these figures are only estimates. There is some difficulty tracking the data, especially in the African American community. The African American community tends to not keep diligent records and has different definitions for mission activities. Thus outside communities will not accept these definitions and their diverse methods of engaging the mission field. For example: Does a Vacation Bible School that leads fifty children a week to Christ qualify as legitimate mission activity?

Still, this preliminary research leads one to ask: Why are we not attracting long-term African American missionaries to international missions? Sutherland suggests that there needs to be an intense effort to educate the African American community about international missions. I believe his point is well taken and should be further explored.

David Cornelius has done some research on the topic, providing a historical survey of African American involvement in international missions. This useful research offers a condensed version of the African American mission experience beginning in the eighteenth century (Cornelius 2002, 48–53). He also identifies nine factors (commitment, cultural, economic, education, family, fear, focus, the perspective, and trust) that he believes contribute to the under representation of African Americans in international missions.

He notes, "While these factors are not unique to the African American Christian community, they do have unique application. This is due, in part, to the unique relationship that has existed between African Americans and white Americans historically—that of slave/owner or slave/master" (2010b). Space does not permit us to explore each in depth. However, it should be noted that there are religious, social, and economic issues associated with the lack of participation. As we have seen, African American participation in formal mission agencies is low. The reasons for this anemic participation vary, but the approach of traditional missionaries generally exacerbates the problem.

Chapter 14

WHERE ARE ALL THE AFRICAN AMERICAN MISSIONARIES?

David Cornelius, retired missional church strategist of the International Missions Board and nine-year missionary to Nigeria, says the question is a repeat of what he has heard from many nationals around the world, especially in Africa. The answer is elusive. An October 2009 *EMQ* article titled, "Where are all the African American Missionaries?" written by Richard Coleman did not provide much help. In the article, Coleman reflects on this complex question presenting cross-cultural missions for the African American as either "a pilgrimage home" (to Africa) or a mere exercise by arrogant, insensitive, "condescending know-it alls" (Coleman 2009, 447–48). I think his observations present a distorted picture of the African American mission experience. I have led teams to both Tanzania and Haiti and have not experienced this from my team members or our indigenous leaders. Nevertheless, I will affirm at the very least that members of his case study team exemplified a limited appreciation or lack of respect for their host culture.

Coleman's assertions may have some merit on a case-by-case basis, but they must not be viewed as a reliable generalization. Interestingly enough the same sentence could be rewritten adding any one of numerous ethnic groups and it would not present a picture of the whole culture. His ideas do not properly highlight the successes, contributions, and lessons learned from the African American community. It leads me to the following question: If the desire is to draw one to cross-cultural missions, will you accomplish the task by using vinegar or honey or a combination of both?

Goatley believes the question is loaded. He makes two observations. First, he says it presumes normalcy in favor of white Americans. He asks, "Is someone going to ask where are all the white Americans?" Sutherland notes with the decline of North American Protestant missionaries in recent years, this question is frequently asked. He adds, "It's a disturbing trend, given population increase and emphasis upon shorter-term missions."

Goatley also notes that this position reveals an inherent cultural bias that exists when the question is framed in this manner. In fact, he notes, the question already determines the approach. It presupposes the dominant culture (e.g., white missionaries) already has the normative approach. Goatley's position is one that is echoed by many African Americans: "He who controls that definition and strategy controls ultimately who is 'in' and who is 'out' of the missional enterprise of God." He asks, "Why is it that someone wants to send 10,000 Americans to do cross-culture missions? When if you do it right you might be able to empower one million indigenous people to do mission in so-called cross-cultural settings where there is not such a cross-cultural gulf?" (2010). While his point presents a valid response to developing indigenous leadership, I believe this model needs to be more nuanced.

Goatley raises the most fundamental issue of all here—are American missionaries actually needed at all (whether African American or white)? While this exceeds my scope, given our contemporary culture, emphasis on contextual theology and missional hermeneutical community, this question needs to be asked and answered honestly before we truly start talking about whether most of them are African American or white. A sincere introspective answer must be garnered, not from some triumphalist perspective, but from a perspective that respects and recognizes the contributions and potential inherent in the body of Christ in every ethnic community. Ultimately, I think African Americans are not found in large numbers in the international mission scene because they have been focusing their efforts on ministering to their own people, realizing that they are the ones who are best qualified to speak to and relate to their own.

And this perspective applies to the white church as well. What if the dominant community realized that it is not the answer to the world, but that the Chinese church can best reach the Chinese, the African church can best reach the Africans, and so on?

However, since we find ourselves in a globalized missional context, where diverse communities are mobilizing diverse people to share the gospel in the Global South and around the world, a possible first step in Goatley's method is to develop a relationship with the local culture. An intercultural approach with the host community built on mutual respect is a vital step in building sustainable relationships. Then, "we need to ask people what they need before ministering to them" (Johnson 2006, 19). In doing so we approach cross-cultural mission assignments with an appreciation for the work God is already doing in a respective community.

The *missio Dei* principle that Karl Barth presented and Karl Hartenstein advanced shed light on this process. It redirects followers of Christ to the fact that God is already active in humanity and that it is their "calling" to join God in the fruits of his labor. I like how Anabaptist missiologist Wilbert Shenk reflects on this point in an often cited quote (McPhee 2001, 8–9):

> The mission of the Triune God is to establish *basileia* over the whole of creation. This being realized through the *missio Dei*. The character of the *missio Dei* is defined by the ministry of God's Messiah, Jesus the *ebed*, whose servanthood was empowered by the Holy Spirit. It is by the Spirit that the church is endowed with spiritual gifts and empowered for ministry as the messianic community. The *missio Dei* will be consummated in the eschaton; but in the interim the eschaton infuses the messianic community with hope and power as it continues its witness amid opposition and suffering. The interaction of these elements represents the mission dynamic, which, in turn, defines the vocation of the disciples of Jesus Christ in the world. (Shenk 1996, 93)

Shenk's salient point should serve as a reminder that we are not the architects of the mission. We are instead willing servants who have submitted our calling to God's will in whatever context we find ourselves. Failure to do so will reveal challenges that all cultures experience when missionaries move ahead of God's direction without understanding or appreciating the context.

Collision of Missions

In December, during an evening break from the Urbana 2009 missions conference in St. Louis, Missouri, I turned the television on to get my fix of the latest National Football League (NFL) scores from the previous day. As I clicked the channels, my Tanzanian-born American roomie said with a jokingly sarcastic tone, "You Americans love your football!" I understood the context and affirmed his point. I then asked if Tanzanians love football. He brightly answered, "Yes!" This communication exchange reveals the importance of understanding the context and meaning of a given word. Depending on the context, the meaning of "football" is different. If we were in Tanzania, where he serves and my family and I led a short-term mission team in 2008, we would understand the meaning of "football" to be what Americans call "soccer." The name would be the same, but the meaning would be different. Likewise the meaning of missions tends to take on different meaning in the African American and white American cultures.

Why does the word "mission" elicit so many different responses? David Bosch asserts that the meaning and praxis of missions has evolved from the first century. For example, white Americans view missions through both a local and international lens. They tend to embrace the social aspect of the gospel. Sutherland again notes, "There is a real crisis of definitions," and, "African Americans have been forced to understand the Great Commission from the context of the Anglo structures" (2010). If this is true, then one may suggest that a transformation of the heart and mind are necessary for both the Anglo and African American to effectively align themselves with God's mission.

History

The history of the African American within the world has been one of assimilation and survival: assimilation in the sense that they have had to change their identity, culture, community, and—in many instances—their religion in order to operate within many oppressive and dehumanizing structures, especially those of slavery, colonization efforts in foreign lands, and Jim Crow in America. I know, I can hear someone saying in the back of his or her mind, "Are we going here? Is this going to be another presentation that bashes the white community for the actions of our forefathers?" The answer to this question is a resounding, "No!" However, if we do not understand the history, we may miss opportunities to understand African Americans' theology and perspective regarding their sense of calling to serve.

The African American has had to survive by learning to navigate the various economic, religious, and political systems of empowerment that have constantly been moving. The same is true as it applies to the African American mission efforts in the late eighteenth through the mid-twentieth centuries.

Michael Johnson, an African American missionary who first served with World Gospel Missions (2002, 12), notes: "African Americans have survived what many of us see as a double standard of Christianity" (Johnson 2006, 29). Walter L. Williams affirms Johnson's position that it has been a long, arduous road of self-revelation and identification for the African American to discern the calling of God to "Go ye therefore, and teach all nations, baptizing them in the name of the Father, and of the Son, and of the Holy Ghost " (Matt 28:19). Despite this swinging pendulum, many former slaves sought ways to fulfill God's calling for international missions.

African American cross-cultural missions have existed since the eighteenth century. For many African American Christians from the North and former slaves living in the South, the obvious choice for cross-cultural missions was to go to communities that were similar to their own. This highlights Donald McGavran's Homogenous Unit Principle (HUP), which suggests people most often communicate and share their faith with people that are similar to them culturally, ethnically, or racially: "They prefer to join churches whose members look, talk, and act like themselves" (1970, 198). While I think McGavran's observations highlight an important principle, it is not mutually exclusive. When we examine the missional efforts of Barnabas, Paul, and others over the ages, we learn that God does not constrain himself for only one group of people to be witnesses in one context. There are other factors that need to be considered.

African Americans served as missionaries both locally and internationally, until they were kicked out of Africa in the late nineteenth and early twentieth centuries by colonial governments and white mission agencies. Locally, there were African American missionaries to slaves in the antebellum South. Goatley notes, "The very existence of the black church in America says that black people have been doing missions. Had we not, we would have been out of business" (2010).

On the other hand, international mission gained its introduction with the service of George Lisle to the West Indies in 1782. But it was the efforts of Lott Carey, a former slave who became a Baptist pastor, that most attributed to the launching of African American service internationally. This service focused mainly on the continent of Africa.

Lott Carey traveled with the American Colonization Society (ACS) in 1821 to the Grain Coast, what is now known as Liberia. He established the first church in the country, Providence Baptist Church in Monrovia. It is not difficult to realize the missional legacy planted by Carey after worshipping in the church during the summer of 2010. For Carey and the other former slaves who traveled with the ACS, the benefits far outweighed the cost associated with evangelizing the unreached under the auspices of the ACS. Consider the word[s] of Lott Carey as he stood on the banks of Virginia, preparing for his forty-four-day ocean voyage to Liberia:

> I am about to leave you, and expect to see your faces no more; I long to preach to the poor Africans the way of life and salvation; I don't know what may befall me, whether I may find a grave in the ocean, or among the savage men, or more savage wild beasts on the coast of Africa; nor am I anxious what may become of me: I feel it my duty to go; and I very much fear that many of those who preach the gospel in this country will blush when the Savior calls them to give an account of their labors in his cause, and tells them, I commanded you to go into all the world, and preach the Gospel to every creature; the Savior may ask, Where have you been? What have you been doing? Have you endeavored, to the utmost of your ability, to fulfill the commands I gave you, or have you sought your own gratification and your own ease, regardless of my commands? (Fitts 1978, 68)

Many felt their hearts touched and moved by the solemn appeal. I believe this reveals the heart of African American missionaries who felt called to serve internationally.

Alexander Crummell has been regarded as the "Civilizing Missionary" and the "Father of black Missions." Wilson Jeremiah Moses coins this term for Crummell because of Crummell's deep love for Western culture and civilization, which he believed to be the best ever to exist in the world. As a missionary to Liberia, Crummell tried to export the virtues of Western culture and civilization to the "heathen" inhabitants of the continent. Rick Gray makes this point in his dissertation, "The Black Manifest Destiny as motivation for mission during the golden age of Black Nationalism" (Gray 1996). During his twenty years in Liberia as a missionary, educator, scholar, and lecturer, Crummell observed over 14,000 African Americans heeding the call to missions in Africa in the late nineteenth and early twentieth centuries. This brief summary of the early history of African Americans runs counter to public perceptions.

For example, this is in stark contrast to the observations of scholar Earl Parvin, who is harshly critical, noting:

> Only a few blacks are giving themselves to full-time Christian service either at home or abroad. A survey of the three largest black denominations, representing one-third of US blacks, reveals that they have fielded only about one dozen missionaries. (Parvin 1985, 76)

Parvin blames a lack of adequate leadership from either the black church or white church as an explanation for the "failure." But Parvin's portrayal exposes his inadequate conversance with the history of African American involvement in missionary enterprises. Moreover it has been claimed that most African American missionaries "did not" plan on returning to the West, and thus they were not official missionaries. Who determines the definition of a missionary? Why would one's stipulation that the missionary must return to their home country (or country of birth) negate the validity of their service? Are missionaries who wholly commit their service to indigenous people placed on a time schedule to return?

I think we gain a glimpse into these questions when we consider the sending of Paul and Barnabas by the church at Antioch. In Acts, Luke presents a picture of the church in community praying, worshipping, and preparing Paul and Barnabas for a life of service. Empowered by the Holy Spirit, these servants engaged the various communities with which they came in contact (Acts 13–16), only returning to Antioch to encourage the new believers. Unlike the church in Antioch and the service of Paul and Barnabas, the fervor celebrated by Lott Carey and Alexander Crummell, but rejected by Parvin, was stamped out by colonial governments and white mission agencies. This leads me to our last section on the history of the African American and the importance of diversity in cross-cultural missions.

AFRICAN AMERICAN MISSIONARIES COLLIDE WITH COLONIALISM

The first way in which Christianity came into collision with colonization was through evangelization (Delavignette 1964, 49). Black missionaries in Africa during this time (mid-nineteenth and early twentieth centuries) operated under the banner of what has been called the three C's: Christianity, commerce, and civilization (Ellis 2005, 22). During the same time, this affinity for missions amongst some was one of the most tenuous times for the colonial government and the African American missionary. There was a developing attitude shared by the mission agencies and the colonial governments that the African American missionaries got in the way of their colonial agenda. In fact, as Sylvia M. Jacobs explains:

> After 1900, with "Jim Crow," lynchings, and disfranchisement of blacks prevalent throughout the United States, White mission boards

frequently and spasmodically displayed mistrust and hostility toward black missionaries in Africa, and opposition to them became widespread. By 1920, the idea of using black missionaries in Africa was all but dead in the White American religious community. These boards were being pressured to recall black missionaries stationed in Africa by the European imperialists who, by 1920 had occupied the entire continent except the Republic of Liberia and Ethiopia. (Jacobs 1982, 20)

In other words, the same racial system that African Americans renounced and wanted to get away from was now operating within the partnerships between the colonial governments and the mission agencies. Hence the systematic structures were changed from evangelizing and meeting the needs of the people to accommodating the government's interests and cultural perceptions. The positive development of the people from "heathens" and "savages" (and other names) to "civilized" people was not truly the issue. The interests of the indigenous people were not in fact the concern for the colonizer. White mission boards were fearful that colonial governments during these early years might reject their agencies because free and outspoken people of color would undermine their economic interest (Johnson 2002, 12).

Earlier it was mentioned that the (economic, ideological, and political) systems are consistently moving, making it difficult for one to hit the mark and stay on point. Despite this tumultuous history and hypocrisy, many African Americans are motivated to serve cross-culturally—locally and internationally. The challenge for the traditional missional community is: Will they be willing to accept the past, while still moving forward to embrace the diversity?

COLLISION AVERTED

In April 2007, we received our short-term team list from Africa Inland Mission (AIM). My family and I had been praying for a team that would be willing to enter the host culture as learners and servants. With some coaching and affirmation this was exactly the team we had.

One team member, Sedrick Huckaby, was an African American man from Fort Worth, Texas. Growing up, Sedrick was part of a small Pentecostal church. He had no understanding of cross-cultural missions until this assignment. When I asked him how he found out about AIM, he said he asked around and searched the Internet for "Missions and Africa." Interestingly enough, this is how I learned about mission organizations in 2005. Judith St. Clair Hull notes, "Most African Americans are not even aware of the Evangelical mission organizations, so African American churches have been in the process of inventing their own approaches" (Hull 2006, 1). This fact offered a sense of confidence for Sedrick. Many African Americans want to know they are not the only ones who do not understand the international mission circles.

Moreover, the learning point I had to figure out about Sedrick was that his inexperience with international missions had both positive and negative effects. The negative effect was that he would disappear during various parts of the day to read his Bible while others were getting to know one another. When I would ask him why he was retreating, he expressed an uncertainty about the assignment and his part in it. This did not mean that he doubted his call to serve but that he needed direction. I encouraged our team that learning the value systems of the host culture would aid them in adjusting to cultural shock. This proved to be a good approach. They were willing to laugh when they made mistakes, and this gave them comfort in learning about others.[2]

Sedrick Huckaby Takes a Header (photo by Gabriel B. Tait © 2007)

The positive effect was that Sedrick was a great learner. His vulnerability to the calling was an asset for the team. When asked, he would do almost

---

2   Sedrick Huckaby takes a header during an intense game of football with the youth on the African Inland Church Tanzania (AICT) grounds in Arusha, Tanzania in 2007. Sedrick was part of the diverse ten-member team led by Gabriel and Ilka Tait. Host Pastor Amos Mabele still maintains contact with many of the team members.

anything because he looked at the opportunity as fulfilling his part of the Great Commission with the community. The true benefit from Sedrick's service came when he incorporated his gift for art into numerous classes for the community. In addition there was his love for the game of soccer and his interactions with the young men (see photo above).

Currently Sedrick works as an artist in residence at the University of Texas at Arlington. During a recent conversation he shared his desire to return to the mission field in Africa saying, "I am waiting on the Lord to release us so we can continue our ministry in Africa." He added, "When my family and I head over (to Africa), we will better understand the process of serving cross-culturally." Until then Sedrick and his wife, Letitia, have committed to support a student at the Lott Carey Mission School in Liberia.

This case study reveals an important part of mobilizing African Americans to international cross-cultural service. They need to know that the missional community finds value in their service. It is one thing for God to equip and call. But it is another when people know the majority community cares about them and is willing to educate them about the nuances of mission service in a different culture. This is the route to building relationships.

So far we have highlighted the fact that African Americans serving cross-culturally need information about mission networks, their potential assignments, the need for companionship, and the need to be appreciated. In the next section we will talk about some of the challenges to incorporating African Americans and other diverse populations in traditional mission organizations.

THE COLLISION OF GROWTH

Michael A. Rynkiewich, my former anthropology professor, likes to highlight that culture is "constructed, contingent, contested, and complex." Of course he goes much deeper than I will about the meaning of each segment of culture and its influence on one's understanding of that culture. But I think his point is that when one is able to understand and use these tools, one will have a greater probability of becoming an agent for change within a given culture.

When we look at traditional, white evangelical mission agencies and the African American church, each has clearly developed into dominant cultures within the Western Christian context. The problem is they are often on different ends of the spectrum. They very rarely interact with one another. I think this is by choice and by circumstance. The choice aspect is that it is easier "to do things the way we have done them for years," while the circumstance aspect reinforces the idea that the other party does not want to be a part of "my organization."

Some, like Earl Parvin have even argued, "Since they (African Americans) have not been a part of cross-cultural missions (international), it may be better if we keep things as status quo" (1985, 75–106). This is the wrong attitude for each participant to bring to God's table of mission service. Paul asks an important question that we must consider, "If we have sown spiritual seed among you, is it too much if we reap a material harvest from you? If others have this right of support from you, shouldn't we have it all the more?" (1 Cor 9:11, 12).

I think Paul's point to the people is that there are laborers in the fields who desire to serve more fully in diverse contexts; and, if we are not willing to embrace our differences, we miss opportunities to more completely serve the kingdom of God. This idea brings out another point: If each is to influence the other, they have to learn to interact and trust one another. The writer of Proverbs offers useful advice for both parties when suggesting that if we are going to move past our differences and gain wisdom we must, "Trust in the Lord with all your heart and lean not on your own understanding; in all your ways acknowledge him, and he will make your paths straight" (Prov 3:5, 6).

Jim Sutherland offers seven strategies (Sutherland 2004) that can aid the missional community in gaining African American missionaries. I support his suggestions but will add three additional points for consideration. Sutherland presents the ideas that the white missional community must:

- Approach African Americans uniquely.
- Build trust.
- Network with campus ministries.
- Promote short-term mission assignments.
- Recruit the church (pastors).
- Provide temporary financial assistance.
- Provide internships and mentoring.

While I acknowledge these points, I do not think they go far enough in addressing the distinctiveness of the African American experience. I believe the majority missional community must also:

- Acknowledge that there have been mistakes.
- Allow unique giftedness in traditional ministry roles.
- Show that you care about the person and not just the body, cultivate relationships.

Acknowledge That There Have Been Mistakes

I think this point should be first and foremost. Without true reconciliation there will be no unified mission. I like how Paul Hiebert addresses the issue of reconciliation in dealing with minority societies when he notes, "If bridges of fellowship are not built between groups from the beginning, the church (or mission for that matter) will be captive to social systems and will contribute to the segregation and oppression that characterizes these systems" (Hiebert and Meneses 1995, 239). In the twenty-first century we are well positioned to embrace our brothers and sisters through the love that Jesus so freely offers.

Allow Unique Giftedness in Traditional Ministry Roles

As described above, Sedrick has a unique gift for creative communication. Many disciples in this postmodern world have similar giftedness. Why not allow them to communicate God's message through art and photography? Photographer Micah Marty reminds us, "Photography, unlike most other arts, involves at its essence the stripping away of the superfluous . . . The photographer starts with everything—an infinitely crowded canvas, as it were—and progressively removes various elements . . . When we decided to focus on God, and our faith, simplicity is less difficult to embrace; pushing things out of the way then reveals rather than diverts us from our goal" (Marty and Marty 1998, 8–9). Perhaps God has allowed the mission community to operate in this state of disarray as a way for traditional missions to diversify its ministries.

Show That You Care about the Person and Not Just the Body: Cultivate Relationships

In John 21:15 and following, Jesus reconnects with his disciple, friend, and soon-to-be bridge of the faith, Peter. Despite Peter's rejection of Jesus while under duress, Jesus reaffirms Peter's calling and commissions him to "Feed my sheep." One can only imagine the sense of joy and refocused purpose Peter felt in receiving this vote of confidence. Likewise we are to develop long-lasting relationships with people that are different than we are. When we do this in the missional community, we run a "great risk" of building lifelong ministry partners.

White mission members and administrators must change traditional attitudes and behaviors in relating to African Americans in general. They must avoid ignoring the African American community, while at the same time avoiding the token poster child mentality. They must be willing to ask themselves hard questions, such as:

- Are they genuinely willing to consider African Americans for administrative positions?
- How many of their white personnel have close African American friends?
- How many of their white personnel have been to an African American church and actually enjoyed it?

The answers to these questions say it all, because behavior always speaks louder than words. Be a true friend—regardless of differences. Only when African Americans sense they are truly being accepted as friends would they feel free to be accepted as coworkers.

For this unity to actually happen, it may mean abandoning the traditional mission model and embracing a new way of doing mission. This would include a fresh new group that starts from the ground up with a mix of whites and African Americans in its ranks and with a totally new ethos—one of respecting each other as equals.

If these points are implemented in the majority missional community, I am sure the results for recruitment and retention will improve.

CONCLUSION

Throughout this paper I have examined some of the historical, ideological, and religious barriers that have caused collisions between white mission agencies and the African American community. This is by no means a comprehensive list, but it does highlight the fact that there are real differences in how the two communities understand or at least practice the Great Commission within an international cross-cultural context. In summary we may note that many African Americans serve in missions. Their contexts may be different, but they are serving. Further, not all African Americans serve in Africa. The present situation derives from the early African American missionaries colliding with colonialism and racism in white mission agencies. The rise of Jim Crow laws and segregation drained the energy of the African American Christian community for international missions. While the door to missions is open, African Americans need 1) information about opportunities, 2) companionship with other African Americans, and 3) to be appreciated for their service.

The mission of God is seen in diverse ways. It embraces many cultures. As an African American serving in Africa, some have stated that because of my skin color and the fact that my physical features are very similar to those throughout the continent of Africa (particularly sub-Saharan) I have added benefits. While I do not subscribe to this rhetoric, I believe many African Americans are well positioned to serve in communities where they can adapt to their host cultures. But the true asset for the African American is more about God using one's giftedness in joining in God's mission. We must have a heart that seeks God's will for us as followers of Christ, utilizing the Scripture, the infallible word of God, as our guide. In Genesis 1:26–27—in what is referred to as *imago Dei*—God said, "Let us make man in our image, in our likeness . . . So God created man in his own image, in the image of God he created him; male and female he created them." As we embrace and nurture this principle, issues of race, ethnicity, and cultural difference will not play as large a role. With this realization we will be one step closer to John's picture in Revelation of a diverse humanity worshipping around the throne of grace.

REFERENCES

Adeney, Miriam. 2009. *Kingdom without borders: The untold story of global Christianity.* Downers Grove: InterVarsity.

Barrett, David, and Todd M. Johnson. 2001. *World Christian trends, AD 30–AD 2200: Interpreting the annual Christian megacensus.* Pasadena: William Carey Library.

CensusScope. 2010. Population by race: Analyzed by the social science data analysis network (SSDAN), http://www.censusscope.org/us/chart_race.html.

Clark, Freddy James. 2007. *Hospitality: An ecclesiological practice of ministry.* Lanham, MD: Hamilton Books.

Coleman, Richard. 2009. Where are all the African American missionaries? *Evangelical Missions Quarterly* 446-48.

Cornelius, David. 2002. A brief historical survey of African American involvement in international missions. In *African American experience in world mission: A call beyond community*, ed. Vaughn J. Stevens and Robert J. Stevens, 48–54. Pasadena: William Carey Library.

———. 2010a. Interview by Gabriel B. Tait, February 22.

———. 2010b. Nine factors which contribute to the under representation of African Americans in international missions. Powerpoint Presentation, February 22, Richmond, VA.

Delavignette, Robert. 1964. *Christianity and colonialism*. New York: Hawthorn Books.

Ellis, Carl F. Jr. 2005. *Going global: Beyond the boundaries*. Chicago: Urban Ministries.

Elmer, Duane. 1993. *Cross-cultural conflict: Building relationships for effective ministry*. Downers Grove: InterVarsity.

Fitts, Leroy. 1978. *Lott Carey: First Black missionary to Africa*. Valley Forge, PA: Judson Press.

———. 1985. *A history of Black Baptists*. Nashville: Broadman Press.

———. 2006. Interview by Gabriel B. Tait, November 12.

Goatley, David E. 2010. Interview by Gabriel B. Tait, February 24.

Gray, Richard. 1996. *The Black Manifest Destiny as Motivation for Mission During the Golden Age of Black Nationalism*. PhD Dissertation, School of World Mission, Fuller Theological Seminary, Pasadena: Unpublished, 1996.

Hiebert, Paul G., and Eloise Hiebert Meneses. 1995. *Incarnational ministry: Planting churches in band, tribal, peasant, and urban societies*. Grand Rapids: Baker Books.

Hull, Judith St. Clair. 2006. *African American strategies and motivations in short term missions*. Chicago: Urban Ministries.

Jacobs, Sylvia M. 1982. *Black Americans and the missionary movement in Africa*. Westport, Connecticut: Greenwood Press.

Johnson, Michael. 2002. Am I my brother's keeper. In *African American experience in world mission: A call beyond community*, ed. Vaughn J. Stevens and Robert J. Stevens, 11–18. Pasadena: William Carey Library.

———. 2005. Missing: African-American missionaries. Blackinformant.com (August 29), http://www.blackinformant.com/uncategorized/missing-african-american-missionaries.

———. 2006. *Making the blind man lame: What Jesus wouldn't do*. Raleigh, NC: Higher Standard Publishers.

Marty, Martin E., and Micah Marty. 1998. *When true simplicity is gained: Finding spiritual clarity in a complex world*. Grand Rapids: Eerdmans.

Mayers, Marvin K. 1974. *Christianity confronts culture: A strategy for cross-cultural evangelism*. Grand Rapids: Zondervan.

McGavran, Donald A. 1970. *Understanding church growth*. Grand Rapids: Eerdmans.

McPhee, Art. 2001. The *missio Dei* and the transformation of the church. *Vision*: 6–12.

Parvin, Earl. 1985. *Missions USA*. Chicago: Moody Press.

Priest, Robert J. 2006. "Experience-near theologizing" in diverse human contexts. In *Globalizing theology: Belief and practice in an era of world Christianity*, ed. Craig Ott and Harold A. Netland, 180–95. Grand Rapids: Baker Academic.

Shenk, Wilbert. 1996. The mission dynamic. In *Mission in bold humility: David Bosch's work considered*, ed. David Jacobus, W. A. Saayman, and J. J. Kritzinger Bosch, 83–93. Maryknoll: Orbis.

Sutherland, James W. 2004. Time for African American missionaries. *Evangelical Missions Quarterly* : 500–11.

———. 2009. The effects of few African American missionaries. Reconciliation Ministries Network, Inc., www.rmni.org/.../Effects%20of%20Few%20AfAm%20Missionaries.pdf.

Sutherland, James W. 2010. Interview by Gabriel B. Tait, February 21.

Van Engen, Charles E. 1996. *Mission on the way: Issues in mission theology*. Grand Rapids: Baker.

Wold, Joseph Conrad. 1968. *God's impatience in Liberia*. Grand Rapids: Eerdmans.

15

THE STORY OF ALMA: DIVERSITY IN EVANGELICAL MISSION TODAY

RODNEY ORR

It is with great joy that I share my experience of building and eventually turning over leadership of the Africa Leadership and Management Academy (ALMA), a graduate school in Harare, Zimbabwe. Being a school of leadership, we modeled our own leadership transition on Paul's statement in 2 Timothy 2:2, "And the things you have heard me say in the presence of many witnesses entrust to reliable men who will be qualified to teach others."

Zimbabwe is a beautiful country landlocked in the heart of southern Africa just north of South Africa. It has about thirteen million people and farming is the main industry. Tobacco is the main crop, although maize and other edible crops are grown. Mining of chrome, gold, platinum, and now diamonds is a profitable industry although there is some question as to how much of these profits actually go towards nation building in Zimbabwe. Political turmoil over the past eleven years has led to economic collapse. Even though set in an adverse setting during a turbulent period, ALMA grew from inception to the three hundred students it has today.

The vision of ALMA began in 1992 when Dr. Dela Adadevoh, a Ghanaian with Campus Crusade for Christ, saw many African national missionaries leaving their mission settings in search of leadership development. He wanted to start a graduate school that would provide a course of study suited to these missionaries; one that would help them become more long term in their missionary careers. The vision of ALMA, which is "to build leaders of integrity who would impact Africa and the world for Christ," grew out of the 1994 Pan-African Christian Leadership Assembly II in Nairobi. PACLA I

(1976) was an African response to the needs of leadership development, and PACLA II occurred at the same time as the Rwandan genocide. This tragedy brought to light the hard question of what difference is missions really having on the African continent.

At PACLA II a group of African Christian leaders from across Africa were given the assignment to wrestle with the question "What is Africa's greatest need?" and they concluded that the answer was *leadership*. Africa needs leaders of integrity, they concluded, who put God before themselves and who want to serve others before their own families. It was in the midst of this questioning that these leaders asked a second question, "If leadership is the greatest need in Africa today then what will we do about it?"

They decided that they would begin a school of leadership that would address these needs in a practical way. This goal would be for all of Africa and its vision would be to help Africa take its place in God's plan for evangelizing the world. The conference director, Kweku Hutchful, also a Ghanaian, was assigned to work with Adadevoh in setting up the curriculum for this new leadership institution. It was not just to build and develop Africa for its own sake, but also to develop Africa's vast resources for God's purposes worldwide. They felt that God wanted to use Africa to further God's purposes worldwide. The unprecedented movement of the Spirit across Africa since 1900 was undeniable, but it is not sustainable without leaders of integrity.

Hutchful and Adadevoh both lived in Harare, Zimbabwe and from there scheduled a number of curriculum design workshops with leaders across the continent. They developed a curriculum that addressed the issues of African leaders. Later I met Hutchful and attended a curriculum design workshop with him, Josphat Yego (Kenyan), Ken Stravens (Seychelles), and Victor Cole (Nigeria) to flesh out the courses that would be used, which were:

- Research Methods and Writing
- Bible, Culture, and Leadership Development (two courses)
- Management Theory and Practice
- Leadership Development
- Transforming Leadership in the African Context
- Personal, Relational, and Public Life in Leadership
- Human Resource Management
- Organizational Development
- Dissertation (15,000 words)

Later additional courses were added in areas of governance, educational leadership, financial management, and strategic planning. The original curriculum was submitted to University of Wales for evaluation at a conference sponsored by Oxford Center for Missions Studies (OCMS) at which the conclusion was that one of ALMA's courses, "Personal, Relational, and Public Life in Leadership," needed revision. They considered the course to be too invasive in the personal life of the leader. However, this was exactly what the African leaders who designed the curriculum wanted. They were concerned that it was the personal areas of failure among African leaders that caused so much grief in African countries. As a result, ALMA chose to look for an African-based accrediting body and ended up submitting the curriculum to the University of Zimbabwe for consideration.

At that time ALMA's master's program had a postgraduate certificate and a postgraduate diploma nested within the Masters of Arts degree. After its review, the University of Zimbabwe required that both of these programs be removed. Finally, in 2004, ALMA became an Associate College of the Faculty of Commerce of the University of Zimbabwe. This relationship with the University of Zimbabwe has been mutually beneficial to both and continues today.

ALMA's next step was to become a chartered university. However, this required having Zimbabweans in the top leadership positions. Though this unwritten fact was communicated indirectly, it made me understand why a succession plan was essential to ALMA's long-term development.

My own background will help you understand my orientation at ALMA. After graduating from Purdue University in 1977, I spent five years on active duty in the United States Air Force as a management engineer. During these years it became clear to me that my calling from God was not mainly building jobs or improving efficiency, but building people by opening their eyes to truth. This framed my mission when I was asked to take over leadership of the then nonexistent entity called ALMA.

It was while I was a student at the University of Edinburgh that I first heard about the vision of ALMA. I thought it was very clear and compelling, and I wanted to be a part of it. I had no idea what the situation in Zimbabwe would be like when I agreed to be executive director and begin the school from nothing. In reality, it was less than nothing, as the school owed $15,000 in debts for the curriculum design conference it had held. And so the first miracle had to take place just to get us going. Many more miracles would occur in the process of building ALMA.

It was a great joy to help start ALMA in 1999 with ten students, even though Zimbabwe was in the midst of severe political unrest that led to eventual economic collapse. Inflation grew to 250 million percent in 2009 when the economy collapsed and US currency replaced the Zim dollar as the common currency. From this small beginning ALMA grew into a graduate school accredited by the University of Zimbabwe, Faculty of Commerce, and currently has 300 graduate students as well as undergraduate diploma in leadership.

I also grew spiritually, mentally, and physically as a result of seeing ALMA grow. Leading ALMA was the best job that I've had in twenty-eight years of missionary experience. It would have been easy to stay there another decade as I enjoyed the work so much. But it became evident to me that my time of effective service was coming to an end. If ALMA was going to grow to the next level it was going to need local leadership. We had trained a Zimbabwean faculty member for five years and the Board of Directors felt he was ready to take over leadership. At the same time, my family and I felt God was saying it was time for us to seek our next assignment closer to home.

One of my greatest fears in stepping down from ALMA was not knowing how I would handle not having a leadership role. I found I could understand Abner Hale, the missionary to Hawaii in James Michener's novel, *Hawaii*. He worked in Hawaii his whole life—including working his wife to an early grave, sending his children away for schooling at his wife's parents, and holding on with all his strength to his church. In a dramatic scene from the movie, Hale speaks of the church he built as his own personal possession, never saying it belonged to God.

In nature we see that animals can become territorial about their grazing area, continually marking their home ground as "no go" areas for potential competitors. Political leaders can also become possessive of their countries or territories and feel they have the right to do whatever they want with the people, land, and other resources. This is a major reason for a separation of powers and limitation of political terms. Missionaries are not immune to this tendency; it seems to be a human trait to varying degrees. In Michener's novel, Hale's mission steps in, taking the church away from him. However, the mission could not make Hale himself leave.

Hale serves as an important counterexample to what we hope for when a leadership transition takes place. I had to consider how I might be lost without having the position of executive director. What helped me overcome this fear is faith that God would help me move to the next step. I felt certain that he had something else for me to do and that if I would take this step of faith he would show me what the next step was.

I formally stepped down as executive director at ALMA in June 2009, handing over the executive director position to Dwight Mutonono, a Zimbabwean. Mutonono was in the second class to matriculate at ALMA, and graduated with honors with the first group to get an ALMA degree. After graduating, he joined ALMA, serving as the chief academic officer for three years and then as a board member. During that time he completed his doctorate at Bakke Graduate School of Management in Seattle, Washington. My current role at ALMA is as a global ambassador who serves and encourages the leadership there, while also raising funds for the school.

It was fulfilling and thrilling to have given my best for ten years to building ALMA. To turn over leadership to someone else and now serve the school from a different perspective has also been a wonderful experience. As a missionary I felt that there is only one thing better than succeeding in the ministry, namely helping someone else succeed. Having a good transition in leadership left the door open for further ministry in Zimbabwe and encouraged other leaders to transition well rather than follow Hale's pattern.

WOMEN IN LEADERSHIP

Diversity in every setting has its own challenges. In African settings, with strong male leadership patterns, gender diversity at an institution like ALMA can play a critical role for the African church. Some of the most dynamic leaders in Africa today are women. One of the two Vice Presidents in Zimbabwe is Mrs. Joyce Mujuru. Liberian President, Ellen Johnson Sirleaf, and many lesser political figures are women—and the numbers in Africa are growing. We are certain that the role of African women in leadership in Africa is only beginning to be realized and that the time is overdue to be proactively training women to have maximum impact wherever God places them.

Roughly 25 percent of the 300 students at ALMA are female, ranging in age from mid-twenty's to mid-fifty's. Our goal at ALMA is to have females comprise 50 percent of our students, 50 percent of our board of directors,

50 percent of our executive committee, and 50 percent of our faculty. We found that the key to reaching these goals is not to limit our focus to recruiting female students, but to recruit women for our highest leadership level (our Board of Directors). There were challenges in finding qualified women for our board because the qualified applicants in Zimbabwe were already serving on numerous boards and often oversubscribed in other areas of their lives. The dearth of females in leadership positions could only be reversed if we proactively trained women and gave them opportunities to rise to the highest levels of leadership in organizations in the country and the world.

Currently, two of the nine members of ALMA's Board of Directors are women. Over the past decade, three have served; a bank manager, a theology lecturer and fulltime staff with Navigators, and a human resource director at a major company in Zimbabwe. When ALMA started, we appointed two women as student representatives to the board (one a human resources director of a government agency and the other leading a Far East Broadcasting Association radio station. We saw these student appointees as leadership development works-in-progress.

Over the decade of ALMA existence, we had a student give a testimony at the beginning of six of our annual board meetings, focusing on asking women to participate in this way. ALMA has assigned one or two teaching assistants for each module it teaches, and we invited a number of our outstanding female students to serve in this capacity. We anticipate that some of these will go for doctoral studies and eventually become lead lecturers for module studies.

ALMA requires every student to have three mentors. We noticed that men usually chose other men as their mentors. Seldom did they choose women as mentors. However, our female students chose both men and women as their mentors. One reason for this might be because of the small number of potential women leaders to select as mentors. If we want this to change, we must be intentional in recruiting women for our board, faculty, students, and administrators in order to provide students with women mentors.

ETHNIC DIVERSITY

In Zimbabwe there are only two major tribes: the Shona comprise about 80 percent of the total population and the Ndebele comprise the remaining 20 percent, though each has many subgroups and dialects. Unknowingly, ALMA hired only Shona over the course of our first nine years. Eventually, when we needed a registrar, we found an Ndebele we wanted to hire. Our Shona employees brought to our attention. When I asked what difference that made, I was informed that this was something I needed to be aware of, as even among Christians there can be conflict between the two ethnic groups. Fortunately, after hiring this person no complications have occurred.

A second ethnic diversity issue that we learned about came with our application for a charter (formal documentation in Zimbabwe establishing and recognizing the institution). Early in ALMA's existence, we were told informally that a university charter could only be granted to a university with a Vice Chancellor who was Zimbabwean. Therefore, I would have to be replaced before a university charter could be granted. Though stated informally, this was an inflexible rule. Thus I began to develop a succession plan eight years before I actually stepped down. Having too many American missionaries filling key leadership positions of the ALMA made it look and feel like an American school rather than an African school.

Finally, we noticed we were hiring people from the same church. It was not intentional, but even so the people from this church regularly were well qualified. When we realized that half of our staff came from the same church, we decided we needed to diversify to avoid being accused of favoring a particular church in our hiring practices.

GENERATIONAL DIVERSITY

Given that the average life expectancy of a male in Zimbabwe is about thirty-eight, generational diversity does not play as significant a role there as in countries with longer average lifespans. In effect there is simply less generational diversity than elsewhere. However, given that the productive working life of a person is shorter than in most countries, that Zimbabwe's inflation rates destroyed retirement savings, and unemployment is eighty percent; anyone with a job is likely supporting an extended family of unemployed people from multiple generations. The extended family is very important in Zimbabwe and most people depend on it for their retirement, benefits, and savings. To lose one's family support is to risk destitution and therefore to be avoided.

There has been a great dependence on the Zimbabwean diaspora sending income to those at home. In fact, some become tired of working and simply wait for relatives to send money to them each month. This stifled their motivation for independence. However, giving many of these an opportunity to help themselves by starting a business or buying seeds to plant could be just what they need to get back on their feet and become productive again. Seeing the importance of family across generational lines in Zimbabwe was amazing to me since in my culture we didn't have this closeness. I often found that having gray hair, a calling from God, and children was often enough to be respected whatever the level of productivity.

SOCIOECONOMIC DIVERSITY

Socioeconomic diversity at ALMA was a key issue. The students came from many different economic levels. Most of them were business people and used to a certain standard of service and performance. Some were civil servants and community leaders. However, about 10 percent of ALMA's student body were pastors, many of whom came from very low economic levels. Though pastors did not have large amounts of money or other material resources, they had a lot of spiritual capital. For example, pastors sometimes did not understand the management and organization of the businesses when discussing them with business people. However, the pastors often challenged business leaders to take responsibility for their communities. This type of diversity in the class made for good growth and discussion.

Because the pastors were not well off economically, we had to establish a scholarship program to help them pay up to fifty percent of their school fees. We even challenged the business people to give to this scholarship fund. They did so, expressing their appreciation for the value that the pastors brought to the classroom and to their education as a whole.

Ben Naagaba, one of the pastors who studied ALMA, was killed in a car accident in Uganda before finishing his program. ALMA established a scholarship fund in his name, giving half each year to scholarship pastors and half to pay the school fees for Naagaba's six surviving children.

The business people also challenged ALMA to maintain high standards for our facility, for our teas, and for our hospitality. They wanted the environment at ALMA to be equal to what they were used to in the business environment. They specifically mentioned teas and how important it was to have high quality teas for the students. Many of them were given expense accounts by their companies to pay for their meals, but the pastors received nothing. To equalize things, we charged for the teas in our tuition structure so that everyone's standards could be maintained at a high level, with no student unable to participate.

ALMA has a goal to become operationally self-funded from tuition revenues and giving from local businesses that have benefited from ALMA students. In process, this teaches leadership by example. A leader knows how to manage his/her resources without having to depend on foreign donors. However, external donors are still able to contribute to capital development projects.

As an institution we also sponsored an orphanage and feeding program during one of the droughts. We felt that giving a portion of what ALMA received as an institution was a good use of our resources and an important way of demonstrating to the local community our commitment to give back. In addition to building leaders for today, we wanted to prepare leaders who would come in the future from the community.

SUMMARY

In summary, what did I learn from growing and turning over leadership at ALMA? First a succession plan needs to be in place as soon as the leader takes the position. This should not be left open ended. Second, if you want to recruit women as students you must make every effort to get them into leadership levels such as board, faculty, and staff. Without this welcoming environment you may only be recruiting women as token students and not as serious leadership contenders.

Third, it is important to attend to ethnic diversity without letting it drive your decisions, and you should be informed about ethnic issues that might adversely affect your institution. Listen to the staff when they inform you about various issues affecting their lives and ask how these same issues might play out on a bigger scale. Fourth, and finally, understanding the socialeconomic makeup of your students or members can help you grow the organization. Being sensitive to the needs of people and the community around you is always a good practice even when you make mistakes.

In my case, I continue to take delight in the fact that Zimbabwe is a beautiful country with beautiful people even as I pray that God will bless this land and the institutions like ALMA that are raising up leaders for kingdom purposes.

16

GENERATIONAL DIVERSITY AND WORLDVIEWS IN MISSIONS TODAY: A STUDY OF THE MILLENNIAL GENERATION

DALE WOLYNIAK

INTRODUCTION

The Bible has the power and capacity to speak truth to every generation and to transform not only the individual but to capture their heart for missions outreach. Understanding the generational cohorts and their experiences, expectations, and approach to life will better enable missional leadership to utilize each person's gifts as it relates to their placement and work relations. In this chapter I attempt to define the generational diversity and worldview of the Millennial generation and share some thoughts on how best to engage, enable, and empower them for fulfilling their call to missions. Based on worldviews and life experiences, as well as a Spirit-directed journey of faith in Christ, individuals and organizations are finding new challenges and opportunities to work with a variety of generations whom God is equipping, calling, and sending to the harvest field.

We will examine what agencies and individuals are saying about the workplace challenges concerning staffing needs and requirements and explore suggested best practices to support fluidity, unity, and growth in missional enterprises. Putting new wine into new wineskins, (Matt 9:17), suggests we may need, in principle and practice, to find new ways of infusing and strengthening our missionary efforts. It is our intention to minister to and with the next generation, in line with the declaration of Psalm 71:18: "Even when I am old and gray, do not forsake me, O God, till I declare your power to the next generation, your might to all who are to come."

GENERATIONAL DIFFERENCES

As much as missional agencies target people groups, we also acknowledge the people groups that God is raising up for missionary enterprises. Just as we identify and define cultures and language groups to reach with the gospel, we also need to understand those whom God is raising up as ambassadors to the far reaches of our postmodern world. An emphasis on understanding the differences between the generations and worldviews needs to be discussed prior to establishing effective ministry outreach teams, agencies, and church planting. Worldviews are how people view the world, based on experience, culture, and personal knowledge. Knowing who we are must come before doing the work of ministry. This will be an ongoing challenge as leadership recruits new personnel and the dynamics of the members of that younger generation taking their place in gospel ministry.

We must be careful that our generalizations do not offend the very people that God is raising up as ambassadors for Christ. Labeling can cause more distance between generations, but it can also help us understand some of the basic cohort beliefs, practices, and experiences needed for ministry planning. We recognize that there is within any age group variety and exceptions and that stereotyping creates barriers. Although I focus on the millennial generation in this chapter, it helps to set the context for our discussion if we make some observations from existing literature and studies more broadly focused on generational issues.

Generations Defined

A short description of each generation may help us in establishing an overview for our discussion. There are volumes of material on this topic but here are a few traits.

- Matures, or the Silent Generation, were born between 1928 and 1945. The label comes from their general compliance and commitment to civic duty. There are 35 million people in this group.
- Boomers are those born between 1945–1964, now with 80 million. This has been the largest population cohort until recently.

- Gen X, or Busters, are the birth cohort born between 1965–1978, with some 45 million today.
- Millennials were born between 1979–2010, and spanned the millennial time change, now 124 million strong. If we limit this group to those born between 1979–2000, there are 75 million of them (Census, 2008).

Table 8 indicates some of the tendencies of workers from the four generations. Note the differences in these areas which reflect experiences and expectations of each generation.

Table 8: Tendencies of Workers from the Four Generations
(Source: Diversity Leadership Guide 2006)

	Matures	Baby Boomers	Gen X-Busters	Millennials
Birth Years	Before 1945	1946–1964	1965–1978	1979–2000
Business Focus	Quality	Long hours	Productivity	Contribution
Motivator	Security	Money	Time off	Time off
Company Loyalty	Highest	High	Low	Low
Money is	Livelihood	Status symbol	Means to an end	Today's payoff
Value	Family/community	Success	Time	Individuality

Postmodernism Defined

Within the concept of generations in the workplace and the American population as a whole, it is also necessary to acknowledge that we are living in a postmodern era. Larry D. Pettegrew gives us a good definition of what postmodernism is, relative to ministry:

> Postmodernism is the vaguely defined new cultural paradigm that asserts that there are no absolutes or certainties, and that exalts pluralism and divergence. It expresses itself in many ways. In philosophy it assumes that perception does not necessarily reflect reality, and there may not be any reality to reflect in the first place. In metaphysics and ethics, postmodernism teaches "that there is no objective truth, that

moral values are relative, and that reality is socially constructed by a host of diverse communities." (Veith 1994) (Pettegrew 2006, 159–75)

It is with this postmodern culture, which is now worldwide, that missional efforts with a new generation of field workers must contend for the faith. In the midst of an increasing resistance to objective truth, and especially biblical truth, the challenge is being met, not with skepticism but hope and a willingness on the part of a younger generation of believers to do their part. As I developed this study, it became apparent that a better understanding of the Millennial generation and their worldview is needed by present leadership in missional organizations.

FOCUS: THE MILLENNIAL GENERATION

As the Millennial generation is coming to the workplace, it is important that agencies and leadership teams understand this culturally diverse group. Cam Marston, in his DVD program, *Mixing Four Generations in the Workplace*, stated that Millennials

> like to align themselves with individuals who will help them achieve their goals. They seek open, constant communication from the boss. Interestingly, they work quite well with members of the Mature generation. New Millennials seek personal fulfillment from their jobs, not necessarily financial security. Among the most overscheduled youth in our nation's history, they seek ways to shed stress in their lives. . . . In the workplace, New Millennials are torn between individuality and fitting in. They want to be like their peers—but with a twist. They are loyal and consider a company's altruistic attitude and culture. They don't want to be hurried and will take the time to search for a unique answer. *New Millennials seek personal fulfillment from their jobs, not necessarily financial security yet.* (Martson, n.d., 10)

Marston identifies the trait of trying to fit in and yet maintaining one's own individuality. This trait, common to every generation, has taken on new significance as the Millennials enter the workforce. Some of the conflict with older generations in missions deals with their worldview of what is important and valued.

Chapter 16

What Management Is Saying

Daniel Rasmus, Microsoft director of information for Work Vision, identifies traits that characterize the Millennial generation:

- Lacks trust in corporations
- Focuses on personal success
- Has a short-term career perspective
- Is quickly bored
- Is team oriented
- Builds community
- Sees no clear boundary between work and life in general
- Is socially responsible
- Will sacrifice economic rewards for work–life balance
- Expects to work anytime, anyplace. (Rasmus 2007, 3)

From this short list we can see both positive attributes as well as those that may cause tension and conflict when it comes to building teams, accomplishing task-related items, and issues of trust and loyalty.

The Millennial attitudes and expectations are different from those of succeeding generations. Rasmus shares the following guidelines that Microsoft developed in the hope that they may help other organizations working with Millennials:

- Create engaging environments that inspire, challenge, and motivate employees
- Integrate Millennials into a variety of projects, assignments, and career opportunities
- Favor flexible work schedules, locations, and arrangements (telework, work at home, and job share)
- Use the diverse experiences and backgrounds of the workforce to create innovative work environments that challenge assumptions and create new opportunities
- Harness personal talents and skills by creating opportunities for people to contribute in a variety of roles
- Involve them in collaborative, team-based projects and environments

- Allow and support the pursuit of personal and social outside activities
- Create effective training and mentoring opportunities
- Harness knowledge created "just in time" through personal networks and recognize contributions from new methods of work. (Rasmus 2007, 3)

Rasmus focuses on meeting expectations of the individual and yet incorporating positive workplace attitudes and delivery systems to accomplish organizational goals. Although his discussion is from a business perspective, the principles apply to a missional context. There is a high value placed on independence and teamwork, both of which needed on the mission field.

Cameron Strang, founder of Relevant Media, expressed his viewpoint quite clearly:

> My generation is discontent with dead religion. We don't want to show up on Sunday, sing two hymns, hear a sermon and go home. The Bible says we're supposed to die for this thing. If I'm going to do that, this has to be worth something. Our generation wants a tangible experience of God who is there. (2004)

This millennial generation wants a real encounter with God as well as an experience with God that will hold them in these changing times. We create ministry outreach to the Millennial generation that is rich, deep, and meaningful. Those who journey into missions will continue to value that type of mobilization effort and personal input by leaders in their places of service.

Margaret Heffernan explains that there are three major areas that need management's attention: "I think that, underneath the dazzling differences, three perennial commonalities remain: the desire for fairness, the need to be stretched, and a yearning for community" (2005). Each of these areas requires support and development for employee satisfaction and for the health and growth of the individuals, and this applies not only to secular settings but to the missionary workforce and ministry as well. Millennials want to be challenged, encouraged, and treated fairly in the workplace. Though the working for an agency in an international location is not what Heffernan's envisioned, the reality of millennial expectations remains the same. Wise field leaders will incorporate these essentials when managing younger workers and ministers on wherever they serve.

A Pew Research Survey (Feb 2010) identified additional the characteristics of the Millennial generation that are informative:

> Other characteristics of Millennials are: confident, liberal, upbeat, open to change. They embrace multiple modes of self-expression: three-quarters have created a profile on a social networking site; one-in-five have posted a video of themselves online; four-in-ten have a tattoo (for most who do, one is not enough—half of those with tattoos have two to five and 18 percent have six or more). They treat their hand-held gadgets almost like a body part with eight-in-ten sleeping with a cell phone glowing by their bed. (Profiling the Millennials, 2010)

Millennials are finding their way in society, utilizing their techno-savvy to feel and stay connected. They bring with them a variety of new skills and creativity that can be used by God's purposes. Susan Heathfield, a management and organizational development consultant in human resources, noted:

> Millennials have a "can-do" attitude about tasks at work and look for feedback about how they are doing frequently—even daily. Millennials want a variety of tasks and expect that they will accomplish every one of them. Positive and confident, Millennials are ready to take on the world. (Heathfield n.d.)

The openness to take risks, and the fluidity or adaptation to new challenges seems to be a hallmark of this generation—which makes them a perfect fit for cross-cultural engagement in Christian missions. Wise missional leadership will take this into consideration when enlisting and engaging this younger generation in the tasks they assign—seeing them as opportunities to tap into the creative and positive approach to life.

Missionary Context and Generational Differences

Many ministries enlist, engage, and empower this younger generation. One only needs to review the ministry groups like YWAM, Avant Ministries, Pioneers,

TEAM, and others, to find a fresh wave of enthusiasm and proactive efforts to mobilize Millennials to share the gospel worldwide.

The story of YWAM, which started in 1960, indicates that there is a place for today's youth. Designed to engage and expose individuals to creative missionary outreach, YWAM is keeping up with the demand to be involved in ministry.

> YWAM is now comprised of people from over 150 countries and a large number of Christian denominations, with over half of the organization's staff coming from "non-Western" countries. There are currently over 16,000 full-time workers in nearly 1,100 operating locations in 171 nations. It has been estimated that over 25,000 individuals participate in YWAM training programs and outreaches each year. (YWAM n.d.)

The InterVarsity-sponsored Urbana Conference of 2009 reported that of the 15,800 college-age students registered 2,676 made a commitment to serve two or more years as a missionary; 4,990 made a commitment to short-term missions; and $900,000 was raised at that event for specific ministries. There were 256 organizations that were representing various mission agencies and parachurch ministries. This five-day event is held every three years and has been since 1946. The goal of Urbana is to engage the younger generation for world missions. This very positive event brings awareness, information, and opportunities to serve Christ globally. Such events are a channel to discovery for this present generation (Urbana 2009).

Value Implications of Age Groups

Murray Decker writes about what Millennials value, how they see the world, how they view missions, and how leadership can best relate to them. Especially revealing is his statement on relationships:

> Students expect that mission training and service will be built upon a foundation of relationship and community. Nothing is more attractive to them than honest and authentic relationships. Students who are generally averse to making commitments will commit to a community typified by honesty, authenticity and intimacy. Further, students have an expectation of intimacy and depth from their prospective leaders.

"Can we hang out?" is the highest compliment a college student can pay you. "Will you make time to spend with me?" is the unasked question that underlies most conversations between them and any potential mentor. (Decker 2007, 317)

It is a characteristic of the younger Millennials that relationships are more important than process, product, or programs. Mission agencies and organizations that are proactive in creating a healthy and safe environment for relationships will be most effective in bringing about healthy teams with Millennials.

One of the fresh efforts of the Millennial generation to engage church culture is "Q." This organization, under the direction of Gabe Lyons, gathers annually to "recover a vision and responsibility to renew and restore cultures," using the following framework:

> Q was created as a place where church and cultural leaders could come together to collaborate and explore ideas about how the Gospel can be expressed within our cultural context. Our method of learning is simple: exposure, conversation and collaboration. We didn't want to create just another conference, but instead, make an intentional effort to platform the best and the brightest ideas that are shaping our world and interact with them. (Q 2010)

Q brings a new and younger Christian worldview to the stage of gospel outreach. It seeks to communicate, equip, and engage the American Christian and church leadership to find new ways to reach our own culture with the gospel as well as the cultures of our world. Many of the topics and essays challenge current practices and programs of the larger church community, which in some ways should engage them in dialogue and assessment for renewal and growth.

Viewpoints on Work in Missions

Mark Clark of Team Ministries notes: "What makes them so different is their excitement and lack of strong fear about reaching out to countries and regions across the world where sharing the Gospel is illegal and life-threatening" (2009). This quality of adventure and lack of fear may indeed be a gift of

God, as many places around the world are hostile and unfriendly places for traditional missionary outreach. It appears that God is raising up a generation that is bold, courageous, and willing to sacrifice for kingdom purposes.

Jim Millirons, of the Southern Baptist Convention, discusses how they need to reach the North American population with new approaches. What he says also applies to cross-cultural settings:

> We can no longer target the population most like us and be effective in fulfilling the mission call of God to reach everyone, everywhere (Matt 28, Acts 1:8). That is not to suggest that our builder and boomer driven models are not successful. The opposite is true as their success is well documented. They continue to effectively reach the modern builder and boomer cultures, but the world is increasingly becoming postmodern and millennial. (Millirons 2006, 5)

Millirons suggests that the SBC review and establish leadership and outreach that will take into consideration the general population's cultural shift. Though his statements are primarily focused on the American church, what he says applies in broader missional contexts. Many of the twenty recommendations Millirons gives for reaching this new generation and changing culture directly apply to international efforts.

James Nored discusses the issue of the message for a postmodern society, and in many ways for a postmodern world. We need to not only reach out to a postmodern world, but develop an understanding of those postmodern individuals who look to serve in international ministry:

> In a world that is skeptical of truth, knowledge, language, power, and personal agendas, we must build trust through honesty, openness, patience, and authenticity. [Stanley] Grenz is correct, however, in asserting that the metanarrative must be recovered, for this metanarrative is central to the Christian story. The metanarrative of God's love and mission can provide shaping to those who have been tossed about by divorce, abuse, loneliness, nihilism, and other destructive elements of culture, providing hope for an open, diverse, but often skeptical and hopeless world. Grenz has analyzed these issues well and

provided a way forward for the church to reach out to postmodern culture. (Nored n.d.)

Trust and authenticity are required of Christian churches and missional efforts to reach a postmodern culture. The larger message, the metanarrative, moves forward through individuals of each generation who are willing to surrender agendas, attitudes, and approaches that are offensive or ineffective in sharing the love and grace of Jesus Christ. So it is not the message that needs to change but the messengers and their methods.

BEST PRACTICES

Success in any endeavor requires one to match skills with the challenge presented. Today we have several generations in the missionary workplace, all trying to fulfill their calling by using their gifts to bring people to Christ and glory to God. Within the concept of enabling a younger generation of missionaries, we need to shift our focus from a "come" to a "go." Tim Neufeld discusses Mark Senter's concept of a "going" mentality:

> Here he uses missiologist George W. Peter's discussion of centripetal and centrifugal approaches to mission. "*Centripetal* efforts draw momentum towards a central point (in other words, the church), while *centrifugal* strategies spin energy toward the periphery (or the non-church)." We can clearly see the historical distinction between church and parachurch. The church has a "come" mentality focusing on the community (centripetal) and the parachurch has a "go" mentality focusing on the unchurched (centrifugal). (Neufeld 2002, 198)

The Millennial generation is more than willing to go with the gospel, which lines up well with the parachurch movement which focuses more on outreach and less on consolidation. Tapping into the positive attitudes of relationship building, community, and exploration, the Millennial generation is perfect for reaching the unchurched. Finding new and creative ways of bringing the life-giving message of hope in Jesus Christ is a key developmental task of this generation.

There is a need on the part of existing church and mission leadership to be intentional in activating its youth and young adults into participative roles. Neufeld continues:

> Regarding the second issue, when students will participate in the ministry and life of the church, Senter says there are two answers: either now or in the future. Some churches decide to activate their adolescents and engage them in the present life and ministry of the congregation. Others understand their mission as one of preparing students for healthy roles in the church of the future. "Simply put, the question boils down to whether young people are the church of the future or of the present." (Senter 2001) (Neufeld 2002, 198)

In the context of our discussion, the Millennial generation is rising to the occasion of world missions and is bringing with them both fresh energy and vision even as they bring new challenges to traditional leadership modes. As Murray Decker indicates that mentors and guides who hope to keep connected with this generation need to: 1. keep it personal, 2. connect one-on-one, 3. remain open to ongoing dialog about the role of women, and finally 4. commit and sacrifice. Each of these will build loyalty with this generation and serve the greater goal of world evangelization. By building awareness of the needs and expectations of new missional workers, organizations can assist these missionaries to fulfill their unique call to follow Christ (2007, 3).

One last venture into how organizations are managing to reach and keep Millennials is the US Military Chaplaincy. Drawing from the insights of from Eddie Gibbs, Chaplain R. M. Coffey (2006, 13) identifies characteristics needed to recruit and retain Millennials. The items in Coffey's list that are of particular importance to mission agencies include:

- Emphasize the need for *depth in teaching* and community activities;
- Focus on *responding to the needs* of the community, especially the poor;
- Be *culturally sensitive* by *either* being multicultural *or* organized according to culture;

- Recognize the need for clear messages of *integrity* coupled with refusal to soften radical impact;
- Have *intentional discipleship or mentoring*—challenging people rather than building a larger crowd;
- Emphasize *networking and technology* to supplement church services;
- Demonstrate *compassionate service*; and,
- Practice *holistic spirituality*—rejection of any dichotomy of spiritual and secular.

SUMMARY THOUGHTS

When we consider the missionary challenges that were met by past generations of actively engaged Christians and organizations, we see a shift in the attitudes and expectations of the Millennial generation. There is a need to connect with each generation and to understand the developmental tasks that must be met—to bring about wholeness and stability for the future of the church. The Millennial generation is open to the Great Commission and sacrificial service and wants to be included in God's work.

Worldviews are shaped by a variety of circumstances and experiences. When we take time to assess our lives through observation and critical evaluation, then we will discover some major shifts in our thinking, belief systems, and action outcomes. Each generation has its own peculiar traits, and yet we must remember that people are individuals and do not always fit broad categories. Paul Hiebert cites Brian Walsh's idea that "worldviews are the plausibility structures that provide answers to our ultimate questions" (Hiebert 2008, 29). These assumptions are seldom studied; they are simply taken for granted. Healthy missional leadership will make an intentional effort to harness an awareness of trends, cultural shifts, generational worldviews, and expectations for each generation of candidates. In doing so, they will not neglect present employees. They do both to bring about wholeness and maturity for the days to come.

It is apparent that North American churches are making the effort to develop new approaches to ministry, with due consideration to the cultural changes in society. Millirons' conclusion fits: "The church will always be challenged to contend for the faith, contextualize the gospel, and communicate the good news in diverse cultural forms providing the opportunity for Jesus to embed, impact, and transform every culture and community" (2006, 12).

It is leadership which rightly understands the differences, dynamics, and gifts of a new generation—a generation well-versed in Scripture and cross-cultural awareness—that will bring about the desired fruit of people entering into vital relationship with Christ and new churches established. New wine is needed, and that new wine needs new wineskins. Traditional approaches to missional efforts must give way and adapt to new forms, new people, but without losing the integrity of the message of salvation in Christ Jesus.

Potential and present missional workers of all generations will need to know who their fellow workers are, and what characteristics or traits they carry with them, to establish effective work teams, outreach ministries, and church-planting efforts. Learning to accommodate new expectations requires leadership to pay attention and orient their ministers and cross-cultural workers to the dynamics of the diversity of generations and worldviews. Effective ministries will produce lasting fruit when assumptions and attitudes of the present workforce are informed, concerned, and gracious to a new generation of harvesters. Generational diversity need not be seen as a problem to overcome, as much as an opportunity to engage, enlist, and empower for a concerted effort in sharing Christ.

REFERENCES

Census. 2008. http://www.census.gov/popest/national/asrh/NC-EST2008/NC-EST2008-01.xls.

Clark, Mark. 2009. Millennial generation shows no fear. http://mnnonline.org/article/13521.

Coffey, Chaplain R. M. 2006. USAWC strategy research project, Chaplain ministry to the millennial generation, United States Army. http://www.dtic.mil/cgibin/GetTRDoc?Location= U2&doc=GetTRDoc.pdf&AD=ADA449547.

Decker, Murray. 2007. The emerging college generation and missions: Issues, attitudes, postures and passions. *Evangelical Missions Quarterly* (July, 2007), 316–325.

Diversity Leadership Guide. 2006. NASA. www.grc.nasa.gov/WWW/diversity.

Heathfield, Susan. n.d. Managing Millennials: Eleven tips for managing Millennials. http://humanresources.about.com/od/managementtips/a/millenials.htm .

Heffernan, Margaret. 2005. Managing generational differences in the workplace. http://www.fastcompany.com/resources/talent/heffernan/managing-generational-differences/052507.html?page=0%2C0.

Hiebert, Paul G. 2008. Transforming worldviews: An anthropological understanding of how people change. Grand Rapids. Baker Academic.

Marston, Cam. n.d. Mixing four generations in the workplace. Learning Communications. http://www.crmlearning.com/mixing-four-generations-in-the-workplace.

Millennials: confident, connected, open to change. 2010. Pew Research Center, http://pewresearch.org/pubs/1501/%20millennials-new-survey-generational-personality-upbeat-open-new-ideas-technology-bound.

Millirons, Jim. 2006. Embracing the missional resurgence of the Southern Baptist Convention without going emergent. An Occasional Paper. http://www.missionalnetworkweb.com/files/Embracing%20the%20Missional%20Resurgance%20of%20SBC%5B1%5D.pdf.

Neufeld, Tim. 2002. Postmodern models of youth ministry. *Direction Journal* 31 (2): 194–205, http://www.directionjournal.org/article/?1265.

Nored, James. n.d. A primer on post-modernism. http://www.missionaloutreachnetwork.com /forum/topics/a-primer-on-postmodernism-by.

Pettegrew, Larry D. 2006. Evangelicalism, paradigms, and the emerging church. http://www.tms.edu/tmsj/tmsj17h.pdf.

Profiling the Millennials. 2010. http://www.parsonage.org/images/pwbe/issues/PWBE-100305.cfm.

Q. 2010. http://www.qideas.org/information/new.aspx.

Rasmus, Daniel W. 2007. The next-generation workforce and project management. ASK Magazine 28 (Fall), http://askmagazine.nasa.gov/issues/28/28i_next_generation.html.

Senter, Mark H. III, ed. 2001. Four views of youth ministry and the church: Inclusive congregational, preparatory, missional, strategic. Grand Rapids: Zondervan.

Strang, Cameron. 2004. Christian cool and the new generation gap. New York Times, http://www.nytimes.com/2004/05/16/weekinreview/16lela.html?pagewanted=1.

Urbana 2009. 2009. http://www.urbana.org/urbana09.

Veith, Gene Edward. 1994. *Postmodern times*. Wheaton: Crossway Books.

YWAM. n.d. http://www.search.com/reference/Youth_With_A_Mission.

17

A BIBLICAL BALANCE BETWEEN CHRISTIAN UNITY AND ETHNIC DIVERSITY

CARLOS G. MARTIN

The United States has often been called the "melting pot" of the world. Those using this concept sought to submerge new Americans and minority ethnic groups into the "American way of life" which resulted in the loss of the unique self-identity and heritage of these groups. However, according to social historians, demographers, and others, there seems to be little reality in the hope that this nation will once again have one unified cultural pattern (Booth 1998). Ethnic groupings will not quickly lose their identities, since their numbers are constantly growing. Today there are appearing new terms such as "stew pot" (Wagner 1979, 51)[1] and "mosaic" (Torres 2004; Belew 1974), indicating some blending of flavor, but retaining many qualities of the original ingredients.

It is a fact that "human beings show an overwhelming predisposition to band together with 'their own kind'" (Kraft 1978, 121). Donald McGavran articulated what is now called "the homogeneous unit principle": people "like to become Christians without crossing racial, linguistic or class barriers" (McGavran 1980, 223; Conn 1983, 86). However, this principle has been challenged for the sake of unity (Elliot 1982, 53–63; Dubose 1978, 121–34; McSwain 1980, 521–38; Fong 1996).

My purpose here is to present a biblical basis by which the church, in its search for an appropriate missionary methodology, must take into account the multilingual, multicultural dimensions of the society. Biblical passages

---

[1] "In a stew pot, each ingredient adds its characteristic flavor to every other ingredient, but all maintain their identities and integrity."

will be discussed in order to understand the relationship between unity and ethnicity. It should be noted here that the main emphasis of this presentation will not be racial but rather cultural and linguistic differences.

THE WORD OF GOD FOR ALL NATIONS

Many passages of the Old Testament illustrate God's purpose to the nations and the church's missionary task among the peoples of the world. Very early God appointed Israel to be a "kingdom of priests" (Ex 19:5–6).[1] The whole nation was to function on behalf of the kingdom of God in a mediatorial role in relation to the nations. Although Israel was supposed to be a "light to lighten the nations," and had a mission to "bring forth justice to the nations," (Isa 42:1–4, 6: 49:6) she forgot her call to be sharers of the blessings, truth, gifts, and the "seed" to the nations. The nations came to Israel, but she did not go out to them.[2]

During the days of the exile, Israelites were dispersed and the Law was taken by the Jews of the Diaspora to the ends of the earth as they knew it. But other changes occurred among the Jews of Babylonia and Persia. The language spoken by them was no longer Hebrew, but Aramaic. The Jews of the West also faced a similar problem: Hebrew was being forgotten, and the children of the Hebrew families came more and more under the influence of Hellenism. The Scriptures were not being read and studied. Hence, there arose a need for a translation from Hebrew into Greek. This translation was done sometime in the third century BC in Alexandria and came to be known as the *Septuagint* (LXX) because it was supposed to have been the work of seventy scholars. The point is, that this translation was made because of the need to communicate the Scriptures in the context of relevant languages of the people.

Many centuries later, after that pioneering translation, as the gospel started to be preached in every land, the problem of communication was felt more decisively every day. For that reason, missionaries and scholars learned languages and aimed to convey God's Word in terms that people could understand. This knowledge has been used to translate the message of God and to produce

---

1   Unless otherwise indicated, all Scripture references are from the New King James Version (NKJV).
2   Various writers say that the Old Testament makes no mention of a missionary mandate. Kane says that in the messages of the prophets before the captivity there is no reference of Israel's going out to spread the knowledge of Israel's ethical monotheism and the glory and power of her God and King" (Kane 1987, 28). Blauw insists on the concept of presence and suggests that Israel's mission was not calling the nations but being the "visible manifestation of the deeds of God in and with Israel" (Blauw 1962, 37). This writer does not agree with this position. For a detailed explanation of Israel's missionary role, see Kaiser 1999 and 2000.

newer versions of the Scriptures. Hundreds of versions and translations have multiplied their testimony—that teaching God's message in a way this revelation is understood and accepted requires using the other person's language. This is making possible the fulfillment of the prophecy: "The earth shall be full of the knowledge of the Lord as the waters cover the sea" (Isa 11:9).

The New Testament keeps the original purpose of saving "the nations." In most cases of the New Testament the word, *ethnos,* is used in the sense of "a people." Synonymous are *phule* (people as a national unity of common descent), *laos* (people as a political unity with a common history and constitution), and *glossa* (people as a linguistic unity). Ethnos is "the most general and therefore the weakest of these terms, having simply an ethnographical sense and denoting the natural cohesion of a people in general" (Schmidt 1983). As the concept of peoples or nations is pushed more into the background, the concept of individual salvation is brought to the front. However, the redemption of the whole world is still God's plan (John 3:16–17).

A SAVIOR FOR ALL NATIONS

Unlike his compatriots, Jesus was free from racial prejudice. Most of his public ministry was spent in "Galilee of the Gentiles," (Matt 4:15) and on many occasions he ministered to Samaritans. The fact that the Jews had no dealings with the Samaritans in no way deterred him from preaching in that part of the country. Following the conversation with the woman of Samaria, he remained there two days and during that time many Samaritans believed (John 4:39–42). On another occasion Jesus healed ten lepers, only one of whom returned to give glory to God, and he was a Samaritan (Luke 17:11–19). On still another occasion, when Samaritan villagers refused to extend hospitality to Jesus, he rebuked his disciples as they suggested that they should be destroyed: "The Son of Man did not come to destroy men's lives but to save them" (Luke 9:56).

His healing ministry went beyond the Samaritans, who were half Jews, to the Romans, who were outright Gentiles. Mark informs us that his teaching and healing ministry extended far beyond the confines of Galilee and Judea to Idumaea, Transjordan, Tyre, and Sidon (Mark 3:7–8). Matthew speaks of his fame as having spread throughout all Syria, with great crowds following him from Galilee and Decapolis (Matt 4:24–25). Even Greeks wished to see Jesus (John 12:20).

Some of Jesus' most beautiful praises were from members of despised ethnic groups. He spoke directly to a Roman centurion whose faith he highly praised (Luke 7:1–10), to a Syrophenician woman (Mark 7:26), and to two Roman officers, including Pilate (John 18:33–38). No race or ethnic group was rejected in his ministry.

At the very heart of Jesus' mission is a focused attempt to break down ethnocentrism, the attitude to ethnicity which holds at a distance those who do not share one's ethnic identity. He does this by redefining the people of God in nonethnic terms, by preparing a faithful remnant of Israel to break through ethnic barriers, and by establishing a foundation for a multiethnic church (Geddert 1988, 73).

What language did he use with that great diversity of people? He must have been at least a bilingual man, at home in Aramaic (Gertz 2004), which was the common Palestinian tongue, and Greek (Robertson 1984), the universal language of his day spoken freely in Galilee of the Gentiles, and possibly Latin (Edersheim 1980, 253).

According to Matthew 28:19–20, Christ's followers were commanded, "Having gone, therefore, disciple all nations" (Lenski 1943, 1170). Those who are to be made disciples are described as *panta ta ethne* (all the nations). There is some disagreement among New Testament scholars about the exact meaning of *panta ta ethne* (Meler 1977, 1). The question is whether it refers to Gentiles only, or to nations, including the Jews.

McGavran, who frequently cites panta ta ethne untranslated, interprets it as referring to "the classes, tribes, lineages, and peoples of earth," and a number of other scholars agree with him (McGavran 1980, 22; Tippett 1970, 30, 32; Yamamori 1980, 49). Thus "ethne" is interpreted in an ethnological or sociological sense; it refers to homogeneous units of people sharing common characteristics, particularly a common racial, linguistic, and class heritage. Other interpretations of "ethne" stress a religious designation, based in the Old Testament, where *goyyim* is to be mostly understood as a designation not for nations but for Gentiles or pagans (Bosch 1983, 236).

This researcher thinks that both interpretations above are extremes. *Ta ethne* refers not to homogeneous units of people nor has a restricted religious sense but simply "all nations" of the earth. "Not just the Jews scattered among the Gentiles, but the Gentiles themselves in every land" (Robertson 1983, 245; Lenski 1943, 1173).

Before ascending into heaven, Jesus commanded his disciples to stay in Jerusalem until they were given power at the Holy Spirit's descent upon them. At Pentecost, when Jews from around the world made pilgrimage to the Holy City, the believers were filled with the Holy Spirit and "began to speak with other tongues, as the Spirit gave them utterance" (Acts 2:4). This event has been described as the birth of language missions (Romo n.d., 10).

Peter's limited viewpoint is seen in his opening statement of explanation to this crowd of people from over fifteen nations: "Men of Judea and all who dwell in Jerusalem" (2:14) and later insists: "Men of Israel, hear these words ... " (2:22). Nonetheless, the Spirit moved three thousand to respond to the message (2:41), and it is reasonable to assume they included many of the nations represented in the crowd.

Luke, the writer of Acts, was likely a Gentile from Syrian Antioch, writing to Theophilus, a fellow Greek (1:1). Thus the issue of ethnicity and religion was bound to influence Acts because both its author and its recipient had non-Palestinian backgrounds.

"But you shall receive power when the Holy Spirit has come upon you; and you shall be witnesses to Me in Jerusalem, and in Judea and Samaria, and to the end of the earth." Kane says that Luke built his entire book around Acts 1:8. The book divides into three clearly defined parts and traces the expansion of Christianity in concentric circles, beginning with Jerusalem (1–7), progressing to Judea (8–12), extending ultimately to the ends of the earth (13–28) (Kane 1987, 51).

A WALL OF SEPARATION

But the church of Jerusalem was reluctant to go into an ethnic world. Don Richardson suggests that the book of Acts actually records the twelve apostles' reluctance to obey the Great Commission instead of their obedience to it (Richardson 1999, 104). Their Jewish proclivities were so deep that some even traveled to other towns with a tendency to make Christianity a sect of Judaism.

Ephesians 2:11–22 refers to the segregation of Jews and Gentiles at worship services in the temple. Loyal Jews erected a wall between the inner court, open only to Jews, and the outer court, open to Gentiles. Thus they tried to prevent contamination of the sanctuary—the boundaries of which did not extend beyond the inner court—by the uncircumcised (Beare 1984, 655). The transgression of this taboo carried with it the penalty of death, a fact to which unsuspecting Gentiles were alerted through bilingual inscriptions (Greek and Latin) at regular intervals on this wall (Josephus 1957, 5:2).

The wall of separation, however, began to show the first signs of cracking. Philip preached the gospel in Samaria and many requested to be baptized (Acts 8:12). How did the Jerusalem church react? They sent Peter and John to them (Acts 8:14). Had not John wanted to call down fire from heaven to destroy the Samaritans when they had rejected Jesus (Luke 9:52–54)? It was this same "Son of Thunder" who joined Peter in visiting Samaria (Acts 8:14). Perhaps the barrier between Jews and Samaritans was really crossed when the apostles' prayer for them was followed by the laying on of hands (8:15). Jews had touched Samaritans!

Another crack of the wall was Peter's visit with the Roman centurion, Cornelius. In following God's directions, Peter entered the Gentile's house, something unthinkable for a Jew (Acts 10:28). Peter, in a somehow official manner, went over the wall into the Gentile yard. Not of his own volition, to be sure, but he did. And he declared, "You are well aware that it is against our law for a Jew to associate with a Gentile or visit him. But God has shown me that I should not call any man impure or unclean." (Acts 10:28). Before Peter could complete his sermon, the Spirit fell upon both Jews and Gentiles.

Disciples scattered by persecution (Acts 8:4) went to Syrian Antioch and spread the news of Jesus among the cosmopolitan citizens of that city (11:19). From Syrian Antioch, at the call of the Spirit and with the concurrence of the congregation, Barnabas and Paul were sent forth as cross-cultural missionaries (13:1–3). They sowed the seed of the gospel in Cyprus (13:4), Iconium (14:1), Lystra (14:8), Derbe (14:20), and other cities of Asia Minor (14:24–25). Then, at the Lord's express direction, Paul and his colleagues bypassed some areas and went on to answer the Macedonian call (16:9). Crossing over into Europe, they evangelized the military center of Philippi (16:12), the seaport city of Thessalonica (17:1), Berea (17:10), sophisticated Athens (17:16), and immoral Corinth (18:1). Later trips included Malta (28:1), and even the imperial Rome (28:31), and Paul wrote of plans for penetrating as far west as Spain (Rom 15:24).

Jews were found in significant numbers throughout the Roman Empire as well as beyond its limits. Jerusalem remained, however, the focus of the Jewish religion. But there was a notable division among the Jews of Jerusalem. Hopler points out that there were Hellenists (Jews influenced by the Greek culture, speaking the Greek language) as well as Mesopotamian Jews, Egyptian Jews, Asian Jews, and others. But the most numerous were Palestinian Jews, who held to their own culture, traditions, and language (Aramaic) (Hopler 1981, 80).

The Talmud speaks of 480 synagogues in Jerusalem (Lenski 1961, 250). Hopler suggests that there were different synagogues for different language groups (such as Aramaic and Greek), for different ethnic groups (such as Egyptian, Mesopotamian, and Creteans—see Acts 6:9), and even for different trades (such as copper workers) in what Hopler calls a de facto segregation (1981, 84). Luke's record shows that the basic ecclesiastical unit for Christians was the house church (Acts 2:46; 5:42; 12:12, 17; 21:18). The pattern of house churches within the early Christian community tended to preserve this cultural diversity as believers gathered to worship in what Wagner would call "homogeneous units" (1979, 122–23). Ethnic tensions naturally arose in this atmosphere.

TENSIONS AMONG CULTURES IN THE EARLY CHURCH

In the early days the church was bicultural, but the Hebrews provided the top leadership. "To summarize this pecking order, Palestinian Jews were on top, followed by the Diaspora Jews (principally Hellenists), with proselytes and God-fearers next, and Samaritans (who Jews regarded as heretics) and Gentiles at the bottom" (Hopler 1981, 81). The first problem related to ethnic tensions put to test the unity of the church. "There arose a murmuring against the Hebrews by the Hellenists, because their widows were neglected in the daily distribution" (Acts 6:1).

Like many missionaries today, who have fallen into the error of assuming the leadership of churches in the new cultures to which they have been called, the apostles were probably talking behind the Hellenist believers' backs in Aramaic, a language the Hellenists could not understand. No wonder friction developed (Wagner 1994, 175)!

Luke described the charge of the Hellenist widows being neglected as a class discrimination offense. There is no defense for the partiality, from either Luke or the apostles. It was just that everyone was too busy. A group of poor women belonging to a particular cultural-language group happened not to receive "the daily distribution" and felt discriminated against.

The apostles called the community gathered in house churches and asked them to choose seven men who would be responsible for the daily distribution (Acts 6:2–6). "Then the twelve summoned the multitude of the disciples" (Acts 6:2). The fact that the apostles called a congregational meeting indicates that they had realized that the problem was serious. The apostles advised the leadership to expand by involving other church members (Acts 6:3–4). "They recognized that the Hellenists felt isolated from the power structure of the whole community" (Hopler 1981, 86), so they chose seven men who probably had already emerged as leaders among their own people group. All seven men elected for office had Greek names (Wagner 1994, 184–86). The unity of the church across cultural barriers was preserved. The immediate result of this form of witnessing was that "the word of God spread, and the number of the disciples multiplied greatly in Jerusalem" (6:7). Luke adds that also many of the priests became obedient to the faith (Acts 6:7). Wagner suggests that "when the Hellenists became indigenized and moved out under their own leadership, the priests now could become a part of a more purely Hebrew Messianic community without compromising their own integrity" (Wagner 1994, 189). The church of Jerusalem manifested both the unity and the diversity of the body of Christ.

Antioch is another example of a multicultural church. Each of the leaders mentioned in Acts 13:1–3 is identified by his ethnic background: an African, an Asian, and a Palestinian. These not only represented different ethnic and geographical areas, but almost certainly different language groups. Since people usually desire to pray in the language of their homeland, it is almost certain that Antioch followed the pattern of house churches started in Jerusalem. It is probable that these three elders in Antioch were elected to represent smaller groups of believers. This would demonstrate a considerable degree of unity and trust within the church in Antioch. Again, just as happened in Jerusalem, Christians demonstrated that "authentic unity is always unity in diversity" (Wagner 1979, 96).

Wagner suggests that had the New Testament churches not been homogeneous unit churches, they could not have multiplied as rapidly as they did (Wagner 1979, 117). In regards to the rapid growth of the church in Antioch, he says that it is "reasonable to postulate" that a cluster of house churches with Gentile membership was established quite separately from the Jewish groups (Wagner 1979, 124–25). Wagner also believes that in Rome (1979, 130–31) and in Thessalonica (1979, 131), house churches were homogeneous units.

In sharp contrast with Wagner's opinions, Rene Padilla says that "the uses of the homogeneous principle for church growth has no biblical foundation" (Padilla 1983, 301) so "exclusive groupings of believers, whether around individual leaders for theological or other reasons (1 Cor 1:10–13) or around homogeneous cultural units, are unacceptable in the Christian church" (Bosch 1983, 240). This writer thinks that both positions are extreme. While it is hard to believe that there was no racial prejudice among early Christians or that they formed pure homogeneous units, it is also clear that there are evidences of ethnic groups which used their language and culture to spread the gospel among their equals.

The fact is that the gospel incorporates all the nations and ethnic and social groups of the earth. That is what the early church discovered. Although they may have begun with a de facto segregation, the Holy Spirit opened their eyes. As the Holy Spirit began to open doors, they walked through them, one-by-one, until the church changed from a sect of Judaism to a universal church that included Samaritans, Ethiopians, Greeks, Asians, Romans—anybody who would come to the faith. That is the story that Luke was telling Theophilus.

Paul was a multicultural and bilingual man from an ethnic minority. He spoke Greek and was a citizen of a city noted for its Greek culture. He was a Roman citizen (Acts 22:25–29; 21:39; 23:7) and probably also spoke in Latin (Robertson 1956). He was a Jew; his education under Rabbi Gamaliel at Jerusalem (Acts 22:3) was Hebraic and surely he also spoke Aramaic. His Hebrew name was Saul; Paul was his Greek name.

Before his conversion, he had been a Jew and continued to be one, but he was also a Hellenistic Jew. His Bible was the Greek Septuagint. Ferdinand Prat says that Paul was familiar with the Bible in two languages, but he almost always quoted it in Greek. Possibly as he wrote in Greek, the Septuagint came to his mind more spontaneously.[3]

Unlike Jesus, Paul traveled throughout the known world of his day, probably as far as Spain (Rom 15:29), and certainly to Italy, Greece, and throughout Asia Minor. He was a marginal man, able to cross cultural and linguistic boundaries with knowledge and sensitivity.

---

[3] Ferdinand Prat (1947, 27) affirms that according to calculations subject to revision, out of eighty-four quotations, thirty-four reproduce exactly the text of the Seventy, thirty-six depart from it very little, ten offer notable differences, and two are given according to the Hebrew text.

> When Paul brings his message, he makes use of the full range of his abilities to reach people of varying tongues and cultures. Recent studies of Paul's life and work clearly show that he could employ Palestinian-Jewish concepts, Hellenistic-Jewish concepts, and Hellenistic-Gentile concepts as the occasion required. (Verkuyl 1987, 113)

Though he is aware of his calling to the Jews, his own people (Rom 1:14), Paul sees himself called especially to be an apostle to the Gentiles (Acts 13:46, 18:6; Rom 11:13). Passages such as Galatians 1:15–16, 2:7–8, and Romans 1:5 show that his chief aim was to bring about the "obedience to the faith among all nations for his name."

A CALL FOR UNITY IN DIVERSITY

Ephesians 2:11–22 is one of the clearest passages of the Bible in favor of brotherhood and unity among races. In verses 14–19 Paul stresses that the death of Jesus Christ annuls the divisions that until then had separated men into superior (fellow citizens) and inferior (strangers and foreigners), privileged and under privileged. It is clear that among believers there should be no barriers based on race, color, or nationality (Tilson 1957, 67).

In many passages, Paul says the church is the body of Christ. He wrote, "You are the body of Christ and members individually" (1 Cor 12:27; also see Rom 12:5; 1 Cor 10:17; Eph 1:23, 3:6, 4:12, 5:23; Col 1:18). Just as the physical body has many parts, a congregation of people, in addition to spiritual gifts, may also have gifts of a cultural heritage and the ability to communicate in a language(s) other than the one used by the dominant group. The use of these gifts should not produce pride or envy, nor cause dissension in the church. The user of these gifts should always keep in mind Paul's statement to the Romans, "For as we have many members in one body, but all the members do not have the same function, so we, being many, are one in Christ, and individually members of one another" (Rom 12:4–5). Romo explains:

> When Paul speaks of Christian believers being "all one in Christ," he is describing the reality that for those in Christ, although they may have ethnic, linguistic and cultural differences, these differences were transcended by their "being-in-Christness." (Romo n.d., 22)

There is a wise equilibrium between Paul's concept of brotherhood/oneness and his understanding of cultural/ethnic differences. On one side, he insists that "there is neither Jew nor Greek, there is neither slave nor free, there is neither male or female; for you are all one in Christ Jesus" (Gal 3:28; also 6:15; Rom 10:12; 1 Cor 8:19; Gal 7:5–6). On the other side, he recalls many times his Jewish heritage (Rom 11:1; Phil 3:4–6; Acts 23:6). Furthermore, this international traveler knew better than many others the need of speaking in languages that people could understand. In 1 Corinthians 14:11, speaking of the gift of tongues, he remembers a simple fact: "If I do not know the meaning of the language, I shall be a foreigner to him who speaks, and he who speaks will be a foreigner to me."

In the epistle to the Galatians, Paul addresses whether Gentile Christians have to become Jews to belong to the Messianic people and, more specifically, do Gentiles have to be circumcised? The Jewish-Christian argument was that the Gentile-Christians must become Jews to be Christians. Paul responded by asserting that all people—Jews and Gentiles—are made righteous with God by the faithfulness of Christ and by the faith response of individuals (2:15–21). This is the basis for receiving the Holy Spirit and for being made children of Abraham (3:1ff). "In Christ" annuls the Jew-Gentile distinction in relation to salvation and inclusion in the people of God (3:26ff). "In Christ" Jews remain Jews and Gentiles remain Gentiles; "they are equal without one having to become the other" (Toews 1988, 79). Paul's message to the church is that ethnicity is a legitimate historical and sociological reality. But ethnicity cannot serve as a criterion for inclusion in the church, or as a barrier in relationship among Christians in the church.

In Revelation 5:9, 7:9, 11:9, 13:7, and 14:6, the four synonyms *ethnos*, *phule*, *laos*, and *glossa* are found together. Revelation also pictures an angel with a scroll in his hand, one foot planted on the sea and the other on the land, thus symbolizing the all-encompassing scope of the claims and work of Jesus Christ (10:1–11). Even the song of Moses, which is picked up in the vicinity of the throne of God, includes the words, "All nations shall come and worship before you" (15:4). From the beginning to the end, the Bible teaches that the world is God's world. The human race is one family—God's family. And the purpose of God will not be fulfilled until every segment of that family has been confronted with the claims of Jesus Christ (14:6).

HOMOGENOUS UNITS OR HETEROGENEOUS UNITS

A debate concerning ethnicity is not about the supremacy of any race or the exclusion of some group of people from the church. The ultimate goal of salvation for all nations is not disputed. What is debated is whether or not Christians should be encouraged to plant churches among people with the same characteristics (homogeneous units).

On one side of the debate there are those who say that Paul was quite blunt about the necessity of breaking down social, religious, economic, and ethnic barriers. They cite Ephesians 2:11–22 and Colossians 3:11 to prove that Paul knew all about the most vicious social, religious, national, and religious hatred and prejudice, and that for him one's willingness to rid oneself of these hatreds was a sure sign of genuine conversion. "Heterogeneous groups become a sign of the kingdom in a dehumanized world" (Rooy 1983, 203).

> It seems clear that smashing racial, religious, ethnic, and tribal pride, prejudice and hatred, while it may seem to block winning more converts, is instead the way to build new Christian social communities (that is, local churches of new converts) in hostile pagan ethnic and caste hotbeds. (Reapsome 1983, 17; Wagner 1978, 12–19)

On the other side there are those who see in "the tribe or caste, the clan or other unit one of God's orders of preservation" (McGavran 1972, 56). Wagner says, concerning the Homogeneous Unit Principle: "If all the scientific hypotheses developed within the Church growth framework, this one as nearly as any approaches a 'law'" (Wagner 1976, 110).

Since the battle for brotherhood is raging so strongly, and Christians are making such heroic efforts to overcome apartheid, ethnic pride, and racism, any recognition of ethnicity meets considerable and sometimes fierce opposition. Any stress on ethnicity is viewed by some as segregation, human separatism, discrimination, and prejudice. In reality there are not such intentions among those who speak of Christian ethnicity.

This writer thinks that just emphasizing unity without respecting ethnicity, denying that there are any significant differences of lifestyles or cultures, forces a "melting pot" response. It is often true that Christians are more comfortable if the ethnic convert becomes as culturally like themselves as possible.

The "melting pot" approach may be good if it can be accomplished without stripping persons of their self-image. If this approach works, it will be because the differences are voluntarily subjected to a cause of oneness. However, that does not come automatically with conversion. McGavran stresses that people do not decide first, "We shall act in a one hundred percent brotherly fashion," and then become Christ's followers. Rather, they become Christ's followers and then filled with the Holy Spirit, and commanded by the Scriptures, work their way toward brotherhood—usually much more slowly than expected (McGavran 1983, 14–23).

Paul stressed many times the principle of unity, but unity does not mean uniformity. Uniformity means the same in every aspect. It implies a lack of diversity or variation. The fact is that there are differences, but as Bishop Kern said, "Differences do not necessarily divide; they may enrich" (Baez-Camargo 1943, 18).

There are many communities where redemption is not open to all people because persons must conform in order to belong. They must have the same language, enjoy the same worship styles, and adjust to the socioeconomic ladder for leadership. They do not reject the Savior, but in such a situation they simply cannot feel comfortable in a church in which they are not accepted. Unity means accepting others just as they are. It means allowing for differences, adjusting to those that may be offensive to our culture, and loving each other amid the diversity (Sahlin 1995, 181). Oscar Romo offers some guidelines for those who work with ethnic/language-culture groups:

> Churches ministering in a pluralistic society consider the principles of inclusiveness, freedom and community from a pragmatic viewpoint. Inclusiveness implies openness to all groups or individual regardless of cultural or linguistic heritage. Freedom implies a type of liberty in which groups or individuals are free to create their own fashion, worship, activity, and et cetera. Community implies recognition that all men and groups have the right to exist and are interdependent. (Romo n.d. 23)

McGavran's concept of homogeneous units is useful for the development of a ministry among ethnic groups, but instead of considering it a "principle," this writer would speak of "homogeneous unit strategy" (Smith 1984, 50–51).

This understanding of homogeneous units makes room for both ethnicity and unit; it allows diversity but the emphasis is not on the differences but on the strategies the church can use to build bridges between different ethnic groups.

CONCLUSION

This writer sees no dichotomy between the belief in unity and the emphasis on ethnicity. Christianity must hold two truths in equal tension. Unity must be the goal; so must ethnicity. What is encouraged here is not segregation. All people should be free to worship in whatever congregation they feel comfortable. To the contrary, no one should be forced to worship in a congregation in which he or she is uncomfortable because of language or culture. Christians must not force a person to abandon culture in order to become a Christian. Paul's theology of call, "But as God has distributed to each one, as the Lord has called each one, so let him walk" (1 Cor 7:17) can be understood as an assurance that to become a believer does not require the negation of one's cultural heritage.

In ministering across ethnic boundaries, Christians should stress unity but at the same time have enough sensitivity to recognize ethnic and cultural differences together with wisdom in order to win others for Christ. Furthermore, we should be willing to witness on the terms which are required, as Paul put it in 1 Corinthians 9:19–22:

> For though I am free from all men, I have made myself a servant to all, that I might win the more; and to the Jews I became as a Jew, that I might win Jews; to those who are under the law, as under the law, that I might win those who are under the law; to those who are without the law, as without the law (not being without law toward God, but under law toward Christ), that I might win those who are without law; to the weak I became as weak, that I might win the weak. I have become all things to all men, that I might by all means save some.

REFERENCES

Baez-Camargo, Gonzalo. 1943. *Christianity and the race problem.* New York: Friendship Press.

Beare, Francis W. 1984. The epistle to the Ephesians. In *The interpreter's Bible*, vol. 10, ed. George Arthur Buttrick, 595–749. Nashville: Abingdon.

Belew, M. Wendell. 1974. *Missions in the mosaic.* Atlanta: Home Mission Board, Southern Baptist Convention.

Blauw, Johannes. 1962. *The missionary nature of the church.* New York: McGraw-Hill.

Booth, William. 1998. One nation, indivisible: Is it history? The myth of the melting pot. Washington Post (February 22), http://washingtonpost.com/wp-srv/national/longterm/meltingpot/melt0222.htm.

Bosch, David J. 1983. The structure of mission: An exposition of Matthew 28:16–20. In *Exploring church growth*, ed. Wilbert R. Shenk, 218–48. Grand Rapids: Eerdmans.

Conn, Harvie M. 1983. Looking for a method: Backgrounds and suggestions. In *Exploring church growth*, ed. Wilbert R. Shenk, 79–94. Grand Rapids: Eerdmans.

Dubose, Francis M. 1978. *How churches grow in an urban world.* Nashville: Broadman.

Edersheim, Alfred. 1980. *The life and times of Jesus the Messiah*, vol. 1. Grand Rapids: Eerdmans.

Elliot, Ralph H. 1982. *Church growth that counts.* Valley Forge, PA: Judson Press.

Fong, Bruce W. 1996. *Racial equality in the church: A critique of the homogeneous unit principle in light of a practical theology perspective.* Lanham, MD: University of America Press.

Geddert, Tim. 1988. Jesus and ethnicity. *Direction* 17: 73–78.

Gertz, Steven. 2004. Christian history Corner: Rediscovering the language Jesus spoke. Christianity Today, March 12, http://www.christianitytoday.com/ct/2004/110/52.0.html.

Hopler, Thom. 1981. *A world of difference: Following Christ beyond your cultural walls.* Downers Grove: InterVarsity.

Josephus, Flavius. 1957. Wars of the Jews. In *The complete works of Flavius Josephus.* Trans. William Whiston. Philadelphia: The John C. Winston Company.

Kaiser, Walter C., Jr. 1999. Israel's missionary call. In *Perspectives on the world Christian movement: A reader*, 3rd ed., eds. Ralph D. Winter and Steven C. Hawthorne, 10–16. Pasadena: William Carey Library.

———. 2000. *Mission in the Old Testament: Israel as a light to the nations*. Grand Rapids: Baker.

Kane, Herbert J. 1987. *Christian missions in biblical perspective*. Grand Rapids: Baker.

Kraft, Charles H. 1978. An anthropological apologetic for the homogeneous principle of missiology. *Occasional Bulletin of Missionary Research* 2: 83–121.

Lenski, R. C. H. 1943. *The interpretation of St. Matthew's Gospel*. Minneapolis: Ausburg.

———. 1961. *The interpretation of the Acts of the Apostles*. Minneapolis: Ausburg.

McGavran, Donald A. 1972. The homogeneous unit in mission theory. In Church growth movement: Proceedings of the eleventh biennial meeting of the Association of Professors of Missions June 12–14, in Nashville.

———. 1980. *Understanding church growth*, rev. ed. Grand Rapids: Eerdmans.

———. 1983. The priority of ethnicity. *Evangelical Missions Quarterly* 19: 14–23.

McSwain, Larry L. 1980. A critical appraisal of the church growth movement. *Review and Expositor* 77: 521–38.

Meler, John P. 1977. Nations or gentiles in Matthew 28:19? *Catholic Biblical Quarterly* 39: 49–50.

Padilla, Rene. 1983. The unity of the church and the homogeneous unit principle. In *Exploring church growth*, ed. Wilbert R. Shenk, 285–303. Grand Rapids: Eerdmans.

Prat, Ferdinand. 1947. *La Teologia de Pablo* [Paul's theology]. 3 vols. Mexico: Editorial Jus.

Reapsome, Jim. 1983. Church planting and "the new man's" life style. *Evangelical Missions Quarterly*: 17.

Richardson, Don. 1999. A man for all peoples. In *Perspectives on the world Christian movement: A reader*, 3rd ed., eds. Ralph D. Winter and Steven C. Hawthorne, 104–7. Pasadena: William Carey Library

Robertson, Archibald Thomas. 1956. Latin. In *The international standard Bible encyclopedia*, ed. James Orr. Grand Rapids: Eerdmans.

———. 1983. *Word pictures in the New Testament*, vol. 1. Grand Rapids: Eerdmans.

———. 1984. Language of the New Testament. In *The international standard Bible encyclopedia*, ed. James Orr. Grand Rapids: Eerdmans.

Romo, Oscar I. n.d. *Missions in ethnic America*. Atlanta, GA: Home Mission Board, Southern Baptist Convention.

Rooy, Sidney. 1983. A theology of humankind. In *Exploring church growth*, ed. Wilbert R. Shenk, 191–206. Grand Rapids: Eerdmans.

Sahlin, Monte. 1995. Diversity needs to include everybody. In *Make us one: Celebrating spiritual unity in the midst of cultural diversity*, ed. Delbert W. Baker, 181–92. Boise, ID: Pacific Press.

Schmidt, Karl Ludwig. 1983. Ethnos: Ethnos in the NT. In *Theological dictionary of the New Testament*, eds. Gerhard Kittel and Geoffrey W. Bromiley. Grand Rapids: Eerdmans.

Smith, Ebbie C. 1984. *Balanced church growth*. Nashville: Broadman.

Tilson, Everett. 1957. *Segregation and the Bible*. Nashville: Abingdon.

Tippett, Alan R. 1970. *Church growth and the Word of God: The biblical basis of the church growth viewpoint*. Grand Rapids: Eerdmans.

Toews, John E. 1988. Paul's perspective on ethnicity. *Direction* 7: 78–80.

Torres, Andrés. 2004. *Between melting pot and mosaic*. Philadelphia: Temple University Press.

Verkuyl, Johannes. 1987. *Contemporary missiology: An introduction*. Grand Rapids: Eerdmans.

Wagner, C. Peter. 1976. *Your church can grow*. Glendale: Gospel Light.

———. 1978. How ethical is the homogenous unit principle? *Occasional Bulletin of Missionary Research* 2: 12–19.

———. 1979. *Our kind of people: The ethical dimensions of church growth in America*. Atlanta: John Knox Press.

——— 1994. *Spreading the fire*. Ventura: Regal.

Yamamori, Tetsunao. 1980. Meaning of the great commission. *Evangelical Missions Quarterly* 16: 49–50.

18

DIVERSITY, DONATIONS, AND DISADVANTAGE: THE IMPLICATIONS OF RACE, CLASS, AND GENDER FOR PERSONAL FUND-RAISING IN EVANGELICAL MISSIONS

SAMUEL L. PERRY

INTRODUCTION

For the majority of missionaries and staff workers who must raise their own financial support to serve in evangelical ministries, the fact that fund-raising experiences differ by race, gender, and (though less obviously) class status is hardly earth-shattering news. In fact, this information appears to be common knowledge among evangelical fund-raisers. As I began my research on the fund-raising experiences of evangelical outreach ministers and missionaries, I found this general awareness of the potential fund-raising challenges associated with race, gender, and class surprising for two reasons. First, with few exceptions, most "how-to" manuals on fund-raising appear unwilling to attribute an individual's success or failure in raising financial support to anything other than issues related to spiritual life (e.g., eternal perspective, faith, prayer life, etc.) or character qualities (e.g., organization, work ethic, budgeting habits, etc.). One would suppose that something so well-known among fund-raisers would be thoroughly discussed in this literature. Second, despite the pervasive understanding among outreach ministers and missionaries that gender, race, and class status may impinge on their experiences raising support, many appear to be ignorant as to exactly how this works. In fact, a common answer to my question of how one's fund-raising experience differed as a [racial minority, single female, or person from a lower-income background] was, "I'm sure it was different, but I'm not sure how."

Although a number of ministry directors assured me that they regularly distribute fund-raising surveys among their staff workers, to my knowledge, no systematic study has been undertaken to assess exactly how and to what extent racial, gender, and socioeconomic factors may inhibit the ability of staff to raise their financial support, thereby impeding efforts to maintain diverse staff teams. Moreover, no such study has been conducted that examines fund-raising experiences from a variety of ministries and missions agencies. In view of this need, this study utilizes data from a mixed-methods survey of almost 720 domestic and overseas ministers and missionaries in order to more fully address the implications of racial, gender, and socioeconomic diversity for personal fund-raising in evangelical outreach ministries.

I divide this study into three sections. The first section lays out the theoretical foundations for my research question and describes my research methodology. I briefly outline the dominant funding strategy of most domestic and overseas parachurch organizations, giving attention to how the present stratification system of our society may potentially impact the experiences and outcomes of would-be support-raisers. I then describe the survey sample and my methods of data collection. In the second section, I present the results of my survey that serve to shed light on the effects of race, class, and gender on personal fund-raising. Specifically, I utilize survey responses in order to examine exactly how (if at all) race, class, and gender affects the fund-raising experiences of missionaries or staff workers and determine to what extent the challenges associated with each ascriptive factor potentially inhibits racial, gender, and class diversity among ministry staff teams. In the final section, I offer suggestions based on these findings as to how ministries might better contextualize fund-raising strategies for staff workers who are racial minorities, single females, or from economically disadvantaged backgrounds.

THEORETICAL FOUNDATIONS AND METHODOLOGY

Personal Fundraising within a Stratified Society

Even if it were not widely recognized among domestic and foreign ministries that personal fund-raising experiences and outcomes often differ by gender, race, and class status, such a fact seems almost intuitive when one recognizes that the funding structure adopted by the majority of evangelical foreign missions agencies and domestic outreach ministries in the United States inheres in a society that remains stratified along the lines of race, gender, and class. Indeed, one might be surprised if such differences were not evident. This section provides a brief overview of the dominant fund-raising strategy employed by evangelical outreach ministries and missions agencies in light of its potential challenges functioning within a society that stratifies individuals according to race, gender, and class.

While the majority of traditional church staff in the United States (e.g., ordained clergy, music directors, administrative personnel, etc.) draw their salaries from funds collected directly from their respective congregations and/or denominations, most foreign and domestic missionaries are required to raise their own salaries through donations obtained from individuals, businesses, events, and/or churches, with a certain percentage of these donations going to fund the home office. Individual character qualities (e.g., work ethic, organization, etc.) being equal, success or failure within this funding structure is contingent upon the ability of a potential missionary to gain access to a sufficient number of prospective donors with both the inclination and the wherewithal to contribute financially to her/his ministry. More specifically, in order to draw enough donated income to continue working for their respective ministry (and for the ministry itself to remain financially solvent) every individual missionary or missionary family must obtain access to enough individuals and/or groups who are in ideological agreement with both the goals of this missionary and their funding strategy (or at least are not too opposed to either), are motivated to contribute, and have the financial capacity to make donations.

Potential staff workers or missionaries, in order to locate and petition a sufficient number of "ready, willing, and able" donors, are trained to compile large lists of potential supporters based on their existing social networks (e.g., immediate and extended family, neighbors, church parishioners, friends of the family, teachers, dentists, college buddies, etc.). They may also ask their current supporters (or other sympathetic individuals) for possible referrals. Once prospective donors have been identified, fund-raisers are instructed, first, to send out letters that initiate the solicitation of financial support; second, to make follow-up phone calls to set up face-to-face appointments;

and third, to make direct requests in person for financial sponsorship, often with specific dollar amounts expressly communicated. These petitions may be made to individuals, couples, small groups, and/or churches, but the process is often the same. The methods of sponsorship most often take the form of monthly contributions, but may also consist of one-time or yearly donations. This individualized model of fund-raising has several advantages over strategies that are predominantly event driven or that depend solely on church or denominational support (e.g., flexibility, consistent monthly income, freedom from denominational restrictions, etc.), and consequently, the approach has been adopted by most evangelical foreign missions agencies and domestic outreach ministries in the United States.

Despite its many advantages, the fund-raising approach described above makes an implicit assumption about fund-raisers (and society itself) that I believe limits its long-term effectiveness, particularly for ministries that are striving to increase their racial, gender, and class diversity. Specifically, this approach is based, at least implicitly, on the supposition that all potential ministers and missionaries start off on a level playing field, and that the money for ministry is available to all who would mail out enough letters, place enough phone calls, and sit down to enough face-to-face support-appointments. Indeed, the reluctance of most "how-to" support-raising manuals to acknowledge obstacles unrelated to an individual fund-raiser's spiritual life or character qualities affirms that this is the case. Describing his former attitude towards ethnic minority missionaries, fund-raising expert Scott Morton penitently explains:

> I have a confession. I used to believe that ethnic-minority missionaries could reach full funding just like anyone else if they simply made a gazillion funding appointments. When they struggled I'd say, "Try harder! Visit more people!" Some did try harder, but they rarely got as many appointments as they needed. Furthermore, their gifts were frequently one-time or pledges that lasted only a month or two. My conclusion: They didn't stick with it long enough. As the years went by, I noticed minority missionaries were leaving our staff. Funding difficulties were usually mentioned as a reason, but so were other issues. I persisted in my view that anyone could raise support if they made enough appointments. (1999, 193)

Morton admits that he previously held a similar belief regarding single women and fund-raising as well. This individualistic (what sociologists would probably call "meritocratic") approach to fund-raising appears to be embraced by most support-raising gurus. For example, the personal fund-raising manuals *People Raising* by William Dillon, *Friend Raising* by Betty Barnett, *Growing Givers' Hearts* by Thomas Jeavons, *More Than Money, More Than Faith* by Paul S. Johnson, and the first edition of Scott Morton's *Funding Your Ministry* (1999) never mention the possible influence of gender, class, or race on one's ability to raise financial support. Even the more systematic and scholarly treatments of personal fund-raising found in McCabe and Campbell's *Inside Outreach* or Miller's *Financing Parachurch Organizations* make no mention of these factors affecting the fund-raising enterprise. In fact, to my knowledge, the only exceptions to this trend are *Getting Sent* by Pete Sommer and Morton's most recent edition of *Funding Your Ministry* (2007).

The meritocratic approach, which, again, implicitly assumes all fund-raisers are on equal footing, would be quite appropriate if all staff workers and missionaries were Anglo, male, and middle class (which was almost invariably the case when this method of fund-raising was devised). Yet, as ministries seek to foster greater diversity among their staff teams, they must recognize that we undeniably live in a society where individuals are stratified according to race, gender, and class status. That is to say, within our society, the characteristics of race (European American, African American, Asian American, or Latino), gender (male or female), and socioeconomic class (underclass, working-class, middleclass, upper-middleclass, etc.) are used to organize individuals hierarchically and disproportionately award them with economic resources, prestige, political power, and other privileges.

This stratification of individuals within society at large will have potentially significant consequences for fund-raising at the individual level. For instance, African Americans, Latinos, and lower income families, because they tend to be among the disadvantaged groups within the United States as a whole, will tend to be at a disadvantage (to Anglo middleclass fund-raisers, for example) when it comes to gaining access to networks of potential donors with the disposable income available to contribute to their ministry. Put another way, for many potential missionaries or staff workers who are Latino, African American, or come from a lower socioeconomic background, their families, neighbors, churches, and friends will tend to have fewer resources to contribute to their support base, thereby making their fund-raising experience more challenging and possibly increasing the turnover among these individuals.

Moreover, while some fund-raising challenges related to racial and class diversity are due more to structural factors (i.e., who has disposable income and who does not) fund-raising may also be affected by theological-cultural differences that are defined along the lines of race and gender. For instance, while soliciting donations in order to work for a missions organization or college student ministry may be acceptable—or even laudable—in some ethnic cultures (e.g., white E\evangelicalism), it is often looked upon with suspicion or disapproval by other ethnic groups who may either be unfamiliar with such a fund-raising strategy (e.g., African American or Latino Protestants) or are culturally offended by the strategy of direct business-like petitions, requesting specific dollar amounts, and soliciting referrals (e.g., Asian American Protestants).

Additionally, there are differing theological-cultural perspectives regarding the role of women in ministry that may also put them at a disadvantage when it comes to fund-raising. For example, while virtually all evangelicals are comfortable with single men working in ministry at any capacity, some potential donors may be suspicious of a single woman working in ministry. They may be apprehensive that the woman would be placed in some sort of leadership role over men, and thus, more reluctant to financially support her ministry.

Sommer's *Getting Sent* and Morton's 2007 edition of *Funding Your Ministry* both affirm that potential staff workers who are racial minorities, single women, and/or individuals from a lower-income background may experience challenges to fund-raising that are not experienced by staff who are Anglo, male, and/or from higher-income backgrounds. For their chapter, "Becoming Conservative, Becoming White," McGlathery and Griffin (2007, 145–61) interviewed a number of African Americans working for an ethnic-specific wing of a well-known campus ministry. Their respondents expressed that raising financial support was particularly difficult for them since supporting individual missionaries was largely unfamiliar to the black church and also violated several strongly held cultural values associated with economic independence and community uplift. The respondents also questioned whether their cultural preferences had been taken into consideration by their predominantly Anglo ministry directors.

Chapter 18

While the few previous investigations of how race, class, and gender may affect the fund-raising experiences of evangelical outreach, ministers and missionaries provided directions for research. Their conclusions are largely based on anecdotal evidence, small sample sizes, and/or responses from only one ministry. This study utilizes a large and diverse sample from a variety of outreach ministries and missions agencies in order to draw conclusions on the implications of race, gender, and socioeconomic diversity for support-raising and how this potentially affects efforts to develop and maintain diverse ministry teams.

METHODS OF DATA COLLECTION AND SAMPLE DESCRIPTION

The data for this study was taken from the Parachurch Ministries Fundraising Survey (hereafter PMFRS), which was fielded in 2009. This survey contained a series of closed-coded and open-ended questions that assessed the fund-raising experiences of individual missionaries and outreach ministry staff. Because telephone or e-mail directories from which to develop a random sample of staff from missions agencies and outreach ministries either do not exist or were inaccessible to the researcher, the data was collected using a purposive sampling procedure. Outreach ministries headquartered in the United States were selected with the criterion that their staff be required to raise their own personal support, as opposed to it being raised by a board of directors (e.g., Fellowship of Christian Athletes) or a denomination (e.g., the International Missions Board of the Southern Baptist Convention).

Ministry directors were contacted by the researcher and were e-mailed a link to access the online survey, which could be completed and returned completely online. The directors were then asked to forward the link to all the staff in their respective organizations, requesting that they participate. The directors were also asked to issue follow-up e-mail reminders to their staff. Ministry staff workers and missionaries were informed that the survey was completely anonymous and that their participation was voluntary. Because the surveys were distributed through the ministry directors, it was impossible to know how many individual workers received a survey and thus response rates are unavailable. The online survey was left open from February 2009 through September 2009. All responses were self-reported.

Because the survey was distributed to outreach ministers and missionaries in the evangelical Protestant tradition, the sample consisted of all college-educated, conservative Protestants, who work full-time for their respective ministry at some capacity. The vast majority (almost 73 percent) of respondents indicated that their primary job was evangelism, discipleship, or church planting; almost 20 percent served in administrative roles; and less than 8 percent indicated that their job was theological education, mercy/service ministry (e.g., building houses, distributing food, clothing, etc.), translation/Bible distribution, or "other" (a catch-all category that could include audio-visual production, website management, fund-development, sports ministry, etc). Although the majority of workers in the sample served in domestic collegiate ministries (e.g., Campus Crusade for Christ, InterVarsity Christian Fellowship, Chi Alpha, etc.), a significant minority worked overseas and/or worked with adults or children. Thus, this study should not be understood as focusing *strictly* on US collegiate ministry workers. After the data was cleaned and prepared for analysis, the resulting sample size was 716.

THE IMPLICATIONS OF RACE, CLASS, AND GENDER FOR PERSONAL FUNDRAISING

Race and Fundraising: Economic Disadvantage and Cultural Barriers

Fundraising challenges associated with racial/ethnic differences were perhaps the most pronounced in the survey results and thus receive the lion's share of attention within this paper. African American, Latino, and Asian American respondents were on average more likely than their Anglo counterparts to feel that their fund-raising experience was more difficult than the average person. Yet findings reveal significant discrepancies not only in fund-raising *experiences*, but in *outcomes*. Minority respondents from all three groups were less likely than Anglos to have reached their full support goal, while African Americans and Latinos were also more likely than Anglos to have to pick up a second job to supplement their income.

As one might expect, about 90 percent of Latinos, African Americans, and Asian Americans believed that their fund-raising experience differed somewhat from that of their Anglo counterparts. When respondents were asked to indicate why, their responses revealed that the fund-raising challenges experienced by ethnic minorities consist of both economic and cultural obstacles that often require greater effort along with greater cultural and even relational sacrifices relative to Anglo Americans. Further, minority respondents frequently questioned whether their predominantly Anglo ministry directors or fund-raising coaches were aware of the barriers that they as minorities encountered.

Economic obstacles affected African American and Latino fund-raisers primarily. African Americans and Latinos repeatedly expressed that they had greater difficulty establishing viable support contacts with enough money to contribute to their ministry. Respondents from both groups repeatedly indicated that although their family, friends, and church networks may have been enthusiastic about contributing to their respective ministries, these contacts did not have the resources to make donations. One Latino respondent expressed, "Working class Latinos were supportive, but they did not have a lot of finances available to help meet my support needs. I had to go outside of my race to raise support; most of my supporters came from a white PCA church." Respondents often connected their inability to find support contacts with the wherewithal to make contributions to the economically disadvantaged situation of African Americans and Latinos within society at large. One Latina respondent, when asked about the most difficult aspect of fund-raising answered plainly, "The Hispanic community; they earn less money and give mostly to the church." The following response from an African American missionary elaborates this idea further:

> There are financial realities generally true of the majority of our White staff and their accompanying contacts that are generally not true of the majority of our Black staff: [Black] Staff do not have financial contacts that can give $2000+ per year; [Black] Staff do not have families that can support them through the tougher years (family sent them to school so that the staff could make money, not so that the family could support the staff) . . . These factors alone mean that the same efforts put in between a "typical" White staff and a "typical" Black staff will produce very different results, results that are financially challenging to the Black staff.

At the end of this excerpt, the respondent asserts that the economic obstacles facing African American fund-raisers (and certainly Latino fund-raisers based on previous responses) are such that the same efforts put forth by a "typical black staff" and a "typical white staff" will produce different results,

results that put African American staff at an economic disadvantage to their Anglo counterparts.

Ethnic minorities also experienced significant cultural barriers to personal fund-raising. Some of these cultural barriers to fund-raising were similar across all three minority groups. For example, minority respondents across all three racial groups expressed that their families and respective minority-group contacts were bewildered and disappointed that the minority fund-raiser did not want to use their college education to make money, but would rather "beg" for a living and avoid getting what they considered a "real job," namely, traditional employment. One Latina fund-raiser explained, "Most of my family don't understand why I completed a bachelor's degree to now ask people who do not have very much (or a degree) for money." An Asian American respondent elaborated further on this cultural conflict:

> The idea of education being wasted is a big thing in the Asian community. If your parents don't pressure you they certainly get the stigma from other parents of not raising you right because their child is begging for money. There is a shame aspect. There is the aspect that the child can't take care of themselves. If they want to do ministry they should do church ministry or be a tent maker or do it on the side. Part of the reason is that we as children are the parents' social security plan. We take care of them in their old age. This is harder to do when you are raising support.

African American respondents provided similar explanations. To be sure, a number of Anglo respondents also indicated in their responses that their family, friends, and various support contacts disapproved of their living off of donated income. Yet, few if any mentioned the idea of a wasted education as a reason. This is likely due to the value historically disadvantaged minority groups tend to place on education as a means of gaining economic independence and contributing to the family and community. To gain a college education and to shirk one's responsibility to achieve financial stability is particularly offensive to the families and affinity groups of these minority respondents.

Family opposition to fund-raising in general was common to all minority groups, but it was most pronounced among Asian Americans. Almost two-thirds of Asian American respondents (64 percent) believed that their family was embarrassed by them raising financial support and over half of Latino respondents (56 percent) affirmed this as well. These percentages were considerably higher than for Anglo respondents (41 percent).

In addition to the cultural stigmas against "begging," "wasting education," and an emphasis on "getting a real job," all minority groups to some degree, African Americans and Latinos more so than Asian American respondents, expressed that both parachurch ministries in general and particularly the funding model of full-time ministers living off of individual donations were largely unfamiliar to their families, social networks, and their respective ethno-religious tradition, as the following excerpts indicate:

> My family and close friends did not understand the individual support raising model of fund development. Typically, in the black community people in ministry, including pastors many times, work full-time to support themselves, in addition to working or volunteering many hours in a ministry. –African American female

> In the Hispanic culture, it is not accustomed to give to individuals but to churches, so it has not been easy to ask for support from people of my own background. Also, because of the same reason, it is also hard for me to ask for support, since it is not that common to be asking others for financial support. –Latino

Although Asian American respondents mentioned the challenge of unfamiliarity considerably less than African American or Latino respondents, the traditional means of supporting ministers (through tithes given to a local church) are culturally familiar for each minority group and therefore generally favored by the family and church networks of minority respondents.

Respondents from each minority group also expressed that their families and respective ethnic group contacts were suspicious of contributing money to what they perceived as a "white ministry." One Latina respondent, referring to the ethnic-specific branch of her campus ministry, asserted, "Some (members of Latino churches) don't like that I am working for a 'white' organization that keeps its ministries 'separate, but equal.'" An Asian American respondent elaborated:

I still feel a tension when raising support in the Asian community because [my ministry] is viewed as a white organization. Until more recently, most of the materials that were published by [my ministry] were of white people and the minorities were the ones being "shared with." I think even now [my ministry] is seen as a white ministry from the perspective of minority groups.

While the previous cultural obstacles to fund-raising were experienced by members of all three minority groups, other cultural barriers to fund-raising appear to be more specific to particular minority groups. African American respondents, for example, repeatedly expressed that the idea of "missions" was foreign to the black church. One such respondent explained, "We've found that many black churches are either not trained in missions giving (especially home missions) or they are self-focused. One black church expected us to "work" for them for the $100/month they gave. When we left the church, they cut our support!" Another African American respondent echoed this sentiment, associating the difficulty with black culture. He asserts: "It goes back to a cultural issue. In the black culture missions is a 'foreign' concept. Legitimate ministry is considered being a pastor of a local congregation. So I did not have a list of individuals or churches that I could approach in my culture to ask for financial support."

African American respondents, possibly due to historic economic disadvantages and a cultural value of economic independence, particularly from Anglos, were unique in their expression of shame and embarrassment associated with having to petition Anglos for financial donations. One African American male asserted, "As an African American male, asking white men for support often felt degrading, embarrassing, and shameful. My 'work ethic' often bothers me still to this day." The following excerpt elaborates this further:

> Some (Black) staff go through painful psychological/social dissonance when they have to ask non-Black peoples (mostly White) to support their ministries, especially when their ministries are mostly to Black students; their potential donors sometimes ask innocent-but-inappropriate questions and have innocent-but-painful perspectives on serving "poor Black students." –African American male

In addition to the cultural stigmas on "begging," values of economic success and independence, and occasional lack of familiarity with the funding strategy, Asian American respondents repeatedly expressed that their most significant cultural barrier to fund-raising was what they perceived as culturally Anglo, business-like techniques used to solicit donations. One Asian American male asserted plainly: "In Asian American culture, people often communicate indirectly and giving is even more based on relationships than the norm. This makes asking in the direct manner in which we are often coached difficult to do."

The culturally Anglo, business-like approach to fund-raising violates the value Asian Americans place on relationships and being indirect in order to protect the honor of a friend or elder, and thus, Asian American fund-raisers must make adjustments and, to some degree, personal sacrifices, either to embrace the unfamiliar and potentially uncomfortable technique of soliciting donations, or in order to contextualize their fund-raising approach to their respective ethnic audience.

The economic and cultural barriers to fund-raising experienced by minority ministers and missionaries inevitably influences who these individuals can petition for financial support. The survey asked respondents to estimate the percentage of their financial support that came from someone of another race. Less than 5 percent of the financial support Anglo respondents received came from non-Anglos, which indicates that Anglo outreach ministers and missionaries rarely have to venture outside of their own racial group for financial support. By contrast, about three-fourths of the financial support received by Latinos (71 percent) and African Americans (74 percent) came from individuals outside of their racial group. While the survey did not ask respondents to indicate the race that contributed the most to their ministry, this is almost certainly Anglos. Asian Americans were between these two extremes at almost 42 percent. Although this does indicate that Asian Americans have greater success raising financial support from their own racial group, it also indicates that they have to venture outside of their own racial circles quite frequently compared to their Anglo counterparts.

Responses indicate that feeling unsupported by one's respective racial group and having to turn to Anglos both for potential contacts and financial support is not without its relational and psychological consequences. This was true particularly for African American respondents who feel a deep connection to the black community. One African American respondent, when asked to describe the most difficult aspect of fund-raising, simply asserted, "Not having my own race to be as supportive and give even when they knew my life and involvement." Two other African American respondents elaborated further:

> For many of our staff of color, the majority of their support comes from White donors and White churches. Over time, this can be a very discouraging fact because these staff don't feel supported by their own family members or communities. Sometimes, our staff of color attend two churches—one church that meets their personal spiritual, cultural and social needs, and another church that has donor prospects that can fund their ministries. This type of arrangement can also become wearying to staff over time. –African American male

> I had to more quickly learn White evangelical culture and look to that culture for support almost entirely. In the Black church world, giving outside the church is foreign and often comes with a pledge that isn't followed through on. This led to increasing distance between myself and Black Christians and the church as I had to build networks outside of my own people group . . . Having as a goal to be fully funded at a high level required moving outside of Black and urban networks and into suburban, professional, and mostly White networks. –African American male

Both excerpts indicate that African American fund-raisers are faced with an internal dissonance that results from feeling unsupported by one's own racial group. For the first respondent, the tension was resolved by having two churches, one predominantly African American, the other largely Anglo. For the second respondent, working for his predominantly Anglo ministry led to his separation from the black community in both identification and association.

Minority respondents also expressed that a challenging aspect of their fund-raising experience was the inconsistent accommodation, and often unfair expectations, of their Anglo ministry directors. One African American respondent, when asked to describe the most difficult aspect of support-raising stated: "[The most difficult aspects of fund-raising were:] very, very few contacts coupled with expectations of my employer that if I worked hard enough the money would come in." Responding to the same question, an Asian

American female indicated something similar, "[The most difficult aspects of fund-raising were:] raising support in the Asian American community: the length of time needed to develop trust in relationships is much longer than what we're led to expect from [my ministry's] training (and what our support coaches expect to see happen)." Another Asian American fund-raiser expressed her suspicion that, despite the thoroughness of the training generally, her Anglo directors or fund-raising coaches were unaware of the extent to which their fund-raising strategy was culturally Anglo. She asserts: "[O]ur support-raising training (which, incidentally, is done very well) comes from a very white (majority culture) perspective. I'm not sure if those doing the training realize this."

Other minority respondents asserted their belief that their fund-raising training, and ipso facto, their ministry directors, have not taken the cultural differences seriously enough to contextualize the fund-raising process or alter their approach significantly. One Asian American female explained, "I think that Asians raising support don't have as much contextualized training as our white colleagues. There isn't much training on how to 'ask' in a way that is effective." Another Asian American male added, "Asians don't want to impose or obligate others—so asking is a difficult part—or [asking] has to be done in sensitive way (asking aspects of our [Ministry Partner Development] training has not taken cultural sensitivities)."

Due to the disparities between the fund-raising training that minority ministers and missionaries receive and the cultural barriers they encounter when soliciting their respective minority networks for financial support, minority fund-raisers are often forced to contextualize themselves and develop their own culturally appropriate approach, as one Asian American respondent explained, "There's an awareness that you have to respect some of the cultural protocols. The [Fund Development] training I received seemed to focus on meeting people who were Euro-American and were in the business world, so asking my Asian friends was an exercise in contextualizing the methods."

GENDER AND FUNDRAISING: THE DEADLY COMBINATION OF SINGLENESS AND FEMALENESS

According to sociologists Robert Wuthnow and Mark Chaves (Wuthnow 1989), the presence of single women in evangelical campus ministries, the mission field, and even evangelical seminaries has become more prevalent within the last few decades. As more single women are recruited to serve in evangelical parachurch organizations, more ministries have begun to recognize that these women face unique challenges in fund-raising. Yet these challenges are not merely due to their being female, but the fact that they are *unmarried* females. Scott Morton theorizes, "American evangelicals have a bias against single women missionaries... Evangelicals generally prefer giving to couples over single women" (2007, 190). One married respondent, when comparing her fund-raising experience as a married woman to her experience as a single woman, expressed that fund-raising was made easier by the presence of her spouse who was, "viewed as the 'face' of our ministry."

Single female respondents were asked on the survey to indicate whether they felt their fund-raising experience differed somewhat from that of their male counterparts and, if so, to explain why. About three-quarters of single female respondents believed that their fund-raising experience was different than that of a single male's. Based on their explanations, it appears that single women tend to be confronted with a number of fund-raising realities due to the combination of their singleness and femaleness. These are: complementarianism, soft patriarchy, issues of confidence, and complex situations involving support-appointments with both single and married members of the opposite sex.

Many evangelicals, and particularly those on the more conservative end of the theological spectrum, hold to a belief often referred to as complementarianism. Among other things, this position affirms that within spiritual contexts leadership over men is limited to other men. Women may exercise leadership over other women (and young boys up to a certain age), but may not exercise authority over men. Consequently, evangelicals who hold firmly to this position are often suspicious of ministry situations in which women may be given spiritual authority over men. Single female fund-raisers frequently indicated that their more theologically conservative support contacts were concerned that they would be put in leadership situations and thus were apprehensive about financially supporting such a ministry. Support barriers involving the complementarian position of evangelicals were most pronounced for respondents who worked for more egalitarian ministries in which women could take leadership roles. One respondent explained:

I feel that I have to justify myself in a ministry/teaching position more than my male co-workers. As I have been fund-raising, I have met many people from different backgrounds, many of which came from churches where women have not be allowed to hold teaching positions or have authority. So not only do I have to raise support, which is counter-cultural in itself, but I have to address this other "women in leadership" issue at the same time. I want to present a ministry that people want to support and get behind, but it's hard enough to ask for money much less ask people to change their doctrinal beliefs by supporting me.

Survey responses of married women indicated that their fund-raising experience differed in the sense that their husband would be permitted to speak at churches and was naturally more comfortable sitting down with businessmen (or just men in general) in order to make direct asks for financial support.

As a corollary to the complementarian position of many evangelicals, single women fund-raisers also often received questions from support contacts that seemed to indicate that they as single women were not taken seriously in ministry. For example, respondents indicated that they were frequently asked about when they were going to get married. For these women, the implication was that doing ministry as a single person, and specifically as a single woman, was merely a holding pattern while they waited for a husband. One respondent asserted:

> [B]eing taken as seriously as a male counterpart is another story. Especially in a hierarchal community. We are seen as "sharing" and I was told that I can lead because males in college aren't men yet. So it depends on the church and their stance on women in leadership as well as cultural context. I think in some ways there is more a concern of whether I can survive and unfortunately that the situation is temporary because someday she'll get married and won't have to raise support. I think I have to present myself much more professionally to be taken seriously.

While complementarianism is viewed primarily as an obstacle to single females raising their financial support, single women frequently indicated that their experience was easier in certain ways, relative to their male counterparts. Several respondents indicated that male pastors or men with families would feel a deep sense of responsibility for them as single women and consequently would contribute large amounts of financial support. One respondent explained, "People feel more obligated to provide for a single female than a single male. Culturally, single males should 'provide for themselves.'" The following excerpts illustrate this further:

> I actually believe that in some cases I had more empathetic ears as a single female. By my singleness, I found I unintentionally drew the hearts of father figures to want to care for my needs and see me succeed after they met me and heard my heart and passion for what I was called to do . . . It was a real blessing to have people "looking out for me!"

> Sometimes I thought that the "single girl" card was convenient because married couples, especially fathers, might be more compassionate and want to be the hero.

> I think that people I've encountered over the years (especially the male spouses) feel a need to help provide/protect. They were concerned that I would have enough money for auto insurance, a reliable car, living in a safe area, etc. This was encouraging for me and their wives would often communicate that their husbands wanted to make sure I'd be okay. It was very sweet. I don't know that a man would experience the same thing.

Sociologists refer to such situations as "soft patriarchy"; that is, situations in which males embrace a protector/provider role towards women. In this case, being a single woman actually helps the fund-raising enterprise. This situation has its drawbacks, however. When supporters adopt this "patriarchal" mentality towards the single woman, getting married often hurts the woman's support base. One respondent explained, "I've actually heard more from many of my friends who have gotten married and lost support as a result of getting married because their supporters thought they didn't need the support any more now that they were married." Another single woman affirmed this comment: "Some of my single girl friends saw a drop in their support when they got engaged or married. The perception being that the fiancé/husband would now provide for them." Responses like this suggest that supporters, and particularly male supporters, feel some sort of responsibility for the single female fund-raiser only until that responsibility is taken off their hands by a spouse.

Single female respondents consistently expressed that they struggled with a lack of confidence throughout the support-raising process. By comparison, they believed male fund-raisers would be far more comfortable in situations with businessmen where direct, face-to-face petitions were made. One respondent explained, "It was difficult for me to make appointments with men in their [contacts'] offices. I felt unsure of myself. This year (after twenty-two years of raising support) is the first time ever that I met with someone in their office." Another respondent elaborated further: "I struggle with confidence, especially in networking, more than my male coworkers. It's taken me a long time to embrace a more relaxed, friendly style of fund-raising since I felt I needed to be very professional and come across as strong and, essentially, masculine."

Sometimes the lack of confidence and perceived relational support during the fund-raising process can have fairly significant emotional and psychological consequences for single females as the following excerpt indicates:

> I'm not sure, but I was extremely lonely raising support by myself as a single woman. I felt vulnerable, physical pain and suffering, and criticized and did not always receive the care and backing I needed or wanted from those who were coaching me. Often it was not that I minded raising support, but that I longed for someone else to do support-raising with, as a team, as a couple.

These responses, and this last response in particular, suggest that single female fund-raisers tend to be more comfortable in more relational situations where they do not feel business-like and unsure and can be affirmed by those around them. Also, support coaches need to be aware of the challenges that single women face in fund-raising and offer understanding and support.

Lastly, single female fund-raisers recounted facing uncomfortable (and some egregious) situations involving romantically interested members of the opposite sex during support appointments. Responses like the following were common:

Some potential male supporters (singles) might think I'm asking them for a date. It gets kind of uncomfortable. They don't understand it's all about ministry. Even if they decide to give, I don't know their real motivation. Sometimes, they expect some special attention in return. And when they know I'm not interested, they stop giving.

Respondents also indicated that support appointments with married men, be they businessmen or pastors, were awkward and tended to be far more comfortable if the wife were present. This situation is relatively unique for single women since it is rare that married or single men find themselves in a situation where they are petitioning a single or married woman for financial support. In an extreme case, one woman indicated that she had been propositioned by a pastor during a support appointment: "I have needed to be careful on where I have support appointments. Unfortunately, I had a pastor make inappropriate comments to me. The appointments need to be in public, i.e., at a cafe, if I'm meeting with guys." The obvious implication for single women, as this respondent suggests, is to make such support appointments public and potentially go to the appointment with a friend.

CLASS STATUS AND FUNDRAISING: A MATTER OF INCOME NETWORKS

Compared to race and gender, the impact of a fund-raisers' class status on their ability to raise financial support is far less pronounced, at least in the survey data. Moreover, as sociologists have long been aware, there are challenges separating the effects of class status from those of race. This was a problem here as well. Nevertheless, some clear trends emerged from the survey results regarding class status and fund-raising. Before discussing these trends, I will discuss some recent research on the issues of income and giving.

Sociological research on social networks and religious giving contribute two useful pieces of information for this study. First, for the past few decades, researchers have investigated a phenomenon called "social homophily." This refers to the observation that persons tend to be embedded within social networks of individuals who are of the same race and socioeconomic status. For example, lower-income African Americans tend to live in neighborhoods, attend churches, and be friends with individuals who are similar in these regards. The same would be true for higher-income African Americans, Anglos, or Latinos. Simply put, people tend to be found in social networks with similar individuals, at least regarding class status and race. Second, research on religious giving has consistently found that giving, in absolute terms, tends to increase or decrease with income. Higher-income individuals are simply able to give more.

Considered together, these two facts have obvious implications for the ways in which one's class status potentially affects their ability to gain access to a sufficient number of donors with the means to contribute financially to one's ministry. Due to the social homophily principle, the class status of a fund-raiser's social networks will be relatively homogenous, suggesting that fund-raisers whose families, friendship networks, and churches tend to be well-off financially will naturally have an advantage when it comes to gaining access to a large number of well-to-do benefactors. Further, the research on giving suggests that these well-to-do individuals and groups tend to give more than their lower-income counterparts. Consequently, fund-raisers from higher-income backgrounds will tend to have an easier time raising their financial support. Overall, the survey results substantiated these theories. That is to say, there was a clear connection between the financial means of one's primary social networks (family, friends, church, etc.) and the ability of a fund-raiser to raise her or his support.

In order to examine the relationship between class background and fund-raising, respondents were asked to estimate the combined income of their parents when the respondent was sixteen years old. For the sake of analysis, respondents whose parents made $40,000 or less were considered to be from a lower-income background. Taking age into consideration, I removed respondents who were forty-five years old or older (because $40,000 per year around 1980 would have been considerably more then). Over 65 percent of respondents who indicated they were from a lower-income background (parents earned less than $40,000 per year at age sixteen) agreed with the statement "My support contacts did not have much money to begin with." These respondents also tended to believe to a greater extent that they did not have very many support contacts.

Over 70 percent of respondents from a lower-income background believed that their fund-raising experience differed somewhat from that of individuals who came from higher-income backgrounds. When respondents were asked to explain why, they typically described the economic disparities between their social networks and even mentioned the aspect of connections identified by social homophily research. One respondent stated plainly, "Wealthier families tend to have connections with wealthier individuals." Another explained, "Because most people socialize with others from similar class and race, family income certainly plays a huge role in who one has access to for fund-raising." Several respondents also elaborated on the practical consequences of being from a lower-income background:

> I simply do not have the connections to families with higher incomes that some of my staff partners have. I don't have connections to churches that have anyone of a higher income. The average monthly gift to my account is $44/month. I have very few donors in a higher range than that and none that have surpassed $4,000 a year.

> My family was not able to sponsor me, nor did they have relationships or networks with higher income people, that might have helped me to get started. I also noticed that I had lower goals, within the allowable range, than other single staff from higher income backgrounds. I am guessing too that staff from higher income backgrounds did not have trouble asking other higher income individuals to help support a relatively lower income missionary salary.

> My average supporter gives around $30 a month. I have friends from metropolitan areas where the average income is higher who average $75 a month per supporter. As well I have over 260 individual supporters and know of staff that have fewer than 70 to raise the same amount of support. This is clearly an indication of the disparity in locations and financial means of various areas of the country.

As these excerpts indicate, the practical consequences of being from a lower-income background for fund-raising appear to amount to donations at lower dollar amounts, which requires a larger support team and inevitably more support appointments, as well as more instances where families, friends, and churches are supportive and encouraging towards a missionary's calling, but unfortunately do not have the economic resources to contribute with any sort of consistency if at all. As the last respondent indicated, class status may also be related to the region of the country in which one is raising support or in which one has support contacts (e.g., rural versus urban; South versus North).

Cultural values associated with a lower-income (or working-class) status may also pose an obstacle to support-raising. Working-class men and women tend to possess a blue-collar work ethic that influences them to value a hard day's work and denigrate those who do not pull their own weight. Consequently, ministers and missionaries from working-class backgrounds may feel uncomfortable with the strategy of soliciting donations from family and friends who may question whether they are "earning" their living. Several respondents described this cultural value:

> I think that it is somewhat of a different experience (at least for me). I see people from higher income groups who are more comfortable raising support. They grew up with the attitude that money was just something that was expected so they had no problem asking. My family grew up relatively poor. I grew up in a culture that you don't ask people for money because no matter how poor you are you take pride in providing for yourself—even if it is very little.

> The expectations of my parents and family upon graduation meant that I was to come home and contribute to the overall well-being of my larger family, not continue to "live off of them." A college degree is a highly valued and rare commodity. That I had secured a higher earning potential than my family and was turning it down in order to "beg" from people who did not even attend college was ludicrous in their eyes. It did not help that even at a low salary, my income was higher than many in my immediate and extended family, making it difficult to justify fund-raising from them.

As I indicated above, race and class status tend to be highly correlated and thus it is notoriously difficult to separate the effects of these two factors. Such was the case in this study as well. For example, about two-thirds of African American and Latino respondents indicated that they were from a lower-income background. As discussed in the section on race and fund-raising above, a large percentage of African American and Latino respondents expressed that they experienced considerable difficulty raising support due to the economic challenges facing their families and communities.

Although one should refrain from making sweeping generalizations, particularly when it comes to racial groups, in many regards the challenges associated with class status and fund-raising tended to hold true for many Latino and African American missionaries and outreach ministers as well. Together, the dual challenges of being from a lower-income background on top of being from a historically disadvantaged minority group clearly present a serious obstacle to fund-raising, and consequently, working for support-based ministries at all. Addressing the challenge of being a minority from a lower-income background, one African American woman explained, "Actually, I was very reluctant to come on staff at first because I saw no possible way to access the kind of support I saw the white staff being able to raise. I knew very few people with money and I was afraid to talk to them." Responses like this suggest that being from a lower-income background can potentially deter would-be outreach ministers and missionaries from working for ministries where they have to raise personal funds.

RECOMMENDATIONS FOR EVANGELICAL MISSIONS

To recapitulate, I have presented an analysis of survey responses from a sample of almost 720 missionaries, campus ministers, and other parachurch workers in order to assess how race, class, and gender affects the fund-raising experiences of missionaries or staff workers and to what extent the challenges associated with these factors potentially inhibit racial, gender, and class diversity among ministry staff teams.

The findings of this study confirm that race, class, and gender affect the fund-raising enterprise in significant and unique ways. More specifically, these findings also indicate that being a racial minority, single female, and/or from a lower-income background can often make one's fund-raising experience more challenging and consequently diminish the likelihood of one's long-term employment with a support-based evangelical missions agency or outreach ministry.

In light of these findings, a broad recommendation would be that evangelical fund-raising manuals and certainly the more focused fund-raising training of evangelical ministries and missions agencies should give greater attention (or any attention at all!) to the fund-raising challenges confronting racial/ethnic minorities, single women, and individuals from lower-income backgrounds. The findings of this study, in combination with the already pervasive awareness among fund-raisers that race, gender, and class potentially impact one's fund-raising experience and outcomes, suggest that future fund-raising manuals and support-raising coaches ignore these issues to their own detriment. These fund-raising challenges are real and to ignore their presence will likely inhibit efforts to maintain diverse ministry teams and will indirectly fortify the race, class, and gender homogeneity of their organizations. With literally dozens of how-to fund-raising manuals on the market, it makes little sense that only two or three give these challenges any sort of attention.

Although the effects of race/ethnicity on respondents' ability to raise financial support were the most pronounced, gender and class certainly have a considerable impact on fund-raising experiences and outcomes and should also be included in discussions of fund-raising policies and strategies of evangelical mission agencies and outreach ministries. With this in mind, I now discuss some implications of this research for evangelical fund-raising and provide suggestions for alternative approaches.

MINORITIES AND LOWER-INCOME FUNDRAISERS: NEGATING ECONOMIC AND CULTURAL BARRIERS

The findings of this study indicate that African American and Latino missionaries and campus workers often come from lower-income backgrounds and thus have fewer contacts with disposable income to contribute to their ministries. Moreover, social networks of all three minority groups tend to be less familiar with the individualized strategy of personal fund-raising employed by most evangelical mission agencies. These two factors in combination contribute to the greater difficulty of minorities obtaining their full support goal. Solutions to the economic barriers that minority fund-raisers face are so similar to those faced by lower-income fund-raisers generally that solutions for these two are appropriately considered together.

First and foremost, support coaches and ministry directors should commit to contextualizing the fund-raising process for their specific staff team and be willing to be creative and experiment with unique methods. Economic and relational situations will differ by person. One size will not fit all. As for specific ideas, in *Funding Your Ministry*, Morton (2007) provides several suggestions. First, he suggests a temporary support-matching program, where the support raised by lower-income minority missionaries is matched by the organization, dollar for dollar, over a period of several months. He also suggests that instead of paying a guaranteed subsidy each month, incentives be made for minority fund-raisers who take serious initiatives to obtain one-on-one appointments, group presentations, etc. as a way of providing cash while the minority missionary is in the initial stages of support-raising. Lastly, he cites how one particular ministry, known for its multicultural emphasis, has used a minority subsidy that takes a small percentage of the support raised by staff and uses it to support ethnic minority staff. I believe these practices are a step in the right direction in that they help to negate the economic-network deficits that minority staff from lower-income backgrounds potentially bring to the fund-raising venture.

On top of these practices I would recommend exploring the possibility of team-based fund-raising patterned after the Acts 2 church. For example, a campus staff team (of say five people: one couple and three singles) could be required to calculate their collective budget (including their living expenses, savings, tithe, etc.) and raise their budget together as a team. In such a situation, staff who come from higher-income backgrounds with connections to individuals who have the means to give and are also familiar with the typical strategy of parachurch fund-raising would be able to contribute a greater amount to the collective budget, while some might only be able to contribute less based on their existing social networks. The team could go to churches together and those with more well-to-do support contacts could share them with those less fortunate.

Two potential problems with this approach might be, first, support-raising is challenging for everyone and such a situation might allow some less-motivated staff to take advantage of other hard-working staff. This is true, but this should be considered an opportunity for testing character and commitment (as in Acts 2) rather than an insurmountable flaw in the strategy itself. Second, one does not want to rob minority or lower-income communities of the opportunity to give to God's work. This should also be considered and fund-raising presentations should be further contextualized on a case-by-case basis for the particular missionary and her or his community.

SINGLE FEMALES: ALTERNATIVES TO ONE-ON-ONE APPOINTMENTS AND CLEAR COMMUNICATION

Scott Morton and Donna Wilson (Morton 1999, 145–56) also provide several helpful recommendations for single females in order to surmount their obstacles of complementarian barriers in evangelical churches and potentially awkward fund-raising appointments. Regarding the complexities of single females and one-on-one support appointments with both married and single male contacts, Morton recommends single females conduct support appointments in groups. He also recommends single females tackle the fund-raising process in groups throughout. This idea fits well with the group-based fund-raising approach that I proposed above. Raising support as a group would allow single female staff to team up and pool resources in order to establish deeper relationships with one another. It might also help them to avoid potentially awkward appointments with a romantically interested male contact. This would also allow them to feel sufficiently relational and that they are not trying to fit into an uncomfortable, decidedly male, business-like approach to soliciting funds.

Findings of this study indicate that within theologically conservative evangelical circles single female fund-raisers are confronted with (1) the suspicion that they will be placed into situations in which they exercise leadership over men and (2) the assumption that single women should get married and not serve in mission as singles, both of which may hinder their ability to reach their support goal. I believe this fund-raising barrier can be confronted with more direct communication on the part of both the ministry itself and single females regarding exactly what their job entails and even their calling regarding ministry itself. Missions agencies and outreach ministries could develop a literature (brochure, CD-Rom, webpage, etc.) outlining their theological position on women in ministry and describing what the job of a single female in the field looks like. Moreover, single females need to express that they are not serving in ministry as a "holding-pattern" until they get married, but feel called by God to serve in the mission field or on the college campus. For ministries who embrace a more egalitarian position on women in leadership, there are fewer ways to get around a rigidly complementarian stance for single female fund-raisers. Yet with clear communication, we increase opportunities for dialogue, which has been known on occasion to dissolve previously insurmountable obstacles.

REFERENCES

Barnett, Betty J. 1991. *Friend raising: Building a missionary support team that lasts.* Seattle: YWAM Publishing.

Chaves, Mark. 1999. *Ordaining women: Culture and conflict in religious organizations.* Cambridge, MA: Harvard University.

Dillon, William. 1993. *People raising: A practical guide to raising support.* Chicago: Moody.

Jeavons, Thomas H., and Rebekah Burch Basinger. 2000. *Growing givers' hearts: Treating fund-raising as a ministry.* San Francisco: Jossey-Bass.

Johnson, Paul I. 2007. More than money, more than faith: Successfully raising missionary support in the twenty-first century. Enumclaw, WA: Pleasant Word.

McCabe, Tom, and Bill Campbell. 1996. *Inside outreach: A guide to financing outreach ministries.* Milwaukee, WI: Christian Stewardship Association.

McGlathery, Marla, and Traci Griffin. 2007. 'Becoming Conservative, Becoming White?' Black Evangelicals and the Para-church Movement. In *This side of heaven: Race, ethnicity, and Christian faith,* ed. R. Priest and A. Nieves, 145-61. New York: Oxford University.

Miller, Sharon L. 1999. Financing parachurch organizations. In *Financing American Religion,* eds. M. Chaves and S. L. Miller, 119-30. Walnut Creek, CA: AltaMira Press.

Morton, Scott. 1999. *Funding your ministry: Whether you're gifted or not,* 1st edition. Colorado Springs: DawsonMedia.

———. 2007. *Funding your ministry,* 2nd edition. Colorado Springs, CO: NavPress.

Perry, Samuel L. 2009. *Parachurch ministries fund-raising survey.*

Sommer, P., ed. 1999. *Getting sent: A relational approach to support raising.* Downers Grove: InterVarsity.

Wilson, Donna. 1999. When Women Raise Support. In *Getting sent: A relational approach to support raising,* ed. P. Sommer, 145–56. Downers Grove: InterVarsity.

Wuthnow, Robert. 1989. *The restructuring of American religion: Society and faith since World War II.* Princeton, NJ: Princeton University.

19

UNDERSTANDING THE EFFECTS OF DIVERSITY IN MISSION FROM A SOCIAL SCIENCE PERSPECTIVE

DAVID R. DUNAETZ

INTRODUCTION

Understanding the effects of diversity in teams is important because missionaries, by nature of their task, form partnerships and teams with people of different cultures and races. In addition, it appears inevitable that missionary teams (teams composed only of missionaries from sending countries) will become more diverse. As the demographics of sending countries evolve, a healthy mission that maintains its ranks (or even grows) will most likely be composed of a more racially diverse missionary force. Increased globalization and the mixing of cultures is occurring throughout out the world. Christian colleges, seminaries, and mission organizations need to be aware of what the likely effects of this will be in order to plan proactively and provide the appropriate training for the missionary workforce.

Yet diversity is much more than the mixing of cultures. Diversity may also include differences in gender, educational level, age, function within the organization, personality, knowledge, and experience. Any characteristic or attribute of individuals that can lead to the perception that one person is different from another is a source of diversity (van Knippenberg and Schippers 2007). If mission team members identify each other as either Anglo or Latino, diversity issues will arise. If missionary team members think of each other as either Bible school trained or university trained, diversity plays a role in the group dynamics, even if all the team members are of the same ethnicity and gender.

Diversity has always been a factor in Christ's church. The early church was immediately confronted with an ethnically and culturally diverse membership (Acts 2:5–11; 6:1–7; 15:1–29) that varied in gender, social standing, function, and gifting (1 Cor 1:26–27; 12:12–30; Gal 3:28). The nature of cross-cultural missionary work, whether it be church planting, relief work, or any other task that requires cooperation, leads to the mixing of individuals with diverse backgrounds, abilities, and perspectives. For centuries, missionaries and scholars have been recording experiences with diverse cultures, explaining the difficulties that have been encountered and proposing solutions to these problems (Carey 1892/2004; Gregory of Tours 591/1974; Taylor 1894/1974). With the advent of modern social science (especially psychology, sociology, anthropology, and the administrative sciences), new sources of information that may be useful to missionaries have become available. The purpose of this review is to summarize what the social sciences have discovered concerning diversity in work groups and to emphasize that which is relevant and potentially beneficial to missionary teams.

The basic problem with diversity of all types is that it very often leads to conflict (Jehn, Northcraft, and Neale 1999) and that conflict, in general, leads to decreased work group performance (de Dreu and Weingart 2003). When a group is composed of diverse members, communication is more difficult because differences between members make misunderstanding and misinterpretation more likely. Cooperation is more difficult because the values of the team members are likely to diverge, and the sources of this divergence might not be comprehensible to the various team members. Unfortunately, Christians do not always want to recognize the difficulties involved with diversity (Dunaetz 2008). As Christians are called to be unified (Phil 2:1–2), a lack of unity indicates some sort of problem. Unfortunately, it often is easier to deny that a problem exists than to find a solution for it. Such a denial in no way lessens our responsibility to resolve the difficulties that diversity brings about.

However, diversity is not always negative; it may lead to increased team performance depending on the context (Joshi and Roh 2009). Diversity can bring to a team a greater range of resources and perspectives. If all missionaries were exactly alike, we would have difficulty coming up with new strategies and solutions to the problems every generation encounters. In addition, openness to diversity creates a larger pool from which mission organizations may recruit new missionaries and evolve with the churches of sending countries. We will examine here the conditions and the contexts that have been discovered which either increase or decrease team performance.

The general approach we will take is to summarize various empirical (data driven) studies and apply them to missionary contexts. Although most of these studies have been done in a secular context, there is little reason to believe that the problems that non-Christians encounter with diversity are different than those which Christians encounter (1 Cor 3:3). Similarly, the benefits that may come to non-Christians from diversity should also be available to Christians as well (Eph 1:3). Empirical studies are driven by statistical analyses of information provided by the observations of many different individuals and teams. By statistically combining the results of many studies such as Joshi and Roh (2009), we gain the advantage of potentially counterbalancing any biases that might exist in individual studies. It is important to note that statistics only indicate general trends that occur under specific conditions. We cannot use this statistical information to determine with certainty what will happen in any specific context. We can only use statistics to predict what the most likely outcome is, given what we have observed in other similar contexts. So even in teams where success does not seem likely, where diversity is threatening all productive cooperation, by the grace of God, the odds may be overcome and these teams may still accomplish the task to which God has called them (2 Cor 5:7–10; Phil 4:13).

BASIC SOCIAL SCIENCE CONCEPTS

The social sciences have produced a number of concepts that are useful in missionary contexts. In this section, we will define and examine these concepts before going on to explain when and under what conditions diversity may have positive effects.

Diversity

The popular notion of diversity held by many North Americans is often the proportion of blacks, Latinos, and perhaps Asians that are in a group. However, diversity can be much broader than a simple schema of racial categorization from a Caucasian point of view. Van Knippenberg and Schippers, organizational scholars from the Netherlands, define diversity as "differences between individuals on any attribute that can lead to the perception that another person is different from self" (2007, 517). Diversity can be measured along various *dimensions*. These dimensions can be defined by categories (e.g., race, gender, nationality, or subject studied in college), by different positions on a continuous attitudinal scale (e.g., priority accorded to evangelism versus social work), or different levels of status or power (e.g., level of education, age, organizational position). It is thus important to identify the dimensions of diversity that are of concern (Harrison and Klein 2007). Once a dimension has been chosen, diversity can be measured in a number of ways. One common measure is an index of heterogeneity (Blau 1977) which is calculated from the proportions of each group identified along the chosen dimension; it represents the probability that any two group members selected at random will be members of different groups. In general, the smaller the largest subgroup is and the more subgroups that are present in a group, the higher will be its diversity.

Team Performance

To measure the effects of diversity on teams, team performance must somehow be measured. Team performance measures to what extent a team accomplishes its mission. If increasing diversity benefits a team, its performance will go up. If diversity is detrimental to a team, its performance will go down. In experimental situations, teams can be told what their mission is (e.g., find the best solution to a problem, earn the most money possible) and their performance can be measured subjectively (by a group of experts, for example) or objectively (as in the case of a multiple choice test that a team works on). In field studies where real teams are observed, the team performance is typically measured by subjective observers (such as team members themselves or their supervisors) or by objective data (such as sales volume or number of parts manufactured).

In a missions context, team performance can be especially hard to measure because the team's mission may not be clear, because there are few clear measures of success, or because any indication of less than optimal results may be detrimental to support raising or contrary to a missionary's theology. Nevertheless, team performance can be measured according to the context. Examples would include the time it takes to plant a church, the number of street children that were housed during a certain period, or the number of students in a school. Although most missions do not have the resources necessary to measure and standardize team performance data, we assume that, all other things being equal, the same factors that affect team performance in situations that have been studied will also affect team performance in mission contexts.

Task Diversity and Relationship Diversity

Two primary types of diversity have been the subject of team performance studies (Joshi and Roh 2009). Task diversity involves those dimensions that are assumed to be relevant to the team's task or mission. These dimensions include educational background (MBA, MDiv, etc.), role within a team or an organization (pastor, worship leader, youth worker, accountant, etc.), and tenure (years with the team's organization). These dimensions represent differences in skills and knowledge. The more task diversity that is found in a team, the more resources the team has to accomplish its mission.

Relationship diversity involves dimensions that are not directly relevant to the team's mission, such as gender, race, and age. These dimensions are similar in that they all are easily observable by others, all team members possess them, and all are unchangeable. They form the basis of social categorization processes. They influence relationships between individuals because cultural norms often dictate how members of these categories should interact with each other. For example, a culture may say that women can say some things to other women that they cannot say to men or that people of one race can say things to each other that they should not say to people outside their race.

Theoretical Frameworks

Human behavior is so complicated that social scientists have little hope of completely understanding it. However, models of behavior are useful to explain what people do "on the average." By looking at trends among large numbers of individuals and situations, generalizations can be made about human behavior. Some of these generalizations, models, or frameworks are better than others. Those which most accurately describe how large numbers of people behave in the given context are superior to those that describe human behavior less accurately. Currently there are two competing theoretical frameworks concerning diversity that have been found to accurately describe human behavior (van Knippenberg et al. 2004; van Knippenberg and Schippers 2007). Both appear to be true under certain conditions.

The *Information/Decision Making Perspective* posits that diverse groups have more access to task relevant knowledge, skills, and abilities. Diversity is thus beneficial to teams. When teams are faced with a new problem, the greater resources of a group will promote the likelihood of the creation of an innovative and effective solution. For this to occur, the team members must be willing to share their perspectives, expend the effort necessary to understand the perspectives of others, and be able to work toward integrating these perspectives to come up with an optimal solution. If the perspectives of all the team members are not considered, premature decision-making will occur and the best solution may not be found. This can occur because of authoritarian leadership (Adorno 1950; Lipman-Blumen and Finder 2005), beliefs in a false consensus (Ross, Greene, and House 1977), or groupthink (Janis 1982). To prevent these premature decisions, the constructive expression of conflicting ideas must be allowed and even encouraged (Turner and Pratkanis 1997).

This perspective corresponds to Paul's theology of spiritual gifts (Rom 12:3–8; 1 Cor 12:1–31). Individual Christians are different and complementary. Proper functioning of the body of Christ requires the input of all members and no one is considered superior to another. Diversity, according to this theoretical framework, is thus necessary for the proper functioning of a team.

The other principle theoretical framework is the *Similarity/Attraction Perspective* (Rajfel and Turner 1986; Tsui, Egan, and O'Reilley 1992). People have a tendency to prefer being with people who are similar to themselves. In-group members are considered more attractive than out-group members. Interpersonal similarity leads to interpersonal attraction (Berscheid and Reis 1998). So the greater similarity people have to each other in a team, the more effectively the team will function. People will be more committed to and enjoy working in teams of people that are similar to them. Because similar team members can readily understand each other, communication is easier and finding solutions requires less effort. Diversity, according to this theoretical framework, is thus detrimental to team performance.

This perspective corresponds to the view presented in the story of the Tower of Babel (Gen 11:1–9). Differences among individuals make communication strained and coordination of efforts more difficult, if not impossible. The proper response to these differences is humility before God and the recognition of our human limitations.

Under certain conditions the *Information/Decision Making Perspective* (i.e., diversity leads to better team performance) is the best model. Under other conditions, the *Similarity/Attraction Perspective* (i.e., diversity leads to worse team performance) is the best model. The focus of much research has been upon determining what these conditions are. In general, the *Information/Decision Making Perspective* describes the effects of task diversity and the *Similarity/Attraction Perspective* describes the effects of relationship diversity (Joshi and Roh 2009). However, these effects are relatively small. We will examine the conditions that amplify these effects in more depth later once we have finished defining the basic concepts.

Faultlines

In most groups, some dimensions of diversity are only slightly correlated. For example, within a mission organization, a person's gender may only be slightly (or not at all) correlated to his or her ethnic origin. In other groups, some dimensions of diversity may be highly correlated. One's level of education may be strongly related to ethnic origin. Or a group may consist mainly of older men and younger women. This type of group is characterized by *faultlines* (Lau and Murnighan 1998), which can be defined as "combinations of correlated dimensions of diversity that yield a clear basis for distinction" (van Knippenberg and Schippers 2007, 523). When faultlines exist, teams easily divide into subgroups because there are many dimensions that clearly separate the subgroups, not just one. When subgroups are present, team members are likely to be affected by similarity/attraction processes that favor their own ingroup and team performance is likely to decrease. Diversity that is not characterized by faultlines is far less disruptive than diversity that has strong faultlines.

Cultural versus Non-Cultural Diversity

Culture is an especially important concept in diversity research. Although a very wide range of definitions exist, culture is usually associated with beliefs/assumptions/values that are shared within a group. A definition of culture which is broad enough to cover groups as large as nations and as small as work teams is provided by Schein: "A pattern of shared basic assumptions that was learned by a group as it solved its problems of external adaptation and internal integration, that has worked well enough to be considered valid and, therefore, to be taught to new members as the correct way to perceive, think, and feel in relation to those problems" (2004, 17). Viewing culture this way underlines the special nature of the dimension of cultural diversity. Whereas few people would think that it is right or wrong to be male or female, to be white or black, to be a business or a Bible major, we all have a tendency to believe that our cultural approaches to problem solving are the right way to deal with the issues and that those approaches that go against what our culture values are wrong ways.

This makes cultural diversity the most difficult dimension of diversity to deal with. As missionaries, we are expected to adapt to our host culture, at least on a superficial level, but our task has a goal—changing people's beliefs (John 3:16) and hence their culture at some level. Within missionary teams it is unlikely that we can abandon our home cultures (which may be very diverse) and adopt our host culture's approach to problem solving. We may also have difficulty in recognizing the cultural differences that exist among team members. It's easy for missionaries to think that they are only dealing with two cultures: their home culture and their host culture, both of which they may highly respect. However, many missionaries may not pay attention to or be aware of the cultural differences that exist among themselves. It can become very complicated when one missionary's perception of the host culture differs from another missionary's perception of the host culture because the two missionaries themselves are from different cultures. Difficult situations like that easily disintegrate into "I'm right and you're wrong" conflicts that are not dealt with constructively.

Status

Another concept that is related to both diversity and culture is *status*, which may be defined as culturally held beliefs concerning performance expectations for an individual, either on a specific task or on all tasks in general (Berger, Cohen, and Zelditch 1972; Berger, Fisek, Norman, and Zelditch 1977; Dunaetz 2009). These culturally held beliefs define who receives status regardless of whether the beliefs conform to reality or not. In North American culture, higher status, whether it is merited or not, is often ascribed to white educated males because it is generally believed that whites, males, and the educated are more task competent in most situations (Berger, Rosenholtz, and Zelditch 1980). In other cultures, status will be given according to the dictates of that culture.

If a person demonstrates within a group his or her competence in a task, his or her status will go up. People accorded status within a group are given more resources and opportunities to lead the group toward the accomplishment of its mission. If the high status person successfully leads the group, his or her status will be maintained and will continue to be able to influence the group. Similarly, if low status members contribute significantly to the achievement of the group's goals (beyond what is expected of them and in spite of the leadership opportunities given them), their status will also go up. But if a high status person consistently performs below expectations, his or her status will go down. Numerous experiments and observational studies have confirmed these phenomena (Ridgeway 2001).

Status is an important concept for understanding the effect of diversity because diversity may not affect all people along a diversity dimension equally. If higher status is associated with members at one end of a dimension and lower status with members at the other end, diversity may impact members of the group differently.

WHEN WILL DIVERSITY MOST LIKELY HAVE POSITIVE EFFECTS ON TEAM PERFORMANCE?

We will now address in more detail the conditions under which diversity is most likely to have positive effects on team performance. This is an important question because, as missionaries, our job is to accomplish the mission we have been given (Matt 28:19–20). We want to seek to accomplish this task using the most effective ways possible, and in the ways that bring the most glory to God. Understanding the effects of diversity allows us to anticipate its effects and make the necessary changes to be the most effective in ministry.

Task Diversity versus Relationship Diversity

As mentioned previously, task diversity generally helps teams accomplish their task while relationship diversity slows the team down. In a meta-analysis combining thirty-nine empirical studies involving over 8,000 teams, Joshi and Roh (2009) found that among the dimensions of relationship diversity, age diversity had the least negative affect while gender and race/ethnicity diversity had stronger negative effects. As for the effects of task dimensions, they found that functional and seniority diversity had positive effects, while educational diversity (different levels or types of education) had negative effects. However, all of these effects were small (accounting for less than 1 percent of the variation in team performance) by themselves, except for the benefits that came from functional diversity (which accounted for nearly 2 percent of the variation in team performance). Having team members that have different roles and responsibilities (functional diversity) had a very significant positive effect on teams.

However, these effects, in themselves, are small compared to the influence that other factors have on team performance. A meta-analysis of ninety-three studies involving more than 3,000 teams (Stewart 2006) has demonstrated that the average level of cognitive ability and the personality traits of the team members have a far greater influence on team performance than diversity. The average level of cognitive ability (measured typically by IQ-related tests, SAT scores, or GRE scores), accounts for 16 percent of the variation in team performance. Groups with brighter people perform better, on the average, than less bright groups. Two personality traits that are especially valuable are what is known as *conscientiousness* (a measure of that predicts how responsible, consistent, and reliable a team member will be) and *agreeableness* (a measure of how sensitive team members are to the concerns of other team members). Average levels of conscientiousness and agreeableness account for over 6 percent of the variation in team performance. This means that in terms of team effectiveness, the influence of personality and cognitive ability of the team members is far more influential than either task or relationship diversity. Bright, conscientious, agreeable people contribute to team performance regardless of the task and relational diversity of the team.

It should also be noted that task and relationship diversity also interact with each other. Task diversity is, in general, beneficial, but this relationship is especially true when relationship diversity is low (van Knippenberg and Schippers 2007). When relationship diversity is high, there is little or no benefit from task diversity. But when relationship diversity is low, the benefits from task diversity multiply. Apparently the more people are similar along the relationship diversity dimensions, the greater the trust and the ability to communicate effectively, enabling the group to better deal with difficult situations. This implies that, as mission teams become more diverse in general, mission organizations will need to provide more training in communication and conflict resolution in order to adjust to the new team dynamics they will encounter.

Faultlines
When diversity occurs along several dimensions that are strongly correlated (strong faultlines), the effects on team performance can be especially negative

(van Knippenberg et al. 2004). For example, a team that consists of only middle-aged adults and older teens would not have a faultline if both the adults and the teens were evenly split between males and females. A team that consists uniquely of middle-aged males and teen females would have a strong faultline and would likely function much less effectively. Faultlines accentuate a sense of identity with subgroups and thus similarity/attraction principles come into play, lowering the group's ability to communicate and to achieve their goals. This is an especially important issue in missions because culture is strongly associated with many dimensions of diversity, increasing the likelihood of faultlines. To avoid these problems, organizations may try to recruit members from different cultural backgrounds while seeking to make sure that average educational background, gender mix, age, and ministry experience for each cultural group is approximately the same.

Beliefs about Diversity

A *diversity mind-set*, the belief that diversity is good, has been shown to increase the team performance, at least for task diversity and gender diversity (van Knippenberg et al. 2004). The effects of a diversity mind-set are less clear for other forms of relationship diversity. Nevertheless, the more that people believe that some forms of diversity are good, the more likely they are to make the necessary changes in their relationships with others. This may be because people with a diversity mind-set tend to be more open-minded. The benefits of open-mindedness will be discussed a little later.

Status of Team Members

Team satisfaction, the degree to which one is satisfied with the team, and team commitment, the degree to which one is committed to a team, are both associated with better team performance. When the average level of team satisfaction or team commitment rises, team performance improves when all other factors are held constant. This is because committed and satisfied team members are more motivated to give themselves to the team and sacrifice their own personal goals for the good of the team. The effects of diversity on team commitment and satisfaction depend on the status of the team members. If a team is composed of high status members, the introduction of low status members (i.e., greater diversity) leads to lower team satisfaction and commitment; if a team consists of low status members, the introduction of high status members (i.e., greater diversity) leads to greater team satisfaction and commitment (Chatman and O'Reilly 2004; Tsui et al. 1992; van Knippenberg and Schippers 2007). The effects of diversity are thus not symmetrical. Low status groups stand to benefit more from diversity than high status groups.

This phenomenon is partially explained by one's sense of social identity which is determined by one's perception of the groups to which one belongs (Hogg and Terry 2000). People tend to be more committed to and satisfied with groups that enhance their social identity, that is, groups that are more attractive or have higher status members. So mission leaders need to be aware of the difficulties that teams consisting of higher status members (for example, white males in North America) might have in integrating members of lower status and the loss that they may feel. A way to make their integration more successful is not to emphasize that the team is becoming more diverse, but to emphasize the skills and the abilities that the new individuals are bringing to the team. If the emphasis is on what the new person can bring rather than how the new person is different, team members will be able focus on integrating the new member into the team because of the contributions that he or she can bring. What the new person can bring to the team will be salient, rather than what the team will lose.

Interdependence

Teams vary in the level of interdependence of their members. Interdependence measures the degree to which team members depend on one another for accomplishing their goals. A missionary team that meets together several times a week and decides by consensus all missionary activity is characterized by high interdependence. A missionary team that meets twice a year for sharing and praying but has no discussion of strategy has low interdependence.

In the meta-analysis of over 8,000 teams previously mentioned (Joshi and Roh, 2009), it was found that medium and high interdependence teams were influenced by diversity in the usual ways: task diversity was beneficial but relationship diversity was a hindrance in accomplishing the team's goals. However, in low interdependence teams, a very surprising result was found: relationship diversity was positively correlated to team performance (while task diversity was not significantly correlated to team performance). Apparently, when there is little interdependence, relationship diversity (including cultural diversity) acts like task diversity by enabling individuals to see other ways of accomplishing the task without having to spend the effort necessary to fully coordinate their work with people that are different from them. Teams low in interdependence can receive the benefits of diversity without the negative consequences of diversity.

The implications of this phenomenon for missions teams are important. If teams consisting of culturally diverse members encourage members to function independently (or interdependently only with others with whom they have a natural affinity), team members from one culture may benefit from the perspectives brought by team members of other cultures. However, if teams consisting of culturally diverse members are expected to work together very closely, it is likely that the cultural diversity will be a source of tension rather than enrichment. Missionaries need to be taught about team dynamics, including interdependence, and be encouraged to structure their teams in ways that will allow them to function most effectively.

Team Duration

A similar effect is found with team duration (Joshi and Roh 2009). Long-term teams, teams that are formed to work together more or less permanently, are helped by task diversity and hindered by relationship diversity. The negative effects of relationship diversity on long-term teams are relatively strong, accounting for 2 percent of the variation in team performance. However, in short-term teams, teams that are only formed for a certain period (as would be the case in summer missions) improve their performance with increased diversity (task diversity has no significant effect).

The reason (or reasons) for this effect is not clear. It is possible that belonging to a relationally diverse, short-term team keeps everyone on their guard, so that everyone remains polite and respectful during their time together which enhances communication processes and team contentment. Or perhaps many short-term teams are organized in a context where team members are especially open to learning and the presence of relationally diverse people provides opportunity to learn and benefit from others. In either case, the beneficial effects of relational diversity disappear with time in long-term teams. The differences between the team members are real and cannot be ignored. Communication is more difficult and mutual comprehension is less likely, both of which are detrimental to team performance.

The Need for Cognition and Open-mindedness

Two personality traits are especially relevant in understanding when diversity can have positive and negative effects. Need for cognition is the "tendency to engage in and enjoy effortful cognitive activity" (Cacioppo et al. 1996, 197). Some people are highly motivated to think deeply and solve problems creatively; others are more motivated to participate in activities that require less mental effort. The need for cognition is different from, but related to, cognitive ability. People high in cognitive ability tend to encounter success more often in cognitive activity and may be more motivated to expend further effort. However, some people low in cognitive ability may still enjoy thinking deeply about problems to find new solutions while some people high in cognitive ability are perfectly happy with popular and traditional approaches to dealing with problems (Cacioppo et al. 1996).

When teams have a high average level of need for cognition, both task and relational diversity predict better team performance (Kearney et al. 2009). However, when teams have a low average level of need for cognition, both task and relational diversity predict worse team performance. Thus diversity is most likely to benefit teams where the members like thinking deeply about issues and working to solve problems by considering various options. Teams composed of members who prefer to do things traditionally or in ways that they've seen previously and who do not enjoy spending the cognitive effort necessary to work through complex problems will likely suffer with increased diversity.

A similar personality trait is openness to experience or open-mindedness (McCrase 1996). People high in open-mindedness tend to seek new information, be creative, have a preference for variety, and have a high level of intellectual curiosity. People low in open-mindedness tend to be conventional and traditional. This trait is closely related to need for cognition; people that are high in need for cognition tend to be more open-minded. Both open-mindedness and need for cognition appear to interact with diversity in similar ways (Goldberg et al. 2008). For example, both blacks and whites who are low in open-mindedness tend to prefer supervisors who are white. The preferences for people high in open-mindedness tend not to be determined by race. Thus more open-minded people are likely to benefit more from diversity than are less open-minded people, as in the case for need for cognition.

This is important because evangelical Christians tend to be low in open-mindedness (Saroglou 2002; Streyffeler and McNally 1998). It is not clear if people low in open-mindedness are attracted to the traditions and conservatism of evangelical Christianity, or if evangelical Christianity with its emphasis on correct doctrine and biblical authority promotes closed-mindedness, or both. This is not to say that all evangelical Christians are closed-minded; many, indeed, are very open-minded. But we need to be aware that closed-mindedness is a trait that characterizes evangelicals more than the population in general. There is little reason to believe that missionaries are much less closed-minded than evangelicals as a whole. Closed-mindedness might actually be useful for persistence and remaining in mission service. In any case, a lack of open-mindedness is likely to interact with diversity to have negative effects in teams.

However, there are a number of things that mission leaders can do to reduce the negative effects of diversity and to promote its benefits when teams have members low in openness (Kearney et al. 2009). They can encourage in-depth processing of new information by stressing the need to be open-minded. They can promote open-mindedness, lifting it up as a virtue, so that when missionaries think creatively they do not risk being labeled as mavericks or rebels. Team leaders may be held accountable, not for assuring the unity of their team, but for leading their team in a manner in which all points of view are expressed, respected, and understood by each member. Mission leaders may also promote open-mindedness by making learning more attractive. Educational and scholarly pursuits can be encouraged and promoted. In addition, open-mindedness is encouraged when leaders have a clear and compelling vision for the team; if the team's goals are lofty enough and honestly sought after, people are more likely to realize that traditional thinking is not sufficient and that creative thinking is necessary to achieve them. This will encourage new ideas to be expressed, rather than suppressed by those who value tradition and conventional methods.

CONCLUSIONS

We have looked at various forms of diversity and their effect on team effectiveness in missionary contexts. Task diversity (function within a team, educational background, etc.) tends to be beneficial for teams because each individual has something to contribute. Relationship diversity (race, culture, gender, etc.) tends to decrease team performance because communication and coordination is more difficult. However, these effects are small compared to the effects of other team characteristics such as average level of cognitive ability and the personality traits of the team members.

A number of factors have been found which reduce the negative effects of diversity and increase the positive effects. When there are few faultlines, diversity has fewer negative effects. When team members believe diversity is good, increased diversity along some dimensions is associated with better team functioning. Teams that are composed of low status members are especially open to increased diversity and reap many benefits from it. Teams with low levels of interdependence are also likely to benefit from increased relational diversity, as well as short-term teams. Teams where open-mindedness and the need for cognition are high and promoted are also more likely to benefit from diversity.

Although increased diversity may require many changes in some mission organizations, these organizations can adapt to and profit from diversity. These organizations will likely be the most effective ones in reaching a diverse world as they reflect the incarnational adaptation that Jesus Christ himself modeled.

REFERENCES

Adorno, Theodor W. 1950. *The authoritarian personality.* New York: Harper.

Berger, Joseph, Bernard P. Cohen, and Morris Zelditch Jr. 1972. Status characteristics and social interaction. *American Sociological Review* 37: 241–55.

Berger, Joseph, M. H. Fisek, R. Z. Norman, and Morris Zelditch Jr. 1977. *Status characteristics and social interaction: An expectation states approach.* New York: Elsevier.

Berger, Joseph, S. J. Rosenholtz, and Morris Zelditch Jr. 1980. Status organizing processes. *Annual Review of Sociology* 6: 479–508.

Berscheid, Ellen, and Harry T. Reis. 1998. Attraction and close relationships. In *The handbook of social psychology*, 4th ed., ed. D. T. Gilbert, S. T. Fiske, and G. Lindzey, 193–281. Boston: McGraw-Hill.

Blau, Peter M. 1977. *Inequality and heterogeneity: A primitive theory of social structure.* New York: Free Press.

Cacioppo, John T., Richard E. Petty, Jeffrey A. Feinstein, and W. Blair G. Jarvis. 1996. Dispositional differences in cognitive motivation: The life and times of individuals varying in need for cognition. *Psychological Bulletin* 119: 197–253.

Carey, W. 1972/2004. *An enquiry into the obligations of Christians to use means for the conversion of the heathens.* Whitefish, MT: Kessinger Publishing Co.

Chatman, Jennifer A., and Charles A. O'Reilly. 2004. Asymmetric reactions to work group sex diversity among men and women. *Academy of Management Journal* 47: 193–208.

deDreu, Carsten K. W., and Laurie R. Weingart. 2003. Task versus relationship conflict, team performance, and team member satisfaction: A meta-analysis. *Journal of Applied Psychology* 88: 741–49.

Dunaetz, David R. 2008. Transforming chaos into beauty: Intentionally developing unity in church plants. *Evangelical Missions Quarterly* 44: 358–65.

———. 2010. Worse instrumental outcomes but better relationships: Age-hierarchy status incongruence in organizational conflicts. Manuscript submitted for publication.

Goldberg, Caren, Christine M. Riordan, and Lu Zhang. 2008. Employees' perceptions of their leaders: Is being similar always better? *Group and Organization Management* 33: 330–55.

Gregory of Tours. 591/1974. *The history of the Franks,* trans. L. Thorpe. New York: Penguin Books.

Harrison, David A., and Katherine J. Klein. 2007. What's the difference? Diversity constructs as separation, variety, or disparity in organizations. *Academy of Management Review* 32: 1199–228.

Hogg, M. A., and D. I. Terry. 2000. Social identity and self-categorization processes in organizational contexts. *Academy of Management Review* 25: 121–40.

Janis, Irving L. 1982. *Groupthink: Psychological studies of policy decisions and fiascoes.* Boston: Houghton Mifflin.

Jehn, Karen A., Gregory B. Northcraft, and Maragret A. Neale. 1999. Why differences make a difference: A field study of diversity, conflict, and performance in workgroups. *Administrative Science Quarterly* 44: 741–63.

Joshi, Aparna, and Hyuntak Roh. 2009. The role of context in work team diversity research: A meta-analytic review. *The Academy of Management Journal* 52: 599–627.

Kearney, E., D. Gebert, and Sven C. Voelpel. 2009. When and how diversity benefits teams: The importance of team members' need for cognition. *The Academy of Management Journal* 52: 581–98.

Lau, Dora C., and J. Keith Murnighan. 1998. Demographic diversity and faultlines: The compositional dynamics of organizational groups. *The Academy of Management Review* 23: 325–40.

Lipman-Blumen, Jean, and A. Finder. 2005. Toxic leadership: When grand illusions masquerade as noble visions. *Leader to Leader* 36: 29–36.

McCrae, Robert R. 1966. Social consequences of experiential openness. *Psychological Bulletin* 120: 323–37.

Ridgeway, Cecilia L. 2001. Social status and group structure. In *Blackwell handbook of social psychology: Group processes*, eds. M. A. Hogg and S. Tindale, 352–75. Malden, MA: Blackwell Publishing.

Ross, Lee, D. Greene, and P. House. 1977. The false consensus effect: An egocentric bias in social perception and attribution processes. *Journal of Experimental Social Psychology* 13: 279–301.

Saroglou, Vassilis. 2002. Religion and the five factors of personality: A meta-analytic review. *Personality and Individual Differences* 32: 15–25.

Schein, Edgar H. 2004. *Organizational culture and leadership*, 3rd ed. San Francisco: Jossey-Bass.

Stewart, Greg L. 2006. A meta-analytic review of relationships between team design features and team performance. *Journal of Management* 32: 29–54.

Streyffeler, L. L., and R. J. McNally. 1998. Fundamentalists and liberals: Personality characteristics of protestant Christians. *Personality and Individual Differences* 24: 579–80.

Tajfel, Henri, and John C. Turner. 1986. The social identity theory of intergroup behavior. In *Psychology of intergroup relations*, 2nd ed., ed. S. Worchel and W. G. Autin, 7–24. Chicago: Nelson-Hall.

Taylor, J. H. (1894/74). *A retrospect/To China with love*, 18th ed. Minneapolis: Dimension Books.

Tsui, Anne S., Terri D. Egan, and Charles A. O'Reilly III. 1992. Being different: Relational demography and organizational attachment. *Administrative Science Quarterly* 549–79.

Turner, M. E. and A. R. Pratkanis. 1997. Mitigating groupthink by stimulating constructive conflict. In *Using conflict in organizations*, ed. C. K. W. de Dreu and E. van de Vliert, 53–71. Thousand Oaks, CA: Sage Publications.

Van Knippenberg, Daan, Carsten K. W. de Dreu, and Astrid C. Homan. 2004. Work group diversity and group performance: An integrative model and research agenda. *Journal of Applied Psychology* 89: 1008–22.

Van Knippenberg, Daan, and M. C. Schippers. 2007. Work group diversity. *Annual Review of Psychology* 58: 515–41.

INDEX

4/14 Window, 58

A
A Fair Country: Telling Truths about Canada, 6
aboriginal, 7
    ideas, 6
    identity, 4
abosom, 37
Abraham, 177, 299
Absolute Reality, 37
acculturation, 43, 48
Achaia, 210, 221, 223
Achaicus, 210, 221
Adadevoh, Dela, 263–64
Adeney, Miriam, 54, 107, 243
Affleck, Mark, 116–17
Africa, 21, 24, 27, 29, 36, 40, 54, 65, 88, 114, 116, 179, 244, 246–47, 251–56, 259–60, 264, 267
    African, 28, 36, 39–40, 45, 48–50, 52–54, 56–57, 127, 129, 132, 248, 252, 264–65, 296
        church, 23, 29, 50, 55, 248, 267
        congregation, 50
        context, 112, 264
        cosmology, 36–38
        hospitality, 50
        immigrant, 29–31, 52
            church, 22
        leadership, 25, 264–67
        perspective, 48
        religion, 40
        school, 269
        worldview, 39, 53
        worship, 25
    East, 125, 244
    modern, 36
    North, 210
    South, 115, 263
    West, 29, 107

African American, 29–30, 52–54, 198, 241–59, 311–12, 314–20, 326–27, 329–31
African Inland Mission (AIM), 245, 254
African Leadership and Management Academy (ALMA), 263, 265–71
African Traditional Religion (ATR), 39
age, 92, 108, 172, 180, 183, 187, 233–35, 238–39, 274, 280, 327, 335, 338–39, 343, 345
AIDS, 104, 113, 115–16
Akan, 37–41, 48, 53, 57
    kente, 60
Alaska, 91–92
Alberta, 65, 72, 80
Alexandria, 210, 221, 290
    · Alexandrian Jew, 212
America(n). *See* United States of America.
American Colonization Society (ACS), 251
American Conservative Baptist, 66, 86
Amish, 7
Anabaptist, 249
ancestors, 37–38, 54, 57
Anderson, Rufus, 220
Anglican Church, 108
Anglophone African, 22
anthropology, 56, 98, 128, 150, 188, 200, 243, 256, 336
Antioch, 210, 221–22, 253, 293–94, 296
    church, 177, 194
Apostolic Church of Ghana, 50
Apollos, 210, 212–13, 221
Apphia, 210, 221
Aquila, 210, 214, 216, 221
Aramaic, 290, 292, 295, 297
Archbishop Kolini, 108
Archippus, 210, 212, 221
Aristarchus, 210, 222
Arlington, 50, 256
Ashkanasy, Neal, 182
Asia, 21, 65, 86, 88, 136, 179, 185–86, 210, 221, 223
    Asian, 86, 132, 134, 179, 185–86, 219, 296–97, 316, 316, 321, 337
    South, 65
Asia Minor, 294, 297
Asian American, 311–14, 314, 316–17, 317, 321
Assemblies of God, 50

assimilation, 9, 13, 23, 27, 40, 42–44, 46, 48, 250
atheism, 28
Athens, 217, 294
Atlanta, 50
Atlas of Global Christianity, 179
attrition, 113, 163–66, 170, 172
Australia
        Australian, 152, 182
authority, 16, 128, 150, 181, 214, 322–23
        biblical, 349
        confusion in, 172
Avant Ministries, 279

B
Babylon, 14, 290
Baptist, 66, 74–75, 79–80, 86, 246, 251, 282, 313
        conservative, 66
baramee, 181
Barna Group, 98–99
Barnabas, 210–12, 221, 251, 253, 294
Barnett, Betty, 311
Barth, Karl, 11, 248
Bediako, Kwame, 52
Beloit College, 92
Benedict, Ruth, 40
Bhagat, Rabi, 182
Bible, 10, 25–26, 77, 95, 100, 112, 170, 177, 190, 202, 246, 255, 264, 273, 278, 295–299, 335, 341
        biblical, 158
               application, 151
               approach, 235
               authority. *See* authority.
               balance, 289
               community, 153, 159
               element, 142
               foundation, 297
               imperatives, 110–11
               interaction, 144
               mandate, 103, 120
               model, 115, 187
               narrative, 12
               norms, 104

　　　　principles, 108
　　　　teaching, 155, 218
　　　　truth, 197, 199–201, 206, 218, 276
　　　　understanding, 159, 209, 220
　　　　view, 151, 202
　　　　worldview, 53
　　distribution, 314
　　Scripture, 12, 56, 95, 100, 158, 200, 202, 218–19, 229, 235, 260, 286, 290–91, 301
　　study, 24, 49, 68
　　translator, 167, 197
bicultural, 4, 22, 28, 51, 192–93, 242, 295
bilingual, 4, 22, 27, 51, 292, 294, 297
Biney, Moses, 35–36, 48
Biola University, 128, 198
Blanchard, Kenneth, 144
Bombay Palaces, 66
Bonk, Jonathon, 9
Book IV, The Cultural Contribution of the Other Ethnic Groups, 4
boomers, 41, 141, 274–75, 282
Borden, William, 101
Bosch, David, 56, 250
Bowling Alone, 94
Bradshaw, Bruce, 116
Brake, Terence, 158
Brampton, 73
Brazil, 26
　　Brazilian, 26, 136, 152
British Columbia, 65, 72, 80
Bronx, 54, 57
Brooklyn, 50
Brown, C. M., 97
Buddhism, 28
Buddhist, 87
Burma, 83
busters, 275

C
Calenberg, Rick, 36, 49
Calgary, 73–74, 78–81
California, 91
　　South, 198

Cambodian
    Cambodian, 7
Cameroon
    Cameroonian, 54
Campbell, Bill, 311
Campus Crusade for Christ, 263, 314
Canada, 4–7, 11, 13, 64–68, 70–71, 74–75, 77–80, 83, 85, 87–89, 178
    Canadian, 3–7, 12, 16, 66, 71, 141
        church, 71, 85
        community, 66
        context, 17
        evangelical community, 9
        experience, 48
        government, 4, 11
        identity, 13
        perspective, 75
        society, 4
        sociologist, 9
        worldview, 13
Canadian Baptists
    of Ontario and Quebec (CBOQ), 74–75, 79–80
    of Western Canada (CBWC), 75, 79–80
Canadian Review of Sociology, 3
Cantonese, 22, 25
Carew, Donald, 144
Carey, Lott, 251, 253
Caribbean, 7, 27
Caucasian, 198, 337
Cenchrae, 210, 214
Centennial College Residence and Conference Centre, 70, 75, 84
Centre for the Study of Christianity in the non-Western World, 87
Chaves, Mark, 321
Cheptebo, 244
Chi Alpha, 314
Chicago, 50
Chile, 26
China, 22, 27–28, 65
    Chinese, 7, 22–28, 30, 39, 47, 65, 243, 248
        cultural center, 70, 84
China-Myanmar border, 26
Chinatown, 24–26, 66
Chinese Bible seminary, 26

Chretien, Jean, 7
Christian(s), 13–14, 28–30, 45, 48, 50–53, 55–57, 59, 87–88, 99, 104–05,
    110, 142, 178–79, 188, 193, 208, 210–12, 214–16, 238, 242, 269,
    285, 289, 295–300, 302, 336–37, 340, 349
    college, 96, 335
    community, 10, 12, 17, 107, 126, 160, 243, 246, 295
        African American, 260
    congregation, 14, 16, 53, 55
    denominations, 280
    holidays, 5
    leader, 11, 16, 180
    material, 26
    ministry, 145
    nation, 86
    non-Christian, 55, 57, 59, 337
    organization, 157
    school, 67
    service, 252
    unity, 289
    witness, 144
    worldview, 281
Christianity, 28, 39, 50, 52, 55, 59–60, 87, 107, 133, 137, 177–79, 250, 253,
    293, 302, 349
church
    Black, 251, 253, 312, 316, 320
    Chinese, 22–28, 248
    ethnic, 23, 44
    Ghanaian, 22, 24–25, 27, 50
    Hispanic, 22–30
    immigrant. *See* immigrant.
    membership, 56, 110
    missional, 71, 74, 78, 247
    mother, 24–26, 29, 50, 55, 65
    Nigerian, 22, 24–25, 27
    nondenominational, 22, 25–26
    nonimmigrant, 23
    planting, 24–25, 68, 71, 74, 88, 143, 220, 286
        diaspora. *See* diaspora.
        vision, 67–68, 70, 72, 79–80
Church of Pentecost, 50
Clark, Freddy James, 242
Clark, Mark, 281

class status, 307, 309, 311, 326–32
Clemens, 210, 212
Clement, 213–14, 222
Coffey, R.M., 284
cognition, 39, 46, 348, 351
        cognitive, 36, 43, 48, 148
                ability, 344, 348, 351
                theory, 188
Cole, Victor, 264
Coleman, Richard, 246–47
Colossae, 210, 212, 218, 221–22
Columbia
        Columbian, 22
Columbus, 50
communication, 30, 41, 43, 80, 95, 100, 128, 134–35, 145–46, 150–51,
        163–65, 167, 170–71, 177, 181, 184, 189, 236, 238, 249, 258, 276,
        290, 333, 336, 340, 344, 347, 349
        skills, 169–71
community, 9, 13–15, 23, 26–29, 31, 39, 41, 44, 46, 48, 50, 53–54, 60, 66,
        76, 78, 82, 83, 85, 94–95, 97, 100, 104–05, 109–10, 112–13, 117,
        125–26, 128, 143, 153, 155, 157, 159, 173, 190–91, 202, 206, 213,
        242–44, 246, 248–50, 253–54, 256, 257–59, 270–71, 275, 277–78,
        280–81, 283–85, 296, 301, 312, 315–16, 323, 332
        Christian. *See* Christian.
        immigrant. *See* immigrant.
        service, 31, 83
Community Health Evangelism, 109
complementarianism, 323
conflict, 47–48, 57, 127–129, 143, 147, 150–52, 167, 172, 174, 197, 200, 269,
        276–77, 316, 336, 342
        conflict resolution, 128, 146–47, 150, 157, 173, 344
Confucianism, 28
conservative, 39, 46, 51, 96, 314, 322, 333
Corinth, 210, 212, 214, 216, 221–23, 294, 299
Cornelius, David, 246–47, 294
cosmology, 37–38, 184
        African. *See* African.
Costa Rica, 167
Coulibaly, David, 107
Cox, Taylor, 133
cross-cultural
        adaptation, 93

        context, 153, 259
        experience, 141, 143, 150
        interaction, 144
        leadership, 115–16, 128, 178
        living, 198
        ministry, 44, 100–01, 212, 219
            teams, 141
        mission, 9, 15, 210, 237, 242–43, 245, 247–48, 251, 253, 255, 256, 294, 336
        misunderstanding, 152
        sensitivity, 137
        situation, 180
        stress, 199, 208
        studies, 125, 169
        teams, 142–43, 145–47, 150, 157, 159–60
        training, 149, 168–69, 185–86, 192
        understanding, 179
Crucial Confrontations, 152
Crucial Conversations, 152
Crummell, Alexander, 252–53
cultural
        differences, 5, 12, 141, 151, 167–68, 185, 191, 193, 197–201, 298, 342
        diversity. *See* diversity.
        fatigue, 180, 184–85, 192
        intelligence (CQ), 15, 147–49, 157
            cognitive, 148
            emotional/motivational, 148–49
            physical, 148–49
        norms, 150–51, 204, 339
        pluralism, 9
        relativism, 188
        training, 147, 149, 180, 185
culturally-competent leaders, 15–17
culture
        based Judging System (CbJS), 197–200, 208
        bureaucratic, 180–81, 183–84
        dominant, 40, 43–44, 46, 247, 256
        egalitarian, 180, 182, 184
        hierarchical, 181, 183
        immigrant. *See* immigrant.
        individualistic, 182–83

Cyprus, 210, 221–22, 294

D
Daniel, 177
Daniels, Gene, 135
Daoism, 28
Dean, Kendra, 100
decision making, 114, 130, 134, 145, 150, 157, 181, 184, 199–200, 230, 234, 239, 340
Decker, Murray, 280, 284
Deity, 37
    divinities, 37–38
    Supreme Being, 37–38
    Ultimate Reality, 37–38
demons, 37–38, 45, 57
Denmark, 87
devil, 37
    Satan, 38, 53, 57
dialogue, 9, 12, 14, 55, 117, 119, 152, 242, 281, 333
    public, 3
diaspora, 28, 36, 49, 52–53, 56, 63–66, 78, 82, 85, 87–89, 193, 269, 290, 295
    church planting, 63–64, 67–68, 70, 72
    Ghanaian, 35, 40, 42–45, 47–50, 59–60
        meaning, 35
Dierck, Lorraine, 181
Dillon, William, 311
Diognetus, 10
Dischinger, T., 97
disciple, 56, 59, 66, 76, 104, 137, 141, 249, 257–58, 291–93, 296
discipleship, 25, 44–45, 56, 64, 66, 76, 100, 285, 314
discrimination, 17, 157, 295, 300
diversity
    cultural, 11, 35–36, 40, 58, 64, 142, 159, 180, 295, 341–42, 347
    ethnic, 36, 40, 210, 213, 230, 232, 235, 268, 271, 289, 343
    gender, 59, 213, 215, 220, 267, 310, 330, 343, 345
    generational, 35, 41–43, 58, 103, 229–32, 269, 273, 286
    in evangelical mission, 88, 263
    linguistic. *See* linguistic.
    non-cultural, 341
    relationship, 339, 341, 343–47, 349
    task, 339, 341, 343–49
    worldview, 45, 273, 286

Diversity Visa Lottery Program (DVLP), 35–36
Doing Member Care Well, 158
Dominican Republic
    Dominican, 22
Douglas, Mary, 128, 180, 197, 199–200, 202
Downes, Donna, 185
Duff, Alexander, 220
Dunn, James, 56, 216
Dyrness, William, 107

E
Earley, 148
ecclesia, 56
Edinburgh, 11, 265
egalitarianism, 6, 129, 159, 180, 182–84, 191, 322, 333
    culture. *See* culture.
Egypt, 14, 210
    Egyptian, 295
Elliot, Elisabeth, 219
Elliot, Jim, 101
Elmer, Duane, 118–19, 144
Elmer, Muriel, 118–19
Elmers' Learning Cycle, 118
Ely, Robin, 159
Emperor Claudius, 214
enculturation, 55
Engel, James, 107
English, 7, 22–25, 27, 29–30, 40, 47–48, 52, 58, 65, 85, 134, 170, 173, 189–90, 194, 237
English as a Second Language (ESL), 23, 106
English as Foreign Language (EFL), 112
Epaphras, 210, 212, 218, 222
Ephesus, 210, 212, 216, 221–23
equality rights, 6
Erastus, 216, 222
Escobar, Samuel, 132–33
Ethiopia, 125, 129, 254, 297
ethnic/ethnicity
    diversity. *See* diversity.
    groups, 4, 22, 27–28, 36, 40, 71, 78, 190, 211, 213, 247, 269, 289, 292, 295, 297, 301–02, 312, 317
    tolerance, 5

ethnocentric/ethnocentrism, 180, 188–89, 235, 243, 292
ethnographic description, 35
ethnos, 291, 299
Euodia, 210, 212–13, 222
Eurocentric, 16
Europe, 24, 52, 65, 88, 142, 179, 294
    Eastern, 26, 231–32
    European, 187, 311
        imperialist, 254
        leaders, 132
    Northern, 21
    Western, 21, 132
evangelical(s), 86, 97–98, 108, 312, 322–23, 333, 349
    community, 9, 97
    denomination, 22, 25
    mission, 88, 255, 256, 263, 307, 309, 330–31
        diversity. *See* diversity.
    outreach ministries, 308–12, 313
    school, 96
Evangelical Missiological Society (EMS), 88
Evangelical Missions Quarterly (EMQ), 189, 247
evangelize, 66, 76, 141, 219
Ewe, 40–41, 48

F
faith, 3, 11, 13–14, 50, 52, 54, 59, 74–80, 87–88, 109, 153, 219, 245, 251, 258, 267, 273, 276, 285, 292, 296–299, 307, 311
Fante, 40
Far East Broadcasting Association, 268
faultlines, 341, 344–45, 351
Fellowship of Christian Athletes, 313
Florissant, 242
Fordham University, 57
Fort Worth, 254
Fortunatus, 210, 222
Foyle, Marjory, 171
France, 65, 141, 149
    French, 4, 7, 48, 80, 141, 149, 152
Fujianese Grace Church, 24
fundraising, 310, 314, 321, 326

G
Ga, 48
    dialect, 40
Galatia, 210, 221–22
Gamaliel, Rabbi, 297
Gazan, Paul, 245
gender, 58–59, 183, 209, 220–23, 307–11, 311–16, 321, 326, 330–33, 335–36, 339, 341, 343, 345
    diversity. *See* diversity.
    inclusion, 187
    roles, 126
generational diversity. *See* diversity.
Gen X, 41, 275
Gen Y, 41
Genesis Community Fellowship, 54
Gentiles, 211–13, 216, 221–23, 291–95, 298–99
Gerlof, Roswith, 52
Germany
    German, 7, 198
Ghana, 30, 35–36
    Ghanaian(s), 35–36, 39, 46–50, 52–55, 59, 263–64
        church. *See* church.
        community, 24, 35, 43, 45, 49, 53, 60
        congregations, 43, 45, 49, 53–54, 56, 58, 60
            diversity in, 35
        diaspora. *See* diaspora.
        diversities
            cultural, 36
            ethnic, 36, 40
            generational, 41
        immigrant, 27, 35, 48
            church, 22, 24
        language, 40, 57
        local born (LBGs), 42–48, 51–52, 57–59
        non-Ghanaians, 41, 51, 58
        overseas born (OBGs), 42–49, 51–53, 58–59
        perception, 40
        worldview, 38
Ghana News Agency (GNA), 36
Gibbs, Eddie, 284
Gibbs, Nancy, 92–93, 95
global, 64, 67–68, 132, 163

    expansion, 106
    North, 106, 109–10, 137, 178–79
    leadership, 15, 131, 177–80, 184, 186–88, 190, 192–94
    management, 132, 185
    migration, 63
    ministry, 27
    mission, 66, 108, 132–33, 135, 164, 230
        assignment, 70
        leadership, 103
        movement, 133, 230
        work, 28
    outreach. *See* outreach.
    perspectives, 39, 75
    presence, 87
    scattering, 87
    South, 104–05, 109, 111, 115–16, 137, 177–80, 185–86, 188–89, 191, 248
    trend, 63
globalization, 43, 99, 103, 115, 125, 128, 130–37, 187–88, 335
Globalization and the Gospel, 21
glocal, 64, 87, 108
    missions, 64, 85, 87
glossa, 291, 299
Goatley, David Emmanuel, 244–45, 247–48, 251
Gora, Tahir Aslam, 5–6
Grachev, Mikhail, 180
Gray, Rick, 252
Great Britain
    British, 132, 152, 198, 201
Great Commandment of Love, 59, 103, 111, 119–20
Great Commission, 56, 59, 67, 86, 103, 111, 119–20, 137, 163, 173, 192, 218, 229, 233, 242, 250, 256, 259, 285, 293
Great Lakes, 7
Great Requirement of Humility, 59
Greek, 7, 16, 119, 213, 220, 290–99, 299
Greenhills Christian Fellowship (GCF), 63–64, 66, 88
    Calgary, 73–74, 78–80
    Canada, 72–83, 85
        Covenant, 75, 77–80
        Ethos, 77
    Canada Leadership Summit, 74–75, 80, 82
        Manifesto, 75, 77, 80

    diasproa church plating, 63–64, 66–68, 70, 72
    Etobicoke, 72, 80–81
    mission statement, 76, 79
    New Zealand, 73
    Ortigas, 66–70, 81
    Peel, 72–75, 78, 80–83
    Philippines, 66–68, 75, 81
    satellite, 66–70, 72–83, 85, 88
        Batangas City, 67, 69
        Parañaque, 67, 69
        Santa Rosa, 67, 69
    South Metro, 67–70
    Toronto, 64–65, 67–75, 79–85, 87–89
    Triple Vision, 72–74, 78
    Vancouver, 72–75, 80–82
    Winnipeg, 72, 74, 78–81
Grenz, Stanley, 282
Grid/Group theory, 202
Griffin, Hayne, 312
Guangdong, 22

H
Habacon, Alden, 12
Haiti, 247
Hale, Abner, 266–67
Hampden-Turner, Charles, 129, 133, 151
Hanciles, Jehu, 133
Harare, 263–64
Harris, Philip, 129
Hartenstein, Karl, 248
Hawaii, 266
Haystack Prayer Meeting, 91
Healthcare Initiative, 104, 108
Hebrew, 290, 295–97
Heffernan, Margaret, 278
Hellenism, 290
Herod, 210
heterogeneous, 40, 50–51, 338
Hiebert, Paul, 38, 56, 218, 258, 285
Hindu, 85, 87
Hinduism, 39, 88
Hispanic, 27, 29, 47, 54, 132, 198, 317

community, 25, 31, 315
    group, 25
    immigrant, 23–24, 26, 28–29
    worship style, 25
HIV, 104, 109, 113, 115–16
Hofstede, Geert, 129, 151
Hofstede, Gert Jan, 129, 151
Holland
    Dutch, 152
Holy Spirit, 51, 57, 77, 101, 155, 160, 200, 245, 249, 253, 293, 297, 299, 301
homogeneous, 40, 50–52, 109, 292, 295, 297, 299–301, 327, 331
Homogenous Unit Principle (HUP), 251, 300
Hong Kong, 7, 22, 25
Hoppe, Michael, 182
Horton, Robin, 36
Horton, Tim, 65
House, Robert, 129
House of Commons, 4
Houston, 50
Huckaby, Sedrick, 254–57
Hudson's Bay, 7
Hull, Judith St. Clair, 255
Hutchful, Kweku, 264

I
identity, 4, 9, 11–12, 14, 17, 44, 48, 52, 99, 101, 155, 188, 190, 193, 250, 289, 292, 345–46
    aboriginal, 4
    individual, 4, 11
Immanuel Baptist Church, 74
immigrant, 5–6, 12, 21–25, 27–31, 35, 42, 48, 52, 54, 65–68, 78, 83–85, 87, 99
    church, 21–24, 26, 30–31
    community, 5–6, 23–24, 28–29
    culture, 5
inclusiveness, 6, 301
India, 39, 65, 83, 166
    Indian, 7, 186
indigenous, 218, 220, 247–48, 253–54
individualism, 43, 46, 205–06
    American. *See* United States of America.
    individualistic, 39, 47–48, 95, 180, 182–83, 311
        culture. *See* culture.

Ingleby, Jonathan, 135
integration, 11, 13, 17, 40, 42–43, 103–04, 341, 346
intercultural, 17, 82, 248
    church, 82
    citizen, 7–8
    competence, 15–16
    dialogue, 12, 14
    relations, 13
    skill, 8–9, 178
Intercultural Development Inventory, 16
interdependence, 135, 346–47, 351
International Leadership Team, 231, 233, 236–37
International Mission Board, 246
internationalization, 127–28, 131, 178, 187–88, 190
Internet, 43, 94–95, 255
interpersonal
    communication, 169
    relationships, 46, 94, 164, 167, 171, 174, 232
InterVarsity, 280, 314
Iran, 65
Ireland, 83
    Irish, 7, 152, 198
Islam, 39, 88
    fundamental groups, 5
    Islamic
        world, 87
Israel, 290, 292–93
Italy, 210, 297
    Italian, 7

J
Jacobs, Sylvia M., 253
Japan
    Japanese, 231
        American, 198
Jeavons, Thomas, 311
Jenkins, Philip, 57, 178
Jerusalem, 71–73, 210–12, 221–22, 293–97
Jesus Christ, 16, 54, 56–57, 76–77, 79, 99–101, 104, 108, 119, 144, 193, 213, 219–20, 229–30, 235, 241–42, 245, 249, 258, 283, 285–86, 291–94, 297–299, 351
    followers, 10–11

Jewish, 21, 87, 144, 177, 211–12, 214, 219, 221–22, 293–94, 296, 298–299
Jim Crow, 250
    laws, 260
    lynchings, 253
John Mark, 210, 222
Johnson, C. Neal, 137
Johnson, Michael, 250
Johnson, Paul S., 311
Joseph, 177
Judson, Ann, 219
Junia, 215, 222

K
Kagame, Paul, 105
Kaiser Family Foundation, 94
    study of youth media consumption, 94
Kane, J. Herbert, 293
Karongi District, 104, 109, 113–14
Katzenbach, John, 142–43
Keller, Tim, 231, 238
Kenya, 8, 125–29, 136, 244, 264
Kim, Dong-hwa, 167
King George III, 7
kingdom of God, 8–10, 14, 17, 59, 87, 89, 91, 99, 104, 120, 126, 135, 164, 166, 193–94, 215–16, 229, 235, 237, 241–42, 245, 257, 271, 282, 290, 300
kirpans, 5
Koch, Bruce, 63
Korea, 136, 166
    Korean, 47, 192, 201
        church, 25
        immigrant church, 23
        missionary movement, 138
    South, 65, 163, 166–74
Korean Research Institute for Missions, 138
Kraft, Charles, 56, 116–17
Kymlicka, Will, 7–8, 13, 16

L
language, 7, 9–11, 22–24, 27, 29, 40, 47–48, 54–55, 57–59, 66, 92, 98, 120, 134, 146–49, 151, 169–70, 172, 177, 180–81, 187, 189–90, 193–94, 197–98, 201, 205, 207, 236–37, 241, 274, 282, 290–93, 295–99, 301–02

ability, 169
laos, 291, 299
Latin America, 21–22, 26, 29–30, 65, 88, 136, 179, 198
Latin American Mobilization Center, 136
Latino/a, 311–14, 314–19, 317, 327, 329–31, 335, 337
Lausanne
    movement , 229
    Occasional Papers, 21
leadership, 17, 25, 44, 54, 68, 74–75, 77, 79, 81, 83, 98, 103–05, 110, 114–17, 119–20, 135–28, 130–34, 136–37, 143, 145–47, 150–57, 159, 165–67, 172–73, 177–81, 183, 186–90, 192–94, 206, 208, 210, 215, 218–19, 229–39, 248, 253, 263–69, 271, 273–74, 276, 279–82, 284–86, 295–96, 301, 312, 322–23, 333, 340, 343
    African. *See* African.
    cross-cultural. *See* cross-cultural.
    global. *See* global.
    spiritual, 66
    style, 129, 153, 156
    women in leadership. *See* women.
Lederleitner, Mary M., 135
Lee, John, 190
Lee, Sang Hyun, 23
LePSAS, 111
Lewis, Richard, 151
liberal, 46, 279
Liberia, 251–52, 254, 256
    Liberian, 54, 267
Liddel, Eric, 101
Light House Church, 50
Lingenfelter, Sherwood, 104, 114, 128, 135, 153–55, 157, 190, 192
lingua franca, 170, 190
linguistic diversity, 40, 44, 47, 58
Lisle, George, 251
Little Saigon, 66
Livermore, David, 98
local, 8–9, 11, 22, 64, 130
    believers, 27, 59
    ministry, 23
    mission, 28, 64
    outreach, 27
Long Island, 25
Lott Carey Foreign Mission Convention, 244

Lott Carey Mission School, 256
Lucius, 210
Luke, 210–11, 216, 221, 253, 293, 295–97
Lundy, J. David, 131, 177, 185–86, 188
Luzbetak, 184
Lyons, Gabe, 281
Lystra, 210, 221, 294

M
Macedonia, 210, 216, 221–23
Maclean's, 3
Madrid, 150
Mandarin, 22
Manean, 210
Manila, 12, 65–67, 69–70, 73, 81, 86
    Pasig City, 66
Manitoba, 72
Marston, Cam, 276
Marty, Micah, 258
Mary, 215, 222
Maryland, 50
Matures, 274–75
Mayers, Marvin, 114, 192, 242
Mayfield Guest House, 244
McCabe, Tom, 311
McDonald, John A., 7
McGavran, Donald, 251, 289, 292, 301
McGlathery, Marla, 312
media, 66, 94–95, 99
    social, 41, 95
        Facebook, 94–95, 99
        Twitter, 95, 99
Medical Ambassadors International, 109
member care, 146, 164–67, 170, 173–74
    missionary, 163
    resources, 163
Mennonite, 201
Mensah-Shalders, Ekow, 57
Methodist, 50
Metis, 6
metropolitan, 13, 74–75, 78, 82, 88, 328
Mexico, 8

Michener, James, 266
migration, 21, 63, 65, 88
millennials, 41, 92, 94–96, 98–101, 273–85
    Emerging Adults, 92, 96
    Mosaics, 92, 98–99
    Net Generation, 92
    New Millennials, 276
Miller, Sharon, 311
Millirons, Jim, 282, 285
Min, Pyong Gap, 23
Mindset List, 92
ministry, 24–29, 35, 43–45, 49, 52, 57, 60, 66–70, 74–77, 81–82, 85–86, 100–01, 107, 109–13, 115, 117, 126–27, 132, 134–35, 137, 141, 43, 145, 147, 163–65, 167–71, 173, 178, 183, 193, 209, 211–12, 215–27, 219–20, 231–35, 249, 256–60, 267, 274–75, 278–80, 282, 284–85, 291–92, 301, 310–23, 326–27, 330–33, 343, 345
    leaders, 16
    local. *See* local.
minority, 29, 64, 66, 167, 169–70, 198, 206, 258, 289, 297, 310, 310, 314, 316–18, 320–21, 330–32
missio Dei, 9, 87–88, 243, 248–49
missio ekklesia, 9
missiological
    analysis, 64, 85
    circles, 98
    implications, 35, 55
    issues, 219
    perspective, 133
    reflections, 9
    training, 171
missiology, 56, 185
Missiology, 134
mission
    cross-cultural. *See* cross-cultural.
    evangelical. *See* evangelical.
    history, 85, 91, 163, 188, 245
    mobilizer, 91, 100
    organization, 26–27, 125, 128, 130–31, 136–37, 177–79, 184, 187–88, 190, 192–93, 217–18, 239, 242, 255–56, 276, 312, 335, 337, 341, 344, 351
    practices, 9, 22, 28, 55–56, 137
    short-term. *See* short-term.

    structure, 26, 107, 137, 239
    team, 8, 107, 113, 215, 220, 249, 335–37, 342, 344, 346–47
    trips, 26, 29, 105
    work, 28, 69, 86, 99, 213–15, 217, 221–23, 237, 336
Mission Handbook, 130
missional, 13, 28, 55, 71, 74–75, 78, 82–83, 85, 87–88, 95, 244, 247–48, 251, 254, 256–57, 259, 273–74, 276, 278–79, 282–86
missionary
    member care. *See* member care.
    retention, 164–65, 173
Mississauga, 73
Missouri, 242, 249
mobilize, 6, 87, 91, 105–06, 109–10, 152, 231, 280
    mission. *See* mission.
Mole-Dagomba, 41
Monrovia, 251
Montreal, 15, 65
Moon, Lottie, 219
Moon, Steve Sang-Cheol, 135, 138, 172
Moose Jaw, 15
Moran, Robert, 129, 133
Moreau, A. Scott, 48, 55, 59
Morton, Scott, 310–12, 322, 331, 333
Mosakowski, Elaine, 148
Moses, 177, 299
Moses, Wilson Jeremiah, 252
mother tongue, 44–45, 47–48, 52, 170, 189, 192
Mueller, Walt, 41, 43, 46
Mujuru, Joyce, 267
Mulroney, Brian, 7
multicultural/multiculturalism, 3–4, 6, 10–11, 13
    city, 63–64, 70
    common spaces, 13–15, 17
    faith communities, 3, 11
    policy, 4–5, 11
    social theory, 3, 9, 11, 17
    society, 6, 12, 40, 51
    state, 7–9
    team, 126, 134, 143, 145, 158, 168, 178–79, 184, 186, 199, 205
        building workshop, 197, 199, 207–08
    training, 186, 193, 197, 206, 208
multinational, 54, 134, 137, 167–70, 172–73, 178

375

Muslim, 6, 85
Mutonono, Dwight, 267
Myanmar, 26–27

N
Nacpil, Emerito, 86
Nairobi, 244, 263
native tongue, 58
Natural Church Development, 77
Navigators, 268
Ndebele, 268–69
Nehemiah, 177
Netherlands, 337
networking, 134–35, 285, 325
    social, 94, 279
Neufeld, Tim, 283–86
New Brunswick, 65
New Testament, 158, 210–11, 214–15, 291–92, 296
New York City, 22, 27–30, 238
    Department of City Planning, 36
    Twin Towers, 92
Newark, 50
Newbigin, Lesslie, 10
Nicholls, 170
Nigeria, 27, 30, 87, 247
    Nigerian, 22, 24–25, 27, 54
non-American, 36, 205, 207
non-Western, 87–88, 134, 185–88, 280
Nored, James, 282
North America, 24, 67, 87–88, 92, 94, 96–97, 108, 128, 130–32, 134, 136–37, 144, 179, 185, 187, 189, 231–33, 237, 242, 247, 282, 285, 337, 342, 346
    youth, 94
North American Mission Leaders Conference (NAMLC), 60

O
obadinto, 40
OC International, 125, 127, 132, 136
O'Donnell, Kelly, 163
Ogden, 50
Ohio, 50
Old Testament, 290, 292

Onesimus, 210, 217, 222
Ontario, 5, 8, 66, 72–75, 79–81
Onyankopon, 38
openness/open-mindedness, 159, 204, 279, 282, 301, 336, 345, 348–50
Operation Mobilization (OM), 185
organizational culture, 128, 130, 134, 159, 184, 186, 190, 192
outreach, 29–30, 83–84, 108, 273–75, 278, 280–84, 286, 307–10, 313, 317, 330–31, 333
    community, 28, 31
    focus, 27
    global, 91
    partnership, 26
overseas mission fields (OMF), 50
Oxford Center for Missions Studies (OCMS), 265

P
Pakistan, 65
    Pakistani-Canadian, 6
Palestine, 210
Palmer, Parker, 14
Pan-African Christian Leadership Assembly II (PACLA II), 264
panta ta ethne, 292
Pantoja, Luis, Jr., 66, 68–70, 73–74, 79, 81
parachurch, 64, 85, 136, 138, 280, 283, 310, 317, 322, 330, 332
Parachurch Ministries Fundraising Survey (PMFRS), 313
Parisi-Carew, Eunice, 144
Parry, Sue, 115
partnership, 26, 75, 79, 81, 85–87, 100, 103–04, 108, 110, 113, 115–16, 118–20, 126–27, 132, 135–37, 166, 192–93, 231–32, 237–38, 254, 335
Parvin, Earl, 252–53, 257
patriarchy/patriarchal, 322, 324
Paul, 177, 190, 211–20, 229, 235, 251, 253, 257, 263, 294, 297–302, 340
    coworkers, 209–11, 213, 215–16, 21
    missionary strategy, 210–11
    Pauline
        scholarly theology, 53
PEACE plan, 103, 105–07, 109, 112–13, 116–17, 119
Pennsylvania, 91
Pentecost, 211, 293
Pentecostal
    church, 54, 254
    movement, 29

tradition, 22
Persia, 290
Persis, 215, 222
Peter, 258, 293–94
Peter, George W., 283
Pettegrew, Larry D., 275
Pew Research study, 94, 99, 279
Philadelphia, 50
Philemon, 210, 212, 217, 221–22
Philippi, 210, 212, 221–23, 294
Philippines, 65–68, 71, 75, 81, 83, 85–86, 89, 136
      Filipino, 7, 64, 66, 69, 71, 84, 86–89
Phoebe, 210, 214, 223
phradet 181
phrakhun, 181
phule, 291, 299
Piekkari, Rebecca, 189
Pioneers, 279
Piper, John, 95, 99
Plueddemann, James, 151–52
pluralism, 6, 9, 40, 44, 51, 275, 301
Pocock, Michael, 137
Pohl, Christine, 14
Pontus, 210
Portland International Church (PIC), 54
Portuguese, 7
postmodernism, 6, 41, 108, 110, 116, 163, 258, 274–76, 282–83
prejudice, 17, 110, 127, 291, 297, 300
Prensky, Marc, 93
Presbyterian, 50
      PCUSA, 50, 52
Presbyterian Church of Ghana (PCG), 50
Priest, R.J., 96–97, 243
Priscilla, 210, 214, 216, 221
problem solving, 134, 145, 158, 342
Protestant, 21, 30, 85, 188, 245, 247, 312–14
Providence Baptist Church, 251
Purdue University, 265
Putnam, Robert, 94

Q
Quebec, 48, 74–75, 79–80

Quebec's Consultation Commission on Accommodation Practices Related to Cultural
    Differences, 5
Queens, 25
Queens University, 7

R
race, 11, 45, 53–54, 59–60, 188–90, 192–93, 241, 292, 298–300, 307–09,
    311–15, 317–20, 326–31, 335, 338–39, 343, 348–49
RAIL, 58
Rasmus, Daniel, 277–78
Rassmussen, S., 97
Reapsome, Jim, 189
Redeemed Church of Jesus Christ, 54
Redeemer Presbyterian Church, 238
relational paradigm, 56
relationships, 17, 56, 65, 77, 85, 94–95, 100, 104, 127, 142–43, 145, 152,
    154–55, 160, 163, 167–68, 171, 174, 180, 184, 193, 200, 207, 209,
    217–18, 230, 234, 238, 242, 248, 256–58, 280–81, 317, 321,
    328, 333, 339, 345
    healthy, 129
    institutionalized, 41
    interpersonal. *See* interpersonal.
    mentoring, 15
    sexual, 41
    team, 126, 129
Relevant Media, 278
religion, 6, 28, 39–40, 47, 49–50, 52, 55, 63, 88, 116, 250, 278, 293–94
religious, 5–6, 13, 21, 36, 40, 56, 59, 65–66, 68, 73, 80, 96, 100, 103, 245–46,
    250, 254, 259, 292, 300, 317, 326–27
    multiplicity, 39
ReMAP, 166
    I, 164–65, 170
    II, 165–66
reverse mission, 50, 54
Richardson, Don, 293
rites, 43
    of passage, 40, 45, 55, 97
    puberty, 43
Robert, Dana, 133
Robertson, Roland, 64
Roembke, Lianne, 143, 145, 153

Roman Catholic, 50, 85
    immigrants, 21
Rome, 210, 214, 216, 221–23, 294, 297
Romo, Oscar, 298, 301
Rowell, John, 135
Royal Commission on Bilingualism and Biculturalism, 4
Rundle, Steven, 137
Russia, 181
    Russian, 180
Rwanda, 103–06, 108, 111, 116, 119
    Department of Health, 104, 108
    genocide, 108, 264
    Western Rwanda Initiative, 115
Rynkiewich, Michael A., 256

S
Saayman, Willem, 110
Saddleback Church, 76, 103–05, 111, 119
Samaria, 71–73, 80, 291, 293–94
    Samaritan, 291, 294–95, 297
Sanneh, Lamin, 52, 133
Santos, Narry, 67, 69
Sapir-Whorf hypothesis, 189
Sarpong, Peter, 40
Saul, 210, 297
Saul, John Ralston, 6
Scandinavian, 7
Scattered: The Filipino Global Presence, 87
Schein, Edgar, 341
Schippers, M. C., 337
Schnabel, Eckhard, 216, 220
School for Urban Biblical Studies (SUBS), 82
Schreiner, Thomas, 213
Schwarz, Christian, 77
Scot, 7
Seattle, 267
segregation, 258, 260, 293, 295, 297, 300, 302
Senter, Mark, 283–84
Septuagint, 290, 297
Seraya, Victor, 54
servanthood, 249
Serving with Eyes Wide Open, 98

sex, 41
    sexting, 41
    sexual
        behavior, 54
        orientation, 99
        relationships, 41
shalom, 9–10, 13, 17
Shalom Church, 242
Sharia law, 5
Shenk, Wilbert, 249
Shona, 268–69
short term missions (STM), 26, 28–29, 96–98, 100, 103, 105, 107, 112–14, 125, 247, 249, 254, 257, 280, 347, 351
Sierra Leone, 87
Sikh(s), 5
Sikhism, 88
SIL, 185, 197–98, 201, 205, 208
Silas, 210, 212, 221
Silver Springs, 50
Simeon, 210
Singapore, 136
Sirleaf, Ellen Johnson, 267
Situational Leadership model, 155–56
Smith, Douglas, 94, 142–43
Snell, Patricia, 94
social
    games, 154–55
    identity, 346
    media. *See* media.
    mobility, 23
    networking. *See* networking.
    structuralism, 188
socialization, 43, 45, 55, 116
Somalia
    Somali, 7
Sommer, Pete, 311–12
South America, 231–33
South Carolina, 91
South Korea. *See* Korea.
Southeast Asian, 168
Southern Baptist Convention, 282, 313
Spanish, 24–25, 29, 152

Speer, Robert, 11
spirits, 37–38, 45
 evil, 37
spiritual gifts, 147, 249, 298, 340
Sri Lanka
 Sri Lankan, 7
St. Lawrence River, 6
St. Louis, 249
status, 14, 23, 30, 46, 126, 150, 180–84, 189, 205, 214, 216, 257, 275, 307, 309, 311, 326–27, 329–30, 338, 342–43, 345–46, 351
Steering Committee (SC), 104–05, 113–14, 116
Stephanas, 210, 223
Stetzer, Ed, 158
Strang, Cameron, 278
Stravens, Ken, 264
Student Volunteer Movement, 91
Sutherland, Jim, 246–47, 250, 257
symbolism, 53, 188
Syntyche, 210, 212–13, 223
Syria, 210–11, 291
 Syrian, 293–94
Syrophenician woman, 292

T
Taiwan, 22, 136
Tanzania, 247, 249
Tarsus, 210–11
Taylor, Charles, 9
Taylor, Williams D., 134
Team Ministries, 281
technology, 24, 43, 93–95, 99, 101, 177, 285
Teen Mania, 98
Ten Years, Ten Values, 68
ter Haar, Gerrie, 52
Texas, 98, 254
The Changing Face of World Missions, 237
The Hamilton Spectator, 5
The Master's College, 94
The Mission Society, 246
The New People Next Door, 21
The Next Christendom, 178
The Purpose Driven Life, 105

theology, 16, 53, 100, 127, 218–19, 243, 248, 250, 268, 302, 338, 340
    theological
        challenges, 50
        diversity, 103
        education, 30, 314
        foundation, 56
        frames, 12
        reflections, 9, 242, 244
        studies, 26
        training, 171
        understanding, 155
Thessalonike, 210, 221
Third Culture Kids, 100
Third World, 163, 168, 170
Thomas, David, 159
Timothy, 210–12, 218, 235
Tiplady, Richard, 151
Titus, 211–13, 218, 221
Togolese, 54
tolerance, 6, 55, 99
    ethnic. *See* ethnic.
Toronto, 15, 64–71, 74, 80–82, 85
transnational, 39, 45, 50, 178
Treaty of Paris, 85
Trinity, 12, 199
Trompenaars, Fons, 129, 133
Trophimus, 210, 223
Trotter, Lilias, 101
Trudeau, Pierre, 6, 9
Tryphaena, 215, 223
Tryphosa, 215, 223
Twi, 40, 48, 52, 57–58
Tychicus, 210, 212, 221
Tyndale Intercultural Ministries (TIM), 82
Tyndale Seminary, 83

U
Ukraine
    Ukrainian, 7
Union Seminary, 86
United Kingdom, 202
United Nations, 5

United Nations Development Program, 63
United States of America, 21–25, 28–30, 35, 40–41, 49, 53, 85, 100, 125, 178, 198, 205, 245, 253, 265, 289, 309–11, 313
   America(n)
      African, 29–30, 52–54, 198, 241–60, 311–12, 314–20, 326, 329–33
      Anglo, 250, 311–12, 314–21, 327
      European, 311
      White, 246–47, 254
University of Aarhus, 87
University of Edinburgh, 87, 265
University of Texas
   Arlington, 256
University of Wales, 265
University of Zimbabwe, 265–66
unreached, 28, 53–55, 193, 211, 219, 231–32, 234, 251
Urbana Mission Conference, 91, 249, 280
US Mobilization Center, 136

V
values
   common, 4, 231–33
   family, 44, 54, 129
Van Engen, Charles, 245
Van Knippenberg, Daan, 337
Vancouver, 15, 65, 73, 81
Vietnam
   Vietnamese, 7
violence, 6, 126
Virginia, 50, 251
Vision 359 Toronto City Catalyst, 80
Volf, Miroslav, 9–10

W
Wakin, Daniel, 50, 52, 54–55
Walls, Andrew F., 87–88, 103, 133
Walsh, Brian, 285
Wan, Enoch, 42, 50, 56, 88
war
   World War II, 41
Ward, Ted, 116
Warren, Rick, 76, 103, 105, 117

Washington, 267
West Indies, 251
Western, 21, 40, 49, 86, 88, 133–34, 167, 179, 185–89, 242, 252, 256, 280
    civilization, 6
    dominance, 16
    mind-set, 38–39
    missionaries, 28, 86, 170, 173, 184, 191, 218
    world, 87, 190, 192
Western Seminary, 89
Wilder, Mary, 89
Williams, Walter L., 250
Wilson, Donna, 333
Winnipeg, 74, 78–79
Winter, Ralph, 63, 133
women
    in leadership, 267–70, 271, 322–23, 333
World Evangelical Fellowship, 134
World Gospel Missions, 250
World Missionary Congress, 11
worldview, 12–13, 6, 38–39, 41, 43–46, 53, 92, 111, 116, 188–90, 194, 198, 273–76, 276, 281, 285–86
    diversity. *See* diversity.
worship, 25, 27–28, 38, 44–45, 50, 52–54, 58, 66–67, 70, 73, 76–79, 229, 235, 241, 251, 253, 295, 299, 301–02, 339
Wuthnow, Robert, 321
Wycliffe Bible Translators (WBT), 205

X
xenophobia, 17

Y
Yego, Josphat, 264
Yount, David, 66, 86
YWAM, 186–87, 279–80

Z
Zehner, Edwin, 97
Zimbabwe, 263–71
    Zimbabwean, 265–67, 269

SCRIPTURE INDEX

Genesis 1:26–27, 260
Genesis 1:31, 144
Genesis 2:1, 144
Genesis 11:1–9, 340
Exodus 19:5–6, 290
Leviticus 19:18, 59
Deuteronomy 6:4, 59
Psalm 71:18, 273
Proverbs 3:5–6, 257
Isaiah 11:9, 291
Isaiah 42:1–4, 6, 290
Isaiah 49:6, 290
Micah 6:8, 59
Matthew 4:15, 291
Matthew 4:24–25, 291
Matthew 5:23–24, 151
Matthew 9:17, 273
Matthew 18:15–18, 151
Matthew 28, 282
Matthew 28:16–20, 59
Matthew 28:19, 250
Matthew 28:19–20, 163, 242, 292, 343
Mark 3:7–8, 291
Mark 7:26, 292
Mark 9:35, 84
Mark 10:43–45, 84
Mark 12:25–31, 59
Mark 16:15–18, 59
Luke 7:1–10, 292
Luke 9:52–54, 294
Luke 9:56, 291
Luke 17:11–19, 291
Luke 24:45–49, 59
John 3:16, 245, 342
John 3:16–17, 291
John 4:39–42, 291
John 12:20, 291
John 17, 158, 160, 193
John 17:13–26, 229

John 17:21, 119
John 18:36, 104
John 20:21, 59
John 21:15, 258
Acts 1:8, 59, 71–72, 282, 293
Acts 2:4, 293
Acts 2:5–11, 336
Acts 2:46, 295
Acts 5:42, 295
Acts 6:1–7, 158, 336
Acts 6:9, 294–96
Acts 8:4, 294
Acts 8:12, 294
Acts 8:14, 294
Acts 10:28, 294
Acts 11:30, 211
Acts 12:12, 17, 295
Acts 13:1–3, 294, 296
Acts 13:5, 211
Acts 13:46, 298
Acts 13–16, 253
Acts 14, 211
Acts 14:1, 211, 294
Acts 15:1–29, 336
Acts 16:1, 212
Acts 16:8–17, 216
Acts 16:9–10, 84
Acts 17:1, 10, 17, 211
Acts 17:16, 217, 294
Acts 17:26–28, 89, 190
Acts 18:1–2, 214, 294
Acts 18:3, 216
Acts 18:5, 211
Acts 18:6, 298
Acts 18:33–38, 292
Acts 19:22, 216, 222
Acts 20:5–15, 216
Acts 21:1–18, 216
Acts 21:18, 295
Acts 21:39, 297
Acts 22:3, 211, 297
Acts 22:25–29, 297

Acts 23:6, 299
Acts 23:7, 297
Acts 27:1–28:16, 216
Romans 1:5, 298
Romans 1:13, 211
Romans 1:14, 298
Romans 1:27, 59
Romans 5:8, 53
Romans 10:12, 299
Romans 11:1, 299
Romans 11:11–24, 53
Romans 11:13, 211, 298
Romans 12:3, 151
Romans 12:3–8, 340
Romans 12:4–5, 298
Romans 12:9–13, 158
Romans 15:16–18, 211
Romans 15:20, 219
Romans 15:24, 294
Romans 15:29, 297
Romans 16:1–3, 212, 214, 223
Romans 16:6, 222
Romans 16:9, 223
Romans 16:12, 223
Romans 16:32, 216
1 Corinthians 1:1, 223
1 Corinthians 1:10–13, 297
1 Corinthians 1:26–27, 336
1 Corinthians 3:3, 337
1 Corinthians 3:10, 209
1 Corinthians 4:12, 215
1 Corinthians 7:17, 302
1 Corinthians 8:19, 299
1 Corinthians 9:11, 12–14, 257
1 Corinthians 9:19–22, 302
1 Corinthians 9:19–23, 71, 177
1 Corinthians 10:17, 298
1 Corinthians 12:1–31, 340
1 Corinthians 12:12–30, 336
1 Corinthians 12:21, 119
1 Corinthians 12:27, 298
1 Corinthians 12–14, 158

1 Corinthians 14:11, 299
1 Corinthians 16:1, 222
1 Corinthians 16:7, 222
1 Corinthians 16:15, 17, 221, 22
1 Corinthians 16:19, 214
2 Corinthians 5:7–10, 337
Galatians 1:15–16, 298
Galatians 2:1–3, 211
Galatians 2:7–8, 298
Galatians 3:28, 119, 213, 220, 29
Galatians 6:15, 223, 299
Galatians 7:5–6, 299
Ephesians 1:3, 337
Ephesians 1:23, 2,4, 298
Ephesians 2:11–22, 293, 298, 30
Ephesians 3:6, 298
Ephesians 3:8, 211
Ephesians 4:12, 298
Ephesians 5:23, 24, 151, 298
Ephesians 6:22, 212
Philippians 2:1–2, 336
Philippians 2:16, 215
Philippians 2:25–30, 222
Philippians 3:4–6, 299
Philippians 4:2–3, 213, 222–23
Philippians 4:13, 337
Colossians 1:18, 298
Colossians 1:29, 215
Colossians 3:11, 300
Colossians 4:14, 216, 222
Colossians 4:17, 212, 221
1 Timothy 2:7, 211
1 Timothy 2:11–15, 215
1 Timothy 3:14–16, 58
1 Timothy 4:19, 214
2 Timothy 2:2, 233, 235
2 Timothy 4:10, 222
2 Timothy 4:19, 214
2 Timothy 4:20, 216
Titus 2:3–5, 214
Philemon 1, 222
1 John 5:11–13, 53

Revelation 5:9, 299
Revelation 7:9, 299
Revelation 11:9, 299
Revelation 13:7, 299
Revelation 14:6, 299
Revelation 19:6–7, 120

www.ingramcontent.com/pod-product-compliance
Lightning Source LLC
Chambersburg PA
CBHW071228070526
44583CB00017B/2084